P9-CKS-424

Global Issues 11/12

Twenty-Seventh Edition

EDITOR

Robert M. Jackson
California State University, Chico

Robert M. Jackson is a professor emeritus of political science and past dean of the School of Graduate, International and Sponsored Programs at California State University, Chico. In addition to teaching courses on third-world politics and globalization, he has published articles on the international political economy, international relations simulations, and political behavior. Dr. Jackson has been responsible for numerous international training programs for professionals from throughout the world. International educational exchanges and study-abroad programs also have been an area of special interest. His research and professional travels include China, Japan, Hong Kong, Taiwan, Singapore, Malaysia, Spain, Portugal, Morocco, Belgium, Germany, the Czech Republic, the Netherlands, Italy, Russia, Mexico, Guatemala, Honduras, Costa Rica, El Salvador, Brazil, Chile, and Argentina.

Connect Learn Succeed™

ANNUAL EDITIONS: GLOBAL ISSUES, TWENTY-SEVENTH EDITION

Published by McGraw-Hill, a business unit of The McGraw-Hill Companies, Inc., 1221 Avenue
of the Americas, New York, NY 10020. Copyright © 2012 by The McGraw-Hill Companies, Inc.
All rights reserved. Previous editions © 2011, 2010, and 2009. No part of this publication may be
reproduced or distributed in any form or by any means, or stored in a database or retrieval system,
without the prior written consent of The McGraw-Hill Companies, Inc., including, but not limited
to, in any network or other electronic storage or transmission, or broadcast for distance learning.

Some ancillaries, including electronic and print components, may not be available to customers
outside the United States.

Annual Editions® is a registered trademark of The McGraw-Hill Companies, Inc.

Annual Editions is published by the **Contemporary Learning Series** group within the
McGraw-Hill Higher Education division.

1 2 3 4 5 6 7 8 9 0 QDB/QDB 1 0 9 8 7 6 5 4 3 2 1

ISBN 978-0-07-805084-8
MHID 0-07-805084-7
ISSN 1093-278X (print)
ISSN 2158-4060 (online)

Managing Editor: *Larry Loeppke*
Developmental Editor II: *Debra A. Henricks*
Permissions Supervisor: *Lenny J. Behnke*
Senior Marketing Communications Specialist: *Mary Klein*
Project Manager: *Robin A. Reed*
Design Coordinator: *Margarite Reynolds*
Buyer: *Susan K. Culbertson*
Media Project Manager: *Sridevi Palani*

Compositor: Laserwords Private Limited
Cover Images: U.S. Coast Guard photo by Petty Officer 3rd Class Patrick Kelley (inset); US Navy
Photo by Mass Communication Specialist First Class Michael B. Watkins (background)

Editors/Academic Advisory Board

Members of the Academic Advisory Board are instrumental in the final selection of articles for each edition of ANNUAL EDITIONS. Their review of articles for content, level, and appropriateness provides critical direction to the editors and staff. We think that you will find their careful consideration well reflected in this volume.

ANNUAL EDITIONS: Global Issues 11/12
27th Edition

EDITOR

Robert M. Jackson
California State University, Chico

ACADEMIC ADVISORY BOARD MEMBERS

Preface

In publishing ANNUAL EDITIONS we recognize the enormous role played by the magazines, newspapers, and journals of the public press in providing current, first-rate educational information in a broad spectrum of interest areas. Many of these articles are appropriate for students, researchers, and professionals seeking accurate, current material to help bridge the gap between principles and theories and the real world. These articles, however, become more useful for study when those of lasting value are carefully collected, organized, indexed, and reproduced in a low-cost format, which provides easy and permanent access when the material is needed. That is the role played by ANNUAL EDITIONS.

The beginning of the new millennium was celebrated with considerable fanfare. The prevailing opinion in much of the world was that there was a great deal for which we could congratulate ourselves. The very act of sequentially watching on television live celebrations from one time zone to the next was proclaimed as a testimonial to globalization and the benefits of modern technology. The tragic events of September 11, 2001, however, were a stark reminder of the methods of destruction available to those determined to challenge the status quo. The subsequent wars in Afghanistan and Iraq along with continuing acts of terror have dampened the optimism that was expressed at the outset of the twenty-first century.

As the second decade of the twenty-first century begins, new challenges are rising to the top of the political agenda. Global climate change, growing pressure on the supply of oil, and the problem of nuclear proliferation are among those most frequently discussed.

While the mass media may focus on the latest crisis for a few weeks or months, the broad forces that are shaping the world are seldom given the in-depth analysis that they warrant. Scholarly research about these historic forces of change can be found in a wide variety of publications, but these are not readily accessible. In addition, students just beginning to study global issues can be discouraged by the terminology and abstract concepts that characterize much of the scholarly literature. In selecting and organizing the materials for this book, we have been mindful of the needs of beginning students and have, thus, selected articles that invite the student into the subject matter.

Each unit begins with an introductory article(s) providing a broad overview of the subject area to be studied. The following articles examine in more detail specific case studies that often identify the positive steps being taken to remedy problems. Recent events are a continual reminder that the world faces many serious challenges, the magnitude of which would discourage even the most stout-hearted individual. While identifying problems is easier than solving them, it is encouraging to know that many are being addressed.

Perhaps the most striking feature of the study of contemporary global issues is the absence of any single, widely held theory that explains what is taking place. As a result, we have made a conscious effort to present a wide variety of points of view. The most important consideration has been to present global issues from an international perspective, rather than from a purely American or Western point of view. By encompassing materials originally published in different countries and written by authors of various nationalities, the anthology represents the great diversity of opinions that people hold. Two writers examining the same phenomenon may reach very different conclusions. It is not just a question of who is right or wrong, but rather understanding that people from different vantage points can have differing perspectives on an issue.

Another major consideration when organizing these materials was to explore the complex interrelationship of factors that produce social problems such as poverty. Too often, discussions of this problem (and others like it) are reduced to arguments about the fallacies of not following the correct economic policy or not having the correct form of government. As a result, many people overlook the interplay of historic, cultural, environmental, economic, and political factors that form complex webs that bring about many different problems. Every effort has been made to select materials that illustrate this complex interaction of factors, stimulating the beginning student to consider realistic rather than overly simplistic approaches to the pressing problems that threaten the existence of civilization.

In addition to an annotated *Table of Contents* and a *Topic Guide,* included in this edition of *Annual Editions: Global Issues* are *Internet References* that can be used to further explore topics addressed in the articles. New to this edition, *Critical Thinking* questions test understanding of key concepts.

Also new to this edition, *Learning Outcomes* for each unit are organized around two principles. The first: all of the articles have a central point of view (usually identified in the opening paragraphs), which is supported by specific reasons and illustrated with examples. The articles typically conclude by reconsidering the point of view in terms of counter arguments, policy implications, and/or forecasts of the future. Basic comprehension of each article requires an understanding of the author's point of view and supporting reasons. In a number of cases, articles are paired to illustrate contending points of view so that the reader is aware of on-going policy debates. The process of comparing and contrasting, therefore, requires a higher level of understanding beyond the comprehension of each article's content of and by itself.

The second principle is the interconnectedness of the units of the book. As identified in the introduction to Unit 1, the Allegory of the Balloon portrays the interconnectedness of the book's four organizing concepts. An ability to identify and articulate these connections is the second focus of the *Learning Outcomes.*

This is the twentieth-seventh edition of *Annual Editions: Global Issues.* When looking back over more than a quarter century of work, a great deal has taken place in world affairs, and the contents and organization of the book reflect these changes. Nonetheless, there is one underlying constant. It is my continuing goal to work with the editors and staff at McGraw-Hill Contemporary Learning Series to provide materials that encourage the readers of this book to develop a life-long appreciation of the complex and rapidly changing world in which we live. This collection of articles is an invitation to further explore the global issues of the twenty-first century and become personally involved in the great issues of our time.

Finally, materials in this book were selected for both their intellectual insights and readability. Timely and well-written materials should stimulate good classroom lectures and discussions. I hope that students and teachers will enjoy using this book. Readers can have input into the next edition by completing and returning the postage-paid article rating form in the back of the book.

Robert M. Jackson
Editor

Contents

UNIT 1
Global Issues in the Twenty-First Century: An Overview

Unit Overview   xx

The concepts in bold italics are developed in the article. For further expansion, please refer to the Topic Guide.

UNIT 2
Population and Food Production

UNIT 3
The Global Environment and Natural Resources Utilization

The concepts in bold italics are developed in the article. For further expansion, please refer to the Topic Guide.

UNIT 4
Political Economy

Unit Overview

72

The concepts in bold italics are developed in the article. For further expansion, please refer to the Topic Guide.

The concepts in bold italics are developed in the article. For further expansion, please refer to the Topic Guide.

UNIT 5
Conflict

UNIT 6
Cooperation

The concepts in bold italics are developed in the article. For further expansion, please refer to the Topic Guide.

UNIT 7
Values and Visions

The concepts in bold italics are developed in the article. For further expansion, please refer to the Topic Guide.

Correlation Guide

The *Annual Editions* series provides students with convenient, inexpensive access to current, carefully selected articles from the public press. **Annual Editions: Global Issues 11/12** is an easy-to-use reader that presents articles on important topics such as *population, environment, political economy,* and many more. For more information on *Annual Editions* and other *McGraw-Hill Contemporary Learning Series* titles, visit www.mhhe.com/cls.

This convenient guide matches the units in **Annual Editions: Global Issues 11/12** with the corresponding chapters in one of our best-selling McGraw-Hill Political Science textbooks by Rourke/Boyer.

Annual Editions: Global Issues 11/12	**International Politics on the World Stage, Brief, 8/e by Rourke/Boyer**
Unit 1: Global Issues in the Twenty-First Century: An Overview	**Chapter 1:** Thinking and Caring about World Politics **Chapter 2:** The Evolution of World Politics **Chapter 5:** Globalization: The Alternative Orientation
Unit 2: Population and Food Production	**Chapter 8:** International Law and Human Rights
Unit 3: The Global Environment and Natural Resources Utilization	**Chapter 12:** Preserving and Enhancing the Biosphere
Unit 4: Political Economy	**Chapter 6:** Power, Statecraft, and the National State: The Traditional Structure **Chapter 7:** Intergovernmental Organizations: Alternative Governance **Chapter 10:** National Economic Competition: The Traditional Road **Chapter 11:** International Economics: The Alternative Road
Unit 5: Conflict	**Chapter 6:** Power, Statecraft, and the National States: The Traditional Structure **Chapter 9:** Pursuing Security
Unit 6: Cooperation	**Chapter 8:** International Law and Human Rights **Chapter 11:** International Economics: The Alternative Road
Unit 7: Values and Visions	**Chapter 3:** Levels of Analysis and Foreign Policy **Chapter 8:** International Law and Human Rights

Topic Guide

This topic guide suggests how the selections in this book relate to the subjects covered in your course. You may want to use the topics listed on these pages to search the Web more easily.

On the following pages a number of websites have been gathered specifically for this book. They are arranged to reflect the units of this Annual Editions reader. You can link to these sites by going to www.mhhe.com/cls

All the articles that relate to each topic are listed below the bold-faced term.

Agriculture
1. Global Trends 2025: A Transformed World: Executive Summary
2. Could Food Shortages Bring Down Civilization?
6. Get Smart
11. The Next Breadbasket?: How Africa Could Save the World—and Itself
14. The Big Melt
21. Can Extreme Poverty Be Eliminated?
22. The Ideology of Development

Communication
19. It's a Flat World, After All
20. Why the World Isn't Flat
37. War in the Fifth Domain

Conservation
2. Could Food Shortages Bring Down Civilization?
3. Navigating the Energy Transition
14. The Big Melt
15. Troubled Waters
16. Acacia Avenue: How to Save Indonesia's Dwindling Rainforests
17. Asian Carp, Other Invasive Species Make a Splash

Cultural Customs and Values
4. Asia's Rise: Rise and Fall
5. Feminists and Fundamentalists
7. The New Population Bomb: The Four Megatrends That Will Change the World
8. Population and Sustainability
9. Why Migration Matters
18. Globalization and Its Contents
19. It's a Flat World, After All
20. Why the World Isn't Flat
21. Can Extreme Poverty Be Eliminated?
22. The Ideology of Development
24. The Case against the West: America and Europe in the Asian Century
40. Geneva Conventions
41. Is Bigger Better?
42. A World *Enslaved*
44. Humanity's Common Values: Seeking a Positive Future
45. Life, Religion and Everything
46. The End of Men

Demographics
1. Global Trends 2025: A Transformed World: Executive Summary
7. The New Population Bomb: The Four Megatrends That Will Change the World
8. Population and Sustainability
9. Why Migration Matters
10. Pandemic Pandemonium

Dependencies, international
4. Asia's Rise: Rise and Fall
9. Why Migration Matters
11. The Next Breadbasket?: How Africa Could Save the World—and Itself
18. Globalization and Its Contents
19. It's a Flat World, After All
20. Why the World Isn't Flat

24. The Case against the West: America and Europe in the Asian Century
25. Bolivia and Its Lithium
26. Not Your Father's Latin America
27. More Aid Is Not the Answer
28. It's Still the One

Development, economic
1. Global Trends 2025: A Transformed World: Executive Summary
2. Could Food Shortages Bring Down Civilization?
4. Asia's Rise: Rise and Fall
5. Feminists and Fundamentalists
10. Pandemic Pandemonium
11. The Next Breadbasket?: How Africa Could Save the World—and Itself
18. Globalization and Its Contents
19. It's a Flat World, After All
20. Why the World Isn't Flat
24. The Case against the West: America and Europe in the Asian Century
25. Bolivia and its Lithium
26. Not Your Father's Latin America
27. More Aid Is Not the Answer
31. On Clean Energy, China Skirts Rules
41. Is Bigger Better?
42. A World *Enslaved*
43. Chile Starts Early

Development, social
5. Feminists and Fundamentalists
11. The Next Breadbasket?: How Africa Could Save the World—and Itself
21. Can Extreme Poverty Be Eliminated?
22. The Ideology of Development
24. The Case against the West: America and Europe in the Asian Century
40. Geneva Conventions
41. Is Bigger Better?
43. Chile Starts Early
44. Humanity's Common Values: Seeking a Positive Future
45. Life, Religion and Everything
46. End of Men

Ecology
3. Navigating the Energy Transition
6. Get Smart
8. Population and Sustainability
12. Climate Change
14. The Big Melt
15. Troubled Waters
16. Acacia Avenue: How to Save Indonesia's Dwindling Rainforests
17. Asian Carp, Other Invasive Species Make a Splash
19. It's a Flat World, After All
21. Can Extreme Poverty Be Eliminated?
30. The End of Easy Oil
45. Life, Religion and Everything

Economics
1. Global Trends 2025: A Transformed World: Executive Summary
2. Could Food Shortages Bring Down Civilization?
3. Navigating the Energy Transition

Internet References

The following Internet sites have been selected to support the articles found in this reader. These sites were available at the time of publication. However, because websites often change their structure and content, the information listed may no longer be available. We invite you to visit www.mhhe.com/cls for easy access to these sites.

Annual Editions: Global Issues 11/12

General Sources

U.S. Information Agency (USIA)
www.america.gov

USIA's home page provides definitions, related documentation, and discussions of topics of concern to students of global issues. The site addresses today's Hot Topics as well as ongoing issues that form the foundation of the field.

World Wide Web Virtual Library: International Affairs

Resources
www.etown.edu/vl

Surf this site and its extensive links to learn about specific countries and regions, to research various think tanks and international organizations, and to study such vital topics as international law, development, the international economy, human rights, and peacekeeping.

UNIT 1: Global Issues in the Twenty-First Century: An Overview

The Henry L. Stimson Center
www.stimson.org

The Stimson Center, a nonpartisan organization, focuses on issues where policy, technology, and politics intersect. Use this site to find varying assessments of U.S. foreign policy in the post–cold war world and to research other topics.

The Heritage Foundation
www.heritage.org

This page offers discussion about and links to many sites having to do with foreign policy and foreign affairs, including news and commentary, policy review, events, and a resource bank.

The North-South Institute
www.nsi-ins.ca/ensi/index.htm

Searching this site of the North-South Institute, which works to strengthen international development cooperation and enhance gender and social equity, will help you find information and debates on a variety of global issues.

UNIT 2: Population and Food Production

The Hunger Project
www.thp.org

Browse through this nonprofit organization's site, whose goal is the sustainable end to global hunger through leadership at all levels of society. The Hunger Project contends that the persistence of hunger is at the heart of the major security issues threatening our planet.

Penn Library: Resources by Subject
www.library.upenn.edu/cgi-bin/res/sr.cgi

This vast site is rich in links to information about subjects of interest to students of global issues. Its extensive population and demography resources address such concerns as migration, family planning, and health and nutrition in various world regions.

World Health Organization
www.who.int

This home page of the World Health Organization will provide you with links to a wealth of statistical and analytical information about health and the environment in the developing world.

WWW Virtual Library: Demography & Population Studies
http://demography.anu.edu.au/VirtualLibrary

A definitive guide to demography and population studies can be found at this site. It contains a multitude of important links to information about global poverty and hunger.

UNIT 3: The Global Environment and Natural Resources Utilization

National Geographic Society
www.nationalgeographic.com

This site provides links to material related to the atmosphere, the oceans, and other environmental topics.

National Oceanic and Atmospheric Administration (NOAA)
www.noaa.gov

Through this home page of NOAA, part of the U.S. Department of Commerce, you can find information about coastal issues, fisheries, climate, and more. The site provides many links to research materials and to other Web resources.

SocioSite: Sociological Subject Areas
www.pscw.uva.nl/sociosite/TOPICS

This huge site provides many references of interest to those interested in global issues, such as links to information on ecology and the impact of consumerism.

United Nations Environment Programme (UNEP)
www.unep.ch

Consult this home page of UNEP for links to critical topics of concern to students of global issues, including desertification, migratory species, and the impact of trade on the environment.

UNIT 4: Political Economy

Belfer Center for Science and International Affairs (BCSIA)
http://ksgwww.harvard.edu/csia

BCSIA is the hub of Harvard University's John F. Kennedy School of Government's research, teaching, and training in international affairs related to security, environment, and technology.

Internet References

U.S. Agency for International Development
www.usaid.gov

Broad and overlapping issues such as democracy, population and health, economic growth, and development are covered on this website. It provides specific information about different regions and countries.

The World Bank Group
www.worldbank.org

News, press releases, summaries of new projects, speeches, publications, and coverage of numerous topics regarding development, countries, and regions are provided at this World Bank site. It also contains links to other important global financial organizations.

UNIT 5: Conflict

DefenseLINK
www.defenselink.mil

Learn about security news and research-related publications at this U.S. Department of Defense site. Links to related sites of interest are provided. The information systems BosniaLINK and GulfLINK can also be found here. Use the search function to investigate such issues as land mines.

Federation of American Scientists (FAS)
www.fas.org

FAS, a nonprofit policy organization, maintains this site to provide coverage of and links to such topics as global security, peace, and governance in the post–cold war world. It notes a variety of resources of value to students of global issues.

ISN International Relations and Security Network
www.isn.ethz.ch

This site, maintained by the Center for Security Studies and Conflict Research, is a clearinghouse for information on international relations and security policy. Topics are listed by category (Traditional Dimensions of Security, New Dimensions of Security, and Related Fields) and by major world region.

The NATO Integrated Data Service (NIDS)
www.nato.int/structur/nids/nids.htm

NIDS was created to bring information on security-related matters to within easy reach of the widest possible audience. Check out this website to review North Atlantic Treaty Organization documentation of all kinds, to read *NATO Review,* and to explore key issues in the field of European security and transatlantic cooperation.

UNIT 6: Cooperation

Carnegie Endowment for International Peace
www.ceip.org

An important goal of this organization is to stimulate discussion and learning among both experts and the public at large on a wide range of international issues. The site provides links to *Foreign Policy,* to the Moscow Center, to descriptions of various programs, and much more.

OECD/FDI Statistics
www.oecd.org/statistics

Explore world trade and investment trends and statistics on this site from the Organization for Economic Cooperation and Development. It provides links to many related topics and addresses the issues on a country-by-country basis.

U.S. Institute of Peace
www.usip.org

USIP, which was created by the U.S. Congress to promote peaceful resolution of international conflicts, seeks to educate people and to disseminate information on how to achieve peace. Click on Highlights, Publications, Events, Research Areas, and Library and Links.

UNIT 7: Values and Visions

Human Rights Web
www.hrweb.org

The history of the human rights movement, text on seminal figures, landmark legal and political documents, and ideas on how individuals can get involved in helping to protect human rights around the world can be found at this valuable site.

InterAction
www.interaction.org

InterAction encourages grassroots action and engages government policymakers on advocacy issues. The organization's Advocacy Committee provides this site to inform people on its initiatives to expand international humanitarian relief, refugee, and development-assistance programs.

World Map

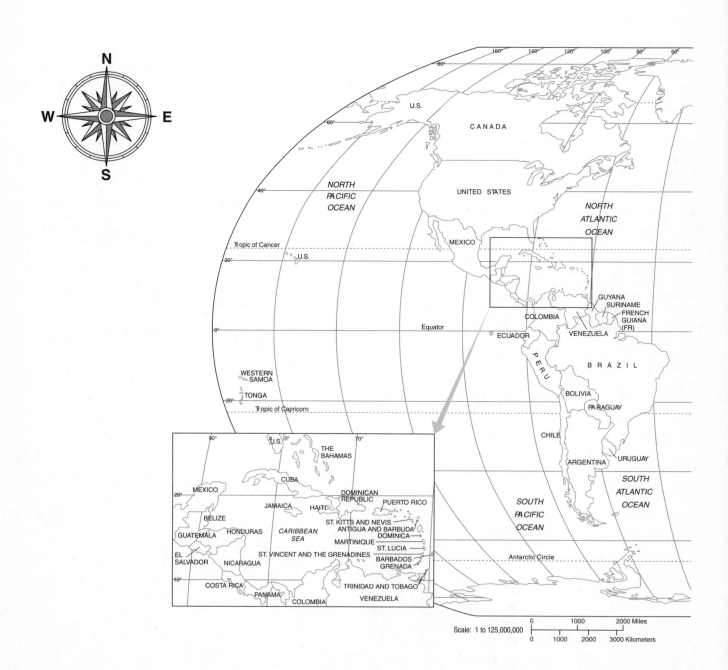

N
W E
S

160° 140° 120° 100° 80° 60°
80°

U.S.
CANADA

60°

40°
NORTH
PACIFIC
OCEAN
UNITED STATES

NORTH
ATLANTIC
OCEAN

Tropic of Cancer
MEXICO

20°
U.S.

GUYANA
SURINAME
FRENCH
GUIANA
(FR)
COLOMBIA

Equator
ECUADOR
VENEZUELA

0°

P E R U
B R A Z I L

WESTERN
SAMOA

BOLIVIA

TONGA
PARAGUAY

20°
Tropic of Capricorn
CHILE

ARGENTINA
URUGUAY

SOUTH
ATLANTIC
OCEAN

SOUTH
PACIFIC
OCEAN

Antarctic Circle

90° 0° 70°
U.S.
THE
BAHAMAS

CUBA

20°
MEXICO
DOMINICAN
REPUBLIC
PUERTO RICO
JAMAICA
HAITI
BELIZE
ST. KITTS AND NEVIS
ANTIGUA AND BARBUDA
DOMINICA
GUATEMALA
HONDURAS
CARIBBEAN
SEA
MARTINIQUE
ST. LUCIA
EL
SALVADOR
NICARAGUA
ST. VINCENT AND THE GRENADINES
BARBADOS
GRENADA
10°
COSTA RICA
PANAMA
TRINIDAD AND TOBAGO
COLOMBIA
VENEZUELA

0 1000 2000 Miles
Scale: 1 to 125,000,000
0 1000 2000 3000 Kilometers

UNIT 1

Global Issues in the Twenty-First Century: An Overview

Unit Selections

1. **Global Trends 2025: A Transformed World: Executive Summary,** *U.S. National Intelligence Council*
2. **Could Food Shortages Bring Down Civilization?,** Lester R. Brown
3. **Navigating the Energy Transition,** Michael T. Klare
4. **Asia's Rise: Rise and Fall,** Paul Kennedy
5. **Feminists and Fundamentalists,** Kavita Ramdas
6. **Get Smart,** Jamais Cascio

Learning Outcomes

After reading this unit you should be able to:

- Elaborate each of the four components of the Allegory of the Balloon (e.g., natural resources) with specific examples from the articles.

- Discuss the relationships between the four categories of the allegory with examples from each of the articles (e.g., the increasing costs of energy resource extraction and changing social structures).

- Identify key change factors that are likely to alter international relations in the next fifty years.

- Discuss how the role of the United States, Europe, and Japan is likely to change in the next fifty years.

- Discuss alternative scenarios of the future.

Student Website

www.mhhe.com/cls

Internet References

The Henry L. Stimson Center
www.stimson.org
The Heritage Foundation
www.heritage.org
The North-South Institute
www.nsi-ins.ca/ensi/index.htm

Imagine yellow paint being brushed onto an inflated, clear balloon. The yellow color, for purposes of this allegory, represents "people." In many ways the study of global issues is first and foremost the study of people. Today, there are more human beings occupying Earth than ever before. In addition, we are in the midst of a period of unprecedented population growth. Not only are there many countries where the majority of people are under age 16, but also due to improved health care, there are a greater number of older people alive today than ever before. The effect of a growing global population, however, goes beyond sheer numbers, for this trend has unprecedented impacts on natural resources and social services. An examination of population trends and the related topic of food production is a good place to begin an in-depth study of global issues.

Imagine that our fictional artist next dips the brush into a container of blue paint to represent "nature." The natural world plays an important role in setting the international agenda. Shortages of raw materials, climate change, regional droughts, and pollution of waterways are just a few examples of how natural resources can have global implications.

Adding blue paint to the balloon reveals one of the most important underlying concepts found in this book. Although the balloon originally was covered by both yellow and blue paint (people and nature as separate conceptual entities), the two combined produce an entirely different color: green. Talking about nature as a separate entity or people as though they were somehow removed from the forces of the natural world is a serious intellectual error. The people–nature relationship is one of the keys to understanding many of today's most important global issues.

The third color to be added to the balloon is red. This color represents "social structures." Factors falling into this category include whether a society is urban or rural, industrial or agrarian, and consumer-oriented or dedicated to the needs of the state. The relationship between this component and the others is extremely important. The impact of political decisions on the environment, for example, is one of the most significant features of the contemporary world. Will the whales or bald eagles survive? Historically, the forces of nature determined which species survived or perished. Today, survival depends on political decisions or indecision. Understanding the complex relationship between social structure and nature (known as ecopolitics) is central to the study of global issues.

Added to the three primary colors is the fourth and final color of white. It represents the "meta" component (i.e., those qualities that make human beings different from other life forms). These include new ideas and inventions, culture and values, religion and spirituality, and art and literature. The addition of the white paint immediately changes the intensity and shade of the mixture of colors, again emphasizing the relationship among all four factors.

© David Zurick

If the painter continues to ply the paintbrush over the miniature globe, a marbling effect becomes evident. From one area to the next, the shading varies because one element is more dominant than another. Further, the miniature system appears dynamic. Nothing is static; relationships are continually changing. This leads to a number of important insights: (1) There are no such things as separate elements, only connections or relationships; (2) changes in one area (such as the climate) will result in changes in all other areas; and (3) complex and dynamic relationships make it difficult to predict events accurately, so observers and policymakers are often surprised by unexpected events.

This book is organized along the basic lines of the balloon allegory. The first unit provides a broad overview of a variety of perspectives on the major forces that are shaping the world of the twenty-first century. From this "big picture" perspective more in-depth analyses follow. Unit 2, for example, focuses on population, disease, and hunger. Unit 3 examines the environment and related natural resource issues. The next three units look at different aspects of the world's social structures. They explore issues of economics, national security, conflict, and international cooperation. In the final unit, a number of "meta" factors are presented.

The reader should keep in mind that, just as it was impossible to keep the individual colors from blending into new colors on the balloon, it is also impossible to separate global issues into discrete chapters in a book. Any discussion of agriculture, for example, must take into account the impact of a growing population on soil and water resources, as well as new scientific breakthroughs in food production. Therefore, the organization of this book focuses attention on issue areas; it does not mean to imply that these factors are somehow separate.

With the collapse of the Soviet empire and the end of the cold war, the outlines of a new global agenda have emerged. Rather than being based on the ideology and interests of

1

the two superpowers, new political, economic, environmental, cultural, and security issues are interacting in an unprecedented fashion. Rapid population growth, environmental decline, uneven economic progress, and global terrorist networks are all parts of a complex state of affairs for which there is no historic parallel. As we enter the second decade of the twenty-first century, signs abound that we are entering a new era. In the words of Abraham Lincoln, "As our case is new, so we must think anew." Compounding this situation, however, is a whole series of old problems such as ethnic and religious rivalries.

The authors in this first unit provide a variety of perspectives on the trends that they believe are the most important to understanding the historic changes at work at the global level. This discussion is then pursued in greater detail in the following units.

Although the authors look at the same world, they often come to different conclusions. This raises an important issue of values and beliefs, for it can be argued that there really is no objective reality, only differing perspectives. In short, the study of global issues will challenge each thoughtful reader to examine her or his own values and beliefs.

Global Trends 2025: A Transformed World

Executive Summary

U.S. NATIONAL INTELLIGENCE COUNCIL

The **international system**—as constructed following the Second World War—will be almost unrecognizable by 2025 owing to the rise of emerging powers, a globalizing economy, a historic transfer of relative wealth and economic power from West to East, and the growing influence of nonstate actors. By 2025, the international system will be a **global multipolar one** with gaps in national power[1] continuing to narrow between developed and developing countries. Concurrent with the shift in power among nation-states, the relative power of various nonstate actors—including businesses, tribes, religious organizations, and criminal networks—is increasing. The players are changing, but so too are the scope and breadth of transnational issues important for continued global prosperity. Aging populations in the developed world; growing energy, food, and water constraints; and worries about climate change will limit and diminish what will still be an historically unprecedented age of prosperity.

Historically, emerging multipolar systems have been more unstable than bipolar or unipolar ones. Despite the recent financial volatility—which could end up accelerating many ongoing trends—we do not believe that we are headed toward a complete breakdown of the international system, as occurred in 1914–1918 when an earlier phase of globalization came to a halt. However, the next 20 years of transition to a new system are fraught with risks. Strategic rivalries are most likely to revolve around trade, investments, and technological innovation and acquisition, but we cannot rule out a 19th century-like scenario of arms races, territorial expansion, and military rivalries.

This is a story with **no clear outcome,** as illustrated by a series of vignettes we use to map out divergent futures. Although the United States is likely to remain the single most powerful actor, the United States' relative strength—even in the military realm—will decline and U.S. leverage will become more constrained. At the same time, the extent to which other actors—both state and nonstate—will be willing or able to shoulder increased burdens is unclear. Policymakers and publics will have to cope with a growing demand for multilateral cooperation when the international system will be stressed by the incomplete transition from the old to a still-forming new order.

Economic Growth Fueling Rise of Emerging Players

In terms of size, speed, and directional flow, the transfer of **global wealth and economic power** now under way—roughly from West to East—is without precedent in modern history. This shift derives from two sources. First, increases in oil and commodity prices have generated windfall profits for the Gulf states and Russia. Second, lower costs combined with government policies have shifted the locus of manufacturing and some service industries to Asia.

Growth projections for Brazil, Russia, India, and China (the BRICs) indicate they will collectively match the original G-7's share of global GDP by 2040–2050. **China** is poised to have more impact on the world over the next 20 years than any other country. If current trends persist, by 2025 China will have the world's second largest economy and will be a leading military power. It also could be the largest importer of natural resources and the biggest polluter. **India** probably will continue to enjoy relatively rapid economic growth and will strive for a multipolar world in which New Delhi is one of the poles. China and India must decide the extent to which they are willing and capable of playing increasing global roles and how each will relate to the other. **Russia** has the potential to be richer, more powerful, and more self-assured in 2025 if it invests in human capital, expands and diversifies its economy, and integrates with global markets. On the other hand, Russia could experience a significant decline if it fails to take these steps and oil and gas prices remain in the $50–70 per barrel range. No other countries are projected to rise to the level of China, India, or Russia, and none is likely to match their individual global clout. We expect, however, to see the political and economic power of other countries—such as Indonesia, Iran, and Turkey—increase.

For the most part, China, India, and Russia are not following the Western liberal model for self-development but instead are using a different model, "**state capitalism.**" State capitalism is a loose term used to describe a system of economic management that gives a prominent role to the state. Other rising powers—South Korea, Taiwan, and Singapore—also used state capitalism to develop their economies. However, the impact of Russia, and particularly China, following this path is potentially much greater owing to their size and approach to "democratization." We remain optimistic about the *long-term* prospects for **greater democratization,** even though advances are likely to be slow and globalization is subjecting many recently democratized countries to increasing social and economic pressures with the potential to undermine liberal institutions.

Many other countries will fall further behind economically. **Sub-Saharan Africa** will remain the region most vulnerable to economic disruption, population stresses, civil conflict, and political instability. Despite increased global demand for commodities for which Sub-Saharan Africa will be a major supplier, local populations are unlikely to experience significant economic gain. Windfall profits arising from sustained increases in commodity prices might further entrench corrupt or otherwise ill-equipped governments in several regions, diminishing the prospects for democratic and market-based reforms. Although many of **Latin America's** major countries will have become middle income powers by 2025, others, particularly those such as Venezuela and Bolivia that have embraced populist policies for a protracted period, will lag behind—and some, such as Haiti, will have become even poorer and less governable. Overall, Latin America will continue to lag behind Asia and other fast-growing areas in terms of economic competitiveness.

Asia, Africa, and Latin America will account for virtually all **population growth** over the next 20 years; less than 3 percent of the growth will occur in the West. Europe and Japan will continue to far outdistance the emerging powers of China and India in per capita wealth, but they will struggle to maintain robust growth rates because the size of their working-age populations will decrease. The US will be a partial exception to the aging of populations in the developed world because it will experience higher birth rates and more immigration. The number of migrants seeking to move from disadvantaged to relatively privileged countries is likely to increase.

The number of countries with youthful age structures in the current "arc of instability" is projected to decline by as much as 40 percent. Three of every four youth-bulge countries that remain will be located in Sub-Saharan Africa; nearly all of the remainder will be located in the core of the Middle East, scattered through southern and central Asia, and in the Pacific Islands.

New Transnational Agenda

Resource issues will gain prominence on the international agenda. Unprecedented global economic growth—positive in so many other regards—will continue to put pressure on a number of **highly strategic resources,** including energy, food, and water, and demand is projected to outstrip easily available supplies over the next decade or so. For example, non-OPEC liquid hydrocarbon production—crude oil, natural gas liquids, and unconventionals such as tar sands—will not grow commensurate with demand. Oil and gas production of many traditional energy producers already is declining. Elsewhere—in China, India, and Mexico—production has flattened. Countries capable of significantly expanding production will dwindle; oil and gas production will be concentrated in unstable areas. As a result of this and other factors, the world will be in the midst of a fundamental energy transition away from oil toward natural gas, coal and other alternatives.

The World Bank estimates that **demand for food** will rise by 50 percent by 2030, as a result of growing world population, rising affluence, and the shift to Western dietary preferences by a larger middle class. Lack of access to stable supplies of water is reaching critical proportions, particularly for agricultural purposes, and the problem will worsen because of rapid urbanization worldwide and the roughly 1.2 billion persons to be added over the next 20 years. Today, experts consider 21 countries, with a combined population of about 600 million, to be either cropland or freshwater scarce. Owing to continuing population growth, 36 countries, with about 1.4 billion people, are projected to fall into this category by 2025.

Climate change is expected to exacerbate resource scarcities. Although the impact of climate change will vary by region, a number of regions will begin to suffer harmful effects, particularly water scarcity and loss of agricultural production. Regional differences in agricultural production are likely to become more pronounced over time with declines disproportionately concentrated in developing countries, particularly those in Sub-Saharan Africa. Agricultural losses are expected to mount with substantial impacts forecast by most economists by late this century. For many developing countries, decreased agricultural output will be devastating because agriculture accounts for a large share of their economies and many of their citizens live close to subsistence levels.

New technologies could again provide solutions, such as viable alternatives to fossil fuels or means to overcome food and water constraints. However, all current technologies are inadequate for replacing the traditional energy architecture on the scale needed, and new energy technologies probably will not be commercially viable and widespread by 2025. The pace of technological innovation will be key. Even with a favorable policy and funding environment for biofuels, clean coal, or hydrogen, the transition to new fuels will be slow. Major technologies historically have had an "adoption lag." In the energy sector, a recent study found that it takes an average of 25 years for a new production technology to become widely adopted.

Despite what are seen as long odds now, we cannot rule out the possibility of an **energy transition** by 2025 that would avoid the costs of an energy infrastructure overhaul. The greatest possibility for a relatively quick and inexpensive transition during the period comes from better renewable generation sources (photovoltaic and wind) and improvements in battery technology. With many of these technologies, the infrastructure cost hurdle for individual projects would be lower, enabling many small economic actors to develop their own energy transformation projects that directly serve their interests—e.g., stationary fuel cells powering homes and offices, recharging plug-in hybrid autos, and selling energy back to the grid. Also, energy conversion schemes—such as plans to generate hydrogen for automotive fuel cells from electricity in the homeowner's garage—could avoid the need to develop complex hydrogen transportation infrastructure.

Prospects for Terrorism, Conflict, and Proliferation

Terrorism, proliferation, and conflict will remain key concerns even as resource issues move up on the international agenda. Terrorism is unlikely to disappear by 2025, but its appeal could diminish if economic growth continues and youth unemployment is mitigated in the Middle East. Economic opportunities for youth and greater political pluralism probably would dissuade some from joining terrorists' ranks, but others—motivated by a variety of factors, such as a desire for revenge or to become "martyrs"—will continue to turn to violence to pursue their objectives.

In the absence of employment opportunities and legal means for political expression, conditions will be ripe for disaffection, growing radicalism, and possible recruitment of youths into **terrorist groups.** Terrorist groups in 2025 will likely be a combination of descendants of long-established groups—that inherit organizational structures, command and control processes, and training procedures necessary to conduct sophisticated attacks—and newly emergent collections of the angry and disenfranchised that become self-radicalized. For those terrorist groups that are active in 2025, the diffusion of technologies and scientific knowledge will place some of the world's most dangerous capabilities within their reach. One of our greatest concerns continues to be that terrorist or other malevolent groups might acquire and employ biological agents, or less likely, a nuclear device, to create mass casualties.

Although **Iran's** acquisition of nuclear weapons is not inevitable, other countries' worries about a nuclear-armed Iran could lead states in the region to develop new security arrangements with external powers, acquire additional weapons, and consider pursuing their own nuclear ambitions. It is not clear that the type of stable deterrent relationship that existed between the great powers for most of the Cold War would emerge naturally in the Middle East with a nuclear-weapons capable Iran. Episodes of low-intensity conflict taking place under a nuclear umbrella could lead to an unintended escalation and broader conflict if clear red lines between those states involved are not well established.

We believe **ideological conflicts** akin to the Cold War are unlikely to take root in a world in which most states will be preoccupied with the pragmatic challenges of globalization and shifting global power alignments. The force of ideology is likely to be strongest in the Muslim world—particularly the Arab core. In those countries that are likely to struggle with youth bulges and weak economic underpinnings—such as Pakistan, Afghanistan, Nigeria, and Yemen—the radical Salafi trend of Islam is likely to gain traction.

Types of **conflict** we have not seen for awhile—such as over resources—could reemerge. Perceptions of energy scarcity will drive countries to take actions to assure their future access to energy supplies. In the worst case, this could result in interstate conflicts if government leaders deem assured access to energy resources, for example, to be essential for maintaining domestic stability and the survival of their regimes. However, even actions short of war will have important geopolitical consequences. Maritime security concerns are providing a rationale for naval buildups and modernization efforts, such as China's and India's development of blue-water naval capabilities. The buildup of regional naval capabilities could lead to increased tensions, rivalries, and counterbalancing moves but it also will create opportunities for multinational cooperation in protecting critical sea lanes. With water becoming more scarce in Asia and the Middle East, cooperation to manage changing water resources is likely to become more difficult within and between states.

The risk of **nuclear weapon use** over the next 20 years, although remaining very low, is likely to be greater than it is today as a result of several converging trends. The spread of nuclear technologies and expertise is generating concerns about the potential emergence of new nuclear weapon states and the acquisition of nuclear materials by terrorist groups. Ongoing low-intensity clashes between India and Pakistan continue to raise the specter that such events could escalate to a broader conflict between those nuclear powers. The possibility of a future disruptive regime change or collapse occurring in a nuclear weapon state such as North Korea also continues to raise questions regarding the ability of weak states to control and secure their nuclear arsenals.

If nuclear weapons are used in the next 15–20 years, the international system will be shocked as it experiences immediate humanitarian, economic, and political-military repercussions. A future use of nuclear weapons probably would bring about significant geopolitical changes as some states would seek to establish or reinforce security alliances with existing nuclear powers and others would push for global nuclear disarmament.

A More Complex International System

The trend toward greater diffusion of authority and power that has been occurring for a couple decades is likely to accelerate because of the emergence of new global players, the worsening institutional deficit, potential expansion of regional blocs, and enhanced strength of nonstate actors and networks. The **multiplicity of actors** on the international scene could add strength—in terms of filling gaps left by aging post-World War II institutions—or further fragment the international system and incapacitate international cooperation. The diversity in type of actor raises the likelihood of fragmentation occurring over the next two decades, particularly given the wide array of transnational challenges facing the international community.

The rising BRIC powers are unlikely to challenge the international system as did Germany and Japan in the 19th and 20th centuries, but because of their growing geopolitical and economic clout, they will have a high degree of freedom to customize their political and economic policies rather than fully adopting Western norms. They also are likely to want to preserve their policy freedom to maneuver, allowing others to carry the primary burden for dealing with such issues as terrorism, climate change, proliferation, and energy security.

Existing multilateral institutions—which are large and cumbersome and were designed for a different geopolitical order—will have difficulty adapting quickly to undertake new missions, accommodate changing memberships, and augment their resources.

Nongovernmental organizations (NGOs)—concentrating on specific issues—increasingly will be a part of the landscape, but NGO networks are likely to be limited in their ability to effect change in the absence of concerted efforts by multilateral institutions or governments. Efforts at greater inclusiveness—to reflect the emergence of the newer powers—may make it harder for international organizations to tackle transnational challenges. Respect for the dissenting views of member nations will continue to shape the agenda of organizations and limit the kinds of solutions that can be attempted.

Greater **Asian regionalism**—possible by 2025—would have global implications, sparking or reinforcing a trend toward three trade and financial clusters that could become quasi-blocs: North America, Europe, and East Asia. Establishment of such quasi-blocs would have implications for the ability to achieve future global World Trade Organization (WTO) agreements. Regional clusters could compete in setting trans-regional product standards for information technology, biotechnology, nanotechnology, intellectual property rights, and other aspects of the "new economy." On the other hand, an absence of regional cooperation in Asia could help spur competition among China, India, and Japan over resources such as energy.

Intrinsic to the growing complexity of the overlapping roles of states, institutions, and nonstate actors is the **proliferation of political identities,** which is leading to establishment of new networks and rediscovered communities. No one political identity is likely to be dominant in most societies by 2025. Religion-based networks may be quintessential issue networks and overall may play a more powerful role on many transnational issues such as the environment and inequalities than secular groupings.

The United States: Less Dominant Power

By 2025 the US will find itself as one of a number of important actors on the world stage, albeit still the most powerful one. Even in the military realm, where the US will continue to possess considerable advantages in 2025, advances by others in science and technology, expanded adoption of irregular warfare tactics by both state and nonstate actors, proliferation of long-range precision weapons, and growing use of cyber warfare attacks increasingly will constrict US freedom of action. A more constrained US role has implications for others and the likelihood of new agenda issues being tackled effectively. Despite the recent rise in anti-Americanism, the US probably will continue to be seen as a much-needed regional balancer in the Middle East and Asia. The US will continue to be expected to play a significant role in using its military power to counter global terrorism. On newer security issues like climate change, US leadership will be widely perceived as critical to leveraging competing and divisive views to find solutions. At the same time, the multiplicity of influential actors and distrust of vast power means less room for the US to call the shots without the support of strong partnerships. Developments in the rest of the world, including internal developments in a number of key states—particularly China and Russia—are also likely to be crucial determinants of US policy.

2025—What Kind of Future?

The above trends suggest major **discontinuities,** shocks, and surprises, which we highlight throughout the text. Examples include nuclear weapons use or a pandemic. In some cases, the surprise element is only a matter of **timing:** an energy transition, for example, is inevitable; the only questions are when and how abruptly or smoothly such a transition occurs. An energy transition from one type of fuel (fossil fuels) to another (alternative) is an event that historically has only happened once a century at most with momentous consequences. The transition from wood to coal helped trigger industrialization. In this case, a transition—particularly an abrupt one—out of fossil fuels would have major repercussions for energy producers in the Middle East and Eurasia, potentially causing permanent decline of some states as global and regional powers.

Other discontinuities are less predictable. They are likely to result from an interaction of several trends and depend on the quality of leadership. We put uncertainties such as whether China or Russia becomes a democracy in this category. China's growing middle class increases the chances but does not make such a development inevitable. Political pluralism seems less likely in Russia in the absence of economic diversification. Pressure from below may force the issue, or a leader might begin or enhance the democratization process to sustain the economy or spur economic growth. A sustained plunge in the price of oil and gas would alter the outlook and increase prospects for greater political and economic liberalization in Russia. If either country were to democratize, it would represent another wave of democratization with wide significance for many other developing states.

Also **uncertain** are the outcomes of demographic challenges facing Europe, Japan, and even Russia. In none of these cases does demography have to spell destiny with less regional and global power an inevitable outcome. Technology, the role of immigration, public health improvements, and laws encouraging greater female participation in the economy are some of the measures that could change the trajectory of current trends pointing toward less economic growth, increased social tensions, and possible decline.

Whether global institutions adapt and revive—another key uncertainty—also is a function of leadership. Current trends suggest a dispersion of power and authority will create a global governance deficit. Reversing those trend lines would require strong leadership in the international community by a number of powers, including the emerging ones.

Some uncertainties would have greater consequences—should they occur—than would others. In this work, we emphasize the overall potential for greater conflict—some forms of which could threaten globalization. We put WMD terrorism and a Middle East nuclear arms race in this category. In the four fictionalized scenarios, we have highlighted new challenges that could emerge as a result of the ongoing global transformation. They present new situations, dilemmas, or predicaments that represent departures from recent developments. As a set, they do not cover all possible futures. ***None of these is inevitable or even necessarily likely;*** but, as with many other uncertainties, the scenarios are potential game-changers.

- In *A World Without the West,* the new powers supplant the West as the leaders on the world stage.
- *October Surprise* illustrates the impact of inattention to global climate change; unexpected major impacts narrow the world's range of options.
- In *BRICs' Bust-Up,* disputes over vital resources emerge as a source of conflict between major powers—in this case two emerging heavyweights—India and China.
- In *Politics Is Not Always Local,* nonstate networks emerge to set the international agenda on the environment, eclipsing governments.

Note

1. National power scores, computed by the International Futures computer model, are the product of an index combining the weighted factors of GDP, defense spending, population, and technology.

Critical Thinking

1. What is the authors' point of view, which is the basis of this article?
2. What reasons are given to support this point of view?
3. Who are the so-called BRIC countries?
4. What is meant by state capitalism?
5. What is the new transnational agenda?
6. In addition to nation-states (i.e., countries), who are some of the new international actors?
7. Are there plausible scenarios of the future that have been left out?
8. In the "note" at the end of the article, the variables are identified that comprise the National Power Score. Assess the centrality of these variables to predicting the future and identify other variables that may have been omitted. Note: this assessment reveals a general outline of your international relations theory. Is it similar or different from the theory underlying the analysis presented in this article?

From *Atlantic Council,* November 2008, pp. vi–xiii.

Could Food Shortages Bring Down Civilization?

Lester R. Brown

One of the toughest things for people to do is to anticipate sudden change. Typically we project the future by extrapolating from trends in the past. Much of the time this approach works well. But sometimes it fails spectacularly, and people are simply blindsided by events such as today's economic crisis.

For most of us, the idea that civilization itself could disintegrate probably seems preposterous. Who would not find it hard to think seriously about such a complete departure from what we expect of ordinary life? What evidence could make us heed a warning so dire—and how would we go about responding to it? We are so inured to a long list of highly unlikely catastrophes that we are virtually programmed to dismiss them all with a wave of the hand: Sure, our civilization might devolve into chaos—and Earth might collide with an asteroid, too!

For many years I have studied global agricultural, population, environmental, and economic trends and their interactions. The combined effects of those trends and the political tensions they generate point to the breakdown of governments and societies. Yet I, too, have resisted the idea that food shortages could bring down not only individual governments but also our global civilization.

I can no longer ignore that risk. Our continuing failure to deal with the environmental declines that are undermining the world food economy—most important, falling water tables, eroding soils, and rising temperatures—forces me to conclude that such a collapse is possible.

The Problem of Failed States

Even a cursory look at the vital signs of our current world order lends unwelcome support to my conclusion. And those of us in the environmental field are well into our third decade of charting trends of environmental decline without seeing any significant effort to reverse a single one.

In six of the past nine years world grain production has fallen short of consumption, forcing a steady drawdown in stocks. When the 2008 harvest began, world carryover stocks of grain (the amount in the bin when the new harvest begins) were at 62 days of consumption, a near record low. In response, world grain prices in the spring and summer of last year climbed to the highest level ever.

As demand for food rises faster than supplies are growing, the resulting food-price inflation puts severe stress on the governments of countries already teetering on the edge of chaos. Unable to buy grain or grow their own, hungry people take to the streets. Indeed, even before the steep climb in grain prices in 2008, the number of failing states was expanding. Many of their problems stem from a failure to slow the growth of their populations. But if the food situation continues to deteriorate, entire nations will break down at an ever increasing rate. We have entered a new era in geopolitics. In the 20th century the main threat to international security was superpower conflict; today it is failing states. It is not the concentration of power but its absence that puts us at risk.

States fail when national governments can no longer provide personal security, food security, and basic social services such as education and health care. They often lose control of part or all of their territory. When governments lose their monopoly on power, law and order begin to disintegrate. After a point, countries can become so dangerous that food relief workers are no longer safe and their programs are halted; in Somalia and Afghanistan, deteriorating conditions have already put such programs in jeopardy.

Failing states are of international concern because they are a source of terrorists, drugs, weapons, and refugees, threatening political stability everywhere. Somalia, number one on the 2008 list of failing states, has become a base for piracy. Iraq, number five, is a hotbed for terrorist training. Afghanistan, number seven, is the world's leading supplier of heroin. Following the massive genocide of 1994 in Rwanda, refugees from that troubled state, thousands of armed soldiers among them, helped to destabilize neighboring Democratic Republic of the Congo (number six).

Our global civilization depends on a functioning network of politically healthy nation-states to control the spread of infectious disease, to manage the international monetary system, to control international terrorism and to reach scores of other common goals. If the system for controlling infectious diseases—such as polio, SARS, or avian flu—breaks down, humanity will be in trouble. Once states fail, no one assumes responsibility for their debt to outside lenders. If enough states disintegrate, their fall will threaten the stability of global civilization itself.

A New Kind of Food Shortage

The surge in world grain prices in 2007 and 2008—and the threat they pose to food security—has a different, more troubling quality than the increases of the past. During the second half of the 20th century, grain prices rose dramatically several times. In 1972, for instance, the Soviets, recognizing their poor harvest early, quietly cornered the world wheat market. As a result, wheat prices elsewhere more than doubled, pulling rice and corn prices up with them. But this and other price shocks were event-driven—drought in the Soviet Union, a monsoon failure in India, crop-shrinking heat in the U.S. Corn Belt. And the rises were short-lived: Prices typically returned to normal with the next harvest.

In contrast, the recent surge in world grain prices is trend-driven, making it unlikely to reverse without a reversal in the trends themselves. On the demand side, those trends include the ongoing addition of more than 70 million people a year; a growing number of people wanting to move up the food chain to consume highly grain-intensive livestock products [see "The Greenhouse Hamburger," by Nathan Fiala; *Scientific American,* February 2009]; and the massive diversion of U.S. grain to ethanol-fuel distilleries.

The extra demand for grain associated with rising affluence varies widely among countries. People in low-income countries where grain supplies 60 percent of calories, such as India, directly consume a bit more than a pound of grain a day. In affluent countries such as the U.S. and Canada, grain consumption per person is nearly four times that much, though perhaps 90 percent of it is consumed indirectly as meat, milk, and eggs from grain-fed animals.

The potential for further grain consumption as incomes rise among low-income consumers is huge. But that potential pales beside the insatiable demand for crop-based automotive fuels. A fourth of this year's U.S. grain harvest—enough to feed 125 million Americans or half a billion Indians at current consumption levels—will go to fuel cars. Yet even if the entire U.S. grain harvest were diverted into making ethanol, it would meet at most 18 percent of U.S. automotive fuel needs. The grain required to fill a 25-gallon SUV tank with ethanol could feed one person for a year.

The recent merging of the food and energy economies implies that if the food value of grain is less than its fuel value, the market will move the grain into the energy economy. That double demand is leading to an epic competition between cars and people for the grain supply and to a political and moral issue of unprecedented dimensions. The U.S., in a misguided effort to reduce its dependence on foreign oil by substituting grain-based fuels, is generating global food insecurity on a scale not seen before.

Water Shortages Mean Food Shortages

What about supply? The three environmental trends I mentioned earlier—the shortage of freshwater, the loss of topsoil, and the rising temperatures (and other effects) of global warming—are making it increasingly hard to expand the world's grain supply fast enough to keep up with demand. Of all those trends, however, the spread of water shortages poses the most immediate threat. The biggest challenge here is irrigation, which consumes 70 percent of the world's freshwater. Millions of irrigation wells in many countries are now pumping water out of underground sources faster than rainfall can recharge them. The result is falling water tables in countries populated by half the world's people, including the three big grain producers—China, India, and the U.S.

Usually aquifers are replenishable, but some of the most important ones are not: The "fossil" aquifers, so called because they store ancient water and are not recharged by precipitation. For these—including the vast Ogallala Aquifer that underlies the U.S. Great Plains, the Saudi aquifer and the deep aquifer under the North China Plain—depletion would spell the end of pumping. In arid regions such a loss could also bring an end to agriculture altogether.

In China the water table under the North China Plain, an area that produces more than half of the country's wheat and a third of its corn, is falling fast. Overpumping has used up most of the water in a shallow aquifer there, forcing well drillers to turn to the region's deep aquifer, which is not replenishable. A report by the World Bank foresees "catastrophic consequences for future generations" unless water use and supply can quickly be brought back into balance.

As water tables have fallen and irrigation wells have gone dry, China's wheat crop, the world's largest, has declined by 8 percent since it peaked at 123 million tons in 1997. In that same period China's rice production dropped 4 percent. The world's most populous nation may soon be importing massive quantities of grain.

But water shortages are even more worrying in India. There the margin between food consumption and survival is more precarious. Millions of irrigation wells have dropped water tables in almost every state. As Fred Pearce reported in New Scientist:

Half of India's traditional hand-dug wells and millions of shallower tube wells have already dried up, bringing a spate of suicides among those who rely on them. Electricity blackouts are reaching epidemic proportions in states where half of the electricity is used to pump water from depths of up to a kilometer [3,300 feet].

A World Bank study reports that 15 percent of India's food supply is produced by mining groundwater. Stated otherwise, 175 million Indians consume grain produced with water from irrigation wells that will soon be exhausted. The continued shrinking of water supplies could lead to unmanageable food shortages and social conflict.

Less Soil, More Hunger

The scope of the second worrisome trend—the loss of topsoil—is also startling. Topsoil is eroding faster than new soil forms on perhaps a third of the world's cropland. This thin layer of essential plant nutrients, the very foundation of civilization, took long stretches of geologic time to build up, yet it is typically only about six inches deep. Its loss from wind and water erosion doomed earlier civilizations.

In 2002 a U.N. team assessed the food situation in Lesotho, the small, landlocked home of two million people embedded within South Africa. The team's finding was straightforward: "Agriculture in Lesotho faces a catastrophic future; crop production is declining and could cease altogether over large tracts of the country if steps are not taken to reverse soil erosion, degradation and the decline in soil fertility."

In the Western Hemisphere, Haiti—one of the first states to be recognized as failing—was largely self-sufficient in grain 40 years ago. In the years since, though, it has lost nearly all its forests and much of its topsoil, forcing the country to import more than half of its grain.

The third and perhaps most pervasive environmental threat to food security—rising surface temperature—can affect crop yields everywhere. In many countries crops are grown at or near their thermal optimum, so even a minor temperature rise during the growing season can shrink the harvest. A study published by the U.S. National Academy of Sciences has confirmed a rule of thumb among crop ecologists: For every rise of one degree Celsius (1.8 degrees Fahrenheit) above the norm, wheat, rice, and corn yields fall by 10 percent.

In the past, most famously when the innovations in the use of fertilizer, irrigation, and high-yield varieties of wheat and rice created the "green revolution" of the 1960s and 1970s, the response to the growing demand for food was the successful application of scientific agriculture: the technological fix. This time, regrettably, many of the most productive advances in agricultural technology have already been put into practice, and so the long-term rise in land productivity is slowing down. Between 1950 and 1990 the world's farmers increased the grain yield per acre by more than 2 percent a year, exceeding the growth of population. But since then, the annual growth in yield has slowed to slightly more than 1 percent. In some countries the yields appear to be near their practical limits, including rice yields in Japan and China.

Some commentators point to genetically modified crop strains as a way out of our predicament. Unfortunately, however, no genetically modified crops have led to dramatically higher yields, comparable to the doubling or tripling of wheat and rice yields that took place during the green revolution. Nor do they seem likely to do so, simply because conventional plant-breeding techniques have already tapped most of the potential for raising crop yields.

Jockeying for Food

As the world's food security unravels, a dangerous politics of food scarcity is coming into play: Individual countries acting in their narrowly defined self-interest are actually worsening the plight of the many. The trend began in 2007, when leading wheat-exporting countries such as Russia and Argentina limited or banned their exports, in hopes of increasing locally available food supplies and thereby bringing down food prices domestically. Vietnam, the world's second-biggest rice exporter after Thailand, banned its exports for several months for the same reason. Such moves may reassure those living in the exporting countries, but they are creating panic in importing countries that must rely on what is then left of the world's exportable grain.

In response to those restrictions, grain importers are trying to nail down long-term bilateral trade agreements that would lock up future grain supplies. The Phillippines, no longer able to count on getting rice from the world market, recently negotiated a three-year deal with Vietnam for a guaranteed 1.5 million tons of rice each year. Food-import anxiety is even spawning entirely new efforts by food-importing countries to buy or lease farmland in other countries.

In spite of such stopgap measures, soaring food prices and spreading hunger in many other countries are beginning to break down the social order. In several provinces of Thailand the predations of "rice rustlers" have forced villagers to guard their rice fields at night with loaded shotguns. In Pakistan an armed soldier escorts each grain truck. During the first half of 2008, 83 trucks carrying grain in Sudan were hijacked before reaching the Darfur relief camps.

No country is immune to the effects of tightening food supplies, not even the U.S., the world's breadbasket. If China turns to the world market for massive quantities of grain, as it has recently done for soybeans, it will have to buy from the U.S. For U.S. consumers, that would mean competing for the U.S. grain harvest with 1.3 billion Chinese consumers with fast-rising incomes—a nightmare scenario. In such circumstances, it would be tempting for the U.S. to restrict exports, as it did, for instance, with grain and soybeans in the 1970s when domestic prices soared. But that is not an option with China. Chinese investors now hold well over a trillion U.S. dollars, and they have often been the leading international buyers of U.S. Treasury securities issued to finance the fiscal deficit. Like it or not, U.S. consumers will share their grain with Chinese consumers, no matter how high food prices rise.

Plan B: Our Only Option

Since the current world food shortage is trend-driven, the environmental trends that cause it must be reversed. To do so requires extraordinarily demanding measures, a monumental shift away from business as usual—what we at the Earth Policy Institute call Plan A—to a civilization-saving Plan B. [see "Plan B 3.0: Mobilizing to Save Civilization," at www.earthpolicy.org/Books/PB3/]

Similar in scale and urgency to the U.S. mobilization for World War II, Plan B has four components: a massive effort to cut carbon emissions by 80 percent from their 2006 levels by 2020; the stabilization of the world's population at eight billion by 2040; the eradication of poverty; and the restoration of forests, soils, and aquifers.

Net carbon dioxide emissions can be cut by systematically raising energy efficiency and investing massively in the development of renewable sources of energy. We must also ban deforestation worldwide, as several countries already have done, and plant billions of trees to sequester carbon. The transition from fossil fuels to renewable forms of energy can be driven by imposing a tax on carbon, while offsetting it with a reduction in income taxes.

Stabilizing population and eradicating poverty go hand in hand. In fact, the key to accelerating the shift to smaller families is eradicating poverty—and vice versa. One way is to ensure at least a primary school education for all children, girls as well as boys. Another is to provide rudimentary, village-level health care, so that people can be confident that their children will survive to adulthood. Women everywhere need access to reproductive health care and family-planning services.

The fourth component, restoring the earth's natural systems and resources, incorporates a worldwide initiative to arrest the fall in water tables by raising water productivity: the useful activity that can be wrung from each drop. That implies shifting to more efficient irrigation systems and to more water-efficient crops. In some countries, it implies growing (and eating) more wheat and less rice, a water-intensive crop. And for industries and cities, it implies doing what some are doing already, namely, continuously recycling water.

At the same time, we must launch a worldwide effort to conserve soil, similar to the U.S. response to the Dust Bowl of the 1930s. Terracing the ground, planting trees as shelterbelts against windblown soil erosion, and practicing minimum tillage—in which the soil is not plowed and crop residues are left on the field—are among the most important soil-conservation measures.

There is nothing new about our four interrelated objectives. They have been discussed individually for years. Indeed, we have created entire institutions intended to tackle some of them, such as the World Bank to alleviate poverty. And we have made substantial progress in some parts of the world on at least one of them—the distribution of family-planning services and the associated shift to smaller families that brings population stability.

For many in the development community, the four objectives of Plan B were seen as positive, promoting development as long as they did not cost too much. Others saw them as humanitarian goals—politically correct and morally appropriate. Now a third and far more momentous rationale presents itself: Meeting these goals may be necessary to prevent the collapse of our civilization. Yet the cost we project for saving civilization would amount to less than $200 billion a year, a sixth of current global military spending. In effect, Plan B is the new security budget.

Time: Our Scarcest Resource

Our challenge is not only to implement Plan B but also to do it quickly. The world is in a race between political tipping points and natural ones. Can we close coal-fired power plants fast enough to prevent the Greenland ice sheet from slipping into the sea and inundating our coastlines? Can we cut carbon emissions fast enough to save the mountain glaciers of Asia? During the dry season their meltwaters sustain the major rivers of India and China—and by extension, hundreds of millions of people. Can we stabilize population before countries such as India, Pakistan, and Yemen are overwhelmed by shortages of the water they need to irrigate their crops?

It is hard to overstate the urgency of our predicament. [For the most thorough and authoritative scientific assessment of global climate change, see "Climate Change 2007. Fourth Assessment Report of the Intergovernmental Panel on Climate Change," available at www.ipcc.ch] Every day counts. Unfortunately, we do not know how long we can light our cities with coal, for instance, before Greenland's ice sheet can no longer be saved. Nature sets the deadlines; nature is the timekeeper. But we human beings cannot see the clock.

We desperately need a new way of thinking, a new mind-set. The thinking that got us into this bind will not get us out. When Elizabeth Kolbert, a writer for the *New Yorker*, asked energy guru Amory Lovins about thinking outside the box, Lovins responded: "There is no box."

There is no box. That is the mind-set we need if civilization is to survive.

Critical Thinking

1. Identify Lester Brown's point of view, which is the basis for this article.

2. What are the primary reasons he offers to support his point of view?

3. What impact on food prices does the demand for crop-based fuels have?

4. What three environmental trends are making it more difficult to expand grain supply?

5. How does this article illustrate the relationship between natural resources and social structures?

6. How is the concept of sustainability illustrated in this article?

7. What alternatives to current practices does Brown propose?

8. Do the authors of Article 1 give the same priority to threats to the food supply that Brown does?

From *Scientific American*, May 2009. Copyright © 2009 by Lester R. Brown. Reprinted by permission of the author.

Navigating the Energy Transition

Michael T. Klare

Between now and 2050 or so, the world will undergo a great social, economic, and technological transition. In place of the fossil fuels—oil, coal, and natural gas—that now satisfy most of our energy needs and define key aspects of contemporary civilization, a new class of renewable energy sources will come to dominate the industrial landscape. Huge arrays of wind turbines and solar panels will replace the smokestacks and refineries that now surround major cities. In place of gasoline, filling stations will provide advanced biofuels or hydrogen to supply fuel cells. High-speed rail lines will connect major cities, while light rail will snake through large and small cities and their suburbs. Our homes, schools, factories, and offices will be designed to use as little energy as possible for heating, cooling, and illumination.

From our vantage point today, we can readily envision the world of 2050, and picture how the development of alternative sources of energy will alter our lives and those of our descendants. What is *less* clear is how we will get from here to there. At the conclusion of the process, the global economy and its myriad transportation systems will have been reconstructed along new lines, and the human population will have learned to live in new and more environmentally sensitive ways. But the transition from our current energy system to one based largely on renewables will be fraught with danger and crisis, as the supply of existing fuels dwindles and that of alternative fuels proves inadequate to make up the difference. Navigating this great transition could well prove the most difficult challenge facing the human community in the twenty-first century—and it is a challenge that has already forced itself upon us.

Why will this prove such a great challenge, and why is it upon us now? Let us begin with the obvious: An abundant supply of affordable energy is essential for the effective functioning of the world economy. Without such a supply, the global economy slows and suffers all sorts of disorders and trauma. We saw ample evidence of this in the spring and summer of 2008, when oil prices reached record levels, causing intense misery for the automotive, airline, and tourism industries, as well as for farmers, truckers, and commuters. High oil prices were not the direct cause of the financial meltdown of late 2008, but they were a significant factor in the subprime mortgage crisis that ultimately triggered the meltdown, in that they boosted the monthly costs faced by hard-pressed homebuyers in remote exurbs (the epicenter of the subprime pandemic). The price of gasoline only dropped when the economic crisis suppressed international demand, and it will stay low only so long as the crisis persists. As soon as economic activity rebounds, oil prices will climb again.

Energy is tied to another critical concern of the emerging era: global climate change. The largest single constituent of the greenhouse gases that are deemed responsible for planetary warming is carbon dioxide (CO_2), and the principal source of the CO_2 now accumulating in the outer atmosphere is the burning of fossil fuels to generate electricity or power motor vehicles. The more we rely on fossil fuels for these purposes, the greater will be the emissions of CO_2 and the faster the warming of the planet. The obvious solution to this peril is to reduce consumption of oil, coal, and natural gas. But this will require accelerating the development of climate-friendly alternatives, and this will take time and a great infusion of capital. Meanwhile, we still need abundant supplies of energy—affordable energy—and this puts a premium on the increased output of fossil fuels.

The intensified pursuit of fossil fuels to satisfy vital economic requirements will also bear on yet another key aspect of the current epoch: growing geopolitical rivalry among the major powers. In a world in which every nation must endeavor to satisfy its requirement for an adequate supply of energy, the competition for access to the world's remaining reserves of oil and natural gas is destined to become increasingly fierce. This has led the major consuming nations to employ every means at their disposal—including military means—to gain advantage in the competitive struggle over diminishing stocks of energy. In some cases, this has led to an influx of arms into areas of instability, as in Africa and Central Asia; in others, to the permanent deployment of military forces, as in the Persian Gulf and Caspian Sea basin. As the competition for fossil fuels increases, these geopolitical rivalries are likely to gain further momentum.

So the three greatest concerns of the moment—the global economy, the environment, and geopolitical competition—are directly tied to the nature of the world's existing energy mix. And this is where the problem lies. The types of energy on which we currently rely to satisfy most of our needs are not likely to prove adequate to meet future requirements—yet the harder we work to increase their availability, the more we doom the planet to catastrophic climate disorder and recurring geopolitical crisis.

Things as They Are

To grasp better these underlying realities, it is essential to examine the world's existing energy balance. At present, most of the world's energy is derived from fossil fuels. According to the US Department of Energy (DOE), fully 86 percent of total world energy consumption was satisfied in 2005, the most recent year for which comprehensive figures are available, by such fuels—36.7 percent by oil, 26.5 percent by coal, and 23.2 percent by natural gas. An additional 7.7 percent was provided by hydropower and renewable sources of energy, and 5.9 percent by nuclear power (see the table World Energy Consumption by Source).

It is the relative abundance of fossil fuels that has largely propelled the great economic expansion of the past 65 years, enabling not only the reconstruction of Europe and Japan after World War II but also the industrialization of Brazil, China, India, South Korea, Taiwan, and other rapidly growing economies. Over the course of this remarkable epoch, the industrialized nations erected a global civilization based on easy access to affordable fuels and electricity to power a vast array of motor vehicles, aircraft, computers, and other power-hungry devices. All this has been made possible because the international energy industry has—until now—largely succeeded in continually expanding the global output of oil, coal, and natural gas. Clearly, if this civilization is to continue to thrive in the years ahead and be extended to even more countries in the developing world, this extraordinary feat of energy-supply expansion will have to be repeated again and again.

Indeed, the DOE projected in the summer of 2008 that worldwide energy demand would grow by 50 percent between 2005 and 2030, from 462 to 695 quadrillion British thermal units (BTUs). This represents an enormous increase—the 233 quadrillion BTUs that must be added over the next quarter century is the equivalent of current energy consumption by the United States, Europe, and Japan combined. Most of this added energy, the DOE assumes, will have to be supplied by the most common and well-developed fuels: oil, coal, and natural gas. According to DOE projections, these three fuels will provide approximately the same share of world energy in 2030—85.8 percent—as they did in 2005.

Only a radical increase in the tempo of change can ensure that alternative sources of energy will be available in 2025.

If the energy industry were capable of supplying all this added fossil-fuel energy in 2030, that would be good news for the global economy, in that the older industrialized nations could maintain their high levels of consumption while the developing world experienced fast consumption growth. But it is extremely unlikely that the industry will be capable of meeting this objective. Although the net supply of fossil fuels may continue to increase, the global availability of oil will probably go into decline well before the end of this period. Natural gas supplies are likely to remain stagnant. This leaves only coal—the most CO_2-intensive of the three fossil fuels—as a rising source of energy. The bottom line: insufficient energy supplies combined with rising greenhouse-gas emissions.

The most troubling aspect of this equation involves oil. Although the DOE and many oil industry officials claim that global petroleum supplies will be sufficient to satisfy international requirements between now and 2030, many experts doubt that this will prove to be the case. In its *World Energy Outlook* released on November 12, 2008, the International Energy Agency (IEA), a Paris-based organization affiliated with the Organization for Economic Cooperation and Development, warned that global oil supplies may not be adequate to meet global needs in the years ahead. The agency gave three reasons that this might be so. First, existing fields are running out of oil at a faster rate than previously thought. Second, most newly developed oil fields are smaller and less productive than those currently in operation. And third, investors are shying away from costly and complex projects in "frontier" oil regions like the deep waters of the Gulf of Mexico, the Gulf of Guinea, Siberia, and the Caspian Sea.

Of the three reasons, perhaps the most startling was the revelation concerning the rapid depletion of existing fields. Although the world possesses tens of thousands of operating wells, most of our oil is drawn from several hundred giant reservoirs that

World Energy Consumption by Source—2005 (Actual) and 2030 (Projected)

Energy Source	2005 (Actual) Consumption Quad BTUs	2005 (Actual) Percent of World Total	2030 (Projected) Consumption Quad BTUs	2030 (Projected) Percent of World Total
Oil and biofuels	169.4	36.7	229.3	33.0
Natural gas	107.4	23.2	164.7	23.7
Coal	122.5	26.5	202.2	29.1
Nuclear	27.5	5.9	39.4	5.7
Hydropower, Renewables, others	35.5	7.7	59.0	8.5
Total, world	462.2	100.0	694.7	100.0

Source: US Department of Energy, *International Energy Outlook 2008* (Washington, DC: 2008), Table A2, p. 97.

produce hundreds of thousands of barrels per day. Almost all of these fields were discovered a quarter of a century or more ago, and many have already passed their peak level of daily output and are now experiencing a steady rate of decline. Previously, energy analysts assumed that this rate of decline was, on average, about 4 to 5 percent per year across the board—a conceivably manageable rate assuming sufficient investment in new oil field development by the major oil companies. But after conducting a survey of the world's 800 top-producing oil fields, the IEA concluded that the natural decline rate of these reservoirs is closer to 9 percent per year, a wholly unexpected and troubling outcome that tells us we are moving far more rapidly toward the end of the Petroleum Age than was previously assumed.

Replacing 4 percent of the world's oil supply every year is one thing; replacing 9 percent is a vastly greater challenge, given the huge cost and difficulty of developing new fields. Although the oil companies are spending greater amounts every year to locate and develop promising deposits, they are finding fewer and smaller fields. And the reservoirs they do manage to bring on line tend to empty out much faster than the giants discovered earlier, in the golden years of discovery following World War II. For example, the two major discoveries of the 1960s, the North Slope of Alaska and the North Sea, are already experiencing rapid rates of output decline. Only two large discoveries have been made since then—the Kashagan field in the Caspian Sea and the Tupi field in Atlantic waters off Rio de Janeiro—and both pose extraordinary technical challenges to the companies hoping to bring them into production.

The only way to ensure adequate supplies of oil in the years ahead is for the world's oil companies to make mammoth investments in drilling rigs, pipelines, and other infrastructure to bring new reservoirs into production. According to the IEA, satisfying anticipated world demand in 2030 will require a minimum of $350 billion per year (in 2007 dollars) in such investments *every year* between now and then. But much of this money will have to be spent on facilities in the hurricane-prone waters of the Gulf of Mexico and the Atlantic, or in conflict-prone areas of Africa, the Middle East, and Central Asia—which gives pause to investors.

Even before the onset of the world's current economic crisis, many investors were deterred by the rising cost of such ventures and, in the case of projects in Africa, the Middle East, and the former Soviet Union, by the potential for big losses as a result of conflict, sabotage, corruption, or governmental intervention. Since the economic crisis erupted, investors have become even more skittish, proving extremely reluctant to commit large sums to any projects that entail risks of this sort. Thus, even though oil resources could prove abundant in some of these areas, it is questionable whether they will be brought on line in time to satisfy global needs. As noted by the IEA in its November 12 report: "It cannot be taken for granted" that the major private oil companies and government-owned oil firms like Saudi Aramco will allocate sufficient funds "to keep up the necessary pace of investment."

What this means, in sum, is that the worldwide supply of petroleum is likely to fall short of projected global requirements in the decades to come. To put this in further perspective, the most recent edition of the DOE's *International Energy Outlook* projects that world oil supply will rise from 83.6 million barrels per day in 2005 to 95.7 million barrels in 2015, 101.3 million in 2020, and 112.5 million in 2030. (This includes conventional oil plus "nonconventional" supplies such as shale oil, Canadian tar sands, and biofuels.) But many experts, drawing on the sort of analysis presented above, now believe that world production will reach a peak in output well before 2030, probably between 2010 and 2015, at a level of about 95 million barrels per day. They believe output will remain at about that level for several years and then commence an irreversible decline—dropping far below the DOE's estimate of 112 million barrels for 2030. This means that, by 2030 or so, the world could be looking at a shortfall of anywhere from 25 to 30 million barrels of oil per day—a huge plunge in the global supply of energy.

More Carbon Needed

Clearly, any effort to satisfy world fuel requirements in the years after 2015 will require a significant increase in the production of *other* sources of energy. In the first instance, this will lead to greater dependence on the two other fossil fuels, natural gas and coal. Many experts believe that the output of gas and coal can be substantially augmented to compensate for the declining availability of oil. But this, too, could prove problematic.

Without going into great detail, any increase in the global output of natural gas will confront many of the same sorts of hurdles encountered in the case of petroleum. Like petroleum, gas is a finite substance produced by natural phenomena over many millions of years and is often found in similar geological formations. Just as the global output of oil is expected to reach a maximum or peak level in the not-too-distant future, so too will natural gas attain a peak in the third or fourth decade of the century.

Competition for access to the world's remaining reserves of oil and natural gas is destined to become increasingly fierce.

Also as in the case of oil, many of the world's largest reservoirs of gas have already been located and exploited, suggesting that less-attractive fields—those in remote locations like northern Alaska, eastern Siberia, and the Arctic Ocean—are all that remain for future development. Some additional gas is trapped in coal beds, shale rock, and other distinctive geological formations that can be mined with appropriate technologies. Industry experts believe it will be possible to exploit all these remote and "nonconventional" sources of gas. However, the cost will be high, and it is doubtful that these sources will ever prove sufficient to replace more than a tiny share of the energy now provided by oil.

Any increase in the consumption of natural gas will also entail significant geopolitical risks. No less than 56 percent of the world's known gas reserves are held by just three countries—Russia, Iran, and Qatar—and these three have recently taken steps to solidify their control over the fuel's future utilization by creating the nucleus of a "natural gas OPEC." Several other leading gas producers, including Algeria, Libya, Saudi Arabia, and the Central Asian states, have also expressed interest in forming such a cartel, suggesting the likelihood of future constraints on natural gas's global availability. This is precisely the sort of environment in which conflict could arise over access to sources of natural gas, much as has been the case in past years over access to sources of petroleum.

Coal presents a rather different set of problems. Coal is expected to remain relatively abundant well into the middle of the century (after which it, too, will reach a peak in production and go into decline). Moreover, large deposits of it are located in major energy-consuming nations like China, India, Russia, and the United States. With existing technology, coal is the cheapest fuel available for producing electricity, so its use is growing in many developing countries as well as in the United States. According to the DOE, China's coal consumption will grow by 120 percent between 2005 and 2030; in India it will grow by 80 percent, and in the United States by 31 percent. Coal can also be used as a feedstock for synthetic gas and diesel fuel, making it an attractive substitute for natural gas and oil as these materials become increasingly scarce.

However, any increase in coal consumption using existing combustion technologies will result in a speed-up of global warming and an onslaught of climatic disasters. This is so because coal releases more carbon dioxide per unit of energy generated than do the other two fossil fuels. Scientists and engineers are working on a technique to separate the carbon from the coal and bury it before combustion occurs—so-called carbon capture and storage (CCS) technology. But plants using this technique are expected to be far more costly than existing ones, and at this point no commercial facility employs this method. As the impacts of global warming grow more severe, power companies will come under greater pressure to use this technology, but it is unlikely that it will have achieved widespread adoption by 2030. What is more likely, at that point, is an increase in conventional coal technology, producing a heightened risk of catastrophic climate change.

Alternating Current

Obviously, the best hope for all of us on the planet (and for our descendents) is for the energy industry—and the world's major governments—to invest in a massive, rapid expansion of alternative sources of energy, especially renewables like solar, wind, geothermal, and advanced (non-edible) biofuels. These sources are not derived from finite materials like oil, natural gas, and coal but are infinitely replaceable, and release very little or no carbon in their operation. Eventually, when the great energy transition is completed, most of the world's energy supply is likely to be derived from these sources. But increasing the amount of energy supplied by these sources will prove an uphill and expensive struggle—and until that process is completed, we could be in for very difficult times.

At present, renewables and hydropower supply only 7.7 percent of the world's energy. According to the latest projections from the DOE, this figure will only rise to 8.5 percent by 2030, not including biofuels; with the addition of bio-fuels, it would rise by another percentage point or two. (Nuclear power provides another 5.9 percent of world supply currently. Although nuclear power is likely to continue playing a small but significant role in satisfying world energy needs, it poses so many safety, non-proliferation, and waste disposal challenges, as well as legal and financial challenges to investors, that it is unlikely to exceed single digits in its net contribution to the global supply.) Even if we assume these figures are overly pessimistic, this is hardly enough to compensate for the decline in oil or our perilous reliance on coal. Only a tripling or quadrupling in the share of energy provided by renewables and advanced biofuels by 2030 can put us far along the path of a successful transition.

Several factors account for the slow pace of renewable energy's development. To begin with, major utilities and their government backers have long been accustomed to relying on oil, coal, gas, and nuclear power, so they have been reluctant to make major investments in alternative sources of power. According to the IEA, three-quarters of the world's projected output of electricity in 2020 (and more than half in 2030) will come from generation facilities that are already in operation today—almost all of them powered by fossil fuels or nuclear energy. Furthermore, most of the new plants under construction—especially in China and India, where the demand for added electricity is greatest—are of this type. It will be very hard, under these circumstances, to increase the share of energy provided by alternative sources.

In addition, wind, solar, biofuels, and other, more advanced sources of energy face many obstacles that must be overcome before they can replace fossil fuels on a very large scale. Wind and solar power pose a common set of problems. Both collect energy intermittently, and so are off line for considerable periods of time. Also, both achieve their maximum effectiveness in remote areas like the American Southwest (in the case of solar power) or high plains (for wind) that are far removed from areas of greatest demand, and so lack adequate connectivity to the electrical grid. Biofuels pose different problems. Most ethanol in the United States is manufactured from corn ears, a valuable source of food for humans and animals; the very process of making it, moreover, entails a large and wasteful input of energy.

To overcome these various obstacles, huge sums must be spent—on developing new storage batteries so that energy collected from wind and the sun can be harvested when the supply is great and later dispersed when it is not; on an expanded (and more efficient) electrical grid connecting vast solar arrays and wind farms to major population centers; and on advanced biofuels using nonfood plant matter as a feedstock, and chemical rather than thermal means of manufacturing ethanol. Additional investment is also needed to develop other promising but as-yet unproven technologies, including hydrogen fuel cells, wave energy, and fusion reactors.

But even with a huge increase in spending on energy alternatives, such as President-elect Barack Obama and his supporters in Congress have proposed, it is highly unlikely that renewables, advanced biofuels, and climate-safe (that is, CCS) coal will be available on a large enough scale in 2030 to make up for what is likely to be an inadequate supply of oil and natural gas. Increased efforts at conservation will help, as will greater reliance on public transportation. But it is hard to escape the conclusion that in the middle stages of the great transition, from roughly 2020 to 2040, global energy supplies—except for climate-threatening coal—will be insufficient to meet global needs.

Competition Heats Up

In a world constrained by inadequate stockpiles of energy, we can expect intense geopolitical competition for whatever supplies *are* available at any given time. As the US National Intelligence Council (NIC) suggested in its November 2008 assessment of the likely strategic environment in 2025: "The rising energy demands of growing populations and economies may bring into question the availability, reliability, and affordability of energy supplies. Such a situation would heighten tensions between states competing for limited resources, especially if accompanied by increased political turbulence in the Middle East and a general loss of confidence in the ability of the marketplace to satisfy rising demands."

The NIC report, *Global Trends 2025: A Transformed World,* is particularly illuminating because it focuses on the same period discussed in this article: the midpoint in the great transition from fossil fuels to a post-petroleum economy. The report suggests, as well, that the world of 2025 will be well on its way toward the adoption of alternative forms of energy, yet will still be highly dependent on fossil fuels to satisfy most day-to-day requirements. At the same time, according to the report, significant problems will have arisen in boosting output of oil and gas to match rising worldwide demand. The result, it predicts, is an environment of perceived scarcity. In such an environment, political leaders will see no option but to employ any means at their disposal to maximize their own country's supplies—even at the risk of conflict with equally desperate competitors.

Most of our oil is drawn from several hundred giant reservoirs and many have already passed their peak.

"In the worst case," observes the NIC report, "this could lead to interstate conflicts if government leaders deem assured access to energy resources to be essential to maintaining domestic stability and the survival of their regime." Even in the absence of war, competition for energy will have important geopolitical implications as states undertake strategies to hedge against the possibility that existing energy supplies will not meet rising demands. For example, "energy-deficient states may employ transfers of arms and sensitive technologies and the promise of a political and military alliance as inducements to establish strategic relationships with energy-producing states."

Read deeper into the NIC report, and you find numerous portrayals of a world torn apart by relentless struggle over precarious supplies of oil and natural gas. Central Asia comes in for particular attention as a site of potential conflict among the United States, Russia, and China for control over that region's hydrocarbon reserves. Africa, a growing source of oil for the United States and China, is also seen as a potential site of geopolitical rivalry. Even the Arctic—increasingly open to oil and gas drilling as a result of global warming—is deemed a possible locale for conflict.

These kinds of rivalries are doubly dangerous. Not only do they risk full-scale war among the major powers, with all the destructive effects that would entail, but they would also consume mammoth sums of money that could otherwise be devoted to the development of energy alternatives, thereby slowing the transition to a post-petroleum industrial system. In fact, a world of recurring energy wars could make a successful transition impossible, or delay it until such time as the world economy had contracted substantially and global warming had advanced much further than it might have otherwise.

It is painfully evident, then, that the current pace of transition is far too slow to achieve the intended results in time to avert global catastrophe. Only a radical increase in the tempo of change can ensure that alternative sources of energy will be available in 2025 and beyond to compensate for the decline in oil and prevent increased dependence on unsafe coal. This will require vastly greater expenditures on efforts to realize the full potential of wind power, solar, geothermal, advanced biofuels, hydrogen, and climate-safe coal, along with increased investment in public transportation. The world of 2050 can be a bright, livable environment in which renewable energy sources power prosperity—but only if we take steps now to accelerate the transition from our current energy system to its unavoidable replacement.

Critical Thinking

1. What is Michael Klare's point of view?
2. What are the primary reasons he offers to support this point of view?
3. What are some of the implications of the projected patterns of world energy consumption in 2030?
4. How is the consumption of oil, coal and natural gas likely to change in the next 30 years?
5. What are some of the political and technical obstacles to developing alternative energy sources? How do these obstacles illustrate the relationships between the four components of the Allegory of the Balloon?
6. Do the authors of Article 1 give the same priority to the challenges of the energy transition that Klare does?

MICHAEL T. KLARE, a *Current History* contributing editor, is a professor at Hampshire College and author of *Rising Powers, Shrinking Planet: The New Geopolitics of Energy* (Metropolitan Books, 2008).

Asia's Rise: Rise and Fall

How are we to understand the shift of power towards Asia and what does it mean for those 'old' power centres in Europe and the United States? The most important historical question is probably why nations gain and lose power. Growth provides the most elegant answer and the means to defend that power.

PAUL KENNEDY

The first time I visited Japan, it was in the still-powerful after glow of the appearance of Ezra Vogel's bestseller, *Japan as Number One,* originally published by Harvard University Press in 1979, but continually re-published in Japan. To a person, Japanese intellectuals and politicians were excited by that prognostication, although also anxious to avoid giving a neuralgic late Ronald Reagan presidential administration any hint that they were looking forward to America's future relative decline.

I therefore found myself being asked coyly, time and again, what I thought about the ever-moving-westwards theory of international politics. When I asked my interlocutors to explain, the reply was always identical: for thousands of years East Asia had been the centre of the world, the most advanced and productive civilisation, etc. . .; then that centre began to shift westwards, through the Indian Ocean, and up to the Mediterranean; but Braudel's famous 'Mediterranean world' of the sixteenth century was eclipsed by nation-states north of the Alps, France, the Netherlands, eventually Britain.

This British predominance was impressively long-lasting, but by around 1900 it was losing out to the massive industrial states of the eastern half of the United States; and yet, after 1945 and as if by force of nature, the world's weight shifted steadily to the western side of the US.

So all that was happening, you see, was that the caravan of world wealth and civilisation was moving westwards again, to Japan. And that was why Professor Vogel's book was so impressive and convincing. And it was not Japan's fault it was overtaking America; it is just that it was now its turn to be Number One. No hard feelings.

When I pointed out, politely, that there was no reason why the westwards shift would not continue—in fact, the logic of the argument made that shift inevitable—and thus see China in future replacing Japan as Number One in the world, the conversations tended to dry up. As we parted company, both sides agreed to think about this matter a bit more.

Growth Counts

I have been thinking about it ever since. Without needing a complicated Toynbeean explanation of changes in world

history—'action-response', the saving grace of religion, and all that—there is something fascinating—and important—to all of us about this shifting dynamic of power and influence over the course of time.

It is a story that has captured the attention of the great writers and thinkers of the past—Ibn Khaldun, Raleigh, Vico, Gibbon, Brooks Adams, Ranke, Wells, Weber, Spengler, Mackinder, Braudel, McNeill—and with good reason. Why does one organised human unit—a nation, an empire, a civilisation, call it what you will—rise to occupy a greater share of power and influence than the others and then, again, begin to lose that pre-eminence? Is this not the most important historical question of all?

It is at this point that the horde of answers charge in, like cavalry-horses answering the bugle: the answer can be culture, or science, or germs and disease, or a breakdown of morals, or the coming of the steam-engine, or a Roman-like capacity for organisation.

To my mind still, and at the risk of sounding like an out-of date Marxist don, I feel that Lenin himself probably came closest when he pointed to the 'uneven rate of development' as the key. Could anyone believe, he asks his readers again and again, that the unification of Germany and the entry of Japan into the ranks of the Great Powers could have occurred without their successful long-term growth? Of course not.

The beauty about Lenin's approach is that he does not get himself embroiled in debates about some cultures and civilisations being superior to others, or Protestantism and capitalism, or relative resistance to disease, or democracy versus autocracy, or any of the other long-winded stuff, to explain the relative rise and decline of particular economies and their influence in the world. He simply points out—as any natural scientist observing a run of data would—that if the record shows one country's productivity and economy growing faster than others, then there will be a steady shift in the balances of power towards it. The antecedent causes are mere intellectualism. It is what is happening that counts.

And this, it seems to me, is the only sensible way we can discuss the most significant political phenomenon of our new century: the relative rise of Asia, perhaps China especially, and its natural concomitant, the relative decline of the west as a whole and more particularly of both of its two greatest components, Europe and the US.

At some stage, somewhere, those two parts need to be treated separately, since their responses to Asia's rise are so different. In Europe—at least according to some recent conferences I have attended—the mood is one of resigned acquiescence, mingled with a weird panglossian assumption that it will all work out well in the end. In the US, the 'declinist' or 'exceptionalist' debate is much more intense, presumably because—as Henry Kissinger might say—the stakes are so high.

It is difficult to judge which of these two debates are the more depressing to watch, or the less intelligible. Probably the European fatalism—occasionally interrupted by Sarkovian calls for the continent to unite or perish—possesses the superior logic.

By contrast, the debate in the US on Asia's rise now borders on the fatuous, but with three quarrelling variants. Either [a] it is not really happening, and the twenty-first century will still be America's century, despite all the statistical evidence and forecasts to the contrary; or [b] it is indeed happening, but there is nothing to worry about since America and Asia are natural and complementary trading partners so they will all get richer at the same time, as if members of some gigantic trans-Pacific Hanseatic League. This displaying a naivete about power-politics that is breathtaking; or [c] the most puzzling variation of all, though trumpeted by dozens of respectable political scientists and economists—not historians—which goes like this. Yes, the global dynamic proceeds apace; and yes, Asia and China are rising fast, so America's share on virtually all indices is shrinking, relatively; but, notwithstanding all that, the US will continue to occupy a special place in world affairs, over and above all the rest, the indispensable nation.

Calling the Tune

Just how one part of the globe can be relatively rising without other parts relatively falling is neither explained nor admitted. Truly, the first generations of a nation grappling with signs of long-term relative decline have an awfully hard time in being reconciled to that idea.

Yet, once one casts those emotions aside, the facts are clear; the accumulating evidence points to a conclusion which realists from Lenin going back to Thucydides—'it was the rising power of Athens'—would completely understand. Year on year, decade over decade, Asia is growing at a significantly faster pace than the mature economies of the US and Europe.

This is so well known that there is no need to throw in a lot of statistics—per capita gross domestic product, annualised growth-rates, Goldman Sachs projections—at this stage. But two changes are worth pointing to, apart from this massive shift in the relative productive outputs of each nation's goods and services.

The first is the stunning transformation of the world's capital balances over the past twenty years. This is not the place to discuss in detail whether the gigantic Asian capital surpluses—China, Japan, South Korea—will last forever, probably not; but no historian can resist pointing out that surplus bank savings

have usually accompanied the alterations in the military-political balances of power, either running ahead of them or following them: from the Lombard cities to Antwerp and Amsterdam; from there to London; from London, after a long time, to New York; and from New York . . . to where? Shanghai? Does it not matter when, as a Great Power, you owe an awful lot of money to someone else? He who pays the piper will, sooner or later, call the tune.

Sea Denial

The second accompanying shift is in military balances, especially at sea. In brief, we see a triangular situation which looks like this: Europe's maritime capacities are evaporating fast, and without there being a single substantive debate on what that means; Asia's maritime capacities are exploding in both power and reach, but no-one wants to talk about it; and the US Navy is worried.

The first of these deserves a far lengthier examination, but in essence the roster of European warships is shrinking so steadily, decade by decade, that it is fair to conclude that the five hundred-year-old Vasco da Gama era in world affairs is now well and truly over; an occasional run-in with Somali pirates by a French frigate makes for little.

Contrast their collective shrinkage, then, with the soaring naval expenditures of all the navies of East Asia, the Pacific, and South Asia, the frenzied attention to gaining naval-base rights, the drumbeat of propaganda on protecting one's vital sea-lines of communication.

Admiral Mahan has gone east. The Japanese Navy, for example, eclipses any European navy, and is in turn eclipsed by the Chinese Navy. What do those Asian governments know about the future of global power-politics that European governments do not? No politician will say.

Then there is the US, frantically trying to figure out what this rise of Asian sea-power means for its own overstretched world position. The bug-a-boo is of course China. Why is Beijing spending so much on defence; though probably about one-eighth of the Pentagon's budget? Why this heavy investment into cyber-warfare?; into military satellites?; into commercial espionage? What about those medium-range sea-skimming missiles that fly below the radar screens of US warships, and those ultra-long-range rockets that can cross the wide Pacific? Or the super-quiet diesel submarines, now wrapped in an anti-detection 'stealth' coating? How valid are all these rumours about the first Chinese aircraft-carrier?

Overall, then, are we not watching an older-fashioned American blue-water surface navy being pushed ever further away from the Asian coasts, and facing the problem of 'sea denial'? The Chinese navy is not planning to anchor off the entrance to Long Beach, California; but it does not imagine that Nimitz's navy will be in the western Pacific for much longer, either.

Strategy Light

Since it is the US which is much more exercised about Asia's rise than the limp but hopeful Europeans, one might expect to glean some idea of Washington's thinking by perusing the two most important documents so far issued on this topic in the present year: namely, [a] the February Quadrennial Defense Review Report, a Pentagon document requested by the Congress, and [b] the May National Security Strategy, emanating from the White House and signed off by President Barack Obama himself. But if one reads and attempts to de-construct those documents, one will have looked in vain; talk about the hunting of the Snark!

The presidential document is especially vacuous. One must wait until pages 43–45—of a 52-page document—to discover a section called Build Cooperation with Other 21st Century Centers of Influence, and indeed there is a paragraph on China and another on India. But they are followed in rapid succession by paragraphs on Russia, Indonesia, Brazil, the Middle East, Africa; interestingly, no reference to Japan, so much for the round-the-world movement of history! And there are a lot more pages on 'our most cherished values . . .' than there are on hard strategic issues.

The Quadrennial Defense Review seems at first to be a bit more relevant, in part because each of the services is putting in a bid for a large slice of the total Pentagon budget, and therefore has to say something about threats and capacities, or lack thereof. Even so, it looks like a bulky, multi-page menu in an expensive Manhattan restaurant; there is something in there for everyone, carriers, air wings, army groups, the Marines. But, in essence, there is little there. Charming sections on 'Supporting Families' and on 'Strengthening Interagency Partnerships' lead to nothing.

For understandable diplomatic reasons, no doubt, there is no discussion on what are the best ways to intimidate China's military growth; or how best to reach out to India to be your largest global ally, like reaching out to Britain after 1941; or how much it might take to get the shifty Russian Prime Minister Vladimir

Putin onto your side, a sublimely Bismarckian stroke that the Joint Chiefs simply dare not suggest. It is all very sad. Since Kissinger, or perhaps since the Bush-Baker-Scowcroft team, nobody in Washington thinks strategically.

So the shift in the world's power balances will go on. Asia will rise, though not without a stumble here and there, and China in particular seems likely to encounter some environmental or social difficulty before resuming its forward path, difficulties which will give hope to all those who hate the idea of the return of the Middle Kingdom. And the rest of Asia—India, Indonesia, Vietnam, Korea—will also advance, in a ragged though obvious direction.

And Europe will sit back, feeling quite exhausted by all these transformations, getting ever more obsessed about immigrants, high taxes and hedge funds. Meanwhile the US will, I fear, not have a clue where it is going, and what to do. Ninety years ago, Mackinder wrote that democracies, unless they are forced into war, simply cannot think strategically. Is that true? I hope it is not. But the evidence increasingly suggests he is right.

And so the centre of the world rolls, always to the west, to Asia and China. If we wait long enough, it might end up again in Lombardy; but that could take quite a while. Today, most roads seem to be leading to Beijing. Truly, as the Chinese curse puts it, we live in interesting times.

Critical Thinking

1. What is Paul Kennedy's point of view?

2. How does he contrast his point of view with other historians?

3. How does sea power figure into Kennedy's argument?

4. How does this article complement or contradict the analysis offered in Article 1? Or to state this differently: What is Kennedy's theory of international relations?

Feminists and Fundamentalists

Reassertions of an idealized past and a restored 'women's place' are occurring, from Kabul to Cambridge, at a time when the international community has concurred that women's rights are a global good.

KAVITA RAMDAS

The women's movement, as we refer to it now, was one of the most successful movements of the past century. It has been successful in many ways. Perhaps the most tangible evidence is that women's rights have become a desirable commodity, something that in the company of civilized nations people are proud to hold up as a model of what they have achieved, much in the way that democracy has become a global good.

In 1995, 189 countries signed a pact accepting the Beijing Declaration and Platform for Action as an expression of their goals. The platform called itself "an agenda for women's empowerment. It aims at removing obstacles to women's active participation in all spheres of public and private life, through a full and equal share in economic, social, cultural, and political decision making. This means the principle of shared power and responsibility should be established at home, in the workplace, and in wider national and international communities. Equality between women and men is a matter of human rights and a condition for social justice. It is also a necessary and fundamental prerequisite for equality, development, and peace."

These are, indeed, the ideals to which we as an international community should aspire. And in achieving this recognition of women's rights as a global good, we have arguably accomplished one of the most essential outcomes for any social movement: a broad and diverse constituency now concurs that it shares certain values and that we should all collectively promote them.

The women's movement has also been successful, maybe a little less so, with respect to a narrower definition of accomplishment: legal progress in a variety of areas. Today we see—and we sometimes take it for granted—that women are admitted to educational institutions where years ago they were not accepted; that women enjoy opportunities to pursue careers in fields formerly closed to them; that they have inheritance rights, the right to open their own bank accounts, and so forth.

Of course, women still have a long way to go in achieving the narrower legal definition of equality, even in America. Something that seems fairly basic—equal pay for equal work—has not been and probably will not be approved. The Equal Rights Amendment languishes still in the halls of the US Congress. And the United States remains one of the few countries that has not signed the Convention on the Elimination of All Forms of Discrimination against Women.

It does seem, however, that most of the world's nations have accepted women's rights as a global good. And yet the question arises: Is this achievement permanent? Is there some development that might threaten this and future advances of the women's movement?

Social Insecurity

While many of us have arrived at an apparent consensus about the good sense of making women's rights central to our enterprise as forward-looking communities, we are also seeing that the world is coping with unprecedented and unbelievably rapid change—change in science and technology, in social structures, in the movement of people and ideas across borders. As a consequence, all kinds of relationships that once were given are today up for grabs: relationships between individuals and communities, between citizens and states, between parents and children, between husbands and wives. Because of this, millions of people at some fundamental level feel less secure.

Now, the world as we know it has been run to this point by men. Therefore, today's pervasive insecurity is also challenging the prevailing structures in which men set the rules, including the rules of public discourse and political engagement. So what we are seeing is a reaction. The world has mostly agreed that women's rights are a good thing. But, at the same time, this frightening sense of change is condensing into one particular evidence of that change. And that evidence is the transformed position of women in our societies.

The result is a variety of efforts to reassert idealized notions of the past. Islamic fundamentalism is one example that attracts considerable attention. But the assertion of an idealized past is happening across the world, across cultures, within different religious traditions, in different countries and languages, and at all levels of society.

Sistani and Summers

Consider the cases of Iraq's Ali al-Sistani and America's Lawrence Summers. Obviously, these are very different men. They do not share a similar worldview, and they come from very different contexts. Grand Ayatollah Sistani, who wants to impose fundamentalist Islamic constraints on Iraqi women, lives in a rapidly transforming postcolonial society. His is a Muslim country, where the past is alive. Summers—the president of Harvard University who infamously wondered aloud whether women have the same innate abilities in math and science as men—lives in a highly developed capitalist society.

Yet America is also a society in which women increasingly challenge academia and male privilege within academia. Both Iraq and the United States are attempting to respond to where women are located within their social structures. I would argue that both Sistani and Summers are trying, at some level, to place boundaries around what women's roles ought to be.

They are doing so because these roles are up for grabs, and because the aspirations of women pose a widespread dilemma. Having more or less signed on in general to the global good of women's rights, many people around the world feel insecure about what women's advances might mean for their own lives, for their own relationships, for decision making in their own institutions.

This is the global threat: the feeling that somehow, if we let women just take off with this idea about women's rights, who knows where it could go? The last US presidential election highlighted a classic example of this fear, with a number of state ballot referendums drawing voters determined to defend the institution of marriage against perceived erosion.

Indeed, for some the very relevance of men to the reproductive process seems under assault. State governments in America continue to impose restrictions on abortion. But what significance do male partners retain if, outside of marriage between "man and wife," a woman can go to a sperm bank and make an independent choice to have a child? And what does this mean for society? And how do you begin to control this?

The Way We Were

It is not an accident that mass rapes became a symbol of the Bosnian war during the 1990s. An estimated 20,000 to 50,000 Bosnian women were raped during that genocidal conflict. Indeed, mass rape has become a feature of modern warfare—a strange phenomenon, when you consider that warfare has also become so highly technologically developed. We have all these amazing smart bombs, yet we also witness one of the most medieval forms of exerting power. What does this represent, in a society, more broadly?

And how do we think about this reassertion of an idealized past, these "fundamentalisms?" They are certainly not unique to one religion; I have watched Hindu fundamentalists in India spend the past eight years eulogizing one male god in a society that has long prided itself on worshipping numerous goddesses as well as gods.

Predictably, the idealized tradition, the fundamentalist challenge, is borne everywhere on the backs of women, and there is widespread reluctance to oppose it. This is what we found in Afghanistan under the Taliban, a brutal form of gender apartheid that was allowed to exist until the United States invaded in the aftermath of 9-11. Even today, we hear many arguments for why we should not impose human rights on societies that have other cultural traditions—why, if women are treated badly, we ought to be careful about making demands because that may be how things are done in those societies.

The kind of violence that women and girls experience on a day-to-day basis around the world, the kind of entrenched discrimination they face—if this behavior were applied against almost any ethnic or national minority, there would be loud and persistent calls for intervention. After the US invasion of Afghanistan, some rhetoric was heard about the liberation of that country's women. But, as Afghan women would point out, that liberation did not happen until two edifices, two towers, were attacked in the United States.

The variety of fundamentalisms notwithstanding, the one thread they share is the attempt to control women's bodies, the ability of women to move freely, and their ability to speak with any kind of free voice within their societies. It is ironic but telling that these reassertions of an idealized past and a restored "women's place" are occurring, from Kabul to Cambridge, at a time when the international community has concurred that women's rights are a global good. They are occurring at a time when every major international foundation and financial institution has agreed that no development goals—whether in economics, political development, or social development—can be achieved without investing in girls' education and the full and equal participation of women.

The Feminist Vanguard

Fortunately, while there is a threat, there is also hope. The hope is that the women's movement and the advancement of women's rights will be the vanguard in the international community's struggle to overcome fundamentalisms.

You can see this hope in the dilemma the US government is struggling with right now. The Bush administration is caught in a tricky contradiction. Because we have all agreed that women's rights are a global good, the administration cannot say that women's rights do not matter. Yet it is deeply beholden to a Christian fundamentalist movement within the United States that truly believes we must return to an idealized notion of the past.

The Southern Baptist Church, for example, has decided to put the word "obey" back in marriage vows; a woman should obey her husband (it is not in the man's vows). Promise Keepers is another movement that harkens back to eighteenth- and nineteenth-century definitions of husbands as hunter-gatherers and women as loyal wives who stay at home and raise the family. President Bush himself has made a number of speeches that evoke idealized images of a time when, as my husband would say, "men were men, and women were women."

The harkening back to a more constrictive order for women continues while the United States claims to be liberating women overseas from uncivilized nations that do not support women's equality. Human rights are held up as a global good even as they are undermined in the everyday lives of women. At the level of implementation, what you actually see are increasing restrictions on the freedom and control that women have—over their reproductive choices and access to contraception, for example—along with cutbacks in spending on health and education that harm women the most.

This is the global threat: the feeling that somehow, if we let women just take off with this idea about women's rights, who knows where it could go?

Some think Title IX has gone too far and want to turn it back. When many hear the term "Title IX," they think it has to do with women in sports. In fact, it has everything to do with President Summers' comments about women in the sciences. Title IX of the 1972 Education Amendments to the 1964 Civil Rights Act required fair access to a wide variety of educational resources—from soccer playing fields to science laboratories.

There are many levels at which, in the face of rhetorical acceptance of women's rights, policies and proposals are being pursued that would undermine achievements that took decades to accomplish. The women's movement has a vital role in resisting rollbacks.

Changing Culture

I work in the international arena, and people often ask me, "Why do other cultures not value women's rights?" And I like to remind them that there is nothing unique about cultures, and that there is no culture I can think of that intrinsically values women's rights.

Reformers in the United States fought for a very long time for women to be recognized as more than just the property of men, just as they struggled for the rights of black people to be recognized as human beings. Cultures are not static. There is nothing that says Western culture is inherently thoughtful and considerate and inclusive of women, minorities, or anyone else.

Why have some cultures evolved to a place where equal rights are regarded as desirable? Because those who have been most oppressed within these cultures have chosen to fight for the right to be treated with equality and dignity. And this is the same thing that is happening today in most of the world. In India, in Afghanistan, in Iraq, in Peru, in the indigenous communities of Mexico, people are struggling to have their culture evolve as a living, breathing thing, and to have women and girls who have not traditionally had voice in those cultures to now have voice.

There is hope in this—in women's rights as a fulcrum on which societies can tip toward modernity, not in the narrowly defined sense of Westernization, but true modernity, in terms of imagining a different conception of how the world can be organized. Women's movements struggle precisely at this fulcrum between modernity and the fundamentalist pressures to regress, and here there is promise.

In my work I have seen women in the most oppressive and closed societies take extraordinary risks and truly challenge the status quo. I have seen them find ways to make their culture more inclusive, more accepting, and more fundamentally equal for all people within their societies.

My organization, the Global Fund for Women, worked with Afghan women's groups during the Taliban's rule, both in refugee camps in Pakistan and in secret schools for girls—and for boys, I might add, inside Afghanistan. (One of the things people often do not think about is that the success of the women's movement accrues to both women and men. When the Taliban pulled women out of schools in Afghanistan, 65 percent of primary school teachers in the country were women. The government's action jeopardized the education of a whole generation of Afghan boys, who then had no alternative but to go to Islamic religious schools.)

What we found in our work over those years with a number of Afghan women's groups is that they are incredibly strategic about building alliances with male allies within their communities. They do not see their fight as a struggle against men. They see it as a struggle against the patriarchal system. They have been extraordinarily creative about choosing their priorities.

I was in Afghanistan in 2003 after the Taliban had been toppled. Like everyone else, I had seen the pictures of women throwing off their burqas, which everyone in the United States was very excited about (but which most women in Afghanistan, in fact, have not done; while in Iraq many more women have put them back on). To me, far more a sign of liberation in Afghanistan was a scene I witnessed in a small classroom in Kabul, where three women taught a class of 45 male teachers—village school teachers from different provinces around Afghanistan.

These three women, their heads covered in scarves, were discussing the pedagogy of successful education. Amid building blocks made out of recycled cigarette cartons, they were talking to the male teachers about how educators need to make learning joyful and pleasurable, something that children can be enthused about.

When it was time for questions and answers, I asked, "What does it feel like to be sitting in a classroom and listening to three women teachers teaching you?" One man raised his hand and said, "I'm a professor of mathematics and science, and for 25 years, Afghan schoolchildren are boys who have learned how to hold an AK-47 before they learned how to do basic math. I haven't been in a school that has had a science laboratory for 25 years." He said, "During these 25 years, it was women who kept education alive in our country, and I think it's time we should be learning from the women." It was an extraordinary statement, and to me, more powerful than any picture of a woman pulling off her burqa.

"Equal to What?"

Across much of the world the leadership of the women's movement has shifted from the kinds of experiences that Western feminists underwent in the 1960s and 1970s, which were very important and in many ways necessary, but which were very much filled with conflict. There is a willingness now in the developing world to be more inclusive, an approach born out of necessity and also from a sense that this is a struggle we have to be in together.

Women's groups in different parts of the world are showing an increasing ability to build on the notion that their states and the international institutions have all signed onto—this idea that women's rights are a global good—while at the same time finding a way to make it real in their own communities, finding a way to say, "Well, so what happens when the old traditions die?"

In Ethiopia, for example, over 90 percent of women go through female genital mutilation (FGM) as a rite of passage, and women's organizations are challenging the practice. But they are not challenging it from the perspective of "this is an evil, ancient, tribal tradition." Rather, they are looking to the root causes of the tradition.

As I heard an Ethiopian mother explain it, "If you know that the only economic security for your daughter is to ensure that she gets married, and if you know that no one will marry her unless she has gone through the process of FGM, because you cannot assure her purity otherwise, then you have no choice as a mother but to make your daughter go through it, even though you don't have to explain to us how painful it is and what the health consequences are, because each of us has lived those experiences."

If, however, we create an environment in which girls can go to school and stay in school longer, and women have opportunities to earn an income and contribute to their families, then girls will not have to depend for their economic prospects on being married off at age 12 or 13. And if we look at the status of widows in Ethiopia and attend to their security, we can also make a difference, because it turns out that it is the widows who get paid for performing the circumcision ceremony. They depend on this ritual as a means of support because people abandon them at the edges of villages.

The environment fostered by educational and microenterprise initiatives is one that emphasizes joint efforts among men and women within a community. It is not one that says men are the problem. Indeed, women often are just as much the perpetrators of traditional values and practices as men are. What has come through clearly for women's organizations in the rest of the world is that we are struggling against a system, and this system oppresses both women and men who are caught within it.

In the 1960s and 1970s, feminists in the United States were saying, "We want to be equal to you, we want to play on your playing fields, we want to play the same game." Today the women's movement internationally is saying something very different. It is asking the question: "Equal to what?" What do we want to be equal to? And what is the game we should be playing together, men and women, to ensure a freer, more just world that offers more opportunities for all of us?

Critical Thinking

1. What is Kavita Ramdas' point of view?
2. What challenges does the movement to empower women face?
3. How do the concepts presented in this article illustrate the "meta" component of the Allegory of the Balloon?
4. Do the authors of Article 1 give the same priority to the empowerment of women as Ramdas does in terms of it being a central change factor/variable?

KAVITA RAMDAS is president and CEO of the Global Fund for Women.

From *Current History,* March 2006, pp. 99–104. Copyright © 2006 by Current History, Inc. Reprinted by permission.

Get Smart

Pandemics. Global Warming. Food shortages. No more fossil fuels. What are humans to do? The same thing the species has done before: evolve to meet the challenge. But this time we don't have to rely on natural evolution to make us smart enough to survive. We can do it ourselves, right now, by harnessing technology and pharmacology to boost our intelligence. Is Google actually making us smarter?

JAMAIS CASCIO

Seventy-four thousand years ago, humanity nearly went extinct. A super-volcano at what's now Lake Toba, in Sumatra, erupted with a strength more than a thousand times that of Mount St. Helens in 1980. Some 800 cubic kilometers of ash filled the skies of the Northern Hemisphere, lowering global temperatures and pushing a climate already on the verge of an ice age over the edge. Some scientists speculate that as the Earth went into a deep freeze, the population of *Homo sapiens* may have dropped to as low as a few thousand families.

The Mount Toba incident, although unprecedented in magnitude, was part of a broad pattern. For a period of 2 million years, ending with the last ice age around 10,000 B.C., the Earth experienced a series of convulsive glacial events. This rapid-fire climate change meant that humans couldn't rely on consistent patterns to know which animals to hunt, which plants to gather, or even which predators might be waiting around the corner.

How did we cope? By getting smarter. The neurophysiologist William Calvin argues persuasively that modern human cognition—including sophisticated language and the capacity to plan ahead—evolved in response to the demands of this long age of turbulence. According to Calvin, the reason we survived is that our brains changed to meet the challenge: we transformed the ability to target a moving animal with a thrown rock into a capability for foresight and long-term planning. In the process, we may have developed syntax and formal structure from our simple language.

Our present century may not be quite as perilous for the human race as an ice age in the aftermath of a super-volcano eruption, but the next few decades will pose enormous hurdles that go beyond the climate crisis. The end of the fossil-fuel era, the fragility of the global food web, growing population density, and the spread of pandemics, as well as the emergence of radically transformative bio- and nanotechnologies—each of these threatens us with broad disruption or even devastation. And as good as our brains have become at planning ahead, we're still biased toward looking for near-term, simple threats. Subtle, long-term risks, particularly those involving complex, global processes, remain devilishly hard for us to manage.

But here's an optimistic scenario for you: if the next several decades are as bad as some of us fear they could be, we can respond, and survive, the way our species has done time and again: by getting smarter. But this time, we don't have to rely solely on natural evolutionary processes to boost our intelligence. We can do it ourselves.

Most people don't realize that this process is already under way. In fact, it's happening all around us, across the full spectrum of how we understand intelligence. It's visible in the hive mind of the Internet, in the powerful tools for simulation and visualization that are jump-starting new scientific disciplines, and in the development of drugs that some people (myself included) have discovered let them study harder, focus better, and stay awake longer with full clarity. So far, these augmentations have largely been outside of our bodies, but they're very much part of who we are today: they're physically separate from us, but we and they are becoming cognitively inseparable. And advances over the next few decades, driven by breakthroughs in genetic engineering and artificial intelligence, will make today's technologies seem primitive. The nascent jargon of the field describes this as "intelligence augmentation." I prefer to think of it as "You + ."

Scientists refer to the 12,000 years or so since the last ice age as the Holocene epoch. It encompasses the rise of human civilization and our co-evolution with tools and technologies that allow us to grapple with our physical environment. But if intelligence augmentation has the kind of impact I expect, we may soon have to start thinking of ourselves as living in an entirely new era. The focus of our technological evolution would be less on how we manage and adapt to our physical world, and more on how we manage and adapt to the immense amount of knowledge we've created. We can call it the Nöocene epoch, from Pierre Teilhard de Chardin's concept of the Nöosphere, a collective consciousness created by the deepening interaction of human minds. As that epoch draws closer, the world is becoming a very different place.

Of course, we've been augmenting our ability to think for millennia. When we developed written language, we significantly increased our functional memory and our ability to share insights and knowledge across time and space. The same thing happened with the invention of the printing press, the telegraph, and the radio. The rise of urbanization allowed a fraction of the populace to focus on more-cerebral tasks—a fraction that grew inexorably as more-complex economic and social practices demanded more knowledge work, and industrial technology reduced the demand for manual labor. And caffeine and nicotine, of course, are both classic cognitive-enhancement drugs, primitive though they may be.

With every technological step forward, though, has come anxiety about the possibility that technology harms our natural ability to think. These anxieties were given eloquent expression in these pages by Nicholas Carr, whose essay "Is Google Making Us Stupid?" (July/August 2008 *Atlantic*) argued that the information-dense, hyperlink-rich, spastically churning Internet medium is effectively rewiring our brains, making it harder for us to engage in deep, relaxed contemplation.

Carr's fears about the impact of wall-to-wall connectivity on the human intellect echo cyber-theorist Linda Stone's description of "continuous partial attention," the modern phenomenon of having multiple activities and connections under way simultaneously. We're becoming so accustomed to interruption that we're starting to find focusing difficult, even when we've achieved a bit of quiet. It's an induced form of ADD—a "continuous partial attention-deficit disorder," if you will.

There's also just more information out there—because unlike with previous information media, with the Internet, creating material is nearly as easy as consuming it. And it's easy to mistake more voices for more noise. In reality, though, the proliferation of diverse voices may actually improve our overall ability to think. In *Everything Bad Is Good for you,* Steven Johnson argues that the increasing complexity and range of media we engage with have, over the past century, made us smarter, rather than dumber, by providing a form of cognitive calisthenics. Even pulp-television shows and video games have become extraordinarily dense with detail, filled with subtle references to broader subjects, and more open to interactive engagement. They reward the capacity to make connections and to see patterns—precisely the kinds of skills we need for managing an information glut.

Scientists describe these skills as our "fluid intelligence"—the ability to find meaning in confusion and to solve new problems, independent of acquired knowledge. Fluid intelligence doesn't look much like the capacity to memorize and recite facts, the skills that people have traditionally associated with brainpower. But building it up may improve the capacity to think deeply that Carr and others fear we're losing for good. And we shouldn't let the stresses associated with a transition to a new era blind us to that era's astonishing potential. We swim in an ocean of data, accessible from nearly anywhere, generated by billions of devices. We're only beginning to explore what we can do with this knowledge-at-a-touch.

Moreover, the technology-induced ADD that's associated with this new world may be a short-term problem. The trouble isn't that we have too much information at our fingertips, but that our tools for managing it are still in their infancy. Worries about "information overload" predate the rise of the Web (Alvin Toffler coined the phrase in 1970), and many of the technologies that Carr worries about were developed precisely to help us get some control over a flood of data and ideas. Google isn't the problem; it's the beginning of a solution.

The trouble isn't that we have too much information at our fingertips, but that our tools for managing it are still in their infancy.

In any case, there's no going back. The information sea isn't going to dry up, and relying on cognitive habits evolved and perfected in an era of limited information flow—and limited information access—is futile. Strengthening our fluid intelligence is the only viable approach to navigating the age of constant connectivity.

When people hear the phrase *intelligence augmentation,* they tend to envision people with computer chips plugged into their brains, or a genetically engineered race of post-human super-geniuses. Neither of these visions is likely to be realized, for reasons familiar to any Best Buy shopper. In a world of ongoing technological acceleration, today's cutting-edge brain implant would be tomorrow's obsolete junk—and good luck if the protocols change or you're on the wrong side of a "format war" (anyone want a Betamax implant?). And then there's the question of stability: Would you want a chip in your head made by the same folks that made your cell phone, or your PC?

Likewise, the safe modification of human genetics is still years away. And even after genetic modification of adult neurobiology becomes possible, the science will remain in flux; our understanding of how augmentation works, and what kinds of genetic modifications are possible, would still change rapidly. As with digital implants, the brain modification you might undergo one week could become obsolete the next. Who would want a 2025-vintage brain when you're competing against hotshots with Model 2026?

Yet in one sense, the age of the cyborg and the super-genius has already arrived. It just involves external information and communication devices instead of implants and genetic modification. The bioethicist James Hughes of Trinity College refers to all of this as "exocortical technology," but you can just think of it as "stuff you already own." Increasingly, we buttress our cognitive functions with our computing systems, no matter that the connections are mediated by simple typing and pointing. These tools enable our brains to do things that would once have been almost unimaginable:

- powerful simulations and massive data sets allow physicists to visualize, understand, and debate models of an 11-dimension universe;

- real-time data from satellites, global environmental databases, and high-resolution models allow geophysicists to recognize the subtle signs of long-term changes to the planer;
- cross-connected scheduling systems allow anyone to assemble, with a few clicks, a complex, multimodal travel itinerary that would have taken a human travel agent days to create.

If that last example sounds prosaic, it simply reflects how embedded these kinds of augmentation have become. Not much more than a decade ago, such a tool was outrageously impressive—and it destroyed the travel-agent industry.

That industry won't be the last one to go. Any occupation requiring pattern-matching and the ability to find obscure connections will quickly morph from the domain of experts to that of ordinary people whose intelligence has been augmented by cheap digital tools. Humans won't be taken out of the loop—in fact, many, many *more* humans will have the capacity to do something that was once limited to a hermetic priesthood. Intelligence augmentation decreases the need for specialization and increases participatory complexity.

As the digital systems we rely upon become faster, more sophisticated, and (with the usual hiccups) more capable, we're becoming more sophisticated and capable too. It's a form of co-evolution: we learn to adapt our thinking and expectations to these digital systems, even as the system designs become more complex and powerful to meet more of our needs—and eventually come to adapt to us.

Consider the Twitter phenomenon, which went from nearly invisible to nearly ubiquitous (at least among the online crowd) in early 2007. During busy periods, the user can easily be overwhelmed by the volume of incoming messages, most of which are of only passing interest. But there is a tiny minority of truly valuable posts. (Sometimes they have extreme value, as they did during the October 2007 wildfires in California and the November 2008 terrorist attacks in Mumbai.) At present, however, finding the most-useful bits requires wading through messages like "My kitty sneezed!" and "I hate this taco!"

But imagine if social tools like Twitter had a way to learn what kinds of messages you pay attention to, and which ones you discard. Over time, the messages that you don't really care about might start to fade in the display, while the ones that you do want to see could get brighter. Such attention filters—or focus assistants—are likely to become important parts of how we handle our daily lives. We'll move from a world of "continuous partial attention" to one we might call "continuous augmented awareness."

As processor power increases, tools like Twitter may be able to draw on the complex simulations and massive data sets that have unleashed a revolution in science. They could become individualized systems that augment our capacity for planning and foresight, letting us play "what-if" with our life choices: where to live, what to study, maybe even where to go for dinner. Initially crude and clumsy, such a system would get better with more data and more experience; just as important, we'd get better at asking questions. These systems, perhaps linked to the cameras and microphones in our mobile devices, would eventually be able to pay attention to what we're doing, and to our habits and language quirks, and learn to interpret our sometimes ambiguous desires. With enough time and complexity, they would be able to make useful suggestions without explicit prompting.

And such systems won't be working for us alone. Intelligence has a strong social component; for example, we already provide crude cooperative information-filtering for each other. In time, our interactions through the use of such intimate technologies could dovetail with our use of collaborative knowledge systems (such as Wikipedia), to help us not just to build better data sets, but to filter them with greater precision. As our capacity to provide that filter gets faster and richer, it increasingly becomes something akin to collaborative intuition—in which everyone is effectively augmenting everyone else.

In pharmacology, too, the future is already here. One of the most prominent examples is a drug called modafinil. Developed in the 1970s, modafinil—sold in the U.S. under the brand name Provigil—appeared on the cultural radar in the late 1990s, when the American military began to test it for long-haul pilots. Extended use of modafinil can keep a person awake and alert for well over 32 hours on end, with only a full night's sleep required to get back to a normal schedule.

While it is FDA-approved only for a few sleep disorders, like narcolepsy and sleep apnea, doctors increasingly prescribe it to those suffering from depression, to "shift workers" fighting fatigue, and to frequent business travelers dealing with time-zone shifts. I'm part of the latter group: like more and more professionals, I have a prescription for modafinil in order to help me overcome jet lag when I travel internationally. When I started taking the drug, I expected it to keep me awake; I didn't expect it to make me feel smarter, but that's exactly what happened. The change was subtle but clear, once I recognized it: within an hour of taking a standard 200-mg tablet, I was much more alert, and thinking with considerably more clarity and focus than usual. This isn't just a subjective conclusion. A University of Cambridge study, published in 2003, concluded that modafinil confers a measurable cognitive-enhancement effect across a variety of mental tasks, including pattern recognition and spatial planning, and sharpens focus and alertness.

I'm not the only one who has taken advantage of this effect. The Silicon Valley insider webzine *Tech Crunch* reported in July 2008 that some entrepreneurs now see modafinil as an important competitive tool. The tone of the piece was judgmental, but the implication was clear: everybody's doing it, and if you're not, you're probably falling behind.

This is one way a world of intelligence augmentation emerges. Little by little, people who don't know about drugs like modafinil or don't want to use them will face stiffer competition from the people who do. From the perspective of a culture immersed in athletic doping wars, the use of such drugs may seem like cheating. From the perspective of those who find that they're much more productive using this form of enhancement, it's no more cheating than getting a faster computer or a better education.

Modafinil isn't the only example; on college campuses, the use of ADD drugs (such as Ritalin and Adderall) as study aids has become almost ubiquitous. But these enhancements are primitive. As the science improves, we could see other kinds of cognitive-modification drugs that boost recall, brain plasticity, even empathy and emotional intelligence. They would start as therapeutic treatments, but end up being used to make us "better than normal." Eventually, some of these may become over-the-counter products at your local pharmacy, or in the juice and snack aisles at the supermarket. Spam e-mail would be full of offers to make your brain bigger, and your idea production more powerful.

Such a future would bear little resemblance to *Brave New World* or similar narcomantic nightmares; we may fear the idea of a population kept doped and placated, but we're more likely to see a populace stuck in overdrive, searching out the last bits of competitive advantage, business insight, and radical innovation. No small amount of that innovation would be directed toward inventing the next, more powerful cognitive-enhancement technology.

This would be a different kind of nightmare, perhaps, and cause waves of moral panic and legislative restriction. Safety would be a huge issue. But as we've found with athletic doping, if there's a technique for beating out rivals (no matter how risky), shutting it down is nearly impossible. This would be yet another pharmacological arms race—and in this case, the competitors on one side would just keep getting smarter.

The most radical form of superhuman intelligence, of course, wouldn't be a mind augmented by drugs or exocortical technology; it would be a mind that isn't human at all. Here we move from the realm of extrapolation to the realm of speculation, since solid predictions about artificial intelligence are notoriously hard: our understanding of how the brain creates the mind remains far from good enough to tell us how to construct a mind in a machine.

But while the concept remains controversial, I see no good argument for why a mind running on a machine platform instead of a biological platform will forever be impossible; whether one might appear in five years or 50 or 500, however, is uncertain. I lean toward 50, myself. That's enough time to develop computing hardware able to run a high-speed neural network as sophisticated as that of a human brain, and enough time for the kids who will have grown up surrounded by virtual-world software and household robots—that is, the people who see this stuff not as "Technology," but as everyday tools—to come to dominate the field.

Many proponents of developing an artificial mind are sure that such a breakthrough will be the biggest change in human history. They believe that a machine mind would soon modify itself to get smarter—and with its new intelligence, then figure out how to make itself smarter still. They refer to this intelligence explosion as "the Singularity," a term applied by the computer scientist and science-fiction author Vernor Vinge. "Within thirty years, we will have the technological means to create superhuman intelligence," Vinge wrote in 1993. "Shortly after, the human era will be ended." The Singularity concept is a secular echo of Teilhard de Chardin's "Omega Point," the culmination of the Nöosphere at the end of history. Many believers in Singularity—which one wag has dubbed "the Rapture for nerds"—think that building the first real AI will be the last thing humans do. Some imagine this moment with terror, others with a bit of glee.

My own suspicion is that a stand-alone artificial mind will be more a tool of narrow utility than something especially apocalyptic. I don't think the theory of an explosively self-improving AI is convincing—it's based on too many assumptions about behavior and the nature of the mind. Moreover, AI researchers, after years of talking about this prospect, are already ultra-conscious of the risk of runaway systems.

More important, though, is that the same advances in processor and process that would produce a machine mind would also increase the power of our own cognitive-enhancement technologies. As intelligence augmentation allows us to make *ourselves* smarter, and then smarter still, AI may turn out to be just a sideshow: we could always be a step ahead.

So what's life like in a world of brain doping, intuition networks, and the occasional artificial mind?

Banal.

Not from our present perspective, of course. For us, now, looking a generation ahead might seem surreal and dizzying. But remember: people living in, say, 2030 will have lived every moment from now until then—we won't jump into the future. For someone going from 2009 to 2030 day by day, most of these changes wouldn't be jarring; instead, they'd be incremental, almost overdetermined, and the occasional surprises would quickly blend into the flow of inevitability.

By 2030, then, we'll likely have grown accustomed to (and perhaps even complacent about) a world where sophisticated foresight, detailed analysis and insight, and augmented awareness are commonplace. We'll have developed a better capacity to manage both partial attention and laser-like focus, and be able to slip between the two with ease—perhaps by popping the right pill, or eating the right snack. Sometimes, our augmentation assistants will handle basic interactions on our behalf; that's okay, though, because we'll increasingly see those assistants as extensions of ourselves.

The amount of data we'll have at our fingertips will be staggering, but we'll finally have gotten over the notion that accumulated information alone is a hallmark of intelligence. The power of all of this knowledge will come from its ability to inform difficult decisions, and to support complex analysis. Most professions will likely use simulation and modeling in their day-to-day work, from political decisions to hairstyle options. In a world of augmented intelligence, we will have a far greater appreciation of the consequences of our actions.

This doesn't mean we'll all come to the same conclusions. We'll still clash with each other's emotions, desires, and beliefs. If anything, our arguments will be more intense, buttressed not just by strongly held opinions but by intricate reasoning. People in 2030 will look back aghast at how ridiculously unsubtle the political and cultural disputes of our present were, just as we might today snicker at simplistic advertising from a generation ago.

Conversely, the debates of the 2030s would be remarkable for us to behold. Nuance and multiple layers will characterize even casual disputes; our digital assistants will be there to catch any references we might miss. And all of this will be everyday, banal reality. Today, it sounds mind-boggling; by then, it won't even merit comment.

What happens if such a complex system collapses? Disaster, of course. But don't forget that we already depend upon enormously complex systems that we no longer even think of as technological. Urbanization, agriculture, and trade were at one time huge innovations. Their collapse (and all of them are now at risk, in different ways, as we have seen in recent months) would be an even greater catastrophe than the collapse of our growing webs of interconnected intelligence.

A less apocalyptic but more likely danger derives from the observation made by the science-fiction author William Gibson: "The future is already here, it's just unevenly distributed." The rich, whether nations or individuals, will inevitably gain access to many augmentations before anyone else. We know from history, though, that a world of limited access wouldn't last forever, even as the technology improved: those who sought to impose limits would eventually face angry opponents with newer, better systems.

Even as competition provides access to these kinds of technologies, though, development paths won't be identical. Some societies may be especially welcoming to biotech boosts; others may prefer to use digital tools. Some may readily adopt collaborative approaches; others may focus on individual enhancement. And around the world, many societies will reject the use of intelligence-enhancement technology entirely, or adopt a cautious wait-and-see posture.

The bad news is that these divergent paths may exacerbate cultural divides created by already divergent languages and beliefs. National rivalries often emphasize cultural differences, but for now we're all still standard human beings. What happens when different groups quite literally think in very, very different ways?

The good news, though, is that this diversity of thought can also be a strength. Coping with the various world-historical dangers we face will require the greatest possible insight, creativity, and innovation. Our ability to build the future that we want—not just a future we can survive—depends on our capacity to understand the complex relationships of the world's systems, to take advantage of the diversity of knowledge and experience our civilization embodies, and to fully appreciate the implications of our choices. Such an ability is increasingly within our grasp. The Nöocene awaits.

Critical Thinking

1. What is Jamais Cascio's point of view?
2. To meet the challenges of the twenty-first century, what are the courses of action proposed by Cascio?
3. How do his proposals fit into the Allegory of the Balloon?
4. What are implications of his proposals in the context of the National Power Score as presented in Article 1?
5. While the specifics are different, are there common themes between this article and the other articles in Unit 1?

JAMAIS CASCIO is an affiliate at the Institute for the Future and a senior fellow at the Institute for Ethics and Emerging Technologies.

UNIT 2

Population and Food Production

Unit Selections

Learning Outcomes

After reading this unit you should be able to:

*   Describe major demographic trends and the variations in these trends between regions of the world.

*   Describe how infectious disease and food shortages threaten human population.

*   Describe how governments and international organizations are working to meet the challenges of disease and famine.

*   Offer examples of how demographic changes impact natural resources and social structures.

*   Assess your initial effort at identifying your theory of international relations and how this unit changes/complements it.

Student Website

www.mhhe.com/cls

Internet References

The Hunger Project
   www.thp.org
Penn Library: Resources by Subject
   www.library.upenn.edu/cgi-bin/res/sr.cgi
World Health Organization
   www.who.int
WWW Virtual Library: Demography & Population Studies
   http://demography.anu.edu.au/VirtualLibrary

After World War II, the world's population reached an estimated 2 billion people. It had taken 250 years to triple to that level. In the six decades following World War II, the population tripled again to 6 billion. When the typical reader of this book reaches the age of 50, demographers estimate that the global population will have reached 8.5 billion! By 2050, or about 100 years after World War II, some experts forecast that 10 to 12 billion people may populate the world. A person born in 1946 (a so-called baby boomer) who lives to be 100 could see a six-fold increase in population.

Nothing like this has ever occurred before. To state this in a different way: In the next 50 years there will have to be twice as much food grown, twice as many schools and hospitals available, and twice as much of everything else just to maintain the current and rather uneven standard of living. We live in an unprecedented time in human history.

One of the most interesting aspects of this population growth is that there is little agreement about whether this situation is good or bad. The government of China, for example, has a policy that encourages couples to have only one child. In contrast, there are a few governments that use various financial incentives to promote large families.

In the second decade of the new millennium, there are many population issues that transcend simple numeric or economic considerations. The disappearance of indigenous cultures is a good example of the pressures of population growth on people who live on the margins of modern society. Finally, while demographers develop various scenarios forecasting population growth, it is important to remember that there are circumstances that could lead not to growth but to a significant decline in global population. The spread of AIDS and other infectious diseases reveals that confidence in modern medicine's ability to control these scourges may be premature. Nature has its own checks and balances to the population dynamic. This factor is often overlooked in an age of technological optimism.

The lead article in this section provides an overview of general demographic trends, with a special focus on issues related to aging. In the second article, the often-overlooked issue of reversing the increase in human population as a strategy for

© Imageplus/Corbis

achieving long-term balance with the environment is described. The third article examines the politically important issue of global patterns in migration.

There are, of course, no greater checks on population growth than the availability of an adequate food supply and control of the spread of infectious diseases. Some experts question whether current agricultural technologies are sustainable over the long run. How much food are we going to need, and how are farmers and fishermen going to provide it? Will markets deliver food to those in greatest need? Finally, the continuous threat of the spread of disease and the ability of national and international public health organizations to contain it are directly related to population issues.

Making predictions about the future of the world's population is a complicated task, for there are a variety of forces at work and considerable variation from region to region. The danger of oversimplification must be overcome if governments and international organizations are going to respond with meaningful policies. Perhaps one could say that there is not a global population problem but rather many population challenges that vary from country to country and region to region.

The New Population Bomb: The Four Megatrends That Will Change the World

JACK A. GOLDSTONE

Forty-two years ago, the biologist Paul Ehrlich warned in The Population Bomb that mass starvation would strike in the 1970s and 1980s, with the world's population growth outpacing the production of food and other critical resources. Thanks to innovations and efforts such as the "green revolution" in farming and the widespread adoption of family planning, Ehrlich's worst fears did not come to pass. In fact, since the 1970s, global economic output has increased and fertility has fallen dramatically, especially in developing countries.

The United Nations Population Division now projects that global population growth will nearly halt by 2050. By that date, the world's population will have stabilized at 9.15 billion people, according to the "medium growth" variant of the UN's authoritative population database World Population Prospects: The 2008 Revision. (Today's global population is 6.83 billion.) Barring a cataclysmic climate crisis or a complete failure to recover from the current economic malaise, global economic output is expected to increase by two to three percent per year, meaning that global income will increase far more than population over the next four decades.

But twenty-first-century international security will depend less on how many people inhabit the world than on how the global population is composed and distributed: where populations are declining and where they are growing, which countries are relatively older and which are more youthful, and how demographics will influence population movements across regions.

These elements are not well recognized or widely understood. A recent article in The Economist, for example, cheered the decline in global fertility without noting other vital demographic developments. Indeed, the same UN data cited by The Economist reveal four historic shifts that will fundamentally alter the world's population over the next four decades: the relative demographic weight of the world's developed countries will drop by nearly 25 percent, shifting economic power to the developing nations; the developed countries' labor forces will substantially age and decline, constraining economic growth in the developed world and raising the demand for immigrant workers; most of the world's expected population growth will increasingly be concentrated in today's poorest, youngest, and

most heavily Muslim countries, which have a dangerous lack of quality education, capital, and employment opportunities; and, for the first time in history, most of the world's population will become urbanized, with the largest urban centers being in the world's poorest countries, where policing, sanitation, and health care are often scarce. Taken together, these trends will pose challenges every bit as alarming as those noted by Ehrlich. Coping with them will require nothing less than a major reconsideration of the world's basic global governance structures.

Europe's Reversal of Fortunes

At the beginning of the eighteenth century, approximately 20 percent of the world's inhabitants lived in Europe (including Russia). Then, with the Industrial Revolution, Europe's population boomed, and streams of European emigrants set off for the Americas. By the eve of World War I, Europe's population had more than quadrupled. In 1913, Europe had more people than China, and the proportion of the world's population living in Europe and the former European colonies of North America had risen to over 33 percent. But this trend reversed after World War I, as basic health care and sanitation began to spread to poorer countries. In Asia, Africa, and Latin America, people began to live longer, and birthrates remained high or fell only slowly. By 2003, the combined populations of Europe, the United States, and Canada accounted for just 17 percent of the global population. In 2050, this figure is expected to be just 12 percent—far less than it was in 1700. (These projections, moreover, might even understate the reality because they reflect the "medium growth" projection of the UN forecasts, which assumes that the fertility rates of developing countries will decline while those of developed countries will increase. In fact, many developed countries show no evidence of increasing fertility rates.) The West's relative decline is even more dramatic if one also considers changes in income. The Industrial Revolution made Europeans not only more numerous than they had been but also considerably richer per capita than others worldwide. According to the economic historian Angus Maddison, Europe, the United States, and Canada together produced about 32 percent of the world's GDP at the beginning of the nineteenth century. By 1950, that proportion had increased to a remarkable 68 percent of the world's total output (adjusted to reflect purchasing power parity).

This trend, too, is headed for a sharp reversal. The proportion of global GDP produced by Europe, the United States, and Canada fell from 68 percent in 1950 to 47 percent in 2003 and will decline even more steeply in the future. If the growth rate of per capita income (again, adjusted for purchasing power parity) between 2003 and 2050 remains as it was between 1973 and 2003—averaging 1.68 percent annually in Europe, the United States, and Canada and 2.47 percent annually in the rest of the world—then the combined GDP of Europe, the United States, and Canada will roughly double by 2050, whereas the GDP of the rest of the world will grow by a factor of five. The portion of global GDP produced by Europe, the United States, and Canada in 2050 will then be less than 30 percent—smaller than it was in 1820.

These figures also imply that an overwhelming proportion of the world's GDP growth between 2003 and 2050—nearly 80 percent—will occur outside of Europe, the United States, and Canada. By the middle of this century, the global middle class—those capable of purchasing durable consumer products, such as cars, appliances, and electronics—will increasingly be found in what is now considered the developing world. The World Bank has predicted that by 2030 the number of middle-class people in the developing world will be 1.2 billion—a rise of 200 percent since 2005. This means that the developing world's middle class alone will be larger than the total populations of Europe, Japan, and the United States combined. From now on, therefore, the main driver of global economic expansion will be the economic growth of newly industrialized countries, such as Brazil, China, India, Indonesia, Mexico, and Turkey.

Aging Pains

Part of the reason developed countries will be less economically dynamic in the coming decades is that their populations will become substantially older. The European countries, Canada, the United States, Japan, South Korea, and even China are aging at unprecedented rates. Today, the proportion of people aged 60 or older in China and South Korea is 12–15 percent. It is 15–22 percent in the European Union, Canada, and the United States and 30 percent in Japan. With baby boomers aging and life expectancy increasing, these numbers will increase dramatically. In 2050, approximately 30 percent of Americans, Canadians, Chinese, and Europeans will be over 60, as will more than 40 percent of Japanese and South Koreans.

Over the next decades, therefore, these countries will have increasingly large proportions of retirees and increasingly small proportions of workers. As workers born during the baby boom of 1945–65 are retiring, they are not being replaced by a new cohort of citizens of prime working age (15–59 years old).

Industrialized countries are experiencing a drop in their working-age populations that is even more severe than the overall slowdown in their population growth. South Korea represents the most extreme example. Even as its total population is projected to decline by almost 9 percent by 2050 (from 48.3

million to 44.1 million), the population of working-age South Koreans is expected to drop by 36 percent (from 32.9 million to 21.1 million), and the number of South Koreans aged 60 and older will increase by almost 150 percent (from 7.3 million to 18 million). By 2050, in other words, the entire working-age population will barely exceed the 60-and-older population. Although South Korea's case is extreme, it represents an increasingly common fate for developed countries. Europe is expected to lose 24 percent of its prime working-age population (about 120 million workers) by 2050, and its 60-and-older population is expected to increase by 47 percent. In the United States, where higher fertility and more immigration are expected than in Europe, the working-age population will grow by 15 percent over the next four decades—a steep decline from its growth of 62 percent between 1950 and 2010. And by 2050, the United States' 60-and-older population is expected to double.

All this will have a dramatic impact on economic growth, health care, and military strength in the developed world. The forces that fueled economic growth in industrialized countries during the second half of the twentieth century—increased productivity due to better education, the movement of women into the labor force, and innovations in technology—will all likely weaken in the coming decades. College enrollment boomed after World War II, a trend that is not likely to recur in the twenty-first century; the extensive movement of women into the labor force also was a one-time social change; and the technological change of the time resulted from innovators who created new products and leading-edge consumers who were willing to try them out—two groups that are thinning out as the industrialized world's population ages.

Overall economic growth will also be hampered by a decline in the number of new consumers and new households. When developed countries' labor forces were growing by 0.5–1.0 percent per year, as they did until 2005, even annual increases in real output per worker of just 1.7 percent meant that annual economic growth totaled 2.2–2.7 percent per year. But with the labor forces of many developed countries (such as Germany, Hungary, Japan, Russia, and the Baltic states) now shrinking by 0.2 percent per year and those of other countries (including Austria, the Czech Republic, Denmark, Greece, and Italy) growing by less than 0.2 percent per year, the same 1.7 percent increase in real output per worker yields only 1.5–1.9 percent annual overall growth. Moreover, developed countries will be lucky to keep productivity growth at even that level; in many developed countries, productivity is more likely to decline as the population ages.

A further strain on industrialized economies will be rising medical costs: as populations age, they will demand more health care for longer periods of time. Public pension schemes for aging populations are already being reformed in various industrialized countries—often prompting heated debate. In theory, at least, pensions might be kept solvent by increasing the retirement age, raising taxes modestly, and phasing out benefits for the wealthy. Regardless, the number of 80- and 90-year-olds—who are unlikely to work and highly likely to require nursing-home and other expensive care—will rise dramatically. And even if 60- and 70-year-olds remain active and employed, they will require procedures and medications—hip replacements, kidney transplants, blood-pressure treatments—to sustain their health in old age.

All this means that just as aging developed countries will have proportionally fewer workers, innovators, and consumerist young households, a large portion of those countries' remaining economic growth will have to be diverted to pay for the medical bills and pensions of their growing elderly populations. Basic services, meanwhile, will be increasingly costly because fewer young workers will be available for strenuous and labor-intensive jobs. Unfortunately, policymakers seldom reckon with these potentially disruptive effects of otherwise welcome developments, such as higher life expectancy.

Youth and Islam in the Developing World

Even as the industrialized countries of Europe, North America, and Northeast Asia will experience unprecedented aging this century, fast-growing countries in Africa, Latin America, the Middle East, and Southeast Asia will have exceptionally youthful populations. Today, roughly nine out of ten children under the age of 15 live in developing countries. And these are the countries that will continue to have the world's highest birthrates. Indeed, over 70 percent of the world's population growth between now and 2050 will occur in 24 countries, all of which are classified by the World Bank as low income or lower-middle income, with an average per capita income of under $3,855 in 2008.

Many developing countries have few ways of providing employment to their young, fast-growing populations. Would-be laborers, therefore, will be increasingly attracted to the labor markets of the aging developed countries of Europe, North America, and Northeast Asia. Youthful immigrants from nearby regions with high unemployment—Central America, North Africa, and Southeast Asia, for example—will be drawn to those vital entry-level and manual-labor jobs that sustain advanced economies: janitors, nursing-home aides, bus drivers, plumbers, security guards, farm workers, and the like. Current levels of immigration from developing to developed countries are paltry compared to those that the forces of supply and demand might soon create across the world.

These forces will act strongly on the Muslim world, where many economically weak countries will continue to experience dramatic population growth in the decades ahead. In 1950, Bangladesh, Egypt, Indonesia, Nigeria, Pakistan, and Turkey had a combined population of 242 million. By 2009, those six countries were the world's most populous Muslim-majority countries and had a combined population of 886 million. Their populations are continuing to grow and indeed are expected to increase by 475 million between now and 2050—during which time, by comparison, the six most populous developed countries are projected to gain only 44 million inhabitants. Worldwide, of the 48 fastest-growing countries today—those with annual population growth of two percent or more—28 are majority Muslim or have Muslim minorities of 33 percent or more.

It is therefore imperative to improve relations between Muslim and Western societies. This will be difficult given that many Muslims live in poor communities vulnerable to radical appeals and many see the West as antagonistic and militaristic. In the 2009 Pew Global Attitudes Project survey, for example, whereas 69 percent of those Indonesians and Nigerians surveyed reported viewing the United States favorably, just 18 percent of those polled in Egypt, Jordan, Pakistan, and Turkey (all U.S. allies) did. And in 2006, when the Pew survey last asked detailed questions about Muslim-Western relations, more than half of the respondents in Muslim countries characterized those relations as bad and blamed the West for this state of affairs.

But improving relations is all the more important because of the growing demographic weight of poor Muslim countries and the attendant increase in Muslim immigration, especially to Europe from North Africa and the Middle East. (To be sure, forecasts that Muslims will soon dominate Europe are outlandish: Muslims compose just three to ten percent of the population in the major European countries today, and this proportion will at most double by midcentury.) Strategists worldwide must consider that the world's young are becoming concentrated in those countries least prepared to educate and employ them, including some Muslim states. Any resulting poverty, social tension, or ideological radicalization could have disruptive effects in many corners of the world. But this need not be the case; the healthy immigration of workers to the developed world and the movement of capital to the developing world, among other things, could lead to better results.

Urban Sprawl

Exacerbating twenty-first-century risks will be the fact that the world is urbanizing to an unprecedented degree. The year 2010 will likely be the first time in history that a majority of the world's people live in cities rather than in the countryside. Whereas less than 30 percent of the world's population was urban in 1950, according to UN projections, more than 70 percent will be by 2050.

Lower-income countries in Asia and Africa are urbanizing especially rapidly, as agriculture becomes less labor intensive and as employment opportunities shift to the industrial and service sectors. Already, most of the world's urban agglomerations—Mumbai (population 20.1 million), Mexico City (19.5 million), New Delhi (17 million), Shanghai (15.8 million), Calcutta (15.6 million), Karachi (13.1 million), Cairo (12.5 million), Manila (11.7 million), Lagos (10.6 million), Jakarta (9.7 million)—are found in low-income countries. Many of these countries have multiple cities with over one million residents each: Pakistan has eight, Mexico 12, and China more than 100. The UN projects that the urbanized proportion of sub-Saharan Africa will nearly double between 2005 and 2050, from 35 percent (300 million people) to over 67 percent (1 billion). China, which is roughly 40 percent urbanized today, is expected to be 73 percent urbanized by 2050; India, which is less than 30 percent urbanized today, is expected to be 55 percent urbanized by 2050. Overall, the world's urban population is expected to grow by 3 billion people by 2050.

This urbanization may prove destabilizing. Developing countries that urbanize in the twenty-first century will have far lower per capita incomes than did many industrial countries when they first urbanized. The United States, for example, did not reach 65 percent urbanization until 1950, when per capita income was nearly $13,000 (in 2005 dollars). By contrast, Nigeria, Pakistan, and the Philippines, which are approaching similar levels of urbanization, currently have per capita incomes of just $1,800–$4,000 (in 2005 dollars).

According to the research of Richard Cincotta and other political demographers, countries with younger populations are especially prone to civil unrest and are less able to create or sustain democratic institutions. And the more heavily urbanized, the more such countries are likely to experience Dickensian poverty and anarchic violence. In good times, a thriving economy might keep urban residents employed and governments flush with sufficient resources to meet their needs. More often, however, sprawling and impoverished cities are vulnerable to crime lords, gangs, and petty rebellions. Thus, the rapid urbanization of the developing world in the decades ahead might bring, in exaggerated form, problems similar to those that urbanization brought to nineteenth-century Europe. Back then, cyclical employment, inadequate policing, and limited sanitation and education often spawned widespread labor strife, periodic violence, and sometimes—as in the 1820s, the 1830s, and 1848—even revolutions.

International terrorism might also originate in fast-urbanizing developing countries (even more than it already does). With their neighborhood networks, access to the Internet and digital communications technology, and concentration of valuable targets, sprawling cities offer excellent opportunities for recruiting, maintaining, and hiding terrorist networks.

Defusing the Bomb

Averting this century's potential dangers will require sweeping measures. Three major global efforts defused the population bomb of Ehrlich's day: a commitment by governments and nongovernmental organizations to control reproduction rates; agricultural advances, such as the green revolution and the spread of new technology; and a vast increase in international trade, which globalized markets and thus allowed developing countries to export foodstuffs in exchange for seeds, fertilizers, and machinery, which in turn helped them boost production. But today's population bomb is the product less of absolute growth in the world's population than of changes in its age and distribution. Policymakers must therefore adapt today's global governance institutions to the new realities of the aging of the industrialized world, the concentration of the world's economic and population growth in developing countries, and the increase in international immigration.

During the Cold War, Western strategists divided the world into a "First World," of democratic industrialized countries; a "Second World," of communist industrialized countries; and a "Third World," of developing countries. These strategists focused chiefly on deterring or managing conflict between the First and the Second Worlds and on launching proxy wars and diplomatic initiatives to attract Third World countries into the First World's camp. Since the end of the Cold War, strategists have largely abandoned this three-group division and have tended to believe either that the United States, as the sole superpower, would maintain a Pax Americana or that the world would become multipolar, with the United States, Europe, and China playing major roles.

Unfortunately, because they ignore current global demographic trends, these views will be obsolete within a few decades. A better approach would be to consider a different three-world order, with a new First World of the aging industrialized nations of North America, Europe, and Asia's Pacific Rim (including Japan, Singapore, South Korea, and Taiwan, as well as China after 2030, by which point the one-child policy will have produced significant aging); a Second World comprising fast-growing and economically dynamic countries with a healthy mix of young and old inhabitants (such as Brazil, Iran, Mexico, Thailand, Turkey, and Vietnam, as well as China until 2030); and a Third World of fast-growing, very young, and increasingly urbanized countries with poorer economies and often weak governments. To cope with the instability that will likely arise from the new Third World's urbanization, economic strife, lawlessness, and potential terrorist activity, the aging industrialized nations of the new First World must build effective alliances with the growing powers of the new Second World and together reach out to Third World nations. Second World powers will be pivotal in the twenty-first century not just because they will drive economic growth and consume technologies and other products engineered in the First World; they will also be central to international security and cooperation. The realities of religion, culture, and geographic proximity mean that any peaceful and productive engagement by the First World of Third World countries will have to include the open cooperation of Second World countries.

Strategists, therefore, must fundamentally reconsider the structure of various current global institutions. The G-8, for example, will likely become obsolete as a body for making global economic policy. The G-20 is already becoming increasingly important, and this is less a short-term consequence of the ongoing global financial crisis than the beginning of the necessary recognition that Brazil, China, India, Indonesia, Mexico, Turkey, and others are becoming global economic powers. International institutions will not retain their legitimacy if they exclude the world's fastest-growing and most economically dynamic countries. It is essential, therefore, despite European concerns about the potential effects on immigration, to take steps such as admitting Turkey into the European Union. This would add youth and economic dynamism to the EU—and would prove that Muslims are welcome to join Europeans as equals in shaping a free and prosperous future. On the other hand, excluding Turkey from the EU could lead to hostility not only on the part of Turkish citizens, who are expected to number 100 million by 2050, but also on the part of Muslim populations worldwide.

NATO must also adapt. The alliance today is composed almost entirely of countries with aging, shrinking populations and relatively slow-growing economies. It is oriented toward the Northern Hemisphere and holds on to a Cold War structure that cannot adequately respond to contemporary threats. The young and increasingly populous countries of Africa, the Middle East, Central Asia, and South Asia could mobilize insurgents much more easily than NATO could mobilize the troops it would need if it were called on to stabilize those countries. Long-standing NATO members should, therefore—although it would require atypical creativity and flexibility—consider the logistical and demographic advantages of inviting into the alliance countries such as Brazil and Morocco, rather than countries such as Albania. That this seems far-fetched does not minimize the imperative that First World countries begin including large and strategic Second and Third World powers in formal international alliances.

The case of Afghanistan—a country whose population is growing fast and where NATO is currently engaged—illustrates the importance of building effective global institutions. Today, there are 28 million Afghans; by 2025, there will be 45 million; and by 2050, there will be close to 75 million. As nearly 20 million additional Afghans are born over the next 15 years, NATO will have an opportunity to help Afghanistan become reasonably stable, self-governing, and prosperous. If NATO's efforts fail and the Afghans judge that NATO intervention harmed their interests, tens of millions of young Afghans will become more hostile to the West. But if they come to think that NATO's involvement benefited their society, the West will have tens of millions of new friends. The example might then motivate the approximately one billion other young Muslims growing up in low-income countries over the next four decades to look more kindly on relations between their countries and the countries of the industrialized West.

Creative Reforms at Home

The aging industrialized countries can also take various steps at home to promote stability in light of the coming demographic trends. First, they should encourage families to have more children. France and Sweden have had success providing child care, generous leave time, and financial allowances to families with young children. Yet there is no consensus among policymakers—and certainly not among demographers—about what policies best encourage fertility.

More important than unproven tactics for increasing family size is immigration. Correctly managed, population movement can benefit developed and developing countries alike. Given the dangers of young, underemployed, and unstable populations in developing countries, immigration to developed countries can provide economic opportunities for the ambitious and serve as a safety valve for all. Countries that embrace immigrants, such as the United States, gain economically by having willing laborers and greater entrepreneurial spirit. And countries with high levels of emigration (but not so much that they experience so-called brain drains) also benefit because emigrants often send remittances home or return to their native countries with valuable education and work experience.

One somewhat daring approach to immigration would be to encourage a reverse flow of older immigrants from developed to developing countries. If older residents of developed countries took their retirements along the southern coast of the Mediterranean or in Latin America or Africa, it would greatly reduce the strain on their home countries' public entitlement systems. The developing countries involved, meanwhile, would benefit because caring for the elderly and providing retirement and leisure services is highly labor intensive. Relocating a portion of these activities to developing countries would provide employment and valuable training to the young, growing populations of the Second and Third Worlds.

This would require developing residential and medical facilities of First World quality in Second and Third World countries. Yet even this difficult task would be preferable to the status quo, by which low wages and poor facilities lead to a steady drain of medical and nursing talent from developing to developed countries. Many residents of developed countries who desire cheaper medical procedures already practice medical tourism today, with India, Singapore, and Thailand being the most common destinations. (For example, the international consulting firm Deloitte estimated that 750,000 Americans traveled abroad for care in 2008.)

Never since 1800 has a majority of the world's economic growth occurred outside of Europe, the United States, and Canada. Never have so many people in those regions been over 60 years old. And never have low-income countries' populations been so young and so urbanized. But such will be the world's demography in the twenty-first century. The strategic and economic policies of the twentieth century are obsolete, and it is time to find new ones.

Reference

Goldstone, Jack A. "The new population bomb: the four megatrends that will change the world." *Foreign Affairs* 89.1 (2010): 31. *General OneFile*. Web. 23 Jan. 2010. http://0-find.galegroup .com.www.consuls.org/gps/start.do?proId=IPS& userGroupName=a30wc.

Critical Thinking

1. Identify the four demographic trends.
2. How does the author argue that international politics is changing due to these trends?
3. Summarize the Afghanistan case study.
4. How are these trends related to Kennedy's analysis in Article 4?
5. How does this discussion of demographic trends relate to the Allegory of the Balloon?

Population and Sustainability

Reversing the rise in human numbers is the most overlooked and essential strategy for achieving long-term balance with the environment. Contrary to widespread opinion, it does not require "population control"

ROBERT ENGELMAN

In an era of changing climate and sinking economies, Malthusian limits to growth are back—and squeezing us painfully. Whereas *more people* once meant more ingenuity, more talent, and more innovation, today it just seems to mean *less for each*. Less water for every cattle herder in the Horn of Africa. (The United Nations projects there will be more than four billion people living in nations defined as water-scarce or water-stressed by 2050, up from half a billion in 1995.) Less land for every farmer already tilling slopes so steep they risk killing themselves by falling off their fields. (At a bit less than six tenths of an acre, global per capita cropland today is little more than half of what it was in 1961, and more than 900 million people are hungry.) Less capacity in the atmosphere to accept the heat-trapping gases that could fry the planet for centuries to come. Scarcer and higher-priced energy and food. And if the world's economy does not bounce back to its glory days, less credit and fewer jobs.

It's not surprising that this kind of predicament brings back an old sore topic: human population and whether to do anything about it. Let's concede up front that nothing short of a catastrophic population crash (think of the film *Children of Men,* set in a world without children) would make much difference to climate change, water scarcity or land shortages over the next decade or so. There are 6.8 billion of us today, and more are on the way. To make a dent in these problems in the short term without throwing anyone overboard, we will need to radically reduce individuals' footprint on the environment through improvements in technology and possibly wrenching changes in lifestyle.

But until the world's population stops growing, there will be no end to the need to squeeze individuals' consumption of fossil fuels and other natural resources. A close look at this problem is sobering: short of catastrophic leaps in the death rate or unwanted crashes in fertility, the world's population is all but certain to grow by at least one billion to two billion people. The low-consuming billions of the developing world would love to consume as Americans do, with similar disregard for the environment—and they have as much of a right to do so. These facts suggest that the coming ecological impact will be of a scale that we will simply have to manage and adapt to as best we can.

Population growth constantly pushes the consequences of any level of individual consumption to a higher plateau, and reductions in individual consumption can always be overwhelmed by increases in population. The simple reality is that acting on both, consistently and simultaneously, is the key to long-term environmental sustainability. The sustainability benefits of level or falling human numbers are too powerful to ignore for long.

In the U.S., this discussion remains muted all the same. Population concerns may lurk within the public anger over illegal immigration or over the unwed California mother of octuplets earlier this year. But to the extent that the news media address domestic population growth at all, it is through euphemisms such as "sprawl" (the theoretical culprit in pollution of the Chesapeake Bay, for example) or the economy (the theoretical driver of increased greenhouse gas emissions). You are more likely to read about population growth in a letter to the editor than in a news story or editorial.

When President-elect Barack Obama pledged in late 2008 to bring U.S. carbon dioxide emissions to their 1990 levels by 2020, environmentalists struggled to swallow their dismay. The European Union, after all, had committed itself to 20 percent *reductions* from 1990 levels. But on a per capita basis, President Obama's pledge was somewhat *more* ambitious than the E.U.'s was. Because of much more rapid population growth than in the E.U., Americans would be cutting their individual emissions by 26 percent under his plan and Europeans by 25 percent under theirs. Any pledges to lower emissions by a uniform percentage among industrial countries will be much harder for the U.S. to achieve, simply because it is gaining people so fast through immigration and a birthrate that is higher than average for a developed nation.

The bitterness of the immigration debate has helped keep U.S. population growth off-limits in the national conversation. In industrial countries outside of North America, however, population is creeping back into public and even political consciousness. In the U.K., an all-party parliamentary panel issued a report called "Return of the Population Growth Factor" and called for stronger efforts to slow that growth. And the concern in the U.K.

is not just about the people "over there" in developing countries. In early 2009 Jonathon Porritt, chair of the government's Sustainable Development Commission, whacked a hornet's nest by calling parents of more than two children "irresponsible" and blasting mainstream environmental groups for "betraying" their members by fearing to call for small families. "It is the ghost at the table," Porritt said of population in an interview with the *Daily Telegraph,* a London broadsheet. Blog comments on his remarks, most of them supportive, soared into the thousands.

Meanwhile, in Australia, as summer temperatures hovered near 117 degrees Fahrenheit (47 degrees Celsius) and murderous flames converted forests into carbon dioxide, a new book entitled *Overloading Australia: How Governments and Media Dither and Deny on Population* issued an unusual ecological battle cry: ignore all admonitions to conserve the country's increasingly scarce water supplies until the government eliminates "baby bonuses" in the tax code and clamps down on immigration. A former premier of New South Wales spoke at the book's launch.

With comments such as these gaining attention—and in some circles, approval—are environmentalists and eventually policy makers likely to renew the decades-old call for "population control"? Would they be wise to do so?

A Number of Us

Two big questions present themselves as population reemerges from the shadows: Can any feasible downshift in population growth actually put the environment on a more sustainable path? And if so, are there measures that the public and policy makers would support that could actually bring about such a change?

Nature, of course, couldn't care less how many of us there are. What matters to the environment are the sums of human pulls and pushes, the extractions of resources and the injections of wastes. When these exceed key tipping points, nature and its systems can change quickly and dramatically. But the magnitudes of environmental impacts stem not just from our numbers but also from behaviors we learn from our parents and cultures. Broadly speaking, if population is the number of us, then consumption is the way each of us behaves. In this unequal world, the behavior of a dozen people in one place sometimes has more environmental impact than does that of a few hundred somewhere else.

Consider how these principles relate to global warming. The greenhouse gases already released into the atmosphere are likely to bring us quite close to the 3.6 degree F (two degree C) increase from the preindustrial global temperature average that many scientists see as the best-guess threshold of potential climate catastrophe. Already the earth is experiencing harsher droughts, fiercer storms and higher sea levels. If the scientists are right, these impacts will worsen for decades or centuries. Indeed, even if we ended all emissions tomorrow, additional warming is on the way thanks to the momentum built into the earth's intricate climate system. (The oceans, for example, have yet to come into equilibrium with the extra heat-trapping capacity of the atmosphere. As the oceans continue to warm, so will the land around them.)

Our species' demographic growth since its birth in Africa 200,000 years ago clearly contributed to this crisis. If world population had stayed stable at roughly 300 million people—a number that demographers believe characterized humanity from the birth of Christ to A.D. 1000 and that equals the population of just the U.S. today—there would not be enough of us to have the effect of relocating the coastlines even if we all drove Hummers. But instead we kept growing our numbers, which are projected to reach 9.1 billion by midcentury.

Humanity's consumption behaviors consequently did and do matter, and in this arena, all people have not been created equal. Greenhouse gas release has been linked overwhelmingly, at least up until recently, to the high-consumption habits of the industrial nations. As a result, in an ethical outrage as big as all outdoors, the coming shifts in climate and sea level will most harm the world's poor, who are least responsible for the atmosphere's composition, and will least harm the wealthy, who bear the biggest responsibility.

All-Consuming Passions

What part can the size of the human race play in finding a happy ending to this morality play? Population scenarios cannot directly address the inequity in emissions patterns—but they are far from unimportant.

Countries with the highest emissions per capita tend to have smaller families on average, whereas those with low emissions per capita tend to have larger ones. Americans, for example, consumed 8.6 tons of oil or its commercial energy equivalent per capita in 2007, according to data kept by British Petroleum; Indians consumed just 0.4 ton per capita. (These figures somewhat distort the gap because they exclude biomass and other noncommercial forms of energy, for which data are unreliable.)

So while India gained 17 million people in that year and the U.S. gained three million, by this simplified math the U.S. growth in population counted for the equivalent of an additional 25.6 million tons of oil consumed, whereas India's much greater growth counted for only 6.6 million additional tons. With such large disparities, the climate would be better served if the Americans emulated Indian consumption than if India emulated U.S. population.

End of story? For a variety of reasons, not quite. Population is not a contrasting force to consumption but something very close to its parent. Alone, each of us has no significant impact on the planet, even when our collective behavior overwhelms its natural processes. Historically, population has grown fastest when per capita consumption is modest. Later, consumption tends to explode on the base of a population that is large, but it is by then growing more slowly. Throughout the 19th century, the U.S. population grew at rates typical of Africa today. That century of rapid growth helped to make 21st-century America (with 307 million people now) a consumption behemoth.

The same one-two punch of population growth followed by consumption growth is now occurring in China (1.34 billion people) and India (1.2 billion). Per capita commercial energy use has been growing so rapidly in both countries (or at least it

Human Population Growth.

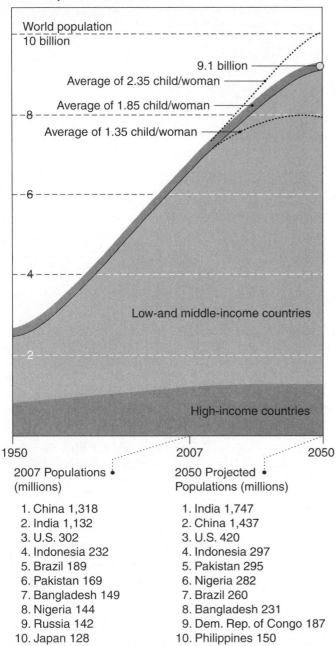

2007 Populations • (millions)

1. China 1,318
2. India 1,132
3. U.S. 302
4. Indonesia 232
5. Brazil 189
6. Pakistan 169
7. Bangladesh 149
8. Nigeria 144
9. Russia 142
10. Japan 128

2050 Projected • Populations (millions)

1. India 1,747
2. China 1,437
3. U.S. 420
4. Indonesia 297
5. Pakistan 295
6. Nigeria 282
7. Brazil 260
8. Bangladesh 231
9. Dem. Rep. of Congo 187
10. Philippines 150

The challenge to sustainability: For most of its history, the human race has numbered no more than several million and has expanded only slowly. As late as A.D. 1000, our species was smaller than the current population of the U.S. Only in the past few centuries have our numbers exploded, especially (during recent decades) in low-and middle-income nations, with increases in consumption habits following suit. Projections suggest that by 2050 or so, the population will probably stabilize around 9.1 billion. But very small changes in fertility could shift that figure up or down by about a billion—with a powerful impact on innumerable sustainability issues.

was through 2007 on the eve of the economic meltdown) that if the trends continue unabated the typical Chinese will outconsume the typical American before 2040, with Indians surpassing

Americans by 2080. Population and consumption thus feed on each other's growth to expand humans' environmental footprint exponentially over time.

Moreover, because every human being consumes and disposes of multiple natural resources, a birth that does not occur averts consumption impacts in every direction. A person reducing her carbon footprint, conversely, does not automatically use less water. A wind turbine displaces coal-fired electricity but hardly prevents the depletion of forests (now disappearing in the tropics at the rate of one Kentucky-size swath a year) or fisheries (at current depletion rates facing exhaustion by the middle of the century). But unlike wind turbines, humans reproduce themselves. So every smaller generation means that the multipliers of consumption linked to population also shrink on into the future.

Because most environmental challenges emerge on scales of decades and centuries, population growth packs a long-term wallop. With respect to saving the planet, over a few short years it is hard for smaller families to beat sharp reductions in per capita consumption. Since the early 1990s, however, published calculations have demonstrated that slower population growth over decades yields significant reductions of greenhouse gas emissions even in countries where per capita fossil-fuel consumption is modest.

Slower population growth that leads to eight billion people in 2050 rather than to the currently projected 9.1 billion would save one billion to two billion tons of carbon annually by 2050, according to estimates by climate scientist Brian O'Neill of the National Center for Atmospheric Research and his colleagues. The subsequent savings in emissions would grow year by year ever afterward—while the billion-plus fewer people would need less land, forest products, water, fish and other foodstuffs.

Those improvements still would not be enough on their own to avert significant climate change. Other similar billion-ton savings in emissions (what Princeton University professors Stephen Pacala and Robert Socolow have dubbed "stabilization wedges") are desperately needed and can come only from reduction in fossil-fuel consumption through energy efficiency, low-carbon technologies and changes in way of life. If two billion automobiles getting 30 miles per gallon traveled only 5,000 miles a year instead of 10,000, that change would save another billion tons of carbon emissions. So would replacing coal-fired power plants that produce 1.4 trillion watts of electricity with equivalent plants burning natural gas. But without a population that stops growing, comparable technology improvements or lifestyle downshifts will be needed indefinitely to keep greenhouse gas emissions sustainable.

The complications that population growth poses to every environmental problem are not to be dismissed. In fact, they are accepted and understood best by the governments of poorer countries, where the impacts of dense and rapidly growing populations are most obvious. During the past few years, most of the reports that developing countries have filed with the U.N. on how they plan to adapt to climate change mention population growth as a complicating factor.

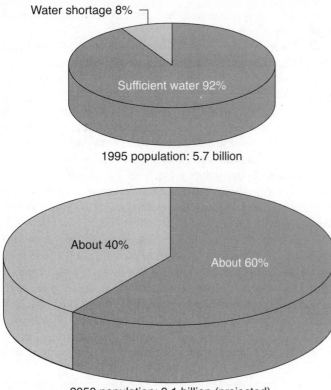

1995 population: 5.7 billion

2050 population: 9.1 billion (projected)

More of the population will suffer water shortages.

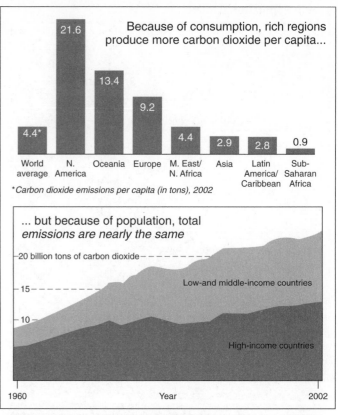

Consumption and the greenhouse gap: Citizens of industrial nations produce far more climate-warming carbon dioxide per capita than their peers in poorer countries. Because of population size, however, the developing world now produces slightly more of the gas. Thus, population exerts a powerful multiplier effect on the toll of consumption on the earth.

Instruments of Policy

A commonsense strategy for dealing with rising environmental risk would be to probe every reasonable opportunity for shifting to sustainability as quickly, easily and inexpensively as possible. No single energy strategy—whether nuclear, efficiency, wind, solar or geothermal—shows much promise on its own for eliminating the release of carbon dioxide into the air. Obstacles such as high up-front costs hamper most of those energy strategies even as part of a collective fix for the climate problem. No single change in land use will turn soils and plants into net absorbers of heat-trapping gases. Without technological breakthroughs in energy or land use, only higher prices for fossil fuels show much potential for edging down per capita emissions—a "solution" that policy makers have yet to grapple with effectively.

Given the long-term contribution that a turnaround in population growth could make in easing our most recalcitrant challenges, why doesn't the idea get more respect and attention? Politicians' apathy toward long-term solutions is part of the answer. But the more obvious reason is the discomfort most of us feel in grappling with the topics of sex, contraception, abortion, immigration and family sizes that differ by ethnicity and income. What in the population mix is *not* a hot button? Especially when the word "control" is added, and when the world's biggest religions have fruitful multiplication embedded in their philosophical DNA. And so critics from left, right and the intellectual center gang up on the handful of environmentalists and other activists who try to get population into national and global discussions.

Population and consumption feed on each other's growth to expand humans' environmental footprint exponentially.

Yet newly released population data from the U.N. show that developed countries, from the U.S. to Spain, have been experiencing (at least up through the beginnings of the economic crisis in 2008), if not baby booms, at least reproductive "rat-a-tat-tats." For the first time since the 1970s, the average number of children born to U.S. women has topped 2.1—the number at which parents replace themselves in the populations of developed and many developing countries. Even if net immigration ended tomorrow, continuation of that fertility rate would guarantee further growth in U.S. population for decades to come.

Those who do consider population to be a key to the problem typically say little about which policies would spare the planet many more billions of people. Should we restructure tax rates to favor small families? Propagandize the benefits of small families for the planet? Reward family-planning workers for clients they have sterilized? Each of those steps alone or in combination might help bend birthrates downward for a time, but none has proved to affect demographic trends over the long term or, critically, to gain and keep public support. When the

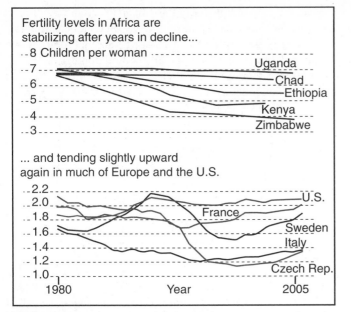

Reason for concern: Declines in fertility rates cannot be taken for granted. In parts of Africa, the rates seem to be flattening out well above the replacement rate. Surprisingly, the U.S. and parts of Europe seem to be experiencling a small but significant increase in fertility, compounding the population increases from immigration.

government of India rewarded health workers for meeting sterilization quotas in 1976, the zeal of some of them for wielding scalpels regardless of their patients' wishes contributed to the downfall of Indira Gandhi's government in 1977.

And how can we reduce consumption? Ideas such as cap-and-trade plans for limiting greenhouse gas emissions and allowing companies to trade emission rights are based on the same principle: raise the price of what harms the environment to reduce consumption of it. Beyond the consumption cuts, however, such schemes don't have much to recommend them. Governments can also eliminate subsidies of polluting behavior, an approach that is more palatable—except to the often powerful interests that benefit from the subsidies. Or governments can subsidize low consumption through tax deductions and credits, but the funds to do so on the needed scale will likely be increasingly scarce.

The Zen of Population

Mostly ignored in the environmental debates about population and consumption is that nearly all the world's nations agreed to an altogether different approach to the problem of growth 15 years ago, one that bases positive demographic outcomes on decisions individuals make in their own self-interest. (If only something comparable could be imagined to shrink consumption.) The strategy that 179 nations signed onto at a U.N. conference in Cairo in 1994 was: forget population control and instead help every woman bear a child in good health when she wants one.

That approach, which powerfully supports reproductive liberty, might sound counterintuitive for shrinking population growth, like handing a teenager the keys to the family car without so much as a lecture. But the evidence suggests that what women want—and have always wanted—is not so much to have *more*

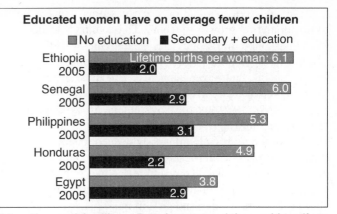

Education and fertility: Data from around the world testify to a robust trend: birthrates fall where women have more access to education. Improving women's access to schooling (and the opportunities it opens) may be one of the most powerful ways to reduce population growth.

children as to have *more for* a smaller number of children they can reliably raise to healthy adulthood. Women left to their own devices, contraceptive or otherwise, would collectively "control" population while acting on their own intentions.

More than 200 million women in developing countries are sexually active without effective modern contraception even though they do not want to be pregnant anytime soon, according to the Guttmacher Institute, a reproductive health research group. By the best estimates, some 80 million pregnancies around the world are unintended. Although the numbers aren't strictly comparable—many unplanned pregnancies end in abortion—the unintended pregnancies exceed the 78 million by which world population grows every year.

In the U.S., which is well informed and spends nearly 20 cents per dollar of economic activity on health care, nearly one out of every two pregnancies is unintended. That proportion has not changed much for decades. In every nation, rich and poor, in which a choice of contraceptives is available and is backed up by reasonably accessible safe abortion for when contraception fails, women have two or fewer children. Furthermore, educating girls reduces birthrates. Worldwide, according to a calculation provided for this article by demographers at the International Institute for Applied Systems Analysis in Austria, women with no schooling have an average of 4.5 children, whereas those with a few years of primary school have just three. Women who complete one or two years of secondary school have an average of 1.9 children apiece—a figure that over time leads to a decreasing population. With one or two years of college, the average childbearing rate falls even further, to 1.7. And when women enter the workforce, start businesses, inherit assets and otherwise interact with men on an equal footing, their desire for more than a couple of children fades even more dramatically.

Forget population control and instead help every woman bear a child in good health when she wants one.

True, old-style population control seems to have helped slow population growth in China. The country's leaders brag that their one-child policy has spared the world's climate 300 million greenhouse gas emitters, the population equivalent of a U.S. that never happened. But most of the drop in Chinese fertility occurred before that coercive policy went into effect in 1979, as the government brought women by the millions into farm and industry collectives and provided them with the family planning they needed to stay on the job. Many developing countries—from Thailand and Colombia to Iran—have experienced comparable declines in family size by getting better family-planning services and educational opportunities to more women and girls in more places.

With President Obama in the White House and Democrats dominant in Congress, the signs are good that the U.S. will support the kind of development abroad and reproductive health at home most likely to encourage slower population growth. Like almost all politicians, however, Obama never mentions population or the way it bridges problems from health and education all the way to food, energy security and climate change.

Bringing population back into the public conversation is risky, but the world has come a long way in understanding that the subject is only one part of most of today's problems and that "population control" can't really control population. Handing control of their lives and their bodies to women—the right thing to do for countless other reasons—can. There is no reason to fear the discussion.

Critical Thinking

1. Identify Robert Engelman's point of view.
2. What are some of the proposed policies to reduce the number of new babies?
3. Summarize his argument that a "downshift" in population will put the environment on a more sustainable path.

ROBERT ENGELMAN is vice president for programs at the Worldwatch Institute and author of *More: Population, Nature, and What Women Want* (Island Press).

Why Migration Matters

The world total of international migrants has more than doubled in just 25 years; about 25 million were added in just the first 5 years of the twenty-first century.

KHALID KOSER

Migration has always mattered—but today it matters more than ever before. The increasing importance of migration derives from its growing scale and its widening global reach, but also from a number of new dynamics. These include the feminization of migration, the growth of so-called irregular migration, and migration's inextricable linkages with globalization in terms of economic growth, development, and security. Climate change, moreover, is certain to raise migration still higher on nations' and international institutions' policy agendas.

The history of migration begins with humanity's very origins in the Rift Valley of Africa. It was from there that Homo sapiens emerged about 120,000 years ago, subsequently migrating across Africa, through the Middle East to Europe and Central and South Asia, and finally to the New World, reaching the Bering Straits about 20,000 years ago. Then, in the ancient world, Greek colonization and Roman expansion depended on migration; significant movements of people were also associated with the Mesopotamian, Incan, Indus, and Zhou empires. Later we see major migrations such as those involving the Vikings along the shorelines of the Atlantic and North Sea, and the Crusaders to the Holy Land.

In more recent history—in other words, in the past two or three centuries—it is possible to discern, according to migration historian Robin Cohen, a series of major migration periods or events. In the eighteenth and nineteenth centuries, one of the most prominent migration events was the forced transportation of slaves. About 12 million people were taken, mainly from West Africa, to the New World (and also, in lesser numbers, across the Indian Ocean and the Mediterranean Sea). One of the reasons this migration is considered so important, other than its scale, is that it still resonates for descendants of slaves and for African Americans in particular. After slavery's collapse, indentured laborers from China, India, and Japan moved overseas in significant numbers—1.5 million from India alone—to work the plantations of the European powers.

European expansion, especially during the nineteenth century, brought about large-scale voluntary migration away from Europe, particularly to the colonies of settlement, dominions, and the Americas. The great mercantile powers—Britain, the Netherlands, Spain, and France—all promoted settlement of their nationals abroad, not just workers but also peasants, dissident soldiers, convicts, and

orphans. Migration associated with expansion largely came to an end with the rise of anticolonial movements toward the end of the nineteenth century, and indeed over the next decades some significant reverse flows back to Europe occurred, for example of the so-called *pieds noirs* to France.

The next period of migration was marked by the rise of the United States as an industrial power. Between the 1850s and the Great Depression of the 1930s, millions of workers fled the stagnant economies and repressive political regimes of northern, southern, and eastern Europe and moved to the United States. (Many fled the Irish famine as well.) Some 12 million of these migrants landed at Ellis Island in New York Harbor. Opportunities for work in the United States also attracted large numbers of Chinese migrants in the first wave of the so-called Chinese diaspora, during the last 50 years of the nineteenth century.

The next major period of migration came after World War II, when the booming postwar economies in Europe, North America, and Australia needed labor. This was the era when, for example, many Turkish migrants arrived to work in Germany and many North Africans went to France and Belgium. It was also the period when, between 1945 and 1972, about 1 million Britons migrated to Australia as so-called "Ten Pound Poms" under an assisted passage scheme. During the same era but in other parts of the world, decolonization continued to have an impact on migration, most significantly in the movement of millions of Hindus and Muslims after the partition of India in 1947 and of Jews and Palestinians after the creation of Israel.

By the late 1970s, and in part as a consequence of the 1973 oil crisis, the international migrant labor boom had ended in Europe, though in the United States it continued into the 1990s. Now, with the global economy's momentum shifting decisively to Asia, labor migration on that continent has grown heavily, and it is still growing. How much longer this will be true, given the current global financial crisis, is a matter open to debate.

More and More

As even this (inevitably selective) overview of international migration's history should make clear, large movements of people have always been associated with significant global events like revolutions, wars, and the rise and fall of empires; with epochal changes like economic expansion, nation building, and political transformations; and with enduring challenges like conflict, persecution, and dispossession.

Nevertheless, one reason to argue that migration matters more today than ever before is sheer numbers. If we define an international migrant as a person who stays outside his usual country of residence for at least one year, there are about 200 million such migrants worldwide. This is roughly equivalent to the population of the fifth-most populous country on earth, Brazil. In fact, 1 in every 35 people in the world today is an international migrant.

Of course, a less dramatic way to express this statistic is to say that only 3 percent of the world's population is composed of international migrants. (In migration, statistics are often used to alarm rather than to inform.) And it is also worth noting that internal migration is a far more significant phenomenon than is international migration (China alone has at least 130 million internal migrants). Still, the world total of international migrants has more than doubled in just 25 years; about 25 million were added in just the first 5 years of the twenty-first century.

And international migration affects many more people than just those who migrate. According to Stephen Castles and Mark Miller, authors of the influential volume *The Age of Migration,* "There can be few people in either industrialized or less developed countries today who do not have personal experience of migration and its effects; this universal experience has become the hallmark of the age of migration." In host countries, migrants' contributions are felt keenly in social, cultural, and economic spheres. Throughout the world, people of different national origins, who speak different languages and practice different customs and religions, are coming into unprecedented contact with each other. For some this is a threat, for others an opportunity.

Migration is also a far more global process than ever before, as migrants today travel both from and to all of the world's regions. In 2005 (the most recent year for which global data are available) there were about 60 million international migrants in Europe, 44 million in Asia, 41 million in North America, 16 million in Africa, and 6 million each in Latin America and Australia. A significant portion of the world's migrants—about 35 million—lived in the United States. The Russian Federation was the second-largest host country for migrants, with about 13 million living there. Following in the rankings were Germany, Ukraine, and India, each with between 6 million and 7 million migrants.

It is much harder to say which countries migrants come from, largely because origin countries tend not to keep count of how many of their nationals are living abroad. It has been estimated that at least 35 million Chinese currently live outside their country, along with 20 million Indians and 8 million Filipinos. But in fact the traditional distinctions among migrants' countries of origin, transit, and destination have become increasingly blurred. Today almost every country in the world fulfills all three roles—migrants leave them, pass through them, and head for them.

A World of Reasons

The reasons for the recent rise in international migration and its widening global reach are complex. The factors include growing global disparities in development, democracy, and demography; in some parts of the world, job shortages that will be exacerbated by the current economic downturn; the segmentation of labor markets in high-income economies, a situation that attracts migrant workers to so-called "3D" jobs (dirty, difficult, or dangerous); revolutions in communications and transportation, which result in more people than ever before knowing about life elsewhere and having the ability to travel there; migration networks that allow existing migrant and ethnic communities to act as magnets for further migration; and a robust migration industry, including migrant smugglers and human traffickers, that profits from international migration.

In addition to being bigger, international migration today is also a more complex phenomenon than it has been in the past, as people of all ages and types move for a wide variety of reasons. For example, child migration appears to be on the increase around the world. Migrants with few skills working "3D" jobs make important contributions to the global economy, but so do highly skilled migrants and students. Some people move away from their home countries permanently, but an increasing proportion moves only temporarily, or circulates between countries. And though an important legal distinction can be made between people who move for work purposes and those who flee conflict and persecution, in reality the two can be difficult to distinguish, as members of the two groups sometimes move together in so-called "mixed flows."

One trend of particular note is that women's representation among migrants has increased rapidly, starting in the 1960s and accelerating in the 1990s. Very nearly half the world's authorized migrants in 2005 were women, and more female than male authorized migrants resided in Europe, North America, Latin America and the Caribbean, the states of the former Soviet Union, and Oceania. What is more, whereas women have traditionally migrated to join their partners, an increasing proportion who migrate today do so independently. Indeed, they are often primary breadwinners for families that they leave behind.

A number of reasons help explain why women comprise an increasing proportion of the world's migrants. One is that global demand for foreign labor, especially in more developed countries, is becoming increasingly gender-selective. That is, more jobs are available in the fields typically staffed by women—services, health care, and entertainment. Second, an increasing number of countries have extended the right of family reunion to migrants, allowing them to be joined by their spouses and children. Third, in some countries of origin, changes in gender relations mean that women enjoy more freedom than previously to migrate independently. Finally, in trends especially evident in Asia, there has been growth in migration of women for domestic work (this is sometimes called the "maid trade"); in organized migration for marriage (with the women sometimes referred to as "mail-order brides"); and in the trafficking of women, above all into the sex industry.

Most Irregular

Another defining characteristic of the new global migration is the growth of irregular migration and the rapid rise of this phenomenon in policy agendas. Indeed, of all the categories of international migrants, none attracts as much attention or divides opinion as consistently as irregular migrants—people often described as "illegal," "undocumented," or "unauthorized."

Almost by definition, irregular migration defies enumeration (although most commentators believe that its scale is increasing).

A commonly cited estimate holds that there are around 40 million irregular migrants worldwide, of whom perhaps one-third are in the United States. There are between 3.5 million and 5 million irregular migrants in the Russian Federation, and perhaps 5 million in Europe. Each year, an estimated 2.5 million to 4 million migrants are thought to cross international borders without authorization.

One reason that it is difficult to count irregular migrants is that even this single category covers people in a range of different situations. It includes migrants who enter or remain in a country without authorization; those who are smuggled or trafficked across an international border; those who seek asylum, are not granted it, and then fail to observe a deportation order; and people who circumvent immigration controls, for example by arranging bogus marriages or fake adoptions.

What is more, an individual migrant's status can change—often rapidly. A migrant can enter a country in an irregular fashion but then regularize her status, for example by applying for asylum or entering a regularization program. Conversely, a migrant can enter regularly then become irregular by working without a permit or overstaying a visa. In Australia, for example, British citizens who have stayed beyond the expiration of their visas account for by far the largest number of irregular migrants.

The Rich Get Richer

International migration matters more today than ever because of its new dimensions and dynamics, but even more because of its increased impact—on the global economy, on international politics, and on society. Three impacts are particularly worth noting: international migration's contribution to the global economy; the significance of migration for development; and the linkages between migration and security.

Kodak, Atlantic Records, RCA, NBC, Google, Intel, Hotmail, Sun, Microsoft, Yahoo, eBay—all these US firms were founded or cofounded by migrants. It has been estimated that international migrants make a net contribution to the US economy of $60 billion, and that half of the scientists, engineers, and holders of PhD degrees in the United States were born overseas. It is often suggested (though this is hard to substantiate) that migrants are worth more to the British economy than is North Sea oil. Worldwide migrant labor is thought to earn at least $20 trillion. In some of the Gulf states, migrants comprise 90 percent of the labor force.

Such a selection of facts and figures can suggest a number of conclusions about international migration's significance for the global economy. First, migrants are often among the most dynamic and entrepreneurial members of society. This has always been the case. In many ways the history of US economic growth is the history of migrants: Andrew Carnegie (steel), Adolphus Busch (beer), Samuel Goldwyn (movies), and Helena Rubenstein (cosmetics) were all migrants. Second, migrants fill labor market gaps both at the top end and the bottom end—a notion commonly captured in the phrase "Mi-grants do the work that natives are either unable or unwilling to do." Third, the significance of migrant labor varies across countries but more importantly across economic sectors. In the majority of advanced economies, migrant workers are over-represented in agriculture, construction, heavy industry, manufacturing, and services—especially food, hospitality, and domestic services. (It is precisely these sectors that the global financial crisis is currently hitting hardest.) Finally, migrant workers contribute significantly more to national economies than they take away (through, for example, pensions and welfare benefits). That is, migrants tend to be young and they tend to work.

This last conclusion explains why migration is increasingly considered one possible response to the demographic crisis that affects increasing numbers of advanced economies (though it does not affect the United States yet). In a number of wealthy countries, a diminishing workforce supports an expanding retired population, and a mismatch results between taxes that are paid into pension and related programs and the payments that those programs must make. Importing youthful workers in the form of migrants appears at first to be a solution—but for two reasons, it turns out to be only a short-term response. First, migrants themselves age and eventually retire. Second, recent research indicates that, within a generation, migrants adapt their fertility rates to those that prevail in the countries where they settle. In other words, it would not take long for migrants to exacerbate rather then relieve a demographic crisis.

The Poor Get Richer

International migration does not affect only the economies of countries to which migrants travel—it also strongly affects the economies of countries from which migrants depart, especially in the realm of development in poorer countries. The World Bank estimates that each year migrants worldwide send home about $300 billion. This amounts to triple the value of official development assistance, and is the second-largest source of external funding for developing countries after foreign direct investment. The most important recipient countries for remittances are India ($27 billion), China ($26 billion), Mexico ($25 billion), and the Philippines ($17 billion). The top countries from which remittances are dispatched are the United States ($42 billion), Saudi Arabia ($16 billion), Switzerland ($14 billion), and Germany ($12 billion).

The impact of remittances on development is hotly debated, and to an extent the impact depends on who receives the money and how it is spent. It is indisputable that remittances can lift individuals and families out of poverty: Annual household incomes in Somaliland are doubled by remittances. Where remittances are spent on community projects such as wells and schools, as is often the case in Mexico, they also have a wider benefit. And remittances make a significant contribution to gross domestic product (GDP) at the national level, comprising for example 37 percent of GDP in Tonga and 27 percent in both Jordan and Lesotho.

Most experts emphasize that remittances should not be viewed as a substitute for official development assistance. One reason is that remittances are private monies, and thus it is difficult to influence how they are spent or invested. Also, remittances fluctuate over time, as is now becoming apparent in the context of the global economic crisis. Finally, it has been suggested that remittances can generate a "culture of migration," encouraging further migration, and even provide a disincentive to work where families come to expect money from abroad. It has to be said, even so, that the net impact of remittances in developing countries is positive.

International migration, moreover, can contribute to development through other means than remittances. For example, it can relieve pressure on the labor markets in countries from which migrants originate, reducing competition and unemployment. Indonesia and the Philippines are examples of countries that deliberately export labor for this reason (as well as to obtain remittance income). In addition, migrants can contribute to their home countries when they return by using their savings and the new skills they have acquired—although the impact they can have really depends on the extent to which necessary infrastructure is in place for them to realize their potential.

At the same time, however, international migration can undermine development through so-called "brain drain." This term describes a situation in which skills that are already in short supply in a country depart that country through migration. Brain drain is a particular problem in sub-Saharan Africa's health sector, as significant numbers of African doctors and nurses work in the United Kingdom and elsewhere in Europe. Not only does brain drain deprive a country of skills that are in high demand—it undermines that country's investment in the education and training of its own nationals.

Safety First

A third impact of international migration—one that perhaps more than any other explains why it has risen toward the top of policy agendas—is the perception that migration constitutes a heightened security issue in the era after 9/11. Discussions of this issue often revolve around irregular migration—which, in public and policy discourses, is frequently associated with the risk of terrorism, the spread of infectious diseases, and criminality.

Such associations are certainly fair in some cases. A strong link, for example, has been established between irregular migrants from Morocco, Algeria, and Syria and the Madrid bombings of March 2004. For the vast majority of irregular migrants, however, the associations are not fair. Irregular migrants are often assigned bad intentions without any substantiation. Misrepresenting evidence can criminalize and demonize all irregular migrants, encourage them to remain underground—and divert attention from those irregular migrants who actually are criminals and should be prosecuted, as well as those who are suffering from disease and should receive treatment.

Irregular migration is indeed associated with risks, but not with the risks most commonly identified. One legitimate risk is irregular migration's threat to the exercise of sovereignty. States have a sovereign right to control who crosses their borders and remains on their territory, and irregular migration challenges this right. Where irregular migration involves corruption and organized crime, it can also become a threat to public security. This is particularly the case when illegal entry is facilitated by migrant smugglers and human traffickers, or when criminal gangs compete for control of migrants' labor after they have arrived.

Irregular migration is indeed associated with risks, but not with the risks most commonly identified.

When irregular migration results in competition for scarce jobs, this can generate xenophobic sentiments within host populations. Importantly, these sentiments are often directed not only at migrants with irregular status but also at established migrants, refugees, and ethnic minorities. When irregular migration receives

a great deal of media attention, it can also undermine public confidence in the integrity and effectiveness of a state's migration and asylum policies.

In addition, irregular migration can undermine the "human security" of migrants themselves. The harm done to migrants by irregular migration is often underestimated—in fact, irregular migration can be very dangerous. A large number of people die each year trying to cross land and sea borders while avoiding detection by the authorities. It has been estimated, for example, that as many as 2,000 migrants die each year trying to cross the Mediterranean from Africa to Europe, and that about 400 Mexicans die annually trying to cross the border into the United States.

People who enter a country or remain in it without authorization are often at risk of exploitation by employers and landlords. Female migrants with irregular status, because they are confronted with gender-based discrimination, are often obliged to accept the most menial jobs in the informal sector, and they may face specific health-related risks, including exposure to HIV/AIDS. Such can be the level of human rights abuses involved in contemporary human trafficking that some commentators have compared it to the slave trade.

Migrants with irregular status are often unwilling to seek redress from authorities because they fear arrest and deportation. For the same reason, they do not always make use of public services to which they are entitled, such as emergency health care. In most countries, they are also barred from using the full range of services available both to citizens and to migrants with regular status. In such situations, already hard-pressed nongovernmental organizations, religious bodies, and other civil society institutions are obliged to provide assistance, at times compromising their own legality.

In Hard Times

What might the future of international migration look like? Tentatively at least, the implications of the current global economic crisis for migration are beginning to emerge. Already a slowdown in the movement of people at a worldwide level has been reported, albeit with significant regional and national variations, and this appears to be largely a result of declining job opportunities in destination countries. The economic sectors in which migrants tend to be overrepresented have been hit first; as a consequence migrant workers around the world are being laid off in substantial numbers.

Migrant workers around the world are being laid off in substantial numbers.

Interestingly, it appears that most workers are nevertheless not returning home, choosing instead to stay and look for new jobs. Those entitled to draw on social welfare systems can be expected to do so, thus reducing their net positive impact on national economies. (It remains to be seen whether national economic stimulus packages, such as the one recently enacted in the United States, will help migrant workers get back to work.) Scattered cases of xenophobia have been reported around the world, as anxious natives increasingly fear labor competition from migrant workers.

In the last quarter of 2008 remittances slowed down. Some project that in 2009 remittances, for the first time in decades, may shrink. Moreover, changes in exchange rates mean that even if the volume of remittances remains stable, their net value to recipients may decrease. These looming trends hold worrying implications for households, communities, and even national economies in poor countries.

Our experience of previous economic downturns and financial crises—including the Great Depression, the oil crisis of the early 1970s, and the Asian, Russian, and Latin American financial crises between 1997 and 2000—tells us that such crises' impact on international migration is relatively short-lived and that migration trends soon rebound. Few experts are predicting that the current economic crisis will fundamentally alter overall trends toward increased international migration and its growing global reach.

Hot in Here

In the longer term, what will affect migration patterns and processes far more than any financial crisis is climate change. One commonly cited prediction holds that 200 million people will be forced to move as a result of climate change by 2050, although other projections range from 50 million to a startling 1 billion people moving during this century.

In the longer term, what will affect migration patterns and processes far more than any financial crisis is climate change.

The relationship that will develop between climate change and migration appears complex and unpredictable. One type of variable is in climate change events themselves—a distinction is usually made between slow-onset events like rising sea levels and rapid-onset events like hurricanes and tsunamis. In addition, migration is only one of a number of possible responses to most climate change events. Protective measures such as erecting sea walls may reduce the impact. Societies throughout history have adapted to climate change by altering their agricultural and settlement practices.

Global warming, moreover, will make some places better able to support larger populations, as growing seasons are extended, frost risks reduced, and new crops sustained. Where migration does take place, it is difficult to predict whether the movement will mainly be internal or cross-border, or temporary or permanent. And finally, the relationship between climate change and migration may turn out to be indirect. For example, people may flee conflicts that arise over scarce resources in arid areas, rather than flee desertification itself.

Notwithstanding the considerable uncertainty, a consensus has emerged that, within the next 10 years, climate-related international migration will become observably more frequent, and the scale of overall international migration will increase significantly. Such migration will add still further complexity to the migration situation, as the new migrants will largely defy current classifications.

One immediately contentious issue is whether people who cross borders as a result of the effects of climate change should be defined as "climate refugees" or "climate migrants." The former conveys the fact that at least some people will literally need to seek refuge from the impacts of climate change, will find themselves in situations as desperate as those of other refugees, and will deserve international assistance and protection. But the current definition of a refugee in international law does not extend to people fleeing environmental pressures, and few states are willing to amend the law. Equally, the description "climate migrant" underestimates the involuntariness of the movement, and opens up the possibility for such people to be labeled and dealt with as irregular migrants.

Another legal challenge arises with the prospect of the total submergence by rising sea levels of low-lying island states such as the Maldives—namely, how to categorize people who no longer have a state. Will their national flags be lowered outside UN headquarters in New York, and will they be granted citizenship in another country?

The complexities of responding to climate-related movements of people illustrate a more general point, that new responses are required to international migration as it grows in scale and complexity. Most of the legal frameworks and international institutions established to govern migration were established at the end of World War II, in response to a migration reality very different from that existing today, and as a result new categories of migrants are falling into gaps in protection. New actors have also emerged in international migration, including most importantly the corporate sector, and they have very little representation in migration policy decisions at the moment.

Perhaps most fundamentally, a shift in attitude is required, away from the notion that migration can be controlled, focusing instead on trying to manage migration and maximize its benefits.

Critical Thinking

1. According to Khalid Koser, why does international migration matter more now than ever before?

2. What are the reasons for this?

3. What countries are the primary recipients of "irregular" migrants?

4. How do immigrants economically benefit their country of origin?

5. What might the future of international migration look like?

KHALID KOSER directs the New Issues in Security program at the Geneva Center for Security Policy. He is also a non-resident fellow at the Brookings Institution and author of *International Migration: A Very Short Introduction* (Oxford University Press, 2007).

Pandemic Pandemonium

JOSH N. RUXIN

Pandemic. The word can spread fear to billions overnight. One of the few public-health terms that gives Hollywood nightmare plotlines. Literally meaning "all people," a pandemic is an extraordinary global health event in which an epidemic of infectious disease spreads across regions and, potentially, the entire planet. Ebola, avian flu, SARS—each had the potential to spread rapidly and each received extraordinary attention during the past several years. Though they did not result in mass casualties, all wrought worldwide fear.

Throughout the course of human history, pandemics have wreaked havoc. The 1918 flu pandemic may have killed over 20 million people. Even then, 50 percent of the mortality difference among countries can be attributed to a single factor: per capita income. Thus, the poorest country hit, India, suffered the most, while Denmark suffered the least. That differential, however, has not yet made for compelling public policy. After all, science made landmark breakthroughs in the twentieth century, often applying scientific insights from previous centuries in innovative ways to control and, in the case of smallpox, eradicate disease. But in the days of porous borders and unprecedented global travel, viruses and other pathogens may once again have the upper hand. One key question on the table is: will the next pandemic be worse than the ones we currently face?

Viewed from where I live in Rwanda, it's clear that the sheer neglect of health of poor people has set an ideal foundation for pandemics to spread for years under the radar, evade surveillance and, as has been the case with HIV/AIDS, enter our airspace and bodies at a startling rate. The history of global health demonstrates that wealthy nations respond best to dramatic, fast-moving outbreaks like Ebola or avian flu. Unfortunately, today wealthy and poor nations alike face pandemics that move slowly and don't necessarily show symptoms during the first few years of infection.

Today's pandemics have evolved to prey on our greatest weakness: our inability to wage sustained fights against pressing health issues. This creates a doubly challenging situation in a world where disease is often socioeconomically stratified. Rich people don't generally get sick from malaria or tuberculosis (TB), so those diseases—which kill millions each year—have until very recently received far-less attention than they deserve. But now the line between rich and poor countries, and rich and poor people within countries, is murky. Dangerous infections such as drug-resistant tuberculosis can cross the globe by air in

a matter of hours. These are the new, rapidly moving vectors of disease, and they provide a direct line of transmission between the most-vulnerable and least-healthy people on the planet and the wealthiest and healthiest. It augurs for the worst that health systems for the poor have failed miserably to generate the quality and accountability needed to address even the most-basic health needs.

What happens when a poor country loses 30 percent of its adult population to AIDS or to a flu epidemic? There are plenty of military models that assess decision making when a country is attacked by an enemy, but few models to assess the chaos that cuts across all segments of society when it's a disease that acts as antagonist. Plans have also not fully taken into account the impact of rapidly changing demographics on disease spread. The poorest, precisely those most at risk, are reproducing the fastest, so the chance of pandemic is growing faster than the numbers may superficially reveal. And of course, the prevalence of megacities means more poor people are living in close proximity to each other—and with greater opportunity for disease transmission.

Leaders of poor countries appear to be completely unaware of the global connections between the health of their populations and the security and stability required to ensure that they do not fall prey to unforeseen health catastrophes. The dearth of strong and transparent leadership among the world's poorest nations augurs poorly for the health of those nations, and of the world.

Meanwhile, the rich countries also continue to think about pandemics in a very linear and scientific way, which fails to account for the comprehensive economic and political chaos that would accompany a major pandemic. The World Health Organization (WHO), Centers for Disease Control, and, for that matter, the Gates Foundation and other donors, are concentrating their efforts on vaccines and, in the case of the WHO, antiviral stockpiles for a possible outbreak of avian flu. Plans are also being developed for isolation and quarantine, running through scenarios for stopping air traffic and the like. Unfortunately, it's unlikely that the pathogens will be as responsive to our efforts as we hope they will be, leading to widespread chaos, morbidity and mortality.

At a time when oil shocks have the ability to globally increase food insecurity, it may be worthwhile to consider how a pandemic could push people living on the edge into poverty and starvation. With food production suffering greatly, the urban centers that are dependent on daily imports of food could rapidly fall victim. If this sounds a bit like Jared Diamond's arguments in *Collapse,* it's intentional. The world is interconnected, but poor countries are hanging by a thread, and it's a thread that could quickly break if a pandemic hits hard enough.

Poor countries are hanging by a thread, and it's a thread that could quickly break if a pandemic hits hard enough.

Adding to the threat, it may well be that the worst pandemics on the planet are not emerging, but have simply been with us so long that we've grown accustomed to their presence and therefore have done little to address them. Women across sub-Saharan Africa continue to stand a 1 percent chance of dying in childbirth—is that a pandemic? Five hundred thousand kids die from measles every year. Africans suffer from an astonishing estimated 300 million episodes of malaria annually, with a death toll of one million. And now throughout the developing world silent killers like heart disease and diabetes are taking hold.

In the best of cases, pursuing a business-as-usual approach, the wealthy countries may get lucky: the spread of contagion may be stopped at borders and when it crosses, advanced, expensive treatment may be available. But no matter what, the economic and potential political destabilization that would result would cross these borders and be felt in everyone's bank accounts. The moral implications of continuing to adopt a merely defensive stance will guarantee that developing countries will suffer millions dead and may also cultivate the pathogens for future pandemics that will evade the best weapons the richer countries can throw at them.

Some might see the call for health improvement in poor nations in order to save our own skins as either a Machiavellian ploy to help poor people or a sad and ironic commentary on the state of humankind. Whatever the case, rich nations must begin taking health systems for the poor seriously because: new bugs and the resurgence of old ones are likely to emerge where people are sickest or treatment is inconsistent; when pandemics strike, they'll do the most harm to those without health services; and when sicknesses like a new strain of influenza inevitably come, the health personnel in these settings will be much-better equipped to identify and contain them.

If they don't, Hollywood fantasies may well come true; America and Western Europe will panic as they hear of outbreaks far away (and which may well reach inside their borders); Asia, a likely epicenter of a new flu outbreak or other zoonotically spread disease, will see its services strained and its globalizing economies wrecked; and Africa will see its people die in higher rates than everywhere else while its nascent economic connections to the rest of the world stumble. This scenario is, sadly, hardly far-fetched. The SARS epidemic alone cost Asian countries more than $16 billion and spread panic worldwide while claiming fewer than one thousand lives. That experience suggests that estimating the toll of an actual pandemic is virtually incalculable.

The Threats
AIDS

For the past decade, AIDS has garnered attention not only because of its clinical impact, but also because of its downstream effects. South African businesspeople report that they have to hire one additional worker for every manager hired because they expect so much of their workforce to die of AIDS. Social services and even traditional societal mechanisms for handling orphans are disintegrating in despair as the wave of millions of orphans builds.

More than a decade after numerous news media outlets optimistically queried whether we had reached the end of AIDS, there are troubling signs that this pandemic may yet prove to be the world's top infectious killer. The World Bank has estimated that for every six new infections, only one person is put on life-saving anti-retrovirals (ARVs). This means the disease continues to spread virtually unchecked. With 40 million infected, in all likelihood we'll continue to see 3 to 5 million people dying annually for years to come. Undeniably, AIDS has hit hardest in sub-Saharan Africa, where nearly 23 million are infected. At current rates of drug rollout, all but a couple million of them will die during the next ten years. The ramifications for each of those deaths are hidden by the numbers: for each death, roughly another six people are immediately affected emotionally and economically. Seen through this lens, nearly one-third of sub-Saharan Africa is already likely to be impacted by the current pandemic.

AIDS presents a perfect case for why all health must be global. It is not simply a philanthropic service to ensure that basic health needs are met worldwide: it's a biological necessity. AIDS may well have been around for the better part of the last century, but it went largely undetected because it was prevalent among populations with minimal access to health care. By the time it reached people with health care, it had spread across the planet, causing an estimated 25 million deaths to date.

The numbers will get worse. In the developing world there may be little data on resistance, but with more treated people, coupled with inconsistent treatments and fewer treatment options, it is likely that drug resistance will emerge as a major problem. The solutions do remain well within the grasp of our current abilities. Good surveillance and improved monitoring for patients on ARVs in developing countries will lessen the possibility of treatment failure and corresponding resistance. Expanded treatment programs that include better monitoring and access to more than first-line therapy ensure that when treatment does fail, patients have other options. This will ensure that they do not become vessels for advanced strains of the disease. But without action, strains of HIV which can tolerate even the most-sophisticated and most-expensive drug regimens available may well emerge and move around the world just as the first strains did. Thus, AIDS in the West could prove to be the definitive killer that it once was, yet again.

Malaria

Malaria, though hardly as expensive as AIDS to address, has joined the ranks of diseases being tackled on a grand scale. The Global Fund has committed $3.1 billion to the malaria fight, and the United States has launched a bold new malaria initiative. Through the use of insecticide-treated bed nets and new drug therapy, several countries have realized steep declines in malaria morbidity and mortality, one among them Rwanda. In 2000, Rwanda saw an estimated one million cases of malaria. Today, thanks in large part to bed nets, that figure has fallen by more than 60 percent. In 2000, an astonishing 10 percent of all children under five succumbed to malaria; today, those deaths have virtually disappeared. For the first time in decades, serious debate and action is emerging to eradicate or diminish the disease. Bill and Melinda Gates have set the world's sights on complete malaria eradication, a feat that will require massive breakthroughs in technology.

However, this is one fight that must be taken to the far reaches of the earth and be resolutely committed to a sustained effort. Today it is widely hypothesized that the extraordinary illness seen from malaria resulted from the failure to continue pushing the disease back with DDT in the 1960s. Instead, after some notable successes, efforts evaporated, individuals and populations lost their natural immunity, and the disease came back with a vengeance. Anything less than persistent, wholesale control and elimination efforts risks exacerbation of the disease. In the worst-case scenario, malaria could be eliminated from much of the African continent, be maintained at low levels in a few places, develop resistance to the best drugs available, and then see efforts to contain it wane. What would follow would be devastating for the continent. Malaria would return to populations lacking any natural immunity, drugs could prove ineffective, and millions of lives would potentially be lost—every year—particularly among very young children.

Tuberculosis

Tuberculosis has plagued humankind since the fourth millennia BCE. While the disease only recently ceased to be a significant public-health threat in the developed world, TB still claims five thousand lives globally every day, more than SARS, Marburg and avian flu ever have. Nine million people develop active TB each year. Although curative treatment has been around for the last several decades, it has been unevenly applied: in many cases health facilities have not ensured that patients receive a full course of treatment, and, overall, those most in need of treatment have not received it at all. Poor treatment has resulted in fiercer, more-resistant strains of TB. Three percent of all newly diagnosed patients have multi-drug-resistant TB (MDR-TB), making their treatment complicated, expensive and uncertain. In September 2006, the WHO announced a further worsening of the MDR-TB pandemic with multiple reports in all regions of the world of the emergence of extensively resistant strains of TB (XDR-TB) immune to virtually all drugs.

It should not shock Americans that this disease is making its way across the globe when every location is just a plane ride away. Yet the growth of XDR-TB, considered virtually untreatable, has gone largely unnoticed in the United States, where there have been only seventeen cases since 2000. In sub-Saharan Africa, where roughly 23 million people are HIV positive, nearly half will develop TB. If treatment is not well administered, these cases will lead to new strains of resistant TB. There is a direct connection between the AIDS pandemic, TB, and the failure of health systems to appropriately diagnose and treat these diseases. However, unlike AIDS, whose transmission relies on behavior (unsafe sex, intravenous-drug usage), TB is airborne. While the immuno-compromised and malnourished are at greater risk for developing active TB, the main risk factor for contracting it is shared by all: breathing. Those in the developed world have every reason to fear for their immunity.

Influenza

The flu may be the world's greatest risk. Recent models based on the 1918 Spanish flu have estimated that the next outbreak will cause between 51 and 157 million excess deaths, with 95 percent of those occurring in developing countries. Critics have suggested that it's overly optimistic to conclude the carnage will be so low in developed nations. Other estimates conclude that total excess deaths could exceed 300 million with 27 million occurring in rich nations and the large remainder in poor. Without sufficient health-care facilities in developing countries—in both urban and rural locations—the higher death estimates will undoubtedly be realized, as a virulent flu spreads easily and rapidly through the air. Whatever the case, a particularly vicious strain of the flu would undoubtedly be the greatest public-health catastrophe of our time.

So what precisely is at the root of the massive inequities that provide the petri dish for global pandemics? Is it simply disease burden? Transmission routes? Poverty? Corruption and poor governance? Selfishness on a grand scale? All of the above?

At the turn of the twenty-first century, the blame for the burden was placed squarely on wealthy countries. The failure to roll out simple solutions required exponential increases in funding and new initiatives—ironically fueled by one of the most-complex diseases ever faced, AIDS. Drugs and big pharmaceuticals were the scapegoats of the last several years; today, experts cite the lack of nurses and human resources. There is a predictable oscillation in the blame game, but one fact is clear: health worldwide has deteriorated.

This is perhaps most troubling in the context of pandemics because just as environmental catastrophes can spur epidemics, and potentially pandemics, pandemics can quickly take down economies and, potentially, countries. In the wake of avian flu, Southeast Asian economies experienced an enormous economic downturn; tourists have been writing me and asking whether it's safe to go to Brazil in light of the dengue epidemic; the economic, social and political cost of AIDS in sub-Saharan Africa remains to be calculated. Thus, there is a vicious cycle: pandemics can encourage chaos and breakdowns of basic systems, particularly in the poorest and poorly governed nations, and these breakdowns can in turn create better conditions for more disease to emerge. Case in point: during the chaos in Kenya at the turn of this year, 60 percent of patients on antiretroviral therapy and 35 percent of patients on TB drugs were lost to follow-up. It is likely that all those patients stopped their treatment midcourse and are now potentially cultivating resistant strains of both infections.

Policy makers are looking at the direct health consequences of pandemics (Who is sick? How do we treat them?) rather than the indirect health consequences (What other services will fail? What will happen to the food supply?). Had SARS hit anywhere in sub-Saharan Africa, where ventilators and surgical masks are a rare commodity, death rates would have been higher than in Asia. Today the response systems being put in place are to protect the wealthy with vaccines and antivirals, but do not treat those most likely to suffer. Thus, we are preparing for the next pandemic rather than doing everything in our power to prevent it.

Foundations and governments can't seem to get their heads around the fact that no disease can be treated in a vacuum: all efforts must be part of an integrated response, otherwise dollars are sure to be poorly spent. The worst-hit area on the planet for health-systems failure remains sub-Saharan Africa, where governments spend paltry amounts on health, the poor are frequently required to pay for services and there's an uncanny history of serious illnesses evolving. HIV is widely recognized today as having its roots in central Africa; resistant malaria parasites are commonplace; and bizarre outbreaks such as Ebola appear from time to time. When sexually transmitted infections go untreated and open sores ensue, the possibility for transmission increases exponentially, and that transmission doesn't stop at borders.

While epidemics get the press—the recent dengue outbreak in Brazil for example—pandemics tend to quietly work their way through populations, doing enormous harm never garnering the resources or the media attention. That's not to say that rich nations shouldn't be concerned about these epidemics, but there is an uncomfortably consistent trend in global public health to place attention on those subjects and diseases that may not pose the greatest threat to human welfare.

In the next couple of decades, with expanded funding for public health, it will be possible to radically alter the course of the future of human health, particularly in poor countries. However, sticking to traditional approaches will fail to provide macro results and may exacerbate health challenges. The uneven delivery of AIDS medications, tuberculosis drugs and antimalarials, for example, could give rise to resistant parasites, bacteria and viruses capable of beating current technology. Further, the singular focus on just a few diseases and the subspecialization that accompanies it may rob us of the expert diagnosticians who can quickly spot an unusual illness before it gets out of control.

The solution to the frightening scenario of national breakdowns and despair is to beef up efforts to build capacity in the poorest nations to handle their current problems, with an eye to avoiding such chaos. Health systems require serious strengthening. Farmers need improved agricultural techniques to push them away from the brink and toward something resembling stability. Basic infrastructure must be massively expanded and improved. The list is a long one but most everywhere you look, we have scarcely begun. It's time to shake up the public-health establishment and place investments in basic health services for the neglected and poor worldwide.

We need to step up efforts and get it right. The world's health and stability depend on it.

Critical Thinking

1. Define pandemic and give an example.
2. What are the four most serious disease threats?
3. Describe some of the impacts a pandemic might have on social structures.

Josh N. Ruxin is an assistant clinical professor of public health at Columbia University's Mailman School of Public Health. He resides in Rwanda where he directs the Access Project and the Millennium Villages Project Rwanda, and advises Rwanda Community Works.

The Next Breadbasket?
How Africa Could Save the World—and Itself

ELIZABETH CHILES SHELBURNE

I t's been 41 years since Paul Ehrlich predicted imminent mass starvation, in his 1968 jeremiad, *The Population Bomb*. In the years that followed, a green revolution drove crop production rapidly upward, while population growth slowed dramatically; Ehrlich's bomb, rather conspicuously, failed to go off.

Nonetheless, we're still multiplying—global population is on track to reach 9.1 billion by 2050, up from 6.8 billion today. And the green revolution seems to have run its course: rice yields, for instance, are growing at only 1 percent a year, down from 2.3 percent in the 1960s, 1970s, and 1980s. For the past several years, grain production has not kept up with demand; if we are to put enough food on the table in the coming decades, something big will need to change.

Much of the world's arable land is being farmed already, so the lion's share of the increase will need to come through higher yields. In many places, yields *can*

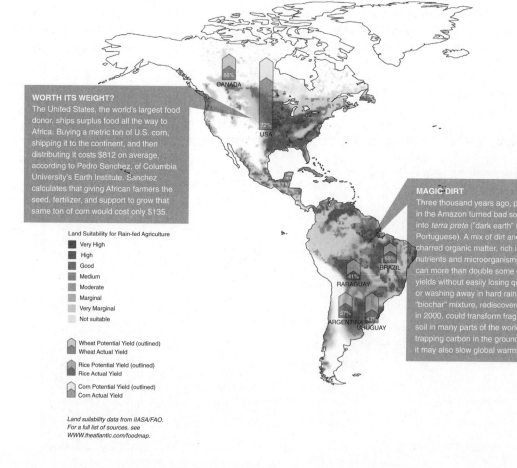

WORTH ITS WEIGHT?
The United States, the world's largest food donor, ships surplus food all the way to Africa. Buying a metric ton of U.S. corn, shipping it to the continent, and then distributing it costs $812 on average, according to Pedro Sanchez, of Columbia University's Earth Institute. Sanchez calculates that giving African farmers the seed, fertilizer, and support to grow that same ton of corn would cost only $135.

MAGIC DIRT
Three thousand years ago, people in the Amazon turned bad soil into *terra preta* ("dark earth" in Portuguese). A mix of dirt and charred organic matter, rich in nutrients and microorganisms, it can more than double some crop yields without easily losing quality or washing away in hard rains. This "biochar" mixture, rediscovered in 2000, could transform fragile soil in many parts of the world. By trapping carbon in the ground, it may also slow global warming.

Land Suitability for Rain-fed Agriculture
- Very High
- High
- Good
- Medium
- Moderate
- Marginal
- Very Marginal
- Not suitable

Wheat Potential Yield (outlined)
Wheat Actual Yield

Rice Potential Yield (outlined)
Rice Actual Yield

Corn Potential Yield (outlined)
Corn Actual Yield

Land suitability data from IIASA/FAO.
For a full list of sources, see
WWW.theatlantic.com/foodmap.

increase—if prices rise high enough to make investment in more-intensive agriculture worthwhile. Still, much of the developed world is approaching the ceiling of what is cheaply possible. Sub-Saharan Africa, despite its long history of food insecurity, is one place where yields could increase dramatically; agricultural basics such as good seed and fertilizer would go far in a region that the green revolution bypassed. "We could increase yields in sub-Saharan Africa threefold tomorrow with off-the-shelf technology," says Kenneth Cassman, a well-regarded agronomist who researches potential yields. The problem is the continent's long history of corruption, poor infrastructure, and lack of market access.

Agricultural investment in Africa—and in a few other high-potential places such as Ukraine and Russia—may be the world's best bet for keeping food plentiful and cheap.

This investment could bring other benefits too; the World Bank estimates that agricultural development is twice as effective at reducing poverty as other sources of growth. In Asia, as cereal yields rose, poverty rates plummeted. Investment in Africa's agriculture—by donors, farmers, and African governments—may allow the continent to feed the world and save itself.

Critical Thinking

1. What is the "green revolution?"
2. Compare Africa to other regions of the world in terms of its ability to increase food production.
3. Does this article complement or contradict Article 2?

ELIZABETH CHILES SHELBURNE is a writer based in Boston.

From *The Atlantic*, September 2009, pp. 72–73. Copyright © 2009 by Atlantic Monthly Group. Reprinted by permission of TMS Reprints.

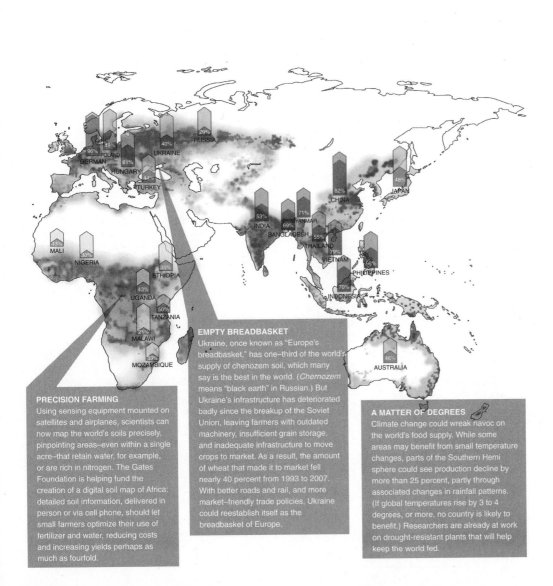

PRECISION FARMING
Using sensing equipment mounted on satellites and airplanes, scientists can now map the world's soils precisely, pinpointing areas–even within a single acre–that retain water, for example, or are rich in nitrogen. The Gates Foundation is helping fund the creation of a digital soil map of Africa; detailed soil information, delivered in person or via cell phone, should let small farmers optimize their use of fertilizer and water, reducing costs and increasing yields perhaps as much as fourfold.

EMPTY BREADBASKET
Ukraine, once known as "Europe's breadbasket," has one–third of the world's supply of chenozem soil, which many say is the best in the world. (*Chernozem* means "black earth" in Russian.) But Ukraine's infrastructure has deteriorated badly since the breakup of the Soviet Union, leaving farmers with outdated machinery, insufficient grain storage, and inadequate infrastructure to move crops to market. As a result, the amount of wheat that made it to market fell nearly 40 percent from 1993 to 2007. With better roads and rail, and more market–friendly trade policies, Ukraine could reestablish itself as the breadbasket of Europe.

A MATTER OF DEGREES
Climate change could wreak havoc on the world's food supply. While some areas may benefit from small temperature changes, parts of the Southern Hemisphere could see production decline by more than 25 percent, partly through associated changes in rainfall patterns. (If global temperatures rise by 3 to 4 degrees, or more, no country is likely to benefit.) Researchers are already at work on drought-resistant plants that will help keep the world fed.

UNIT 3

The Global Environment and Natural Resources Utilization

Unit Selections

Learning Outcomes

After reading this unit you should be able to

- Discuss the basic pro and con arguments regarding the causes of climate change.

- Describe the impact of human activities on glaciers, oceans, tropical forests and other ecological systems.

- Identify some of the policy debates related to mitigating climate change impacts.

- Describe a case study of an invasive species.

- Assess your on-going effort at identifying your theory of international relations and how this unit changes/complements it.

Student Website

www.mhhe.com/cls

Internet References

National Geographic Society
  www.nationalgeographic.com
National Oceanic and Atmospheric Administration (NOAA)
  www.noaa.gov
SocioSite: Sociological Subject Areas
  www.pscw.uva.nl/sociosite/TOPICS
United Nations Environment Programme (UNEP)
  www.unep.ch

In the eighteenth century, the modern nation-state emerged, and, over many generations, it evolved to the point where it is now. It is difficult to imagine a world without national governments. These legal entities have been viewed as separate, self-contained units that independently pursue their "national interests." Scholars often described the world as a political community of sovereign units that interact with each other (a concept described as a billiard ball model).

This perspective of the international community as comprised of self-contained and self-directed units has undergone major rethinking in the past 35 years. One of the reasons for this is the international consequences of the growing demands being placed on natural resources. The Middle East, for example, contains a majority of the world's known oil reserves. The United States, Western Europe, China, India, and Japan are dependent on this vital source of energy. The unbalanced oil supply and demand equation has created an unprecedented lack of self-sufficiency for the world's major economic powers.

The increased interdependence of countries is further illustrated by the fact that air and water pollution do not respect political boundaries. One country's smoke is often another country's acid rain. The concept that independent political units control their own destiny makes less sense than it might have 100 years ago. In order to more fully understand why this is so, one must first look at how Earth's natural resources are being utilized and how this may be affecting the climate.

The first two articles examine the debate surrounding global climate change and the challenges facing policymakers. Climate change directly or indirectly impacts everyone, and if these changes are to be successfully addressed, international collaboration will be required. The consequences of basic human activities such as growing and cooking food are profound when multiplied billions of times every day. A single country or even a few countries working together cannot have a significant impact on redressing these problems. Solutions will have to be conceived that are truly global in scope. Just as there are shortages

© Stephen Reynolds

of natural resources, there are also shortages of new ideas for solving many of these problems.

Unit 3 continues by examining specific case studies. Implicit in these discussions is the challenge of moving from the perspective of the environment as primarily an economic resource to be consumed to a perspective that has been defined as "sustainable development." This change is easily called for, but in fact it goes to the core of social values and basic economic activities. Developing sustainable practices, therefore, is a challenge of unprecedented magnitude.

Nature is not some object "out there" to be visited at a national park. It is the food we eat and the energy we consume. Human beings are joined in the most intimate of relationships with the natural world in order to survive from one day to the next. It is ironic how little time is spent thinking about this relationship. This lack of attention, however, is not likely to continue, for rapidly growing numbers of people and the increased use of energy-consuming technologies are placing unprecedented pressures on Earth's carrying capacity.

Climate Change

BILL MCKIBBEN

"Scientists Are Divided"

No, they're not. In the early years of the global warming debate, there was great controversy over whether the planet was warming, whether humans were the cause, and whether it would be a significant problem. That debate is long since over. Although the details of future forecasts remain unclear, there's no serious question about the general shape of what's to come.

Every national academy of science, long lists of Nobel laureates, and in recent years even the science advisors of President George W. Bush have agreed that we are heating the planet. Indeed, there is a more thorough scientific process here than on almost any other issue: Two decades ago, the United Nations formed the Intergovernmental Panel on Climate Change (IPCC) and charged its scientists with synthesizing the peer-reviewed science and developing broad-based conclusions. The reports have found since 1995 that warming is dangerous and caused by humans. The panel's most recent report, in November 2007, found it is "very likely" (defined as more than 90 percent certain, or about as certain as science gets) that heat-trapping emissions from human activities have caused "most of the observed increase in global average temperatures since the mid-20th century."

If anything, many scientists now think that the IPCC has been too conservative—both because member countries must sign off on the conclusions and because there's a time lag. Its last report synthesized data from the early part of the decade, not the latest scary results, such as what we're now seeing in the Arctic.

In the summer of 2007, ice in the Arctic Ocean melted. It melts a little every summer, of course, but this time was different—by late September, there was 25 percent less ice than ever measured before. And it wasn't a one-time accident. By the end of the summer season in 2008, so much ice had melted that both the Northwest and Northeast passages were open. In other words, you could circumnavigate the Arctic on open water. The computer models, which are just a few years old, said this shouldn't have happened until sometime late in the 21st century. Even skeptics can't dispute such alarming events.

"We Have Time"

Wrong. Time might be the toughest part of the equation. That melting Arctic ice is unsettling not only because it proves the planet is warming rapidly, but also because it will help speed up the warming. That old white ice reflected 80 percent of incoming solar radiation back to space; the new blue water left behind absorbs 80 percent of that sunshine. The process amps up. And there are many other such feedback loops. Another occurs as northern permafrost thaws. Huge amounts of methane long trapped below the ice begin to escape into the atmosphere; methane is an even more potent greenhouse gas than carbon dioxide.

Such examples are the biggest reason why many experts are now fast-forwarding their estimates of how quickly we must shift away from fossil fuel. Indian economist Rajendra Pachauri, who accepted the 2007 Nobel Peace Prize alongside Al Gore on behalf of the IPCC, said recently that we must begin to make fundamental reforms by 2012 or watch the climate system spin out of control; NASA scientist James Hansen, who was the first to blow the whistle on climate change in the late 1980s, has said that we must stop burning coal by 2030. Period.

All of which makes the Copenhagen climate change talks that are set to take place in December 2009 more urgent than they appeared a few years ago. At issue is a seemingly small number: the level of carbon dioxide in the air. Hansen argues that 350 parts per million is the highest level we can maintain "if humanity wishes to preserve a planet similar to that on which civilization developed and to which life on Earth is adapted." But because we're already past that mark—the air outside is currently about 387 parts per million and growing by about 2 parts annually—global warming suddenly feels less like a huge problem, and more like an Oh-My-God Emergency.

"Climate Change Will Help as Many Places as It Hurts"

Wishful thinking. For a long time, the winners-and-losers calculus was pretty standard: Though climate change will cause some parts of the planet to flood or shrivel up, other frigid, rainy regions would at least get some warmer days every year. Or so the thinking went. But more recently, models have begun to show that after a certain point almost everyone on the planet will suffer. Crops might be easier to grow in some places for a few decades as the danger of frost recedes, but over time the threat of heat stress and drought will almost certainly be stronger.

A 2003 report commissioned by the Pentagon forecasts the possibility of violent storms across Europe, megadroughts across the Southwest United States and Mexico, and unpredictable monsoons causing food shortages in China. "Envision Pakistan, India, and China—all armed with nuclear weapons—skirmishing at their borders over refugees, access to shared rivers, and arable land," the report warned. Or Spain and Portugal "fighting over fishing rights—leading to conflicts at sea."

Of course, there are a few places we used to think of as possible winners—mostly the far north, where Canada and Russia could theoretically produce more grain with longer growing seasons, or perhaps explore for oil beneath the newly melted Arctic ice cap. But even those places will have to deal with expensive consequences—a real military race across the high Arctic, for instance.

Want more bad news? Here's how that Pentagon report's scenario played out: As the planet's carrying capacity shrinks, an ancient pattern of desperate, all-out wars over food, water, and energy supplies would reemerge. The report refers to the work of Harvard archaeologist Steven LeBlanc, who notes that wars over resources were the norm until about three centuries ago. When such conflicts broke out, 25 percent of a population's adult males usually died. As abrupt climate change hits home, warfare may again come to define human life. Set against that bleak backdrop, the potential upside of a few longer growing seasons in Vladivostok doesn't seem like an even trade.

"It's China's Fault"

Not so much. China is an easy target to blame for the climate crisis. In the midst of its industrial revolution, China has overtaken the United States as the world's biggest carbon dioxide producer. And everyone has read about the one-a-week pace of power plant construction there. But those numbers are misleading, and not just because a lot of that carbon dioxide was emitted to build products for the West to consume. Rather, it's because China has four times the population of the United States, and per capita is really the only way to think about these emissions. And by that standard, each Chinese person now emits just over a quarter of the carbon dioxide that each American does. Not only that, but carbon dioxide lives in the atmosphere for more than a century. China has been at it in a big way less than 20 years, so it will be many, many years before the Chinese are as responsible for global warming as Americans.

What's more, unlike many of their counterparts in the United States, Chinese officials have begun a concerted effort to reduce emissions in the midst of their country's staggering growth. China now leads the world in the deployment of renewable energy, and there's barely a car made in the United States that can meet China's much tougher fuel-economy standards.

For its part, the United States must develop a plan to cut emissions—something that has eluded Americans for the entire two-decade history of the problem. Although the U.S. Senate voted down the last such attempt, Barack Obama has promised that it will be a priority in his administration. He favors some variation of a "cap and trade" plan that would limit the total amount of carbon dioxide the United States could release, thus putting a price on what has until now been free.

Despite the rapid industrialization of countries such as China and India, and the careless neglect of rich ones such as the United States, climate change is neither any one country's fault, nor any one country's responsibility. It will require sacrifice from everyone. Just as the Chinese might have to use somewhat more expensive power to protect the global environment, Americans will have to pay some of the difference in price, even if just in technology. Call it a Marshall Plan for the environment. Such a plan makes eminent moral and practical sense and could probably be structured so as to bolster emerging green energy industries in the West. But asking Americans to pay to put up windmills in China will be a hard political sell in a country that already thinks China is prospering at its expense. It could be the biggest test of the country's political maturity in many years.

"Climate Change Is an Environmental Problem"

Not really. Environmentalists were the first to sound the alarm. But carbon dioxide is not like traditional pollution. There's no Clean Air Act that can solve it. We must make a fundamental transformation in the most important part of our economies, shifting away from fossil fuels and on to something else. That means, for the United States, it's at least as much a problem for the Commerce and Treasury departments as it is for the Environmental Protection Agency.

And because every country on Earth will have to coordinate, it's far and away the biggest foreign-policy issue we face. (You were thinking terrorism? It's hard to figure out a scenario in which Osama bin Laden destroys Western civilization. It's easy to figure out how it happens with a rising sea level and a wrecked hydrological cycle.)

Expecting the environmental movement to lead this fight is like asking the USDA to wage the war in Iraq. It's not equipped for this kind of battle. It may be ready to save Alaska's Arctic National Wildlife Refuge, which is a noble undertaking but on a far smaller scale. Unless climate change is quickly deghettoized, the chances of making a real difference are small.

"Solving It Will Be Painful"

It depends. What's your definition of painful? On the one hand, you're talking about transforming the backbone of the world's industrial and consumer system. That's certainly expensive. On the other hand, say you manage to convert a lot of it to solar or wind power—think of the money you'd save on fuel.

And then there's the growing realization that we don't have many other possible sources for the economic growth we'll need to pull ourselves out of our current economic crisis. Luckily, green energy should be bigger than IT and biotech combined.

Almost from the moment scientists began studying the problem of climate change, people have been trying to estimate the costs of solving it. The real answer, though, is that it's such a huge transofrmation that no one really knows for sure. The bottom line is, the growth rate in energy use worldwide could be cut in half during the next 15 years and the steps would, net, save more money than they cost. The IPCC included a cost estimate in its latest five-year update on climate change and looked a little further into the future. It found that an attempt to keep carbon levels below about 500 parts per million would shave a little bit off the world's economic growth—but only a little. As in, the world would have to wait until Thanksgiving 2030 to be as rich as it would have been on January 1 of that year. And in return, it would have a much-transformed energy system.

Unfortunately though, those estimates are probably too optimistic. For one thing, in the years since they were published, the science has grown darker. Deeper and quicker cuts now seem mandatory.

But so far we've just been counting the costs of fixing the system. What about the cost of doing nothing? Nicholas Stern, a renowned economist commissioned by the British government to study the question, concluded that the costs of climate change could eventually reach the combined costs of both world wars and the Great Depression. In 2003, Swiss Re, the world's biggest reinsurance company, and Harvard Medical School explained why global warming would be so expensive. It's not just the infrastructure, such as sea walls against rising oceans, for example. It's also that the increased costs of natural disasters begin to compound. The diminishing time between monster storms in places such as the U.S. Gulf Coast could eventually mean that parts of "developed countries would experience developing nation conditions for prolonged periods." Quite simply, we've already done too much damage and waited too long to have any easy options left.

"We Can Reverse Climate Change"

If only. Solving this crisis is no longer an option. Human beings have already raised the temperature of the planet about a degree Fahrenheit. When people first began to focus on global warming (which is, remember, only 20 years ago), the general consensus was that at this point we'd just be standing on the threshold of realizing its consequences—that the big changes would be a degree or two and hence several decades down the road. But scientists seem to have systematically underestimated just how delicate the balance of the planet's physical systems really is.

The warming is happening faster than we expected, and the results are more widespread and more disturbing. Even that rise of 1 degree has seriously perturbed hydrological cycles: Because warm air holds more water vapor than cold air does, both droughts and floods are increasing dramatically. Just look at the record levels of insurance payouts, for instance. Mosquitoes, able to survive in new places, are spreading more malaria and dengue. Coral reefs are dying, and so are vast stretches of forest.

None of that is going to stop, even if we do everything right from here on out. Given the time lag between when we emit carbon and when the air heats up, we're already guaranteed at least another degree of warming.

The only question now is whether we're going to hold off catastrophe. It won't be easy, because the scientific consensus calls for roughly 5 degrees more warming this century unless we do just about everything right. And if our behavior up until now is any indication, we won't.

Critical Thinking

1. What is Bill McKibben's point of view?
2. What reasons does McKibben offer to support his point of view?
3. Identify some of the challenges to reversing climate change?

Reprinted in entirety by McGraw-Hill with permission from *Foreign Policy,* January/February 2009, pp. 32–38. www.foreignpolicy.com. © 2009 Washingtonpost.Newsweek Interactive, LLC.

The Other Climate Changers

JESSICA SEDDON WALLACK AND VEERABHADRAN RAMANATHAN

Why Black Carbon and Ozone Also Matter

At last, world leaders have recognized that climate change is a threat. And to slow or reverse it, they are launching initiatives to reduce greenhouse gases, especially carbon dioxide, the gas responsible for about half of global warming to date. Significantly reducing emissions of carbon dioxide is essential, as they will likely become an even greater cause of global warming by the end of this century. But it is a daunting task: carbon dioxide remains in the atmosphere for centuries, and it is difficult to get governments to agree on reducing emissions because whereas the benefits of doing so are shared globally, the costs are borne by individual countries. As a result, no government is moving fast enough to offset the impact of past and present emissions. Even if current emissions were cut in half by 2050—one of the targets discussed at the 2008 UN Climate Change Conference— by then, humans' total contribution to the level of carbon dioxide in the atmosphere would still have increased by a third since the beginning of this century.

Meanwhile, little attention has been given to a low-risk, cost-effective, and high-reward option: reducing emissions of light-absorbing carbon particles (known as "black carbon") and of the gases that form ozone. Together, these pollutants' warming effect is around 40-70 percent of that of carbon dioxide. Limiting their presence in the atmosphere is an easier, cheaper, and more politically feasible proposition than the most popular proposals for slowing climate change—and it would have a more immediate effect.

Time is running out. Humans have already warmed the planet by more than 0.5 degrees Celsius since the nineteenth century and produced enough greenhouse gases to make it a total of 2.4 degrees Celsius warmer by the end of this century. If the levels of carbon dioxide and nitrous oxide in the atmosphere continue to increase at current rates and if the climate proves more sensitive to greenhouse gases than predicted, the earth's temperature could rise by as much as five degrees before the century ends.

A temperature change of two to five degrees would have profound environmental and geopolitical effects. It would almost—certainly melt all the Arctic summer sea ice. As a result, the Arctic Ocean would absorb more sunlight, which, in turn, would further amplify the warming. Such a rise could eliminate the Himalayan and Tibetan glaciers, which feed the major water systems of some of the poorest regions of the world. It would also accelerate the melting of the Greenland and Antarctic ice sheets, raising the sea level worldwide and provoking large-scale emigration from low-lying coastal regions. Cycles of droughts and floods triggered by global warming would spell disaster for agriculture-dependent economies.

Some of global warming's environmental effects would be irreversible; some of its societal impacts, unmanageable. Given these consequences, policymakers worldwide seeking to slow climate change must weigh options beyond just reducing carbon dioxide, especially those that would produce rapid results. Cutting black carbon and ozone is one such strategy.

Powerful Pollutants

The warming effect of carbon dioxide has been known since at least the 1900s, and that of ozone since the 1970s, but the importance of black carbon was discovered only recently. During the past decade, scientists have used sophisticated instruments on drones, aircraft, ships, and satellites to track black carbon and ozone from their sources to remote locations thousands of miles away and measure and model how much atmospheric heating they cause. Black carbon, a widespread form of particulate air pollution, is what makes sooty smoke look blackish or brownish. It is a byproduct of incomplete, inefficient combustion—a sign of energy waste as much as energy use. Vehicles and ships fueled by diesel and cars with poorly maintained engines release it. So do forest fires and households and factories that use wood, dung, crop waste, or coal for cooking, heating, or other energy needs.

Black carbon alters the environment in two ways. In the sky, the suspended particles absorb sunlight, warming up the atmosphere and in turn the earth itself. On the earth's surface, deposits of black carbon on snowpacks and ice absorb sunlight, thereby heating the earth and melting glaciers. The Arctic sea ice and the Himalayan and Tibetan glaciers, for example, are melting as much as a result of black carbon as they are as a result of the global warming caused by carbon dioxide. The warming effect of black carbon is equal to about 20–50 percent of the effect of carbon dioxide, making it the second- or third-largest contributor to global warming. No one knows exactly how much warming it causes, but even the most conservative estimates indicate a nontrivial impact. And its large contribution to the melting of glaciers and sea ice, one of the most alarming near-term manifestations of climate change, is well documented.

The ozone in the lower level of the atmosphere is another major contributor to global warming that deserves attention. (This is different from the ozone in the stratosphere, which shields life on earth from the sun's ultraviolet rays.) A potent greenhouse gas, its warming effect is equal to about 20 percent of that of carbon dioxide. Unlike black carbon, which exists as particles, ozone is a gas. Ozone in the atmosphere is not emitted directly but formed from other gases, "ozone precursors," such as carbon monoxide (from the burning of fossil fuels or biomass), nitrogen oxides (from lightning, soil, and the burning of fossil fuels), methane (from agriculture, cattle, gas leaks, and the burning of wood), and other hydrocarbons (from the burning of organic materials and fossil fuels, among other sources).

Most important, black carbon and ozone stay in the atmosphere for a much shorter time than does carbon dioxide. Carbon dioxide remains in the atmosphere for centuries—maybe even millennia—before it is absorbed by oceans, plants, and algae. Even if all carbon dioxide emissions were miraculously halted today, it would take several centuries for the amount of carbon dioxide in the atmosphere to approach its preindustrial-era level. In contrast, black carbon stays in the atmosphere for only days to weeks before it is washed away by rain, and ozone (as well as some of its precursors) only stays for weeks to months before being broken down. Nonetheless, because both are widespread and continuously emitted, their atmospheric concentrations build up and cause serious damage to the environment.

Although reducing the emissions of other greenhouse gases, such as methane and halocarbons, could also produce immediate results, black carbon and ozone are the shortest-lived climate-altering pollutants, and they are relatively under-recognized in efforts to stem climate change. Reducing the emissions of these pollutants on earth would quickly lower their concentrations in the atmosphere and, in turn, reduce their impact on global warming.

An Easier Extra Step

Another promising feature of black carbon and ozone precursor emissions is that they can be significantly limited at relatively low cost with technologies that already exist. Although the sources of black carbon and ozone precursors vary worldwide, most emissions can be reduced without necessarily limiting the underlying activity that generated them. This is because, unlike carbon dioxide, black carbon and ozone precursors are not essential byproducts of energy use.

The use of fossil fuels, particularly diesel, is responsible for about 35 percent of black carbon emissions worldwide. Technologies that filter out black carbon have already been invented: diesel particulate filters on cars and trucks, for example, can reduce black carbon emissions by 90 percent or more with a negligible reduction in fuel economy. A recent study by the Clean Air Task Force, a U.S. nonprofit environmental research organization, estimated that retrofitting one million semitrailer trucks with these filters would yield the same benefits for the climate over 20 years as permanently removing over 165,000 trucks or 5.7 million cars from the road.

The remaining 65 percent of black carbon emissions are associated with the burning of biomass—through naturally occurring forest fires, man-made fires for clearing cropland, and the use of organic fuels for cooking, heating, and small-scale industry. Cleaner options for the man-made activities exist. The greenest options for households are stoves powered by the sun or by gas from organic waste, but updated designs for biomass-fueled stoves can also substantially cut the amount of black carbon and other pollutants emitted. Crop waste, dung, wood, coal, and charcoal are the cheapest, but also the least efficient and dirtiest, fuels, and so households tend to shift away from them as soon as other options become reliably available. Thus, the challenge in lowering black carbon emissions is not convincing people to sacrifice their lifestyles, as it is with convincing people to reduce their carbon dioxide emissions. The challenge is to make other options available.

Man-made ozone precursors are mostly emitted through industrial processes and fossil-fuel use, particularly in the transportation sector. These emissions can be reduced by making the combustion process more efficient (for example, through the use of fuel additives) or by removing these gases after combustion (for example, through the use of catalytic converters). Technologies that both minimize the formation of ozone precursors and filter or break down emissions are already widely used and are reducing ozone precursors in the developed world. The stricter enforcement of laws that forbid adulterating gasoline and diesel with cheaper, but dirtier, substitutes would also help.

Fully applying existing emissions-control technologies could cut black carbon emissions by about 50 percent. And that would be enough to offset the warming effects of one to two decades' worth of carbon dioxide emissions. Reducing the human-caused ozone in the lower atmosphere by about 50 percent, which could be possible through existing technologies, would offset about another decade's worth. Within weeks, the heating effect of black carbon would lessen; within months, so, too, would the greenhouse effect of ozone. Within ten years, the earth's overall warming trend would slow down, as would the retreat of sea ice and glaciers. The scientific argument for reducing emissions of black carbon and ozone precursors is clear.

A Political Possibility

Reducing emissions of black carbon and ozone precursors is also a politically promising project. It would yield significant benefits apart from slowing climate change, giving governments economic and developmental incentives to reduce them. Reducing ozone precursors, for its part, would have recognizable agricultural benefits. Ozone lowers crop yields by damaging plant cells and interfering with the production of chlorophyll, the pigment that enables plants to derive energy from sunlight. One recent study estimated that the associated economic loss (at 2000 world prices) ranged from $14 billion to $26 billion, three to five times as large as that attributed to global warming. For policymakers concerned about agricultural productivity and food security, these effects should resonate deeply.

In countries where a large portion of the population still depends on biomass fuels, reducing black carbon emissions from households would improve public health and economic productivity. Nearly 50 percent of the world's population, and up to 95 percent of the rural population in poor countries, relies on solid fuels, including biomass fuels and coal. The resulting indoor air pollution is linked to about a third of the fatal acute respiratory infections among children under five, or about seven percent of child deaths worldwide. Respiratory illnesses associated with the emissions from solid fuels are the fourth most important cause of excess mortality in developing countries (after malnutrition, unsafe sex, and waterborne diseases).

These health problems perpetuate poverty. Exposure to pollutants early in life harms children's lung development, and children who suffer from respiratory illnesses are less likely to attend school. Air pollution leaves the poor, who often earn a living from manual labor, especially worse off. Collectively, workers in India lose an estimated 1.6–2.0 billion days of work every year to the effects of indoor air pollution. Reducing black carbon emissions from households would thus promote economic growth and, particularly for rural women and children, improve public health.

Furthermore, both black carbon and ozone precursor emissions tend to have localized consequences, and governments are more likely to agree to emissions-reduction strategies that can deliver local benefits. With carbon dioxide and other long-lasting, far-spreading greenhouse gases, emissions anywhere contribute to global warming everywhere. But the effects of black carbon and ozone are more confined. When it first enters the atmosphere, black carbon spreads locally and then, within a week, dissipates more regionally before disappearing from the atmosphere entirely in the form of precipitation. Ozone precursors, too, are more regionally confined than carbon dioxide, although background levels of ozone are increasing around the globe.

Because the effects of black carbon and ozone are mostly regional, the benefits from reducing them would accrue in large part to the areas where reductions were achieved. The melting of the Himalayan and Tibetan glaciers is almost reason enough for countries in South and East Asia to take rapid action to eliminate black carbon emissions. So is the retreat of the Arctic sea ice for countries bordering the Arctic Ocean. Regional groupings are also more likely than larger collections of countries to have dense networks of the economic, cultural, and diplomatic ties that sustain difficult negotiations. Moreover, both black carbon and ozone can be contained through geographically targeted strategies because many of the sources of black carbon and ozone are largely fixed. And so even if one country in a region seeks to regulate emissions, that country's polluting activities are unlikely to move to another country with less stringent policies—a common concern with agreements to reduce carbon dioxide emissions.

Cleaning Up

So what can be done to curb black carbon and ozone precursor emissions? A logical first step is for governments, international development agencies, and philanthropists to increase financial support for reduction efforts. Although some money for this is currently available, neither pollutant has emerged as a mainstream target for public or private funding. Simply recognizing black carbon and ozone as environmental problems on par with carbon dioxide would make policymakers more inclined to spend development funds and the "green" portions of stimulus packages on initiatives to tackle them. Developed countries could put their contributions toward customizing emissions-reduction technologies for the developing world and promoting their deployment—an important gesture of goodwill that would kick-start change.

Regardless of the source of the funding, aid should support the deployment of clean-energy options for households and small industries in the developing world and of emissions-reduction technologies for transportation around the world. This could mean distributing solar lanterns and stoves that use local fuel sources more efficiently or paying for small enterprises to shift to cleaner technologies. The specific fixes for small-scale industry will vary by economic activity—making brick kilns cleaner is different from making tea and spice driers more efficient—but the number of possible customers for the new technologies offers some economies of scale. When it comes to transportation, policy options include subsidizing engine and filter upgrades, shifting to cleaner fuels, and removing the incentives, created by government subsidies that favor some fuels over others, for adulterating fuel and for using diesel.

Deploying technologies to reduce emissions from so many culturally embedded activities, from cooking to driving, will not be easy. Enforcing emissions controls on many small, mobile polluters is harder than regulating larger sources, such as power plants. And in customizing technologies, close attention will need to be paid to the varied needs of households and industry. But creating and enforcing regulations and subsidizing and disseminating energy-efficient technologies are challenges that have been met before. The "green revolution"—the remarkable growth in agricultural productivity that occurred in the second half of the twentieth century—introduced radical changes to small-scale farming. Other development initiatives have influenced fertility, gender equality, schooling, and other household decisions more sensitive than those about cooking and driving.

Moreover, the infrastructure for international financial and technological transfers already exists in the form of the World Bank, regional development banks, and UN programs that have supported development around the world for decades. The Global Environment Facility, a development and environmental fund that started as a World Bank program and is now the world's largest funder of environmental projects, is well suited to finance cleaner technologies.

Governments and international agencies should also finance technology that tracks air quality, which is generally under-monitored. In the major cities of most developing countries, the number of sensors has not kept up with the growth in population or economic activity. In rural areas, air pollution is not tracked at all. Improving the monitoring of air quality and disseminating the data would inform policymakers and environmental activists. And tracking individuals' emissions—through indoor air-pollution monitors or devices attached to cars' tailpipes—could help motivate people to curb their emissions. Experimental initiatives to measure individuals' carbon footprints and energy use have been shown to change people's behavior in some settings.

Aid alone will not be enough, however. International organizations must also help governments identify and act on opportunities that mitigate climate change and promote development. International development institutions, such as the UN Environment Program and the multilateral and regional development banks, could sponsor research, set up interministerial working groups, and establish standards for monitoring and reporting public expenditures. These initiatives would make it easier to identify possible areas of coordination among public health, agricultural, environmental, and anti-poverty programs. In most countries, domestic institutions are not designed to encourage cooperation among different authorities. Pitching the reduction of black carbon and ozone precursor emissions as public health and agricultural policies could help such efforts compete for scarce funds; enabling the clearer calculation of the environmental benefits of development policies would make policymaking more informed. Much in the same way that international development organizations currently support good governance to improve infrastructure and services, they should also promote better environmental governance.

Responding Regionally

The current piecemeal approach to climate science—in particular, the tendency to treat air pollution and climate change as separate issues—has at times led to bad policy. The decision of many countries to promote diesel as a means to encourage fuel efficiency, for example, may have had the inadvertent effect of increasing black carbon emissions. And air-pollution laws designed to reduce the use of sulfate aerosols, which cause acid rain, have ironically led to more warming because sulfates also have a cooling effect. Had policymakers instead integrated efforts to reduce air pollution with those to slow global warming, they could have ensured that the reduction of sulfates was accompanied by an equivalent reduction in greenhouse gases.

A single global framework would be the ideal way to integrate various strategies for mitigating climate change. Bilateral or multilateral agreements are more feasible for getting started on reducing black carbon and ozone precursor emissions. These can strengthen governments' incentives to act by discouraging free-riding and by motivating governments to take into account the larger-scale impacts of their own emissions. Because the sources of black carbon and ozone vary from region to region, agreements to reduce them need to be tailored to suit regional conditions. In the Northern Hemisphere, for example, ozone precursors mostly come from industrial processes and transportation, whereas in the Southern Hemisphere, especially tropical regions, they mostly come from natural emissions (soils, plants, and forest fires). The sources of black carbon vary by region, too: in Europe and North America, transportation and industrial activity play a larger role than the burning of biomass, whereas the reverse is true in developing regions.

The impact of emissions on the climate is scientifically complex, and it depends on a number of factors that have not yet been adequately taken into account when devising climate models. The challenge, then, is to quickly create agreements that consider the complex links between human activities, emissions, and climate change and that can adjust over time as the scientific understanding of the problem evolves. Regional air-pollution agreements are easier to update than global agreements with many signatories. The UN Convention on Long-Range Transboundary Air Pollution (most of whose signatories are European or Central Asian states) and its subsequent pollutant-specific protocols provide a ready model for regional agreements on short-lived climate-changing pollutants. The specific provisions of these agreements are based on the costs of reductions, scientists' knowledge of the sources and distribution of air pollution, and the ability to measure reductions—considerations that should also inform the regulation of black carbon and ozone precursor emissions. Moreover, these agreements commit countries to particular actions, not just specific outcomes. This is wise, given that emissions are difficult to monitor and quantify precisely.

Black carbon and ozone can also be built into existing bilateral discussions. The High-Level India-EU Dialogue, a working group of scientists and policymakers from Europe and India, is one such existing forum. In February 2009, it was already urging governments from Europe and India to work together to recognize and reduce the threat from black carbon. Participants proposed an interdisciplinary research project that would determine the effects of biomass-based cooking and heating on health and the climate and assess the obstacles to a large-scale deployment of cleaner stoves. Black carbon and ozone are also natural candidates for U.S.-Chinese cooperation on energy and climate change: China would reap public health and agricultural benefits from reducing emissions, and the United States would earn goodwill for helping China do so.

By building on existing air-pollution agreements, the risk of distracting climate-change negotiations from the substantial task of promoting the reduction of carbon dioxide emissions could be avoided. Putting black carbon and ozone on the table in high-level climate talks could backfire if developing nations thought that they would be tacitly admitting responsibility for global warming by committing to reducing emissions of black carbon and ozone precursors or believed that the issue was an effort by developed countries to divert attention from the need for them to reduce their carbon dioxide emissions. Therefore, efforts to reduce emissions of black carbon and ozone precursors should be presented not as substitutes for commitments to reducing carbon dioxide emissions but as ways to quickly achieve local environmental and economic benefits.

The Low-Hanging Fruit

Historically, initiatives to slow global warming have focused on reducing the emissions of carbon dioxide and other greenhouse gases and largely ignored the role played by air pollution. This strategy makes sense for the long run, since carbon dioxide emissions are, and will continue to be, the most important factor in climate change. But in the short run, it alone will not be enough. Some scientists have proposed geoengineering—manipulating the climate through the use of technology—as a potential option of last resort, but the reduction of black carbon and ozone precursor emissions offers a less risky opportunity for achieving the same end.

Such an approach would quickly lower the level of black carbon and ozone in the atmosphere, offsetting the impact of decades of greenhouse gas emissions, decelerating the rush toward a dangerously warm planet, and giving efforts to reduce carbon dioxide emissions time to get off the ground. These pollutants are also tractable policy targets: they can be reduced through the use of existing technologies, institutions, and strategies, and doing so would lead to local improvements in air quality, agricultural output, and public health. In short, reducing black carbon and ozone precursor emissions is a low-risk, high-potential addition to the current arsenal of strategies to mitigate climate change.

At the current rate of global warming, the earth's temperature stands to career out of control. Now is the time to look carefully at all the possible brakes that can be applied to slow climate change, hedge against near-term climate disasters, and buy time for technological innovations. Of the available strategies, focusing on reducing emissions of black carbon and ozone precursors is the low-hanging fruit: the costs are relatively low, the implementation is feasible, and the benefits would be numerous and immediate.

Critical Thinking

1. What other contributors to climate change are there in addition to greenhouse gases?

2. How does black carbon alter the environment?

3. Why is it less expensive to combat black carbon and ozone precursor emissions than greenhouse gases?

4. What can be done by governments and international organizations to curb these pollutants?

JESSICA SEDDON WALLACK is Director of the Center for Development Finance at the Institute for Financial Management and Research, in Chennai, India. VEERABHADRAN RAMANATHAN is Distinguished Professor of Climate and Atmospheric Sciences at the Scripps Institute of Oceanography at the University of California, San Diego; Distinguished Visiting Fellow at the Energy and Resources Institute, in New Delhi; and a recipient of the 2009 Tyler Prize for Environmental Achievement.

The Big Melt

Brook Larmer

Glaciers in the high heart of Asia feed its greatest rivers, lifelines for two billion people. Now the ice and snow are diminishing.

The gods must be furious.

It's the only explanation that makes sense to Jia Son, a Tibetan farmer surveying the catastrophe unfolding above his village in China's mountainous Yunnan Province. "We've upset the natural order," the devout, 52-year-old Buddhist says. "And now the gods are punishing us."

On a warm summer afternoon, Jia Son has hiked a mile and a half up the gorge that Ming-yong Glacier has carved into sacred Mount Kawagebo, looming 22,113 feet high in the clouds above. There's no sign of ice, just a river roiling with silt-laden melt. For more than a century, ever since its tongue lapped at the edge of Mingyong village, the glacier has retreated like a dying serpent recoiling into its lair. Its pace has accelerated over the past decade, to more than a football field every year—a distinctly unglacial rate for an ancient ice mass.

"This all used to be ice ten years ago," Jia Son says, as he scrambles across the scree and brush. He points out a yak trail etched into the slope some 200 feet above the valley bottom. "The glacier sometimes used to cover that trail, so we had to lead our animals over the ice to get to the upper meadows."

Around a bend in the river, the glacier's snout finally comes into view: It's a deathly shade of black, permeated with pulverized rock and dirt. The water from this ice, once so pure it served in rituals as a symbol of Buddha himself, is now too loaded with sediment for the villagers to drink. For nearly a mile the glacier's once smooth surface is ragged and cratered like the skin of a leper. There are glimpses of blue-green ice within the fissures, but the cracks themselves signal trouble. "The beast is sick and wasting away," Jia Son says. "If our sacred glacier cannot survive, how can we?"

It is a question that echoes around the globe, but nowhere more urgently than across the vast swath of Asia that draws its water from the "roof of the world." This geologic colossus—the highest and largest plateau on the planet, ringed by its tallest mountains—covers an area greater than western Europe, at an average altitude of more than two miles. With nearly 37,000 glaciers on the Chinese side alone, the Tibetan Plateau and its surrounding arc of mountains contain the largest volume of ice outside the polar regions. This ice gives birth to Asia's largest and most legendary rivers, from the Yangtze and the Yellow to the Mekong and the Ganges—rivers that over the course of history have nurtured civilizations, inspired

religions, and sustained ecosystems. Today they are lifelines for some of Asia's most densely settled areas, from the arid plains of Pakistan to the thirsty metropolises of northern China 3,000 miles away. All told, some two billion people in more than a dozen countries—nearly a third of the world's population—depend on rivers fed by the snow and ice of the plateau region.

But a crisis is brewing on the roof of the world, and it rests on a curious paradox: For all its seeming might and immutability, this geologic expanse is more vulnerable to climate change than almost anywhere else on Earth. The Tibetan Plateau as a whole is heating up twice as fast as the global average of 1.3°F over the past century—and in some places even faster. These warming rates, unprecedented for at least two millennia, are merciless on the glaciers, whose rare confluence of high altitudes and low latitudes make them especially sensitive to shifts in climate.

For thousands of years the glaciers have formed what Lonnie Thompson, a glaciologist at Ohio State University, calls "Asia's freshwater bank account"—an immense storehouse whose buildup of new ice and snow (deposits) has historically offset its annual runoff (withdrawals). Glacial melt plays its most vital role before and after the rainy season, when it supplies a greater portion of the flow in every river from the Yangtze (which irrigates more than half of China's rice) to the Ganges and the Indus (key to the agricultural heartlands of India and Pakistan). But over the past half century, the balance has been lost, perhaps irrevocably. Of the 680 glaciers Chinese scientists monitor closely on the Tibetan Plateau, 95 percent are shedding more ice than they're adding, with the heaviest losses on its southern and eastern edges. "These glaciers are not simply retreating," Thompson says. "They're losing mass from the surface down."

The ice cover in this portion of the plateau has shrunk more than 6 percent since the 1970s—and the damage is still greater in Tajikistan and northern India, with 35 percent and 20 percent declines respectively over the past five decades. The rate of melting is not uniform, and a number of glaciers in the Karakoram Range on the western edge of the plateau are actually advancing. This anomaly may result from increases in snowfall in the higher latitude—and therefore colder—Karakorams, where snow and ice are less vulnerable to small temperature increases. The gaps in scientific knowledge are still great, and in the Tibetan Plateau they are deepened by the region's remoteness and political sensitivity—as well as by the inherent complexities of climate science.

Though scientists argue about the rate and cause of glacial retreat, most don't deny that it's happening. And they believe the worst may be yet to come. The more dark areas that are exposed by melting, the more sunlight is absorbed than reflected, causing temperatures to rise faster. (Some climatologists believe this warming feedback loop could intensify the Asian monsoon, triggering more violent storms and flooding in places such as Bangladesh and Myanmar.) If current trends hold, Chinese scientists believe that 40 percent of the plateau's glaciers could disappear by 2050. "Full-scale glacier shrinkage is inevitable," says Yao Tandong, a glaciologist at China's Institute of Tibetan Plateau Research. "And it will lead to ecological catastrophe."

The potential impacts extend far beyond the glaciers. On the Tibetan Plateau, especially its dry northern flank, people are already affected by a warmer climate. The grasslands and wetlands are deteriorating, and the permafrost that feeds them with spring and summer melt is retreating to higher elevations. Thousands of lakes have dried up. Desert now covers about one-sixth of the plateau, and in places sand dunes lap across the highlands like waves in a yellow sea. The herders who once thrived here are running out of options.

Along the plateau's southern edge, by contrast, many communities are coping with too much water. In alpine villages like Mingyong, the glacial melt has swelled rivers, with welcome side effects: expanded croplands and longer growing seasons. But such benefits often hide deeper costs. In Mingyong, surging meltwater has carried away topsoil; elsewhere, excess runoff has been blamed for more frequent flooding and landslides. In the mountains from Pakistan to Bhutan, thousands of glacial lakes have formed, many potentially unstable. Among the more dangerous is Imja Tsho, at 16,400 feet on the trail to Nepal's Island Peak. Fifty years ago the lake didn't exist; today, swollen by melt, it is a mile long and 300 feet deep. If it ever burst through its loose wall of moraine, it would drown the Sherpa villages in the valley below.

This situation—too much water, too little water—captures, in miniature, the trajectory of the overall crisis. Even if melting glaciers provide an abundance of water in the short run, they portend a frightening endgame: the eventual depletion of Asia's greatest rivers. Nobody can predict exactly when the glacier retreat will translate into a sharp drop in runoff. Whether it happens in 10, 30, or 50 years depends on local conditions, but the collateral damage across the region could be devastating. Along with acute water and electricity shortages, experts predict a plunge in food production, widespread migration in the face of ecological changes, even conflicts between Asian powers.

The nomads' tent is a pinprick of white against a canvas of green and brown. There is no other sign of human existence on the 14,000-foot-high prairie that seems to extend to the end of the world. As a vehicle rattles toward the tent, two young men emerge, their long black hair horizontal in the wind. Ba O and his brother Tsering are part of an unbroken line of Tibetan nomads who for at least a thousand years have led their herds to summer grazing grounds near the headwaters of the Yangtze and Yellow Rivers.

Inside the tent, Ba O's wife tosses patties of dried yak dung onto the fire while her four-year-old son plays with a spool of sheep's wool. The family matriarch, Lu Ji, churns yak milk into cheese, rocking back and forth in a hypnotic rhythm. Behind her are two weathered Tibetan chests topped with a small Buddhist shrine: a red prayer wheel, a couple of smudged Tibetan texts, and several yak butter candles whose flames are never allowed to go out. "This is the way we've always done things," Ba O says. "And we don't want that to change."

But it may be too late. The grasslands are dying out, as decades of warming temperatures—exacerbated by overgrazing—turn prairie into desert. Watering holes are drying up, and now, instead of traveling a short distance to find summer grazing for their herds, Ba O and his family must trek more than 30 miles across the high plateau. Even there the grass is meager. "It used to grow so high you could lose a sheep in it," Ba O says. "Now it doesn't reach above their hooves." The family's herd has dwindled from 500 animals to 120. The next step seems inevitable: selling their remaining livestock and moving into a government resettlement camp.

Across Asia the response to climate-induced threats has mostly been slow and piecemeal, as if governments would prefer to leave it up to the industrialized countries that pumped the greenhouse gases into the atmosphere in the first place. There are exceptions. In Ladakh, a bone-dry region in northern India and Pakistan that relies entirely on melting ice and snow, a retired civil engineer named Chewang Norphel has built "artificial glaciers"—simple stone embankments that trap and freeze glacial melt in the fall for use in the early spring growing season. Nepal is developing a remote monitoring system to gauge when glacial lakes are in danger of bursting, as well as the technology to drain them. Even in places facing destructive monsoonal flooding, such as Bangladesh, "floating schools" in the delta enable kids to continue their education—on boats.

But nothing compares to the campaign in China, which has less water than Canada but 40 times more people. In the vast desert in the Xinjiang region, just north of the Tibetan Plateau, China aims to build 59 reservoirs to capture and save glacial runoff. Across Tibet, artillery batteries have been installed to launch rain-inducing silver iodide into the clouds. In Qinghai the government is blocking off degraded grasslands in hopes they can be nurtured back to health. In areas where grasslands have already turned to scrub desert, bales of wire fencing are rolled out over the last remnants of plant life to prevent them from blowing away.

Along the road near the town of Madoi are two rows of newly built houses. This is a resettlement village for Tibetan nomads, part of a massive and controversial program to relieve pressure on the grasslands near the sources of Chinas three major rivers—the Yangtze, Yellow, and Mekong—where nearly half of Qing-hai Province's 530,000 nomads have traditionally lived. Tens of thousands of nomads here have had to give up their way of life, and many more—including, perhaps, Ba O—may follow.

The subsidized housing is solid, and residents receive a small annual stipend. Even so, Jixi Lamu, a 33-year-old woman in a traditional embroidered dress, says her family is stuck in limbo, dependent on government handouts. "We've spent the $400 we had left from selling off our animals," she says. "There was no future with our herds, but there's no future here either." Her husband is away looking for menial work. Inside the one-room house, her mother sits on the bed, fingering her prayer beads. A Buddhist shrine stands on the other side of the room, but the candles have burned out.

It is not yet noon in Delhi, just 180 miles south of the Himalayan glaciers. But in the narrow corridors of Nehru Camp, a slum in this city of 16 million, the blast furnace of the north Indian summer has already sent temperatures soaring past 105 degrees Fahrenheit. Chaya, the 25-year-old wife of a fortune-teller, has spent seven hours joining the mad scramble for water that, even today, defines life in this heaving metropolis—and offers a taste of what the depletion of Tibet's water and ice portends.

Chaya's day began long before sunrise, when she and her five children fanned out in the darkness, armed with plastic jugs of every size. After daybreak, the rumor of a tap with running water sent her stumbling in a panic through the slum's narrow corridors. Now, with her containers still empty and the sun blazing overhead, she has returned home for a moment's rest. Asked if she's eaten anything today, she laughs: "We haven't even had any tea yet."

Suddenly cries erupt—a water truck has been spotted. Chaya leaps up and joins the human torrent in the street. A dozen boys swarm onto a blue tanker, jamming hoses in and siphoning the water out. Below, shouting women jostle for position with their containers. In six minutes the tanker is empty. Chaya arrived too late and must move on to chase the next rumor of water.

Delhi's water demand already exceeds supply by more than 300 million gallons a day, a shortfall worsened by inequitable distribution and a leaky infrastructure that loses an estimated 40 percent of the water. More than two-thirds of the city's water is pulled from the Yamuna and the Ganges, rivers fed by Himalayan ice. If that ice disappears, the future will almost certainly be worse. "We are facing an unsustainable situation," says Diwan Singh, a Delhi environmental activist. "Soon—not in thirty years but in five to ten—there will be an exodus because of the lack of water."

The tension already seethes. In the clogged alleyway around one of Nehru Camp's last functioning taps, which run for one hour a day, a man punches a woman who cut in line, leaving a purple welt on her face. "We wake up every morning fighting over water," says Kamal Bhate, a local astrologer watching the melee. This one dissolves into shouting and finger-pointing, but the brawls can be deadly. In a nearby slum a teenage boy was recently beaten to death for cutting in line.

As the rivers dwindle, the conflicts could spread. India, China, and Pakistan all face pressure to boost food production to keep up with their huge and growing populations. But climate change and diminishing water supplies could reduce cereal yields in South Asia by 5 percent within three decades. "We're going to see rising tensions over shared water resources, including political disputes between farmers, between farmers and cities, and between human and ecological demands for water," says Peter Gleick, a water expert and president of the Pacific Institute in Oakland, California. "And I believe more of these tensions will lead to violence."

The real challenge will be to prevent water conflicts from spilling across borders. There is already a growing sense of alarm in Central Asia over the prospect that poor but glacier-heavy nations (Tajikistan, Kyrgyzstan) may one day restrict the flow of water to their parched but oil-rich neighbors (Uzbekistan, Kazakhstan, Turkmenistan). In the future, peace between Pakistan and India may hinge as much on water as on nuclear weapons, for the two countries must share the glacier-dependent Indus.

The biggest question mark hangs over China, which controls the sources of the region's major rivers. Its damming of the Mekong has sparked anger downstream in Indochina. If Beijing follows through on tentative plans to divert the Brahmaputra, it could provoke its rival, India, in the very region where the two countries fought a war in 1962.

For the people in Nehru Camp, geopolitical concerns are lost in the frenzied pursuit of water. In the afternoon, a tap outside the slum is suddenly turned on, and Chaya, smiling triumphantly, hauls back a full, ten-gallon jug on top of her head. The water is dirty and bitter, and there are no means to boil it. But now, at last, she can give her children their first meal of the day: a piece of bread and a few spoonfuls of lentil stew. "They should be studying, but we keep shooing them away to find water," Chaya says. "We have no choice, because who knows if we'll find enough water tomorrow."

Fatalism may be a natural response to forces that seem beyond our control. But Jia Son, the Tibetan farmer watching Mingyong Glacier shrink, believes that every action counts—good or bad, large or small. Pausing on the mountain trail, he makes a guilty confession. The melting ice, he says, may be his fault.

When Jia Son first noticed the rising temperatures—an unfamiliar trickle of sweat down his back about a decade ago—he figured it was a gift from the gods. Winter soon lost some of its brutal sting. The glacier began releasing its water earlier in the summer, and for the first time in memory villagers had the luxury of two harvests a year.

Then came the Chinese tourists, a flood of city dwellers willing to pay locals to take them up to see the glacier. The Han tourists don't always respect Buddhist traditions; in their gleeful hollers to provoke an icefall, they seem unaware of the calamity that has befallen the glacier. Still, they have turned a poor village into one of the region's wealthiest. "Life is much easier now," says Jia Son, whose simple farmhouse, like all in the village, has a television and government-subsidized satellite dish. "But maybe our greed has made Kawagebo angry."

He is referring to the temperamental deity above his village. One of the holiest mountains in Tibetan Buddhism, Kawagebo has never been conquered, and locals believe its summit—and its glacier—should remain untouched. When a Sino-Japanese expedition tried to scale the peak in 1991, an avalanche near the top of the glacier killed all 17 climbers. Jia Son remains convinced the deaths were not an accident but an act of divine retribution. Could Mingyong's retreat be another sign of Kawagebo's displeasure?

Jia Son is taking no chances. Every year he embarks on a 15-day pilgrimage around Kawagebo to show his deepening Buddhist devotion. He no longer hunts animals or cuts down trees. As part of a government program, he has also given up a parcel of land to be reforested. His family still participates in the village's tourism cooperative, but Jia Son makes a point of telling visitors about the glacier's spiritual significance. "Nothing will get better," he says, "until we get rid of our materialistic thinking."

It's a simple pledge, perhaps, one that hardly seems enough to save the glaciers of the Tibetan Plateau—and stave off the water crisis that seems sure to follow. But here, in the shadow of one of the world's fastest retreating glaciers, this lone farmer has begun, in his own small way, to restore the balance.

Critical Thinking

1. What is the relationship of glacier melt to much of Asia's agricultural production and urban lifestyle?
2. How is the loss of glaciers a potential source of conflict between some of Asia's major political powers?
3. How does this article illustrate the relationship between natural resources and social structures?
4. How does this article complement or contradict articles 1, 2, and 4?

Troubled Waters

The sea is suffering, mostly at the hand of man, says John Grimond.

All of us have in our veins the exact same percentage of salt in our blood that exists in the ocean . . .
And when we go back to the sea . . . we are going back from whence we came.

THE ECONOMIST

Human beings no longer thrive under the water from which their ancestors emerged, but their relationship with the sea remains close. Over half the world's people live within 100 kilometres (62 miles) of the coast; a tenth are within 10km. On land at least, the sea delights the senses and excites the imagination. The sight and smell of the sea inspire courage and adventure, fear and romance. Though the waves may be rippling or mountainous, the waters angry or calm, the ocean itself is eternal. Its moods pass. Its tides keep to a rhythm. It is unchanging.

Or so it has long seemed. Appearances deceive, though. Large parts of the sea may indeed remain unchanged, but in others, especially in the surface and coastal waters where 90% of marine life is to be found, the impact of man's activities is increasingly plain. This should hardly be a surprise. Man has changed the landscape and the atmosphere. It would be odd if the seas, which he has for centuries used for food, for transport, for dumping rubbish and, more recently, for recreation, had not also been affected.

The evidence abounds. The fish that once seemed an inexhaustible source of food are now almost everywhere in decline: 90% of large predatory fish (the big ones such as tuna, swordfish and sharks) have gone, according to some scientists. In estuaries and coastal waters, 85% of the large whales have disappeared, and nearly 60% of the small ones. Many of the smaller fish are also in decline. Indeed, most familiar sea creatures, from albatrosses to walruses, from seals to oysters, have suffered huge losses.

All this has happened fairly recently. Cod have been caught off Nova Scotia for centuries, but their systematic slaughter began only after 1852; in terms of their biomass (the aggregate mass of the species), they are now 96% depleted. The killing of turtles in the Caribbean (99% down) started in the 1700s. The hunting of sharks in the Gulf of Mexico (45–99%, depending on the variety) got going only in the 1950s.

The habitats of many of these creatures have also been affected by man's activities. Cod live in the bottom layer of the ocean. Trawlermen in pursuit of these and other groundfish like pollock and haddock drag steel weights and rollers as well as nets behind their boats, devastating huge areas of the sea floor as they go. In the Gulf of Mexico, trawlers ply back and forth year in year out, hauling vast nets that scarify the seabed and allow no time for plant and animal life to recover. Off New England, off west Africa, in the Sea of Okhotsk north of Japan, off Sri Lanka, wherever fish can still be found, it is much the same story.

Coral reefs, whose profusion of life and diversity of ecosystems make them the rainforests of the sea, have suffered most of all. Once home to prolific concentrations of big fish, they have attracted human hunters prepared to use any means, even dynamite, to kill their prey. Perhaps only 5% of coral reefs can now be considered pristine, a quarter have been lost and all are vulnerable to global warming.

A hotter atmosphere has several effects on the sea. First, it means higher average temperatures for surface waters. One consequence for coral reefs is that the symbiosis between the corals and algae that constitute a living reef is breaking down. As temperatures rise, the algae leave or are expelled, the corals take on a bleached, white appearance and may then die.

Hotter Water, Slimier Slime

Warming also has consequences for ice: it melts. Melting sea ice affects ecosystems and currents. It does not affect sea levels, because floating ice is already displacing water of a weight equal to its own. But melting glaciers and ice sheets on land are bringing quantities of fresh water into the sea, whose level has been rising at an average of nearly 2 millimetres a year for over 40 years, and the pace is getting faster. Recent studies suggest that the sea level may well rise by a total of 80 centimetres this century, though the figure could plausibly be as much as 2 metres.

The burning over the past 100 years or so of fossil fuels that took half a billion years to form has suddenly, in geological terms, put an enormous amount of carbon dioxide into the atmosphere. About a third of this CO_2 is taken up by the sea, where it forms carbonic acid. The plants and animals that have evolved over time to thrive in slightly alkaline surface waters—their pH is around 8.3—are now having to adapt to a 30% increase in the acidity of their surroundings. Some will no doubt flourish, but if the trend continues, as it will for at least some decades, clams, mussels, conches and all creatures that grow shells made of calcium carbonate will struggle. So will corals, especially those whose skeletons are composed of aragonite, a particularly unstable form of calcium carbonate.

Man's interference does not stop with CO_2. Knowingly and deliberately, he throws plenty of rubbish into the sea, everything from sewage to rubber tyres and from plastic packaging to toxic waste. Inadvertently, he also lets flame retardants, bunker oil, and heavy metals seep into the mighty ocean, and often invasive species too. Much of the harm done by such pollutants is invisible to the eye: it shows up only in the analysis of dead polar bears or in tuna served in New York sushi bars.

Increasingly, though, swimmers, sailors, and even those who monitor the sea with the help of satellites are encountering highly visible algal blooms known as red tides. These have always occurred naturally, but they have increased in frequency, number and size in recent years, notably since man-made nitrogen fertilisers came into widespread use in the 1950s. When rainwater contaminated with these fertilisers and other nutrients reaches the sea, as it does where the Mississippi runs into the Gulf of Mexico, an explosion of toxic algae and bacteria takes place, killing fish, absorbing almost all the oxygen, and leaving a microbially dominated ecosystem, often based on a carpet of slime.

Each of these phenomena would be bad enough on its own, but all appear to be linked, usually synergistically. Slaughter one species in the food web and you set off a chain of alterations above or below. Thus the near extinction of sea otters in the northern Pacific led to a proliferation of sea urchins, which then laid waste an entire kelp forest that had hitherto sustained its own ecosystem. If acidification kills tiny sea snails known as pteropods, as it is likely to, the Pacific salmon that feed upon these planktonic creatures may also die. Then other fish may move in, preventing the salmon from coming back, just as other species did when cod were all but fished out in Georges Bank, off New England.

Whereas misfortunes that came singly might not prove fatal, those that come in combination often prove overwhelming. The few coral reefs that remain pristine seem able to cope with the warming and acidification that none can escape, but most of the reefs that have also suffered overfishing or pollution have succumbed to bleaching or even death. Biodiversity comes with interdependence, and the shocks administered by mankind in recent decades have been so numerous and so severe that the natural balance of marine life is everywhere disturbed.

Are these changes reversible? Most scientists believe that fisheries, for instance, could be restored to health with the right policies, properly enforced. But many of the changes are speeding up, not slowing down. Some, such as the acidification of the seas, will continue for years to come simply because of events already in train or past. And some, such as the melting of the Arctic ice cap, may be close to the point at which an abrupt, and perhaps irreversible, series of happenings is set in motion.

It is clear, in any event, that man must change his ways. Humans could afford to treat the sea as an infinite resource when they were relatively few in number, capable of only rather inefficient exploitation of the vasty deep and without as yet a taste for fossil fuels. A world of 6.7 billion souls, set to become 9 billion by 2050, can no longer do so. The possibility of widespread catastrophe is simply too great.

Critical Thinking

1. Describe some of the human activities that are damaging the world's surface and coastal waters.

2. What is meant by "synergistically linked"? Give examples to illustrate this concept. Apply the concept to other case studies in the first three units of this book.

Acacia Avenue

How to Save Indonesia's Dwindling Rainforests

As a spectacle, the four-hour drive to Teluk Binjai from Pekanbaru, capital of Riau province on the island of Sumatra, tends to the monochrome. Mile after mile of palm-oil plantation alternates with mile after mile of regimented lines of acacia trees, grown for pulpwood. Only an occasional banana grove or superannuated rubber plantation offers a spot of variety. Mountainously laden timber lorries ply the interprovincial highway, their loads of acacia logs almost brushing as they pass. In one direction is the mill of Indah Kiat Pulp and Paper, a subsidiary of APP, part of the Sinar Mas group; in the other that of APRIL, Sumatra's other big pulp-and-paper producer.

Off the main road, small patches of "natural" forest survive alongside the swathe of broad sandy corridor cut by a logging company. Some has been cleared fairly recently. Shrouded in white smoke, the peat soil still smoulders under the blackened tree-stumps. Gaunt and barkless, some trees still stand, like skeletal ghosts stalking a battlefield. Underneath, already oil palms are pushing up, planted by local farmers to feed Indonesia's latest commodity boom.

In Teluk Binjai, a village of 400 families sprawling along the bank of the Kampar river, and its neighbour, Teluk Meranti, farmers feel squeezed. Living inside a logging concession, their access to the forest behind their farms is already curtailed. They want to be granted rights to 5,000 hectares of forest on the other side of the river, in the Kampar peninsula. This area of 700,000 hectares of peat forest, home to tigers, sunbears, hawk-eagles, and other endangered species, is now being fought over by plantation companies, forest residents, and local and international NGOs.

The stretch the villagers have their eye on is also part of a concession. They admit they have no legal right to the land, but they say the concession to convert it to acacia is illegal, since the area is supposedly protected. And the villagers claim customary rights. Their families have used the forest for generations. They still depend on it for rattan, fuel, honeybees, hunting, and wood to build their houses and boats. But they use the resource responsibly, claims Muhammad Yusuf, a local farmers' leader: "We only take the best trees." And no more than they need.

Illegally, some farmers are already staking out claims across the river in the sought-after stretch of forest. One, in his second year there, says the village chief in Meranti granted him a six-hectare claim after his coconut grove in Teluk Binjai was destroyed in a land-clearing fire. He is planting oil palms. Speaking in a tiny hut, against the whine of a chainsaw from the nearby rainforest, he says he is too poor to send his 12- and 14-year-old sons to school. They are working in his fields, helping convert another small patch of peatland, and adding to Indonesia's alarming emissions of carbon dioxide.

Stop It, for Peat's Sake

Indonesia's logging of its rainforests has long been identified as a big contributor to the world's emissions of greenhouse gases (GHGs), and hence to global warming. This is one reason for the shocking statistic that Indonesia trails only China and America as an emitter of carbon. But now attention is also turning to the soil beneath the trees, and especially to peat. Al Gore, a former American vice-president and a vigorous climate-change campaigner, has pointed to evidence that the top two metres of soil contain three times as much carbon as the entire vegetation on the planet, and that soil degradation, such as the burning of peatland, is the main cause of Indonesia's high level of emissions.

According to Greenpeace, an environmental NGO, Riau's peatlands have the highest concentration of carbon stored per hectare anywhere in the world. As elsewhere in Indonesia, peat in Riau is disappearing. The trees growing on it are harvested and the land is either abandoned or converted to a plantation. Every year 1.8 billion tonnes of GHG emissions are released by the degradation and burning of Indonesia's peatlands. By the calculation of WWF, an NGO, between 1990 and 2007 Riau alone produced more CO_2 per year than Germany is saving to meet its commitments under the Kyoto protocol.

Small-scale settlers like those clearing the bit of forest opposite Teluk Binjai are a tiny part of the problem. Far more significant, in Riau ("the deforestation centre of Indonesia," according to Yumiko Uryo of WWF) and across Indonesia, are large-scale commercial operations: illegal logging and the conversion of forest land by big plantation companies. By WWF's estimate of the forest cover in Riau lost in the past 25 years, 29% cleared for palm-oil plantations and 24% for pulpwood big producers themselves—not counting large areas their suppliers.

The extent of illegal logging, like every Indonesia's forests, is disputed. By one re $1.6 billion-worth of forest products (no whose export is banned) the EU imported from Indonesia last year came from illegally felled timber. But that is a guess, derived by deducting the timber that can be shown to be legal, a process complicated by the often murky ownership of the original forest lands. The Indonesian government reckons that no more than 10% of exports are illegal. It is working with the EU to devise a licensing system for timber exporters which would then be applied globally. Indonesia also faces difficulties in America. Congress, inspired by an unlikely coalition of domestic timber producers and NGOs, last year amended the Lacey act, a law dating from 1900 that bans the illegal commercial transportation of wildlife. It now covers the produce of illegal logging as well.

Protection of the forest against illegal loggers and enforcement of the law are said to have improved since 1997, when forest fires in Sumatra and Kalimantan (Indonesian Borneo) smothered much of South-East Asia in a noxious, choking haze. The fires were spread by a prolonged drought brought by an El Niño weather pattern. Many were lit to clear land illegally logged. And even now the legal arrival of a logging company in an area is often accompanied by criminals chopping away at the edge of the concession. Decentralisation has complicated efforts to enforce the law. Local authorities resent efforts by the central government to assert control.

Hotspots of Bother

Indonesia's government denies it is doing as much to cook the planet as its critics allege. Agus Purnomo, a former director of WWF in Indonesia who now heads the secretariat of the National Council on Climate Change, says that the country's third place in the carbon-emissions tables is a hangover from the disastrous El Niño of the late 1990s. With no serious forest fire for four years, he claims Indonesia has slid down to number 15 or 20. He reckons that the "hotspots" (small-scale forest fires) recorded this year—3,764 in Riau alone by July, according to a count by satellite—are "not a big issue." Hotspots are now designated as crime scenes, he says, so that no one is allowed to plant oil palms there. If caught, those who caused them are prosecuted and sometimes jailed.

He points out that it is in Indonesia's own interests to do its bit to reduce GHG-emissions and hence global warming. A study this year by the Economy and Environment Programme for South-East Asia, based in Singapore, mapped vulnerability to climate change across the region, divided into 530 subnational districts. Of the ten most endangered by climate change, seven were on Indonesia's most populous island, Java, which would become increasingly prone to droughts, floods, landslides and a rise in the sea level.

Even more immediately, Riau, for example, is suffering a localised haze at the moment. It is not quite the eye-stinging, throat-burning, aviation-disrupting peasouper seen in 1997, but still the town of Dumai recorded a surge in acute respiratory illnesses in June and July.

Blucher Doloksaribu, who heads the provincial government's geophysical, Climatology and Meteorology Board, reckons

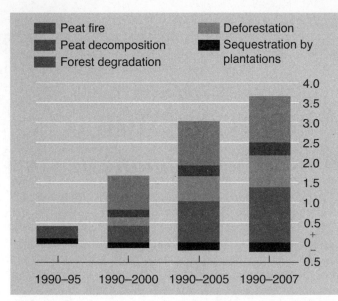

Watch It Grow   Cumulative carbon-dioxide emissions in Riau provice; gigatonnes
Source: WWF

Riau is already suffering its own local, accelerated version of global warming. As forest cover has shrunk from 78% in 1982 to 27% today, minimum temperatures in Riau have increased, he estimates, by an average of 2°C.

After a de facto two-year moratorium for an investigation into alleged corruption, logging has resumed in earnest in Riau this year. Green activists link this to the elections and the need for parties to raise funds.

The big pulp-and-paper and palm-oil companies have several lines of defence against attacks from greens. Responding to growing concern about the impact of palm-oil plantations, the big producers and consumers have joined a round-table on sustainable production. The firms insist that they do follow the law, logging only the "production" forests for which they have bought concessions. But their critics allege that they also buy from less scrupulous subcontractors, and that this year the pressure is especially intense since the moratorium had forced pulp companies to eat into their plantation forests earlier than they would normally have done.

The firms also defend their own practices as responsible and sustainable. Sinar Mas, for example, has set aside some 72,000 hectares (an area bigger than Singapore) of "production forest" as a protected "biosphere," where the trees and wildlife will be preserved. Some even argue that palm-oil and acacia plantations can actually help reduce GHG emissions, though scientists scoff at this notion when the plantations are on cleared natural forest and, especially, peatland.

But Gandhi Sulistyanto, Sinar Mas's managing director, also points to the huge economic benefits his business brings Indonesia, directly and indirectly supporting millions of people and producing more than one-tenth of Indonesia's exports. More than half of Sinar Mas's exports go to China and India. So, despite boasting of his firm's green credentials, and his concern for minimising carbon emissions and saving biodiversity, he cannot conceal his impatience with NGOs: "They care about the orangutans [which are indeed threatened by the spread of plantations], not the *orangs* [people]."

The Great Green Hope: REDD

Mr Sulistyanto hopes Sinar Mas's biosphere in Riau may yet bring the firm some income from an initiative known as Reduced Emissions from Deforestation and Degradation (REDD). This is an idea that sounds almost too sensible to have gained currency. Since developed countries have become rich partly by cutting down their trees, and since old forests are better at storing carbon than new ones, it seems fair for the rich world to pay the poor world to stop logging (rather than, as at present, merely to plant new trees, under the so-called Clean Development Mechanism). There is a lot to preserve. More than half of Indonesia is still covered in forest. Sumatra may be a lost cause, like much of Kalimantan. But there is still, for example, Papua.

REDD forms part of the negotiations on a successor to the Kyoto protocol, which will reach a climax at meetings in Copenhagen this December. The idea may be better known in Indonesia than anywhere else. Businesses are already earmarking scraps of their concessions; Merrill Lynch, a big American investment bank, is nurturing a project; less established "carbon traders" are setting up shop in Indonesia; villagers in places like Teluk Binjai have visions of leisurely retirement at the international taxpayer's expense; and the government is creating a complex bureaucratic infrastructure. The forestry ministry has already issued rules on the sort of conservation projects that might be eligible, as well as guidelines on splitting the revenue.

But so far forest carbon credits remain a small, voluntary market. Gordon Brown, Britain's prime minister, has said a deal at Copenhagen should include transfers of $100 billion a year to the developing world, which would include funds for preserving forests. But there are plenty of question-marks still: the price of carbon, for one thing; how the money should best be used; and whether it would really be paid in perpetuity.

Agus Purnomo of Indonesia's climate-change council is a sceptic. He finds it hard to believe that the sort of money needed to compensate for the loss of deforestation revenue would be forthcoming. The range at present under discussion—$3–10 per tonne of carbon emissions saved—would be wholly inadequate. He agrees with many that the main point of Copenhagen must be "deep, deep cuts" in rich-world emissions. "You cannot leave saving the atmosphere to poor people."

So it is not easy to be optimistic about Indonesia's forests. Ahead of big international gatherings the government makes big promises. It has, for example, banned the conversion of land where the peat is more than three metres deep. But green groups say that hardly helps, since peat bogs have varying depths, and draining a shallow part will erode the rest. The commercial pressures are bound to grow. The conversion of acacia and eucalyptus as cellulose for biofuels will add a new market, and the development of palm-oil micro-refineries will make it much easier to get the fruit to a refinery within 24 hours of harvesting. Perhaps most urgently, a renewed El Niño is brewing, threatening drought and devastating forest fires.

For the government, carbon emissions will become an ever more galling issue. Just as the country seems ready to take its place on the international stage, gaining credit for its peacefulness, its stability and its pluralism, it will find itself under attack, however unfairly, as a vandal on a planetary scale.

Critical Thinking

1. How does the logging of rainforests contribute to the emission of greenhouse gases?

2. How is logging related to the burning of peat?

3. Briefly describe the politics of Indonesian logging practices. Who are the players?

Asian Carp, Other Invasive Species Make a Splash

David Harrison

Last month, a commercial angler netted a 19-pound Asian carp on Chicago's Lake Calumet, part of the waterway system that connects the Mississippi River to Lake Michigan. The fisherman's haul was ominous, suggesting that the carp, a prehistoric-looking behemoth, had somehow gotten past an underwater electric fence designed to keep the species from entering the Great Lakes.

Since then, officials from the Great Lakes states have been fretting about the invasive fish, which has been working its way up the Mississippi River since it was first introduced in the Southeast almost 20 years ago, crowding out native species along the way. Asian carp are just the latest alien species to threaten the lakes, following other creatures such as the zebra and quagga mussel and the sea lamprey, all of which have found homes in the lakes' waters.

But the carp have attained a degree of notoriety that has eluded the other species, owing to their size and their distressing habit of thrashing out of the water at the sound of passing motorboats. Politicians have cast the fish as a voracious invader that would annihilate the lakes' ecosystems and cause the collapse of the $7 billion fishing and tourism industry.

Scientists have disputed that claim, noting that other invasive species already have depleted food sources in the Great Lakes so much that carp could find the waters to be inhospitable. The uproar nevertheless has brought renewed attention to the problem of invasive species, which have been washing into U.S. waters for years thanks to international shipping.

Michigan Attorney General Mike Cox has been particularly vocal, calling on Illinois to close locks and gates on the Chicago River that connect the Mississippi River with the lakes. But behind his rhetoric lies the disconcerting fact that states are powerless to combat most invasive species. Fish and mollusks don't respect state sovereignty, which makes it impossible for one state to completely seal off its waters from another. The best way to effectively control the spread of invasive species, advocates say, is for the federal government to step in.

In an attempt to force Washington's hand, Michigan, Minnesota, Ohio, Pennsylvania and Wisconsin filed a lawsuit against the federal government last week to force the U.S. Army Corps of Engineers to speed up its efforts to protect the lakes from the fish. "President Obama and the Army Corps of Engineers have failed to fight Asian carp aggressively," Cox said in a statement. "Asian carp will kill jobs and ruin our way of life."

This is not the first time Cox has used the courts to combat Asian carp. Late last year, Michigan sued Illinois in the U.S. Supreme Court to try to force Illinois to close the Chicago-area locks, which are crucial to shipping. Right now, carp are massed behind an electric fence and officials fear that all it would take is a power outage for them to flood into the lakes. The court declined to take the case.

The Illinois Chamber of Commerce has criticized the latest lawsuit, calling it politically motivated — Cox is running for governor in Michigan. The state of Illinois did not join the suit. Instead, Illinois Governor Pat Quinn has suggested harvesting the fish and sending them to China, where they are considered a delicacy.

Big Eaters

Despite all the attention they've gotten recently, Asian carp are not the most dangerous invasive species to threaten the Great Lakes. Their impact pales in comparison to that of the quagga mussel which first showed up in the lakes in the late 1990s and has become ensconced there. The mussels reproduce rapidly and devour plankton, disrupting the lower levels of a food chain that native species rely upon.

"We're probably looking at one of the biggest invasions in the Great Lakes right now with the quagga mussels," says Gary Fahnenstiel, a senior ecologist at the National Oceanic and Atmospheric Administration.

Notwithstanding the dire warnings from politicians, Fahnenstiel says, should Asian carp make it to Lake Michigan they probably would have a difficult time competing with the quagga mussels for food. "They beat them to the buffet table, you might say," Fahnenstiel says.

Also, while state officials argue about sealing the lakes from the Mississippi, the biggest threat is likely to come from the north, where the Saint Lawrence Seaway connects the Great Lakes to the Atlantic Ocean. Many of the 185 invasive species in the lakes hitched rides in the cargo holds of ships sailing through the seaway.

Transatlantic cargo vessels often unload their cargo in New York or New Jersey, then take on ocean water to settle themselves. They travel through the seaway to the Great Lakes where they unload the ballast water and pick up cargo before embarking on their return trips. Over time, the mud and residual water that settles in the ships' holds becomes an ideal place for invasive species to settle before they get flushed out into the Great Lakes. That's how quagga and zebra mussels from Eastern Europe arrived on the shores of Michigan, Wisconsin and other Great Lakes states.

Heading West

Unfortunately, it now seems that the mussels' journey didn't end there. About three years ago, a recreational boater drove a mussel-encrusted boat from the Great Lakes to Lake Mead in Nevada. That introduced the species to the inland West, where it is continuing to spread as boaters move their craft from one waterway to the next. Quagga and zebra mussels have been found in Colorado, Nebraska and Utah.

They haven't come to Wyoming or Idaho yet, and those two states want to keep it that way. Recently, officials there started inspecting boats and requiring boaters to buy stickers certifying that their boats are mussel-free.

Yet officials in these states are afraid the mussels will inevitably evade their efforts. Like their Great Lakes counterparts, Western states are blaming what is widely believed to be an inadequate federal response.

"We're doing everything we can to protect our waterways here and the federal government is doing nothing," says Idaho state Representative Eric Anderson, who lives on a lake at the northern tip of the state. "To me it's an absolute crime."

One possible solution would be for the federal government to enforce strict rules on treating the ballast water of international cargo ships. Environmentalists have called on the U.S. Environmental Protection Agency, the Coast Guard or Congress to address the issue without success so far. Some also have suggested closing the Saint Lawrence Seaway to ocean ships, forcing them to transfer their cargo to lake vessels.

States have put in place a patchwork of their own ballast-water rules, which have been upheld in court challenges. But that system encourages shipping companies to find the state with the weakest regulations, putting all the other Great Lakes states at risk, says Nick Schroeck, executive director of the Great Lakes Environmental Law Center.

"Why can't we just get a national standard and be done with it?" Schroeck says. "That's what makes the most sense."

In 2008, the U.S. House of Representatives passed a bill that would have regulated treatment of ballast water, but the measure died in the Senate.

"I don't know that there's much of an appetite right now to take that up again," says Schroek. "You'd think that with the Asian carp situation there would be, but I guess they've got a lot on their plate."

Critical Thinking

1. What is an invasive species?
2. What challenges to governmental agencies does the Asian carp present?
3. What are some other examples of invasive species?

UNIT 4
Political Economy

Unit Selections

Learning Outcomes

After reading this unit you should be able to:

- Describe the basic structure of the contemporary global political economy.

- Describe the process of globalization and the arguments about the costs and benefits of this economic/social process.

- Describe the debate about alternative approaches to alleviating extreme poverty.

- Compare and contrast the insights into the global political economy that the various case studies offer.

- Describe the central role of fossil fuels in the global political economy.

- Identify the challenges in managing the energy transition to alternative, sustainable sources.

- Assess your on-going effort at identifying your theory of international relations and how this unit changes/complements it.

Student Website

www.mhhe.com/cls

Internet References

Belfer Center for Science and International Affairs (BCSIA)
> http://ksgwww.harvard.edu/csia

U.S. Agency for International Development
> www.usaid.gov

The World Bank Group
> www.worldbank.org

A defining characteristic of the twentieth century was the intense struggle between proponents of two economic ideologies. At the heart of the conflict was the question of what role government should play in the management of a country's economy. For some, the dominant capitalist economic system appeared to be organized primarily for the benefit of a few wealthy people. From their perspective, the masses were trapped in poverty, supplying cheap labor to further enrich the privileged elite. These critics argued that the capitalist system could be changed only by gaining control of the political system and radically changing the ownership of the means of production. In striking contrast to this perspective, others argued that the best way to create wealth and eliminate poverty was through the profit motive, which encouraged entrepreneurs to create new products and businesses. An open and competitive marketplace, from this point of view, minimized government interference and was the best system for making decisions about production, wages, and the distribution of goods and services.

Violent conflict at times characterized the contest between capitalism and socialism/communism. The Russian and Chinese revolutions overthrew the old social order and created radical changes in the political and economic systems in these two important countries. The political structures that were created to support new systems of agricultural and industrial production (along with the centralized planning of virtually all aspects of economic activity) eliminated most private ownership of property. These two revolutions were, in short, unparalleled experiments in social engineering.

The economic collapse of the Soviet Union and the dramatic market reforms in China have recast the debate about how to best structure contemporary economic systems. Some believe that with the end of communism and the resulting participation of hundreds of millions of new consumers in the global market, an unprecedented new era has been entered. Many have noted that this process of "globalization" is being accelerated by a revolution in communication and computer technologies. Proponents of this view argue that a new global economy is emerging that will ultimately eliminate national economic systems.

Others are less optimistic about the prospects of globalization. They argue that the creation of a single economic system where there are no boundaries to impede the flow of both capital and goods and services does not mean a closing of the gap between the world's rich and poor. Rather, they argue that multinational corporations and global financial institutions will have fewer legal constraints on their behavior, and this will lead to not only increased risks of global financial crises but also greater exploitation of workers and the accelerated destruction of the environment. Further, these critics point out that the unintended globalization of drug trafficking and other criminal behaviors is developing more rapidly than appropriate remedies can be developed.

The use of the term "political economy" for the title of this unit recognizes that economic and political systems are not

© Courtesy of Department of Energy

separate. All economic systems have some type of marketplace where goods and services are bought and sold. Government (either national or international) regulates these transactions to some degree; that is, government sets the rules that regulate the marketplace.

One of the most important concepts in assessing the contemporary political economy is "development." For the purposes of this unit, the term *development* is defined as an improvement in the basic aspects of life: lower infant mortality rates, longer life expectancy, lower disease rates, higher rates of literacy, healthier diets, and improved sanitation. Judged by these standards, some countries are more developed than others. A fundamental question that a thoughtful reader must consider is whether globalization is resulting in increased development not only for a few people but also for all of those participating in the global political economy.

The unit is organized into three sections. The first is a general discussion of the concept of globalization. How is it defined and what are some of the differing perspectives on this process? For example, is the idea of a global economy wishful thinking by those who sit on top of the power hierarchy, self-deluded into believing that globalization is an inexorable force that will evolve in its own way, following its own rules? Or will there continue to be the traditional tensions of nation–state power politics that transcend global economic processes; that is, conflict between the powerful and those who are either ascending or descending in power?

Following the first section are two sets of case studies. The first focuses on specific countries and/or economic sectors. The second set of case studies examines the global energy sector. All of the case studies have been selected to challenge the reader to develop her or his own conclusions about the positive and negative consequences of the globalization process. Does the contemporary global political economy result in increasing the gap between economic winners and losers, or can everyone positively benefit from its system of wealth creation and distribution?

Globalization and Its Contents

PETER MARBER

Ask ten different people to define the term "globalization" and you are likely to receive ten different answers. For many, the meaning of globalization has been shaped largely by media coverage of an angry opposition: from right-wing nationalist xenophobes and left-wing labor leaders who fear rampant economic competition from low-wage countries to social activists who see a conspiracy on the part of multinational corporations to seek profits no matter what the cost to local cultures and economic equality to environmentalists who believe the earth is being systematically ravaged by capitalism run amok. "Globalization"—as if it were a machine that could be turned off—has been presented as fundamentally flawed and dangerous. But "globalization" is a term that encompasses all cross-border interactions, whether economic, political, or cultural. And behind the negative headlines lies a story of human progress and promise that should make even the most pessimistic analysts view globalization in an entirely different light.

Two decades ago, globalization was hardly discussed. At the time, less than 15 percent of the world's population participated in true global trade. Pessimism colored discussions of the Third World, of "lesser developed" or "backward" countries. Pawns in the Cold War's global chess game, these countries conjured images of famine, overpopulation, military dictatorship, and general chaos. At the time, the prospect of the Soviet Union or Communist China integrating economically with the West, or of strongman regimes in Latin America or Asia abandoning central planning, seemed farfetched. The possibility of these countries making meaningful socioeconomic progress and attaining Western standards of living appeared utterly unrealistic. Yet the forces of globalization were already at work.

On average, people are living twice as long as they did a century ago. Moreover, the world's aggregate material infrastructure and productive capabilities are hundreds—if not thousands—of times greater than they were a hundred years ago.[1] Much of this acceleration has occurred since 1950, with a powerful upsurge in the last 25 years. No matter how one measures wealth—whether by means of economic, bio-social, or financial indicators—there have been gains in virtually every meaningful aspect of life in the last two generations, and the trend should continue upward at least through the middle of the twenty-first century.

Most people are living longer, healthier, fuller lives. This is most evident in poor parts of the world. For example, since 1950, life expectancy in emerging markets (countries with less than one-third the per capita income of the United States, or nearly 85 percent of the world's population) has increased by more than 50 percent, reaching levels the West enjoyed only two generations ago. These longevity gains are linked to lower infant mortality, better nutrition (including an 85 percent increase in daily caloric intake), improved sanitation, immunizations, and other public health advances.

Literacy rates in developing countries have also risen dramatically in the last 50 years. In 1950, only a third of the people in Eastern Europe and in parts of Latin [America] living in these countries (roughly 800 million) could read or write; today nearly two-thirds—more than 3.2 billion people—are literate. And while it took the United States and Great Britain more than 120 years to increase average formal education from 2 years in the early nineteenth century to 12 years by the mid-twentieth century, some fast-growing developing countries, like South Korea, have accomplished this feat in fewer than 40 years.

The world now has a far more educated population with greater intellectual capacity than at any other time in history. This is particularly clear in much of Asia, where mass public education has allowed billions of people to increase their productivity and integrate in the global economy as workers and consumers. Similar trends can be seen in Eastern Europe and in parts of Latin America. This increase in human capital has led to historic highs in economic output and financial assets per capita.

During the twentieth century, economic output in the United States and other West European countries often doubled in less than 30 years, and Japan's postwar economy doubled in less than 16 years. In recent decades, developing country economies have surged so quickly that some—like South Korea in the 1960s and 1970s, or China in recent years—have often doubled productive output in just 7 to 10 years.

We often forget that poverty was the human living standard for most of recorded history. Until approximately two hundred years ago, virtually everyone lived at a subsistence level. As the economist John Maynard Keynes wrote in 1931 in *Essays in Persuasion*: "From the earliest times of which we have record—back, say, to two thousand years before Christ—down to the beginning of the eighteenth century, there was no very great change in the standard life of the average man living in civilized centers of the earth. Ups and downs certainly. Visitation

	1950	2000	2050
Global Output, Per Capita ($)	586	6,666	15,155
Global Financial Market Capitalization, Per Capita ($)	158	13,333	75,000
Percent of Global GDP			
Emerging Markets	5	50	55
Industrial Countries	95	75	45
Life Expectancy (years)			
Emerging Markets	41	64	76
Industrial Countries	65	77	82
Daily Caloric Intake			
Emerging Markets	1200	2600	3000
Industrial Countries	2200	3100	3200
Infant Mortality (per 1000)			
Emerging Markets	140	65	10
Industrial Countries	30	8	4
Literacy Rate (per 100)			
Emerging Markets	33	64	90
Industrial Countries	95	98	99

Sources: Bloomberg, World Bank, United Nations, and author's estimates. Output and financial market capitalization figures are inflation-adjusted.

Figure 1 Measured Global Progress, 1950–2050E.

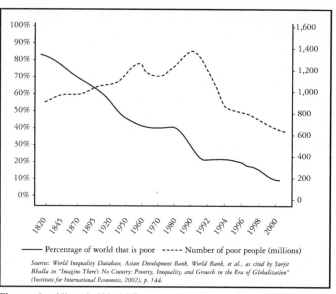

Percentage of world that is poor ———   Number of poor people (millions) - - - -

Sources: World Inequality Database, Asian Development Bank, World Bank, et al., as cited by Surjit Bhalla in "Imagine There's No Country: Poverty, Inequality, and Growth in the Era of Globalization" (Institute for International Economics, 2002), p. 144.

Figure 2 Historic World Poverty Levels, 1820–2000.

of plague, famine, and war. Golden intervals. But no progressive violent change. This slow rate of progress was due to two reasons—to the remarkable absence of technical improvements and the failure of capital to accumulate." Beginning in the early nineteenth century, this picture began to change. The proportion of the world's population living in poverty declined from over 80 percent in 1820 to under 15 percent in 2000; moreover, the actual number of people living in poverty over that period declined, even as the world's population exploded from something over 1 billion to more than 6 billion.

The application of mass production technology, together with excess capital (or "profit") and a free market technologies—is at the root of our modern prosperity. Upon further examination, one can see the virtuous cycle that connects human progress, technology, and globalization. Let's take two countries, one being richer than the other. The richer country has a more educated workforce, with nearly 99 percent literacy, while the poor one has only 50 percent literacy. Due to its less educated workforce and lack of infrastructure, the poor country might only be able to participate in global trade through exporting commodities—let's say fruits and vegetables. The rich country grows fruits and vegetables as well, but it also produces clothing and light manufactured goods such as radios. In the classic Ricardo/Smith models of comparative advantage and free trade, the wealthy country should utilize its skilled workforce to produce more clothing and radios for domestic consumption and export, and it should import more fruits and vegetables from the poorer country. This would, in turn, provide the poorer country with capital to improve education and infrastructure.

As this trade pattern creates profits for both countries, human capital can be mutually developed. Eventually, the poorer country (by boosting literacy and education) should develop its own ability to produce clothes and radios. Over time, the wealthier country—having reinvested profits in higher education, research and development, etc.—will begin to produce higher-tech goods rather than clothes and radios, perhaps televisions and cars. At this stage, the wealthy country would export its cars and televisions, and import clothes and radios. In turn, the poorer country begins to import agricultural products from an even poorer third country while exporting clothing and radios to both countries. As participating countries make progress through crossborder trade and the continuous upgrading of their workforces, it follows naturally that patterns of labor and employment will evolve over time.

It is sometimes argued that free trade harms economic growth and the poor by causing job losses, particularly in wealthier countries. But trade liberalization works by encouraging a shift of labor and capital from import-competitive sectors to more dynamic export industries where comparative advantages lie. Therefore, the unemployment caused by open trade can be expected to be temporary, being offset by job creation in other export sectors (which often requires some transition time). Output losses due to this transitional unemployment should also be small relative to long-term gains in national income (and lower prices) due to production increases elsewhere. In other words, these short-term labor adjustments should be seen as lesser evils when compared to the costs of continued economic stagnation and isolation that occur without open trade.

The shifting U.S. labor pattern from low-wage agricultural labor to manufacturing to higher-paid office and service employment during the nineteenth and twentieth centuries resulted largely from trade. Similar shifts are now seen all over the globe. In the 1950 and 1960s, the United States imported electronics from Japan, and exported cars and other heavy goods. In the 1970s, we began importing small cars from Japan. In the last 30-odd years, Japan has seen its dominance in electronics and economy cars wither amid competition from China and South

Korea. But Japan has made a successful push upmarket into larger, pricier luxury cars and sport utility vehicles. While these markets were shifting over the last three decades, jobs were lost, gained, and relocated in the United States and abroad. But living standards in America, Japan, South Korea, and China have all improved dramatically over that same time.

Working Less, Producing More

There is a growing consensus that international trade has a positive effect on per capita income. A 1999 World Bank study estimates that increasing the ratio of trade to national output by one percentage point raises per capita income by between 0.5 and 2 percent.[2] But the most dramatic illustration of how greater prosperity is spread through globalization is by our increased purchasing power. Ultimately, what determines wealth is the ability to work less and consume more. The time needed for an average American worker to earn the purchase price of various goods and services decreased dramatically during the twentieth century.

In 1919, it took an American worker 30 minutes of labor to earn enough to buy a pound of ground beef. This number dropped to 23 minutes in 1950, 11 minutes in 1975, and 6 minutes in 1997.[3] But this downward trend is even more impressive with respect to manufactured goods and services. For example, in 1895 the list price for an American-made bicycle in the Montgomery Ward catalog was $65. Today an American can buy a Chinese-manufactured 21-speed bike at any mass retailer for the same amount. But an average American needed to work some 260 hours in 1895 to earn the purchase price of the old bicycle, whereas it would take the average worker less than 5 hours to earn enough to buy today's bicycle.[4] In our own lifetimes, the costs of goods and services, everything from televisions to household appliances to telephone calls, computers, and airplane travel have plummeted relative to income—and not just in the United States.

Around the world, both basic commodities and items once considered luxury items now fill store shelves and pantries as increasing output and income have lifted most people above the subsistence level. The 50 most populous countries average more than 95 televisions per 100 households. In the 25 wealthiest countries, there are approximately 450 automobiles per 1,000 people, and China is now among the fastest-growing markets for cars, clothes, computers, cellular phones, and hundreds of household items.

This deflationary effect has also led to a radically improved quality of life. In 1870, the average American worker labored 3,069 hours per year—or six 10-hour days a week. By 1950, the average hours worked had fallen to 2,075.[5] Today, that number is closer to 1,730.[6] This pattern has been repeated around the world. In 1960, the average Japanese worker toiled 2,432 hours a year over a six-day work week; by 1988, this figure had dropped to 2,111 hours a year, and by 2000 it was down to 1,878 hours. There were even more dramatic reductions in European countries like France, Germany, and Sweden.[7] The Nobel Prize–winning economist Robert William Fogel estimates that the average American's lifetime working hours will have declined from 182,100 in 1880 to a projected 75,900 by 2040, with similar trends in other wealthy industrial countries. Fogel notes that while work took up 60 percent of an American's life in 1870, by 1990 it only took up about 30 percent. Between 1880 and 1990, the average American's cumulative lifetime leisure time swelled from 48,300 hours to a remarkable 246,000 hours, or 22 years.[8] This is a pattern of improvement in the human condition that we first saw in the industrialized West and then in Japan, and which is now spreading to dozens of developing countries that are integrating into the global economy.

A Thriving Middle Class

The recent surge in progress is certainly tied to technological advances, but it is also due to the adoption of free-market practices. Cross-border trade has ballooned by a factor of 20 over the past 50 years and now accounts for more than 20 percent of global output, according to the World Bank. Indeed, trade—which grew twice as fast as global output in the 1990s—will continue to drive economic specialization and growth. The global economy is becoming more sophisticated, segmented, and diversified.

The adoption of free-market practices has gone hand-in-hand with greater political freedoms. At the beginning of the twentieth century, less than 10 percent of the world's population had the right to vote, according to Freedom House. By 1950, approximately 35 percent of the global population in less than a quarter of the world's countries enjoyed this right. By 2000, more than two-thirds of the world's countries had implemented universal suffrage.

These symbiotic developments have helped completely recompose the world's "middle class"—those with a per capita income of roughly $10–40 per day, adjusted for inflation and purchasing power parity (PPP). According to the United Nations, in 1960 two-thirds of the world's middle-class citizens lived in the industrialized world—that is, in the United States, Canada, Western Europe, Japan, and Australia. By 1980, over 60 percent of the global middle class lived in developing countries, and by 2000 this number had reached a remarkable 83 percent. It is anticipated that India and China combined could easily produce middle classes of 400–800 million people over the next two generations—roughly the size of the current middle-class populations of the United States, Western Europe, and Japan combined.

A thriving middle class is an important component of economic, political, and social stability that comes with globalization. According to the World Bank, a higher share of income for the middle class is associated with increased national income and growth, improved health, better infrastructure, sounder economic policies, less instability and civil war, and more social modernization and democracy. There are numerous studies that also suggest that increasing wealth promotes gender equality, greater voter participation, income equality, greater concern for the environment, and more transparency in the business and political arenas, all of the quality-of-life issues that concern globalization skeptics.[9]

Measuring Inequality

Even if they concede that the world is wealthier overall, many critics of globalization cite the dangers of growing income inequality. Although the science of analyzing such long-term trends is far from perfect, there are indicators that point toward measurable progress even on this front.[10] The preoccupation with income or gross national product (GNP) as the sole measure of progress is unfortunate. Income is one measure of wealth, but not the only one. And income comparisons do not always reflect informal or unreported economic activity, which tends to be more prevalent in poor countries.

Many social scientists use Gini coefficients (a measure of income dispersion between and within countries) to bolster their arguments about inequality. The lower the Gini figure (between one and zero), the more equal income distribution tends to be. Unfortunately, the Gini index does not take into consideration purchasing power parity, the age dispersion of a population, and other variables that affect the overall picture. When adjusted for PPP, the Gini index for world income distribution decreased from 0.59 to 0.52 between 1965 and 1997, an improvement of nearly 12 percent.[11] Poverty rate trends are also cited by condemners of globalization, but this approach is problematic as well. The impoverished are often defined as those who earn 50 percent less than the median income in a country. But because 50 percent of median American income is very different than 50 percent of median income in Bangladesh, poverty rates may not tell us as much about human progress as we might think.

We can better gauge human progress by examining broader trends in bio-social development than income-centered analyses. A yardstick like the United Nations Development Program's human development index (HDI), for example, which looks at not only income but also life expectancy and education (including literacy and school enrollment), with the higher numbers denoting greater development, provides a clearer picture of global well-being:

	1960	1993	2002
OECD Countries	.80	.91	.91
Developing Countries	.26	.56	.70
Least Developed Countries	.16	.33	.44

What these numbers show is not only that human development has improved overall but that differentials between rich and poor countries are closing. While the HDI figure for wealthy OECD countries in 1960 was five times greater than that for the least developed countries (and three times higher than that for developing countries), those gaps were nearly halved by 1993. And in the most intense period of recent globalization, from 1993 to 2002, these gaps closed even further.

This by no means negates the reality of poverty in many parts of the world. There are still an estimated 1 billion people living in "abject" poverty today, but the World Bank estimates that this number should decline by 50 percent by 2015, if current growth trends hold.

Potholes on the Road to Globalization

The great gains and momentum of the last 25 years should not be seen as sufficient or irreversible. There are still formidable impediments to continued progress, the four most serious being protectionism, armed conflict, environmental stress, and demographic imbalances.

- *Protectionism.* One of the responses to globalization has been the attempt to pull inward, to save traditional industries and cultures, and to expel foreigners and foreign ideas. In India, consumers have protested against McDonald's restaurants for violating Hindu dietary laws. In France, angry farmers have uprooted genetically engineered crops, saying they threatened domestic control over food production.

  Possibly the most harmful protectionism today relates to global agricultural policy. Farming subsidies in wealthy countries now total approximately $350 billion a year, or seven times the $50 billion that such countries provide annually in foreign aid to the developing world.[12] Global trade policies may exclude developing countries from $700 billion in commerce annually, denying them not only needed foreign currency but also the commercial and social interaction necessary to bio-social progress.[13]

  Protectionism in the form of tariffs, rigid labor and immigration laws, capital controls, and regressive tax structures also should be resisted. Wealthy countries should not cling to old industries like apparel or agriculture; it is far more profitable, economically and socially, to look forward and outward, to focus on growing higher-skill industries—like aviation, pharmaceuticals, and entertainment—and to embrace new markets. In turn, poorer countries have generally grown richer through economic interaction with foreign countries, by refocusing nationalistic energies and policies toward future-oriented, internationally engaged commercial activity. The late-twentieth-century march away from closed economies has improved the lives of billions of people. To bow to nationalistic calls for protectionist policies could slow and even reverse this momentum.

- *Armed Conflict.* Countries cannot compete economically, cultivate human capital, or develop financial markets in the midst of armed conflict. According to the Stockholm International Peace Research Institute, there were 57 major armed conflicts in 45 different locations between 1990 and 2001; all but 3 of these were civil wars, which inflict deep economic damage and stunt development. In addition to ongoing civil wars, there are a number of potential cross-border powder kegs (beyond the recent U.S. invasions of Afghanistan and Iraq): Kashmir, over which nuclearized India and Pakistan have been at odds for decades; Taiwan, over which China claims sovereignty; Israel and its Arab neighbors; and the Korean peninsula. The economic, political, and cultural uncertainty surrounding these areas of potential conflict restricts the flow of capital, and paralyzes businesses, investors, and consumers.

To the extent that defense budgets continue to grow in tandem with global tensions and economic resources are used for military purposes, there will be fewer resources devoted to the development of human capital and economic competitiveness.

• *Environmental Stress.* There is no getting around the fact that the success of globalization is underscored by dramatic increases in consumption. With increased consumption comes environmental degradation. Damage to the environment, current or projected, can impede economic progress in many ways. Climatic changes attributed to greenhouse gas emissions and pressure on natural resources are serious problems. Resource scarcity is only one issue we will have to confront as 2–3 billion more people consume like middle-class Americans over the next 50 years. In the face of these environmental dangers, a host of new regulations may be enacted locally or globally. Increased environmental awareness among wealthier populations may lead to domestic policies that will raise costs to businesses and consumers, which in turn could curb economic expansion.

One step in the right direction would be increased public spending on alternative and renewable energy sources in the wealthier countries. The world is clearly underpowered, and the need for diversified energy grows as we speak. The benefits of a burgeoning alternative energy sector could be multiplicative. First, it might spur new economic growth areas for employment in rich countries, supplying them with potential technologies for export while reducing their reliance on foreign oil. Second, it might encourage developing countries that are over-reliant on oil exports to develop and modernize their economies and societies. Third, it would allow developing countries to build their infrastructures with a more diversified, sustainable energy approach than the first wave of industrializing countries.

• *Demographic Imbalances.* There are sharply contrasting population trends around the globe: developing nations are experiencing a youth bulge while industrialized countries are aging rapidly. This divergence may present a variety of challenges to globalization. In poorer developing countries, the youth bulge equals economic opportunity but is also potentially disruptive. In more than 50 of these countries, 50 percent of the population is under the age of 25. In some cases, half the population is under 20, and in extreme cases, even younger. These developing nations are also among the poorest, the fastest urbanizing, and the least politically or institutionally developed, making them susceptible to violence and instability. The large number of unemployed, disenfranchised young men in these countries may explain the growth of Islamic fundamentalism and the existence of pillaging bands of armed warriors in sub-Saharan Africa. Large young

populations may also lead to unregulated, unlawful migration that can create long-lasting instability.[14]

While the youth bulge can cause problems that derail global progress, the richest countries may fall victim to their past success. Prosperity, while providing more lifestyle choices and wellness, also results in lower birth rates and increasing longevity which could dampen long-term economic demand. The aging of wealthier populations also stresses public pension schemes that were conceived under different demographic circumstances—eras of robust population and consumption growth. In economies where populations are stagnant or shrinking, the specter of lengthy "aging recessions"—characterized by vicious cycles of falling demand for consumer goods (and deflation), collapsing asset values (including real estate), shrinking corporate profits, deteriorating household and financial institution balance sheets, weakening currencies, and soaring budget pressures—looms large.

Preparing for the Best, Not the Worst

Globalization and its major engines—burgeoning human capital, freer markets, increasing cross-border interaction—have created a new world order that has incited passionate debate, pro and con. However, both sides have more in common than one might imagine.

First, if human capital is a key component of improved living standards, it is arguable that increased spending on education should become a priority in rich and poor countries alike. Wealthier nations continually need to boost productivity and comparative advantage, while poorer countries need to develop skills to compete in the global economy. By adding to the numbers of the educated, there will be a wider base of workers and consumers to contribute to the virtuous cycle of prosperity we have witnessed in the last 50 years.

Second, boosting human capital in poor countries through increased financial and technical aid should also help broaden the marketplace in terms of workers and consumers. Appropriating an extra $100 billion in aid each year—a drop in the bucket for the 20 richest countries—could help some 2 billion people overcome their daily struggles with malnutrition, HIV/AIDS, malaria, and dirty drinking water, thereby increasing the number of healthy, productive workers and consumers.

Third, reorienting wealthy country subsidies away from low-tech areas like agriculture and mining toward higher-tech industries (including alternative energy development) would accelerate comparative advantage and stimulate greater trade. With wealthy countries focusing on higher-value-added industries for domestic consumption and export, poorer countries could pick up the slack in lower-skilled sectors where they can begin to engage the global economy. Over time, the poorer countries would become larger markets for goods and services. This, along with the two attitudinal and policy shifts mentioned above, could have a positive effect on the well-being of the world's population.

Even with its positive trends, globalization is not a perfect process. It is not a panacea for every problem for every person at every moment in time. It is a messy, complicated web of inter-dependent relationships, some long-term, some fleeting. But globalization is too often cited as creating a variety of human miseries such as sweatshop labor, civil war, and corruption—as if such ills never existed before 1980. Poverty is more at the root of such miseries. That is why the wholesale rejection of globalization—without acknowledging its tremendously posi-tive record in alleviating poverty—is shortsighted. Indeed, one could see how simply embracing globalization as inevitable—rather than debating its definition and purported shortcom-ings—could potentially foster more cross-border coordination on a variety of issues such as drug trafficking, ethnic cleansing, illegal immigration, famine, epidemic disease, environmental stress, and terrorism.

Emotion and confusion have unfortunately tainted the glo-balization debate both in the United States and abroad, and the focus is often on anecdotal successes or failures. Anxieties and economies may ebb and flow in the short run, but the responsi-bility to manage these progressive evolutions and revolutions—with worldwide human prosperity as the goal—should be our consistent aim in both government and the marketplace.

Notes

Many of the issues and arguments presented here in abbrevi-ated form are examined at greater length in my book, *Money Changes Everything: How Global Prosperity Is Reshaping Our Needs, Values, and Lifestyles* (Upper Saddle River, NJ: FT Pren-tice Hall, 2003).

1. See Angus Maddison, *Monitoring the World Economy: 1820–1992* (Paris: OECD, 1995).

2. Jeffrey A. Frankel and David Romer, "Does Trade Growth Cause Growth?" *American Economic Review,* vol. 89 (June 1999), pp. 379–99.

3. W. Michael Cox and Richard Alm, *Time Well Spent: The Declining Real Cost of Living in America*, annual report (Dallas: Federal Reserve Bank, 1997), p. 4.

4. Based on average U.S. industrial wages of approximately $15 per hour in 2000.

5. W. Michael Cox and Richard Alm, *These Are the Good Old Days: A Report on US Living Standards*, annual report (Dallas: Federal Reserve Bank, 1994), p. 7.

6. Robert William Fogel, *The Fourth Great Awakening and the Future of Egalitarianism* (Chicago: University of Chicago Press, 2000), p. 185.

7. Ibid., p. 186.

8. Ibid., pp. 184–90.

9. See Marber, *Money Changes Everything*. For more on specific shifts in attitudes and values relative to economic development, the University of Michigan's Ron Inglehart's seminal Human Values Surveys are an invaluable resource.

10. For a balanced study of this subject, see Arne Mechoir, Kjetil Telle, and Henrik Wiig, *Globalisation and Inequality: World Income and Living Standards, 1960–1998*, Norwegian Ministry of Foreign Affairs, Report 6B:2000, October 2000, available at http://odin.dep.no/archive/udvedlegg/01/01/rev_016.pdf.

11. Ibid., p. 14.

12. James Wolfensohn, "How Rich Countries Keep the Rest of the World in Poverty," *Irish Independent*, September 30, 2002.

13. Ibid.

14. See Michael Teitelbaum, "Are North/South Population Growth Differentials a Prelude to Conflict?" at http://csis.org/gai/Graying/speeches/teitelbaum.html.

Critical Thinking

1. What is Peter Marber's point of view?

2. What reasons does he offer to support his point of view?

3. Identify some of the "potholes" to the continuation of globalization.

4. How is this article related to articles 1 and 4?

PETER MARBER is an author, professional money manager, and faculty member at the School of International and Public Affairs at Columbia University.

From *World Policy Journal*, Winter 2004/2005, pp. 29–30, 33–37. Copyright © 2005 by The World Policy Institute. Reprinted by permission.

It's a Flat World, After All

THOMAS L. FRIEDMAN

In 1492 Christopher Columbus set sail for India, going west. He had the Nina, the Pinta and the Santa Maria. He never did find India, but he called the people he met "Indians" and came home and reported to his king and queen: "The world is round." I set off for India 512 years later. I knew just which direction I was going. I went east. I had Lufthansa business class, and I came home and reported only to my wife and only in a whisper: "The world is flat."

And therein lies a tale of technology and geoeconomics that is fundamentally reshaping our lives—much, much more quickly than many people realize. It all happened while we were sleeping, or rather while we were focused on 9/11, the dot-com bust and Enron—which even prompted some to wonder whether globalization was over. Actually, just the opposite was true, which is why it's time to wake up and prepare ourselves for this flat world, because others already are, and there is no time to waste.

I wish I could say I saw it all coming. Alas, I encountered the flattening of the world quite by accident. It was in late February [2004], and I was visiting the Indian high-tech capital, Bangalore, working on a documentary for the Discovery Times channel about outsourcing. In short order, I interviewed Indian entrepreneurs who wanted to prepare my taxes from Bangalore, read my X-rays from Bangalore, trace my lost luggage from Bangalore and write my new software from Bangalore. The longer I was there, the more upset I became—upset at the realization that while I had been off covering the 9/11 wars, globalization had entered a whole new phase, and I had missed it. I guess the eureka moment came on a visit to the campus of Infosys Technologies, one of the crown jewels of the Indian outsourcing and software industry. Nandan Nilekani, the Infosys C.E.O., was showing me his global video-conference room, pointing with pride to a wall-size flat-screen TV, which he said was the biggest in Asia. Infosys, he explained, could hold a virtual meeting of the key players from its entire global supply chain for any project at any time on that supersize screen. So its American designers could be on the screen speaking with their Indian software writers and their Asian manufacturers all at once. That's what globalization is all about today, Nilekani said. Above the screen there were eight clocks that pretty well summed up the Infosys workday: 24/7/365. The clocks were labeled U.S. West, U.S. East, G.M.T., India, Singapore, Hong Kong, Japan, Australia.

"Outsourcing is just one dimension of a much more fundamental thing happening today in the world," Nilekani explained. "What happened over the last years is that there was a massive investment in technology, especially in the bubble era, when hundreds of millions of dollars were invested in putting broadband connectivity around the world, undersea cables, all those things." At the same time, he added, computers became cheaper and dispersed all over the world, and there was an explosion of e-mail software, search engines like Google and proprietary software that can chop up any piece of work and send one part to Boston, one part to Bangalore and one part to Beijing, making it easy for anyone to do remote development. When all of these things suddenly came together around 2000, Nilekani said, they "created a platform where intellectual work, intellectual capital, could be delivered from anywhere. It could be disaggregated, delivered, distributed, produced and put back together again—and this gave a whole new degree of freedom to the way we do work, especially work of an intellectual nature. And what you are seeing in Bangalore today is really the culmination of all these things coming together."

At one point, summing up the implications of all this, Nilekani uttered a phrase that rang in my ear. He said to me, "Tom, the playing field is being leveled." He meant that countries like India were now able to compete equally for global knowledge work as never before—and that America had better get ready for this. As I left the Infosys campus that evening and bounced along the potholed road back to Bangalore, I kept chewing on that phrase: "The playing field is being leveled."

"What Nandan is saying," I thought, "is that the playing field is being flattened. Flattened? Flattened? My God, he's telling me the world is flat!"

Here I was in Bangalore—more than 500 years after Columbus sailed over the horizon, looking for a shorter route to India using the rudimentary navigational technologies of his day, and returned safely to prove definitively that the world was round—and one of India's smartest engineers, trained at his country's top technical institute and backed by the most modern technologies of his day, was telling me that the world was flat, as flat as that screen on which he can host a meeting of his whole global supply chain. Even more interesting, he was citing this development as a new milestone in human progress and a great opportunity for India and the world—the fact that we had made our world flat!

This has been building for a long time. Globalization 1.0 (1492 to 1800) shrank the world from a size large to a size medium, and the dynamic force in that era was countries globalizing for resources and imperial conquest. Globalization 2.0 (1800 to 2000) shrank the world from a size medium to a size small, and it was spearheaded by companies globalizing for markets and labor. Globalization 3.0 (which started around 2000) is shrinking the world from a size small to a size tiny and flattening the playing field at the same time. And while the dynamic force in Globalization 1.0 was countries globalizing and the dynamic force in Globalization 2.0 was companies globalizing, the dynamic force in Globalization 3.0—the thing that gives it its unique character—is individuals and small groups globalizing. Individuals must, and can, now ask: where do I fit into the global competition and opportunities of the day, and how can I, on my own, collaborate with others globally? But Globalization 3.0 not only differs from the previous eras in how it is shrinking and flattening the world and in how it is empowering individuals. It is also different in that Globalization 1.0 and 2.0 were driven primarily by European and American companies and countries. But going forward, this will be less and less true. Globalization 3.0 is not only going to be driven more by individuals but also by a much more diverse—non-Western, nonwhite—group of individuals. In Globalization 3.0, you are going to see every color of the human rainbow take part.

"Today, the most profound thing to me is the fact that a 14-year-old in Romania or Bangalore or the Soviet Union or Vietnam has all the information, all the tools, all the software easily available to apply knowledge however they want," said Marc Andreessen, a co-founder of Netscape and creator of the first commercial Internet browser. "That is why I am sure the next Napster is going to come out of left field. As bioscience becomes more computational and less about wet labs and as all the genomic data becomes easily available on the Internet, at some point you will be able to design vaccines on your laptop."

Andreessen is touching on the most exciting part of Globalization 3.0 and the flattening of the world: the fact that we are now in the process of connecting all the knowledge pools in the world together. We've tasted some of the downsides of that in the way that Osama bin Laden has connected terrorist knowledge pools together through his Qaeda network, not to mention the work of teenage hackers spinning off more and more lethal computer viruses that affect us all. But the upside is that by connecting all these knowledge pools we are on the cusp of an incredible new era of innovation, an era that will be driven from left field and right field, from West and East and from North and South. Only 30 years ago, if you had a choice of being born a B student in Boston or a genius in Bangalore or Beijing, you probably would have chosen Boston, because a genius in Beijing or Bangalore could not really take advantage of his or her talent. They could not plug and play globally. Not anymore. Not when the world is flat, and anyone with smarts, access to Google and a cheap wireless laptop can join the innovation fray.

When the world is flat, you can innovate without having to emigrate. This is going to get interesting. We are about to see creative destruction on steroids.

How did the world get flattened, and how did it happen so fast?

It was a result of 10 events and forces that all came together during the 1990's and converged right around the year 2000. Let me go through them briefly. The first event was 11/9. That's right—not 9/11, but 11/9. Nov. 9, 1989, is the day the Berlin Wall came down, which was critically important because it allowed us to think of the world as a single space. "The Berlin Wall was not only a symbol of keeping people inside Germany; it was a way of preventing a kind of global view of our future," the Nobel Prize-winning economist Amartya Sen said. And the wall went down just as the windows went up—the breakthrough Microsoft Windows 3.0 operating system, which helped to flatten the playing field even more by creating a global computer interface, shipped six months after the wall fell.

The second key date was 8/9. Aug. 9, 1995, is the day Netscape went public, which did two important things. First, it brought the Internet alive by giving us the browser to display images and data stored on websites. Second, the Netscape stock offering triggered the dot-com boom, which triggered the dot-com bubble, which triggered the massive overinvestment of billions of dollars in fiber-optic telecommunications cable. That overinvestment, by companies like Global Crossing, resulted in the willy-nilly creation of a global undersea-underground fiber network, which in turn drove down the cost of transmitting voices, data and images to practically zero, which in turn accidentally made Boston, Bangalore and Beijing next-door neighbors overnight. In sum, what the Netscape revolution did was bring people-to-people connectivity to a whole new level. Suddenly more people could connect with more other people from more different places in more different ways than ever before.

No country accidentally benefited more from the Netscape moment than India. "India had no resources and no infrastructure," said Dinakar Singh, one of the most respected hedge-fund managers on Wall Street, whose parents earned doctoral degrees in biochemistry from the University of Delhi before emigrating to America. "It produced people with quality and by quantity. But many of them rotted on the docks of India like vegetables. Only a relative few could get on ships and get out. Not anymore, because we built this ocean crosser, called fiber-optic cable. For decades you had to leave India to be a professional. Now you can plug into the world from India. You don't have to go to Yale and go to work for Goldman Sachs." India could never have afforded to pay for the bandwidth to connect brainy India with high-tech America, so American shareholders paid for it. Yes, crazy overinvestment can be good. The overinvestment in railroads turned out to be a great boon for the American economy. "But the railroad overinvestment was confined to your own country and so, too, were the benefits," Singh said. In the case of the digital railroads, "it was the foreigners who benefited." India got a free ride.

The first time this became apparent was when thousands of Indian engineers were enlisted to fix the Y2K—the year 2000—computer bugs for companies from all over the world. (Y2K should be a national holiday in India. Call it "Indian Interdependence Day," says Michael Mandelbaum, a foreign-policy analyst at Johns Hopkins.) The fact that the Y2K work could be outsourced to Indians was made possible by the first two flatteners, along with a third, which I call "workflow." Workflow is shorthand for all the software applications, standards and electronic transmission pipes, like middleware, that connected all those computers and fiber-optic cable. To put it another way, if the Netscape moment connected people to people like never before, what the workflow revolution did was connect applications to applications so that people all over the world could work together in manipulating and shaping words, data and images on computers like never before.

Indeed, this breakthrough in people-to-people and application-to-application connectivity produced, in short order, six more flatteners—six new ways in which individuals and companies could collaborate on work and share knowledge. One was "outsourcing." When my software applications could connect seamlessly with all of your applications, it meant that all kinds of work—from accounting to software-writing—could be digitized, disaggregated and shifted to any place in the world where it could be done better and cheaper. The second was "offshoring." I send my whole factory from Canton, Ohio, to Canton, China. The third was "open-sourcing." I write the next operating system, Linux, using engineers collaborating together online and working for free. The fourth was "insourcing." I let a company like UPS come inside my company and take over my whole logistics operation—everything from filling my orders online to delivering my goods to repairing them for customers when they break. (People have no idea what UPS really does today. You'd be amazed!). The fifth was "supply-chaining." This is Wal-Mart's specialty. I create a global supply chain down to the last atom of efficiency so that if I sell an item in Arkansas, another is immediately made in China. (If Wal-Mart were a country, it would be China's eighth-largest trading partner.) The last new form of collaboration I call "informing"—this is Google, Yahoo and MSN Search, which now allow anyone to collaborate with, and mine, unlimited data all by themselves.

So the first three flatteners created the new platform for collaboration, and the next six are the new forms of collaboration that flattened the world even more. The 10th flattener I call "the steroids," and these are wireless access and voice over Internet protocol (VoIP). What the steroids do is turbocharge all these new forms of collaboration, so you can now do any one of them, from anywhere, with any device.

The world got flat when all 10 of these flatteners converged around the year 2000. This created a global, Web-enabled playing field that allows for multiple forms of collaboration on research and work in real time, without regard to geography, distance or, in the near future, even language. "It is the creation of this platform, with these unique attributes, that is the truly important sustainable breakthrough that made what you call the flattening of the world possible," said Craig Mundie, the chief technical officer of Microsoft.

No, not everyone has access yet to this platform, but it is open now to more people in more places on more days in more ways than anything like it in history. Wherever you look today—whether it is the world of journalism, with bloggers bringing down Dan Rather; the world of software, with the Linux code writers working in online forums for free to challenge Microsoft; or the world of business, where Indian and Chinese innovators are competing against and working with some of the most advanced Western multinationals— hierarchies are being flattened and value is being created less and less within vertical silos and more and more through horizontal collaboration within companies, between companies and among individuals.

Do you recall "the IT revolution" that the business press has been pushing for the last 20 years? Sorry to tell you this, but that was just the prologue. The last 20 years were about forging, sharpening and distributing all the new tools to collaborate and connect. Now the real information revolution is about to begin as all the complementarities among these collaborative tools start to converge. One of those who first called this moment by its real name was Carly Fiorina, the former Hewlett-Packard C.E.O., who in 2004 began to declare in her public speeches that the dot-com boom and bust were just "the end of the beginning." The last 25 years in technology, Fiorina said, have just been "the warm-up act." Now we are going into the main event, she said, "and by the main event, I mean an era in which technology will truly transform every aspect of business, of government, of society, of life."

As if this flattening wasn't enough, another convergence coincidentally occurred during the 1990's that was equally important. Some three billion people who were out of the game walked, and often ran, onto the playing field. I am talking about the people of China, India, Russia, Eastern Europe, Latin America and Central Asia. Their economies and political systems all opened up during the course of the 1990s so that their people were increasingly free to join the free market. And when did these three billion people converge with the new playing field and the new business processes? Right when it was being flattened, right when millions of them could compete and collaborate more equally, more horizontally and with cheaper and more readily available tools. Indeed, thanks to the flattening of the world, many of these new entrants didn't even have to leave home to participate. Thanks to the 10 flatteners, the playing field came to them!

It is this convergence—of new players, on a new playing field, developing new processes for horizontal collaboration—that I believe is the most important force shaping global economics and politics in the early 21st century. Sure, not all three billion can collaborate and compete. In fact, for most people the world is not yet flat at all. But even if we're talking about only 10 percent, that's 300 million people—about twice the size of the American work force. And be advised: the Indians and Chinese are not racing us to the bottom. They are racing us to the top. What China's leaders really want is that the next generation of underwear and airplane wings not just be "made in China" but also be "designed in China." And that is where things are heading. So in 30 years we will have gone from "sold in China" to "made in China" to "designed in China" to "dreamed up in China"—or from China as collaborator with the worldwide manufacturers on nothing to China as a low-cost, high-quality, hyperefficient collaborator with worldwide manufacturers on everything. Ditto India. Said

Craig Barrett, the C.E.O. of Intel, "You don't bring three billion people into the world economy overnight without huge consequences, especially from three societies"—like India, China and Russia—"with rich educational heritages."

That is why there is nothing that guarantees that Americans or Western Europeans will continue leading the way. These new players are stepping onto the playing field legacy free, meaning that many of them were so far behind that they can leap right into the new technologies without having to worry about all the sunken costs of old systems. It means that they can move very fast to adopt new, state-of-the-art technologies, which is why there are already more cellphones in use in China today than there are people in America.

If you want to appreciate the sort of challenge we are facing, let me share with you two conversations. One was with some of the Microsoft officials who were involved in setting up Microsoft's research center in Beijing, Microsoft Research Asia, which opened in 1998—after Microsoft sent teams to Chinese universities to administer I.Q. tests in order to recruit the best brains from China's 1.3 billion people. Out of the 2,000 top Chinese engineering and science students tested, Microsoft hired 20. They have a saying at Microsoft about their Asia center, which captures the intensity of competition it takes to win a job there and explains why it is already the most productive research team at Microsoft: "Remember, in China, when you are one in a million, there are 1,300 other people just like you."

The other is a conversation I had with Rajesh Rao, a young Indian entrepreneur who started an electronic-game company from Bangalore, which today owns the rights to Charlie Chaplin's image for mobile computer games. "We can't relax," Rao said. "I think in the case of the United States that is what happened a bit. Please look at me: I am from India. We have been at a very different level before in terms of technology and business. But once we saw we had an infrastructure that made the world a small place, we promptly tried to make the best use of it. We saw there were so many things we could do. We went ahead, and today what we are seeing is a result of that. There is no time to rest. That is gone. There are dozens of people who are doing the same thing you are doing, and they are trying to do it better. It is like water in a tray: you shake it, and it will find the path of least resistance. That is what is going to happen to so many jobs—they will go to that corner of the world where there is the least resistance and the most opportunity. If there is a skilled person in Timbuktu, he will get work if he knows how to access the rest of the world, which is quite easy today. You can make a website and have an e-mail address and you are up and running. And if you are able to demonstrate your work, using the same infrastructure, and if people are comfortable giving work to you and if you are diligent and clean in your transactions, then you are in business."

Instead of complaining about outsourcing, Rao said, Americans and Western Europeans would "be better off thinking about how you can raise your bar and raise yourselves into doing something better. Americans have consistently led in innovation over the last century. Americans whining—we have never seen that before."

Rao is right. And it is time we got focused. As a person who grew up during the cold war, I'll always remember driving down the highway and listening to the radio, when suddenly the music would stop and a grim-voiced announcer would come on the air and say: "This is a test. This station is conducting a test of the Emergency Broadcast System." And then there would be a 20-second high-pitched siren sound. Fortunately, we never had to live through a moment in the cold war when the announcer came on and said, "This is a not a test."

That, however, is exactly what I want to say here: "This is not a test."

The long-term opportunities and challenges that the flattening of the world puts before the United States are profound. Therefore, our ability to get by doing things the way we've been doing them—which is to say not always enriching our secret sauce—will not suffice any more. "For a country as wealthy as we are, it is amazing how little we are doing to enhance our natural competitiveness," says Dinakar Singh, the Indian-American hedge-fund manager. "We are in a world that has a system that now allows convergence among many billions of people, and we had better step back and figure out what it means. It would be a nice coincidence if all the things that were true before were still true now, but there are quite a few things you actually need to do differently. You need to have a much more thoughtful national discussion."

If this moment has any parallel in recent American history, it is the height of the cold war, around 1957, when the Soviet Union leapt ahead of America in the space race by putting up the Sputnik satellite. The main challenge then came from those who wanted to put up walls; the main challenge to America today comes from the fact that all the walls are being taken down and many other people can now compete and collaborate with us much more directly. The main challenge in that world was from those practicing extreme Communism, namely Russia, China and North Korea. The main challenge to America today is from those practicing extreme capitalism, namely China, India and South Korea. The main objective in that era was building a strong state, and the main objective in this era is building strong individuals.

Meeting the challenges of flatism requires as comprehensive, energetic and focused a response as did meeting the challenge of Communism. It requires a president who can summon the nation to work harder, get smarter, attract more young women and men to science and engineering and build the broadband infrastructure, portable pensions and health care that will help every American become more employable in an age in which no one can guarantee you lifetime employment.

We have been slow to rise to the challenge of flatism, in contrast to Communism, maybe because flatism doesn't involve ICBM missiles aimed at our cities. Indeed, the hot line, which used to connect the Kremlin with the White House, has been replaced by the help line, which connects everyone in America to call centers in Bangalore. While the other end of the hot line might have had Leonid Brezhnev threatening nuclear war, the other end of the help line just has a soft voice eager to help you sort out your AOL bill or collaborate with you on a new piece of software. No, that voice has none of the menace of Nikita Khrushchev pounding a shoe on the table at the United Nations, and it has none of the sinister snarl of the bad guys in "From Russia with Love." No, that voice on the help line just has a friendly Indian lilt that masks any sense of threat or challenge. It simply says: "Hello, my name is Rajiv. Can I help you?"

No, Rajiv, actually you can't. When it comes to responding to the challenges of the flat world, there is no help line we can call. We have to dig into ourselves. We in America have all the basic economic and educational tools to do that. But we have not been improving those tools as much as we should. That is why we are in what Shirley Ann Jackson, the 2004 president of the American Association for the Advancement of Science and president of Rensselaer Polytechnic Institute, calls a "quiet crisis"—one that is slowly eating away at America's scientific and engineering base.

"If left unchecked," said Jackson, the first African-American woman to earn a Ph.D. in physics from M.I.T., "this could challenge our pre-eminence and capacity to innovate." And it is our ability to constantly innovate new products, services and companies that has been the source of America's horn of plenty and steadily widening middle class for the last two centuries. This quiet crisis is a product of three gaps now plaguing American society. The first is an "ambition gap." Compared with the young, energetic Indians and Chinese, too many Americans have gotten too lazy. As David Rothkopf, a former official in the Clinton Commerce Department, puts it, "The real entitlement we need to get rid of is our sense of entitlement." Second, we have a serious numbers gap building. We are not producing enough engineers and scientists. We used to make up for that by importing them from India and China, but in a flat world, where people can now stay home and compete with us, and in a post-9/11 world, where we are insanely keeping out many of the first-round intellectual draft choices in the world for exaggerated security reasons, we can no longer cover the gap. That's a key reason companies are looking abroad. The numbers are not here. And finally we are developing an education gap. Here is the dirty little secret that no C.E.O. wants to tell you: they are not just outsourcing to save on salary. They are doing it because they can often get better-skilled and more productive people than their American workers.

These are some of the reasons that Bill Gates, the Microsoft chairman, warned the governors' conference in a Feb. 26 speech that American high-school education is "obsolete." As Gates put it: "When I compare our high schools to what I see when I'm traveling abroad, I am terrified for our work force of tomorrow. In math and science, our fourth graders are among the top students in the world. By eighth grade, they're in the middle of the pack. By 12th grade, U.S. students are scoring near the bottom of all industrialized nations. . . . The percentage of a population with a college degree is important, but so are sheer numbers. In 2001, India graduated almost a million more students from college than the United States did. China graduates twice as many students with bachelor's degrees as the U.S., and they have six times as many graduates majoring in engineering. In the international competition to have the biggest and best supply of knowledge workers, America is falling behind."

We need to get going immediately. It takes 15 years to train a good engineer, because, ladies and gentlemen, this really is rocket science. So parents, throw away the Game Boy, turn off the television and get your kids to work. There is no sugarcoating this: in a flat world, every individual is going to have to run a little faster if he or she wants to advance his or her standard of living. When I was growing up, my parents used to say to me, "Tom, finish your dinner—people in China are starving." But after sailing to the edges of the flat world for a year, I am now telling my own daughters, "Girls, finish your homework—people in China and India are starving for your jobs."

I repeat, this is not a test. This is the beginning of a crisis that won't remain quiet for long. And as the Stanford economist Paul Romer so rightly says, "A crisis is a terrible thing to waste."

Critical Thinking

1. What does Thomas Friedman mean by a "flat" world?

2. What are some of the primary reasons for this so-called flattening?

THOMAS L. FRIEDMAN is the author of "*The World Is Flat: A Brief History of the Twenty-First Century,*" to be published this week by Farrar, Straus & Giroux and from which this article is adapted. His column appears on the Op-Ed page of *The Times,* and his television documentary "Does Europe Hate Us?" was shown on the Discovery Channel on April 7, 2005.

Why the World Isn't Flat

Globalization has bound people, countries, and markets closer than ever, rendering national borders relics of a bygone era—or so we're told. But a close look at the data reveals a world that's just a fraction as integrated as the one we thought we knew. In fact, more than 90 percent of all phone calls, Web traffic, and investment is local. What's more, even this small level of globalization could still slip away.

PANKAJ GHEMAWAT

Ideas will spread faster, leaping borders. Poor countries will have immediate access to information that was once restricted to the industrial world and traveled only slowly, if at all, beyond it. Entire electorates will learn things that once only a few bureaucrats knew. Small companies will offer services that previously only giants could provide. In all these ways, the communications revolution is profoundly democratic and liberating, leveling the imbalance between large and small, rich and poor. The global vision that Frances Cairncross predicted in her *Death of Distance* appears to be upon us. We seem to live in a world that is no longer a collection of isolated, "local" nations, effectively separated by high tariff walls, poor communications networks, and mutual suspicion. It's a world that, if you believe the most prominent proponents of globalization, is increasingly wired, informed, and, well, "flat."

It's an attractive idea. And if publishing trends are any indication, globalization is more than just a powerful economic and political transformation; it's a booming cottage industry. According to the U.S. Library of Congress's catalog, in the 1990s, about 500 books were published on globalization. Between 2000 and 2004, there were more than 4,000. In fact, between the mid-1990s and 2003, the rate of increase in globalization-related titles more than doubled every 18 months.

Amid all this clutter, several books on the subject have managed to attract significant attention. During a recent TV interview, the first question I was asked—quite earnestly—was why I still thought the world was round. The interviewer was referring of course to the thesis of *New York Times* columnist Thomas L. Friedman's bestselling book *The World Is Flat*. Friedman asserts that 10 forces—most of which enable connectivity and collaboration at a distance—are "flattening" the Earth and leveling a playing field of global competitiveness, the likes of which the world has never before seen.

It sounds compelling enough. But Friedman's assertions are simply the latest in a series of exaggerated visions that also include the "end of history" and the "convergence of tastes." Some writers in this vein view globalization as a good thing—an escape from the ancient tribal rifts that have divided humans, or an opportunity to sell the same thing to everyone on Earth. Others lament its cancerous spread, a process at the end of which everyone will be eating the same fast food. Their arguments are mostly characterized by emotional rather than cerebral appeals, a reliance on prophecy, semiotic arousal (that is, treating everything as a sign), a focus on technology as the driver of change, an emphasis on education that creates "new" people, and perhaps above all, a clamor for attention. But they all have one thing in common: They're wrong.

In truth, the world is not nearly as connected as these writers would have us believe. Despite talk of a new, wired world where information, ideas, money, and people can move around the planet faster than ever before, just a fraction of what we consider globalization actually exists. The portrait that emerges from a hard look at the way companies, people, and states interact is a world that's only beginning to realize the potential of true global integration. And what these trend's backers won't tell you is that globalization's future is more fragile than you know.

The 10 Percent Presumption

The few cities that dominate international financial activity—Frankfurt, Hong Kong, London, New York—are at the height of modern global integration; which is to say, they are all relatively well connected with one another. But when you examine the numbers, the picture is one of extreme connectivity at the local level, not a flat world. What do such statistics reveal? Most types of economic activity that could be conducted either within or across borders turn out to still be quite domestically concentrated.

One favorite mantra from globalization champions is how "investment knows no boundaries." But how much of all the capital being invested around the world is conducted by companies outside of their home countries? The fact is, the total amount of the world's capital formation that is generated from foreign direct investment

(FDI) has been less than 10 percent for the last three years for which data are available (2003–05). In other words, more than 90 percent of the fixed investment around the world is still domestic. And though merger waves can push the ratio higher, it has never reached 20 percent. In a thoroughly globalized environment, one would expect this number to be much higher—about 90 percent, by my calculation. And FDI isn't an odd or unrepresentative example.

The levels of internationalization associated with cross-border migration, telephone calls, management research and education, private charitable giving, patenting, stock investment, and trade, as a fraction of gross domestic product (GDP), all stand much closer to 10 percent than 100 percent. The biggest exception in absolute terms— the trade-to-GDP—recedes most of the way back down toward 20 percent if you adjust for certain kinds of double-counting. So if someone asked me to guess the internationalization level of some activity about which I had no particular information, I would guess it to be much closer to 10 percent—than to 100 percent. I call this the "10 Percent Presumption."

More broadly, these and other data on cross-border integration suggest a semiglobalized world, in which neither the bridges nor the barriers between countries can be ignored. From this perspective, the most astonishing aspect of various writings on globalization is the extent of exaggeration involved. In short, the levels of internationalization in the world today are roughly an order of magnitude lower than those implied by globalization proponents.

A Strong National Defense

If you buy into the more extreme views of the globalization triumphalists, you would expect to see a world where national borders are irrelevant, and where citizens increasingly view themselves as members of ever broader political entities. True, communications technologies have improved dramatically during the past 100 years. The cost of a three-minute telephone call from New York to London fell from $350 in 1930 to about 40 cents in 1999, and it is now approaching zero for voice-over-Internet telephony. And the Internet itself is just one of many newer forms of connectivity that have progressed several times faster than plain old telephone service. This pace of improvement has inspired excited proclamations about the pace of global integration. But it's a huge leap to go from predicting such changes to asserting that declining communication costs will obliterate the effects of distance. Although the barriers at borders have declined significantly, they haven't disappeared.

To see why, consider the Indian software industry—a favorite of Friedman and others. Friedman cites Nandan Nilekani, the CEO of the second-largest such firm, Infosys, as his muse for the notion of a flat world. But what Nilekani has pointed out privately is that while Indian software programmers can now serve the United States from India, access is assured, in part, by U.S. capital being invested— quite literally—in that outcome. In other words, the success of the Indian IT industry is not exempt from political and geographic constraints. The country of origin matters—even for capital, which is often considered stateless.

Or consider the largest Indian software firm, Tata Consultancy Services (TCS). Friedman has written at least two columns in the *New York Times* on TCS's Latin American operations: "[I]n today's world, having an Indian company led by a Hungarian-Uruguayan servicing American banks with Montevidean engineers managed by Indian technologists who have learned to eat Uruguayan veggie is

just the new normal," Friedman writes. Perhaps. But the real question is why the company established those operations in the first place. Having worked as a strategy advisor to TCS since 2000, I can testify that reasons related to the tyranny of time zones, languages, and the need for proximity to clients' local operations loomed large in that decision. This is a far cry from globalization proponents' oft-cited world in which geography, language, and distance don't matter.

Trade flows certainly bear that theory out. Consider Canadian-U.S. trade, the largest bilateral relationship of its kind in the world. In 1988, before the North American Free Trade Agreement (NAFTA) took effect, merchandise trade levels between Canadian provinces—that is, within the country—were estimated to be 20 times as large as their trade with similarly sized and similarly distant U.S. states. In other words, there was a built-in "home bias." Although NAFTA helped reduce this ratio of domestic to international trade—the home bias—to 10 to 1 by the mid-1990s, it still exceeds 5 to 1 today. And these ratios are just for merchandise; for services, the ratio is still several times larger. Clearly, the borders in our seemingly "borderless world" still matter to most people.

Geographical boundaries are so pervasive, they even extend to cyberspace. If there were one realm in which borders should be rendered meaningless and the globalization proponents should be correct in their overly optimistic models, it should be the Internet. Yet Web traffic within countries and regions has increased far faster than traffic between them. Just as in the real world, Internet links decay with distance. People across the world may be getting more connected, but they aren't connecting with each other. The average South Korean Web user may be spending several hours a day online—connected to the rest of the world in theory—but he is probably chatting with friends across town and e-mailing family across the country rather than meeting a fellow surfer in Los Angeles. We're more wired, but no more "global."

Just look at Google, which boasts of supporting more than 100 languages and, partly as a result, has recently been rated the most globalized website. But Google's operation in Russia (cofounder Sergey Brin's native country) reaches only 28 percent of the market there, versus 64 percent for the Russian market leader in search services, Yandex, and 53 percent for Rambler.

Indeed, these two local competitors account for 91 percent of the Russian market for online ads linked to Web searches. What has stymied Google's expansion into the Russian market? The biggest reason is the difficulty of designing a search engine to handle the linguistic complexities of the Russian language. In addition, these local competitors are more in tune with the Russian market, for example, developing payment methods through traditional banks to compensate for the dearth of credit cards. And, though Google has doubled its reach since 2003, it's had to set up a Moscow office in Russia and hire Russian software engineers, underlining the continued importance of physical location. Even now, borders between countries define—and constrain—our movements more than globalization breaks them down.

Turning Back the Clock

If globalization is an inadequate term for the current state of integration, there's an obvious rejoinder: Even if the world isn't quite flat today, it will be tomorrow. To respond, we have to look at trends, rather than levels of integration at one point in time. The results are telling. Along a few dimensions, integration reached its all-time high many years ago. For example, rough calculations suggest that the number of long-term international migrants amounted to 3 percent of the world's population in 1900—the high-water mark of an earlier era of migration—versus 2.9 percent in 2005.

Along other dimensions, it's true that new records are being set. But this growth has happened only relatively recently, and only after long periods of stagnation and reversal. For example, FDI stocks divided by GDP peaked before World War I and didn't return to that level until the 1990s. Several economists have argued that the most remarkable development over the long term was the declining level of internationalization between the two World Wars. And despite the records being set, the current level of trade intensity falls far short of completeness, as the Canadian-U.S. trade data suggest. In fact, when trade economists look at these figures, they are amazed not at how much trade there is, but how little.

It's also useful to examine the considerable momentum that globalization proponents attribute to the constellation of policy changes that led many countries—particularly China, India, and the former Soviet Union—to engage more extensively with the international economy. One of the better-researched descriptions of these policy changes and their implications is provided by economists Jeffrey Sachs and Andrew Warner:

"The years between 1970 and 1995, and especially the last decade, have witnessed the most remarkable institutional harmonization and economic integration among nations in world history. While economic integration was increasing throughout the 1970s and 1980s, the extent of integration has come sharply into focus only since the collapse of communism in 1989. In 1995, one dominant global economic system is emerging."

Yes, such policy openings are important. But to paint them as a sea change is inaccurate at best. Remember the 10 Percent Presumption, and that integration is only beginning. The policies that we fickle humans enact are surprisingly reversible. Thus, Francis Fukuyama's *The End of History,* in which liberal democracy and technologically driven capitalism were supposed to have triumphed over other ideologies, seems quite quaint today. In the wake of Sept. 11, 2001, Samuel Huntington's *Clash of Civilizations* looks at least a bit more prescient. But even if you stay on the economic plane, as Sachs and Warner mostly do, you quickly see counterevidence to the supposed decisiveness of policy openings. The so-called Washington Consensus around market-friendly policies ran up against the 1997 Asian currency crisis and has since frayed substantially—for example, in the swing toward neopopulism across much of Latin America. In terms of economic outcomes, the number of countries—in Latin America, coastal Africa, and the former Soviet Union—that have dropped out of the "convergence club" (defined in terms of narrowing productivity and structural gaps vis-à-vis the advanced industrialized countries) is at least as impressive as the number of countries that have joined the club. At a multilateral level, the suspension of the Doha round of trade talks in the summer of 2006—prompting *The Economist* to run a cover titled "The Future of Globalization" and depicting a beached wreck—is no promising omen. In addition, the recent wave of cross-border mergers and acquisitions seems to be encountering more protectionism, in a broader range of countries, than did the previous wave in the late 1990s.

Of course, given that sentiments in these respects have shifted in the past 10 years or so, there is a fair chance that they may shift yet again in the next decade. The point is, it's not only possible to turn back the clock on globalization-friendly policies, it's relatively easy to imagine it happening. Specifically, we have to entertain the possibility that deep international economic integration may be inherently incompatible with national sovereignty—especially given the tendency of voters in many countries, including advanced ones, to support more protectionism, rather than less. As Jeff Immelt, CEO of GE, put it in late 2006, "If you put globalization to a popular vote in the U.S., it would lose." And even if cross-border integration continues on its upward path, the road from here to there is unlikely to be either smooth or straight. There will be shocks and cycles, in all likelihood, and maybe even another period of stagnation or reversal that will endure for decades. It wouldn't be unprecedented.

The champions of globalization are describing a world that doesn't exist. It's a fine strategy to sell books and even describe a potential environment that may someday exist. Because such episodes of mass delusion tend to be relatively short-lived even when they do achieve broad currency, one might simply be tempted to wait this one out as well. But the stakes are far too high for that. Governments that buy into the flat world are likely to pay too much attention to the "golden straitjacket" that Friedman emphasized in his earlier book, *The Lexus and the Olive Tree,* which is supposed to ensure that economics matters more and more and politics less and less. Buying into this version of an integrated world—or worse, using it as a basis for policymaking—is not only unproductive. It is dangerous.

Critical Thinking

1. What is Pankaj Ghemawat's point of view?

2. What is the "10 percent presumption"?

3. How do the reasons Ghemawat offers differ from Friedman's reasons?

4. How does the point of view of this article fit into the discussion of alternative futures presented in Article 1?

PANKAJ GHEMAWAT is the Anselmo Rubiralta professor of global strategy at IESE Business School and the Jaime and Josefina Chua Tiampo professor of business administration at Harvard Business School. His new book is *Redefining Global Strategy* (Boston: Harvard Business School Press, September 2007).

Can Extreme Poverty Be Eliminated?

**Market economics and globalization are lifting the bulk
of humanity out of extreme poverty, but special measures
are needed to help the poorest of the poor.**

JEFFREY D. SACHS

Almost everyone who ever lived was wretchedly poor. Famine, death from childbirth, infectious disease and countless other hazards were the norm for most of history. Humanity's sad plight started to change with the Industrial Revolution, beginning around 1750. New scientific insights and technological innovations enabled a growing proportion of the global population to break free of extreme poverty.

Two and a half centuries later more than five billion of the world's 6.5 billion people can reliably meet their basic living needs and thus can be said to have escaped from the precarious conditions that once governed everyday life. One out of six inhabitants of this planet, however, still struggles daily to meet some or all of such critical requirements as adequate nutrition, uncontaminated drinking water, safe shelter and sanitation as well as access to basic health care. These people get by on $1 a day or less and are overlooked by public services for health, education and infrastructure. Every day more than 20,000 die of dire poverty, for want of food, safe drinking water, medicine or other essential needs.

For the first time in history, global economic prosperity, brought on by continuing scientific and technological progress and the self-reinforcing accumulation of wealth, has placed the world within reach of eliminating extreme poverty altogether. This prospect will seem fanciful to some, but the dramatic economic progress made by China, India and other low-income parts of Asia over the past 25 years demonstrates that it is realistic. Moreover, the predicted stabilization of the world's population toward the middle of this century will help by easing pressures on Earth's climate, ecosystems and natural resources—pressures that might otherwise undo economic gains.

EXTREME POVERTY could become a thing of the past in a few decades if the affluent countries of the world pony up a small percentage of their wealth to help the planet's 1.1 billion indigent populations out of conditions of dire poverty.

Although economic growth has shown a remarkable capacity to lift vast numbers of people out of extreme poverty, progress is neither automatic nor inevitable. Market forces and free trade are not enough. Many of the poorest regions are ensnared in a poverty trap: they lack the financial means to make the necessary investments in infrastructure, education, health care systems and other vital needs. Yet the end of such poverty is feasible if a concerted global effort is undertaken, as the nations of the world promised when they adopted the Millennium Development Goals at the United Nations Millennium Summit in 2000. A dedicated cadre of development agencies, international financial institutions, nongovernmental organizations and communities throughout the developing world already constitute a global network of expertise and goodwill to help achieve this objective.

This past January my colleagues and I on the U.N. Millennium Project published a plan to halve the rate of extreme poverty by 2015 (compared with 1990) and to achieve other quantitative targets for reducing hunger, disease and environmental degradation. In my recent book, *The End of Poverty,* I argue that a large-scale and targeted public investment effort could in fact eliminate this problem by 2025, much as smallpox was eradicated globally. This hypothesis is controversial, so I am pleased to have the opportunity to clarify its main arguments and to respond to various concerns that have been raised about it.

Beyond Business as Usual

Economists have learned a great deal during the past few years about how countries develop and what roadblocks can stand in their way. A new kind of development economics needs to emerge, one that is better grounded in science—a "clinical economics" akin to modern medicine. Today's medical professionals understand that disease results from a vast array of interacting factors and conditions: pathogens, nutrition, environment, aging, individual and population genetics, and lifestyle. They also know that one key to proper treatment is the

Crossroads for Poverty

The Problem

- Much of humankind has succeeded in dragging itself out of severe poverty since the onset of the Industrial Revolution in the mid-18th century, but about 1.1 billion out of today's 6.5 billion global inhabitants are utterly destitute in a world of plenty.
- These unfortunates, who get by on less than $1 a day, have little access to adequate nutrition, safe drinking water and shelter, as well as basic sanitation and health care services. What can the developed world do to lift this huge segment of the human population out of extreme poverty?

The Plan

- Doubling affluent nations' international poverty assistance to about $160 billion a year would go a long way toward ameliorating the terrible predicament faced by one in six humans. This figure would constitute about 0.5 percent of the gross national product (GNP) of the planet's rich countries. Because these investments do not include other categories of aid, such as spending on major infrastructure projects, climate change mitigation or post conflict reconstruction, donors should commit to reaching the long stand target of 0.7 percent of GNP by 2015.
- These donations, often provided to local groups, would need to be closely monitored and audited to ensure that they are correctly targeted toward those truly in need.

ability to make an individualized diagnosis of the source of illness. Likewise, development economists need better diagnostic skills to recognize that economic pathologies have a wide variety of causes, including many outside the traditional ken of economic practice.

Public opinion in affluent countries often attributes extreme poverty to faults with the poor themselves—or at least with their governments. Race was once thought the deciding factor. Then it was culture: religious divisions and taboos, caste systems, a lack of entrepreneurship, gender inequities. Such theories have waned as societies of an ever widening range of religions and cultures have achieved relative prosperity. Moreover, certain supposedly immutable aspects of culture (such as fertility choices and gender and caste roles) in fact change, often dramatically, as societies become urban and develop economically.

Most recently, commentators have zeroed in on "poor governance," often code words for corruption. They argue that extreme poverty persists because governments fail to open up their markets, provide public services and clamp down on bribe taking. It is said that if these regimes cleaned up their acts, they, too, would flourish. Development assistance efforts have become largely a series of good governance lectures.

The availability of cross-country and time-series data now allows experts to make much more systematic analyses. Although debate continues, the weight of the evidence indicates that governance makes a difference but is not the sole determinant of economic growth. According to surveys conducted by Transparency International, business leaders actually perceive many fast-growing Asian countries to be more corrupt than some slow-growing African ones.

Geography—including natural resources, climate, topography, and proximity to trade routes and major markets—is at least as important as good governance. As early as 1776, Adam Smith argued that high transport costs inhibited development in the inland areas of Africa and Asia. Other geographic features, such as the heavy disease burden of the tropics, also interfere. One recent study by my Columbia University colleague Xavier Sala-i-Martin demonstrated once again that tropical countries saddled with malaria have experienced slower growth than those free from the disease. The good news is that geographic factors shape, but do not decide, a country's economic fate. Technology can offset them: drought can be fought with irrigation systems, isolation with roads and mobile telephones, diseases with preventive and therapeutic measures.

The other major insight is that although the most powerful mechanism for reducing extreme poverty is to encourage overall economic growth, a rising tide does not necessarily lift all boats. Average income can rise, but if the income is distributed unevenly the poor may benefit little, and pockets of extreme poverty may persist (especially in geographically disadvantaged regions). Moreover, growth is not simply a free-market phenomenon. It requires basic government services: infrastructure, health, education, and scientific and technological innovation. Thus, many of the recommendations of the past two decades emanating from Washington—that governments in low-income countries should cut back on their spending to make room for the private sector—miss the point. Government spending, directed at investment in critical areas, is itself a vital spur to growth, especially if its effects are to reach the poorest of the poor.

The Poverty Trap

So what do these insights tell us about the region most afflicted by poverty today, Africa? Fifty years ago tropical Africa was roughly as rich as subtropical and tropical Asia. As Asia boomed, Africa stagnated. Special geographic factors have played a crucial role.

Foremost among these is the existence of the Himalaya Mountains, which produce southern Asia's monsoon climate and vast river systems. Well-watered farmlands served as the starting points for Asia's rapid escape from extreme poverty during the past five decades. The Green Revolution of the 1960s and 1970s introduced high-yield grains, irrigation and fertilizers, which ended the cycle of famine, disease and despair.

It also freed a significant proportion of the labor force to seek manufacturing jobs in the cities. Urbanization, in turn, spurred growth, not only by providing a home for industry and innovation but also by prompting greater investment in a healthy and skilled labor force. Urban residents cut their fertility rates and

Globalization, Poverty and Foreign Aid

Average citizens in affluent nations often have many questions about the effects of economic globalization on rich and poor nations and about how developing countries spend the aid they receive. Here are a few brief answers:

Is Globalization Making the Rich Richer and the Poor Poorer?

Generally, the answer is no. Economic globalization is supporting very rapid advances of many impoverished economies, notably in Asia. International trade and foreign investment inflows have been major factors in China's remarkable economic growth during the past quarter century and in India's fast economic growth since the early 1990s. The poorest of the poor, notably in sub-Saharan Africa, are not held back by globalization; they are largely bypassed by it.

Is Poverty the Result of Exploitation of the Poor by the Rich?

Affluent nations have repeatedly plundered and exploited poor countries through slavery, colonial rule and unfair trade practices. Yet it is perhaps more accurate to say that exploitation is the result of poverty (which leaves impoverished countries vulnerable to abuse) rather than the cause of it. Poverty is generally the result of low productivity per worker, which reflects poor health, lack of job-market skills, patchiness of infrastructure (roads, power plants, utility lines, shipping ports), chronic malnutrition and the like. Exploitation has played a role in producing some of these conditions, but deeper factors [geographic isolation, endemic disease, ecological destruction, challenging conditions for food production] have tended to be more important and difficult to overcome without external help.

Will Higher Incomes in Poor Countries Mean Lower Incomes in Rich Countries?

By and large, economic development is a positive-sum process, meaning that all can partake in it without causing some to suffer. In the past 200 years, the world as a whole has achieved a massive increase in economic output rather than a shift in economic output to one region at the expense of another. To be sure, global environmental constraints are already starting to impose themselves. As today's poor countries develop, the climate, fisheries and forests are coming under increased strain. Overall global economic growth is compatible with sustainable management of the ecosystems on which all humans depend—indeed, wealth can be good for the environment—but only if public policy and technologies encourage sound practices and the necessary investments are made in environmental sustainability.

Do U.S. Private Contributions Make Up for the Low Levels of U.S. Official Aid?

Some have claimed that while the U.S. government budget provides relatively little assistance to the poorest countries, the private sector makes up the gap. In fact, the Organization for Economic Cooperation and Development has estimated that private foundations and nongovernmental organizations give roughly $6 billion a year in international assistance, or 0.05 percent of U.S. gross national product (GNP). In that case, total U.S. international aid is around 0.21 percent of GNP—still among the lowest ratios of all donor nations.

—J.D.S.

thus were able to spend more for the health, nutrition and education of each child. City kids went to school at a higher rate than their rural cousins. And with the emergence of urban infrastructure and public health systems, city populations became less disease-prone than their counterparts in the countryside, where people typically lack safe drinking water, modern sanitation, professional health care and protection from vector-borne ailments such as malaria.

Africa did not experience a green revolution. Tropical Africa lacks the massive floodplains that facilitate the large-scale and low-cost irrigation found in Asia. Also, its rainfall is highly variable, and impoverished farmers have been unable to purchase fertilizer. The initial Green Revolution research featured crops, especially paddy rice and wheat, not widely grown in Africa (high-yield varieties suitable for it have been developed in recent years, but they have not been disseminated sufficiently). The continent's food production per person has actually been falling, and Africans' caloric intake is the lowest in the world; food insecurity is rampant. Its labor force has remained tethered to subsistence agriculture.

Compounding its agricultural woes, Africa bears an overwhelming burden of tropical diseases. Because of climate and the endemic mosquito species, malaria is more intensively transmitted in Africa than anywhere else. And high transport costs isolate Africa economically. In East Africa, for example, the rainfall is greatest in the interior of the continent, so most people live there, far from ports and international trade routes.

Much the same situation applies to other impoverished parts of the world, notably the Andean and Central American highlands and the landlocked countries of Central Asia. Being economically isolated, they are unable to attract much foreign investment (other than for the extraction of oil, gas and precious minerals). Investors tend to be dissuaded by the high transport costs associated with the interior regions. Rural areas therefore remain stuck in a vicious cycle of poverty, hunger, illness and illiteracy. Impoverished areas lack adequate internal savings to make the needed investments because most households live hand to mouth. The few high-income families, who do accumulate savings, park them overseas rather than at home. This capital flight includes not only financial capital but also the human variety, in the form of skilled workers—doctors, nurses, scientists and engineers, who frequently leave in search of improved economic opportunities abroad. The poorest countries are often, perversely, net exporters of capital.

Put Money Where Mouths Are

The technology to overcome these handicaps and jump-start economic development exists. Malaria can be controlled using bed nets, indoor pesticide spraying and improved medicines. Drought-prone countries in Africa with nutrient depleted soils can benefit enormously from drip irrigation and greater use of fertilizers. Landlocked countries can be connected by paved highway networks, airports and fiber-optic cables. All these projects cost money, of course.

Many larger countries, such as China, have prosperous regions that can help support their own lagging areas. Coastal eastern China, for instance, is now financing massive public investments in western China. Most of today's successfully developing countries, especially smaller ones, received at least some backing from external donors at crucial times. The critical scientific innovations that formed the underpinnings of the Green Revolution were bankrolled by the Rockefeller Foundation, and the spread of these technologies in India and elsewhere in Asia was funded by the U.S. and other donor governments and international development institutions.

We in the U.N. Millennium Project have listed the investments required to help today's impoverished regions cover basic needs in health, education, water, sanitation, food production, roads and other key areas. We have put an approximate price tag on that assistance and estimated how much could be financed by poor households themselves and by domestic institutions. The remaining cost is the "financing gap" that international donors need to make up.

For tropical Africa, the total investment comes to $110 per person a year. To place this into context, the average income in this part of the world is $350 per annum, most or all of which is required just to stay alive. The full cost of the total investment is clearly beyond the funding reach of these countries. Of the $110, perhaps $40 could be financed domestically, so that $70 per capita would be required in the form of international aid.

Adding it all up, the total requirement for assistance across the globe is around $160 billion a year, double the current rich-country aid budget of $80 billion. This figure amounts to approximately 0.5 percent of the combined gross national product (GNP) of the affluent donor nations. It does not include other humanitarian projects such as postwar Iraqi reconstruction or Indian Ocean tsunami relief. To meet these needs as well, a reasonable figure would be 0.7 percent of GNP, which is what all donor countries have long promised but few have fulfilled. Other organizations, including the International Monetary Fund, the World Bank and the British government, have reached much the same conclusion.

When polled, Americans greatly overestimate how much foreign aid the U.S. gives—by as much as 30 times.

Foreign Aid: How Should the Money Be Spent?

Here is a breakdown of the needed investment for three typical low-income African countries to help them achieve the Millennium Development Goals. For all nations given aid, the average total annual assistance per person would come to around $110 a year. These investments would be financed by both foreign aid and the countries themselves.

Investment Area	Average per Year between 2005–2015 ($ per capita)		
	Ghana	Tanzania	Uganda
Hunger	7	8	6
Education	19	14	5
Gender equality	3	3	3
Health	25	35	34
Water supply and sanitation	8	7	5
Improving slum conditions	2	3	2
Energy	15	16	12
Roads	10	22	20
Other	10	10	10
Total	100	117	106

Calculated from data from Investing in Development [U.N. Millennium Project, Earth Scan Publications, 2005]. Numbers do not sum to totals because of rounding.

We believe these investments would enable the poorest countries to cut poverty by half by 2015 and, if continued, to eliminate it altogether by 2025. They would not be "welfare payments" from rich to poor but instead something far more important and durable. People living above mere subsistence levels would be able to save for their futures; they could join the virtuous cycle of rising incomes, savings and technological inflows. We would be giving a billion people a hand up instead of a handout.

If rich nations fail to make these investments, they will be called on to provide emergency assistance more or less indefinitely. They will face famine, epidemics, regional conflicts and the spread of terrorist havens. And they will condemn not only the impoverished countries but themselves as well to chronic political instability, humanitarian emergencies and security risks.

The debate is now shifting from the basic diagnosis of extreme poverty and the calculations of financing needs to the practical matter of how assistance can best be delivered. Many people believe that aid efforts failed in the past and that care is needed to avoid the repetition of failure. Some of these concerns are well grounded, but others are fueled by misunderstandings.

When pollsters ask Americans how much foreign aid they think the U.S. gives, they greatly overestimate the amount by as much as 30 times. Believing that so much money has been donated and so little has been done with it, the public concludes that these programs have "failed." The reality is rather different.

U.S. official assistance to sub-Saharan Africa has been running at $2 billion to $4 billion a year, or roughly $3 to $6 for every African. Most of this aid has come in the form of "technical cooperation" (which goes into the pockets of consultants), food contributions for famine victims and the cancellation of unpaid debts. Little of this support has come in a form that can be invested in systems that improve health, nutrition, food production and transport. We should give foreign aid a fair chance before deciding whether it works or not.

A second common misunderstanding concerns the extent to which corruption is likely to eat up the donated money. Some foreign aid in the past has indeed ended up in the equivalent of Swiss bank accounts. That happened when the funds were provided for geopolitical reasons rather than development; a good example was U.S. support for the corrupt regime of Mobutu Sese Seko of Zaire (now the Democratic Republic of the Congo) during part of the cold war. When assistance has been targeted at development rather than political goals, the outcomes have been favorable, ranging from the Green Revolution to the eradication of smallpox and the recent near-eradication of polio.

The aid package we advocate would be directed toward those countries with a reasonable degree of good governance and operational transparency. In Africa, these countries include Ethiopia, Ghana, Mali, Mozambique, Senegal and Tanzania. The money would not be merely thrown at them. It would be provided according to a detailed and monitored plan, and new rounds of financing would be delivered only as the work actually got done. Much of the funds would be given directly to villages and towns to minimize the chances of their getting diverted by central governments. All these programs should be closely audited.

Western society tends to think of foreign aid as money lost. But if supplied properly, it is an investment that will one day yield huge returns, much as U.S. assistance to Western Europe and East Asia after World War II did. By prospering, today's impoverished countries will wean themselves from endless charity. They will contribute to the international advance of science, technology and trade. They will escape political instability, which leaves many of them vulnerable to violence, narcotics trafficking, civil war and even terrorist takeover. Our own security will be bolstered as well. As U.N. Secretary-General Kofi Annan wrote earlier this year: "There will be no development without security, and no security without development."

Critical Thinking

1. How does Jeffery Sachs propose that extreme poverty be eliminated?
2. According to Sachs, what are the key economic and public policy issues that need to be addressed?

The author, **JEFFREY D. SACHS,** directs the Earth Institute at Columbia University and the United Nations Millennium Project. An economist, Sachs is well known for advising governments in Latin America, Eastern Europe, the former Soviet Union, Asia and Africa on economic reforms and for his work with international agencies to promote poverty reduction, disease control and debt reduction in poor countries. A native of Detroit, he received his BA, MA and PhD degrees from Harvard University.

The Ideology of Development

WILLIAM EASTERLY

A dark ideological specter is haunting the world. It is almost as deadly as the tired ideologies of the last century—communism, fascism, and socialism—that failed so miserably. It feeds some of the most dangerous trends of our time, including religious fundamentalism. It is the half-century-old ideology of Developmentalism. And it is thriving.

Like all ideologies, Development promises a comprehensive final answer to all of society's problems, from poverty and illiteracy to violence and despotic rulers. It shares the common ideological characteristic of suggesting there is only one correct answer, and it tolerates little dissent. It deduces this unique answer for everyone from a general theory that purports to apply to everyone, everywhere. There's no need to involve local actors who reap its costs and benefits. Development even has its own intelligentsia, made up of experts at the International Monetary Fund (IMF), World Bank, and United Nations.

The power of Developmentalism is disheartening, because the failure of all the previous ideologies might have laid the groundwork for the opposite of ideology—the freedom of individuals and societies to choose their destinies. Yet, since the fall of communism, the West has managed to snatch defeat from the jaws of victory, and with disastrous results. Development ideology is sparking a dangerous counterreaction. The "one correct answer" came to mean "free markets," and, for the poor world, it was defined as doing whatever the IMF and the World Bank tell you to do. But the reaction in Africa, Central Asia, Latin America, the Middle East, and Russia has been to fight against free markets. So, one of the best economic ideas of our time, the genius of free markets, was presented in one of the worst possible ways, with unelected outsiders imposing rigid doctrines on the xenophobic unwilling.

The backlash has been so severe that other failed ideologies are gaining new adherents throughout these regions. In Nicaragua, for instance, IMF and World Bank structural adjustments failed so conspicuously that the pitiful Sandinista regime of the 1980s now looks good by comparison. Its leader, Daniel Ortega, is back in power. The IMF's actions during the Argentine financial crisis of 2001 now reverberate a half decade later with Hugo Chavez, Venezuela's illiberal leader, being welcomed with open arms in Buenos Aires. The heavy-handed directives of the World Bank and IMF in Bolivia provided the soil from which that country's neosocialist president, Evo Morales, sprung. The disappointing payoff following eight structural adjustment loans to Zimbabwe and $8 billion in foreign aid during the 1980s and 1990s helped Robert Mugabe launch a vicious counterattack on democracy. The IMF-World Bank—Jeffrey Sachs application of "shock therapy" to the former Soviet Union has created a lasting nostalgia for communism. In the Middle East, $154 billion in foreign aid between 1980 and 2001, 45 structural adjustment loans, and "expert" advice produced zero per capita GDP growth that helped create a breeding ground for Islamic fundamentalism.

This blowback against "globalization from above" has spread to every corner of the Earth. It now threatens to kill sensible, moderate steps toward the freer movement of goods, ideas, capital, and people.

Development's Politburo

The ideology of Development is not only about having experts design your free market for you; it is about having the experts design a comprehensive, technical plan to solve all the problems of the poor. These experts see poverty as a purely technological problem, to be solved by engineering and the natural sciences, ignoring messy social sciences such as economics, politics, and sociology.

Sachs, Columbia University's celebrity economist, is one of its main proprietors. He is now recycling his theories of overnight shock therapy, which failed so miserably in Russia, into promises of overnight global poverty reduction. "Africa's problems," he has said, "are . . . solvable with practical and proven technologies." His own plan features hundreds of expert interventions to solve every last problem of the poor—from green manure, breast-feeding education, and bicycles to solar-energy systems, school uniforms for AIDS orphans, and windmills. Not to mention such critical interventions as "counseling and information services for men to address their reproductive health needs." All this will be done, Sachs says, by "a united and effective United Nations country team, which coordinates in one place the work of the U.N. specialized agencies, the IMF, and the World Bank."

So the admirable concern of rich countries for the tragedies of world poverty is thus channeled into fattening the international aid bureaucracy, the self-appointed priesthood of Development. Like other ideologies, this thinking favors collective goals such as national poverty reduction, national economic growth, and the global Millennium Development Goals, over the aspirations of individuals. Bureaucrats who write poverty-reduction frameworks outrank individuals who actually reduce poverty by, say, starting a business. Just as Marxists favored world revolution and socialist internationalism, Development stresses world goals over the autonomy of societies to choose their own path. It favors doctrinaire abstractions such as "market-friendly policies," "good investment climate," and "pro-poor globalization" over the freedom of individuals.

Development also shares another Marxist trait: It aspires to be scientific. Finding the one correct solution to poverty is seen as a scientific problem to be solved by the experts. They are always sure they know the answer, vehemently reject disagreement, and then later change their answers. In psychiatry, this is known as Borderline Personality Disorder. For the Development Experts, it's a way of life. The answer at first was aid-financed investment and industrialization in poor countries, then it was market-oriented government policy reform, then it was fixing institutional problems such as corruption, then it was globalization, then it was the Poverty Reduction Strategy to achieve the Millennium Development Goals.

One reason the answers keep changing is because, in reality, high-growth countries follow a bewildering variety of paths to development, and the countries with high growth rates are constantly changing from decade to decade. Who could be more different than successful developers such as China and Chile, Botswana and Singapore, Taiwan and Turkey, or Hong Kong and Vietnam? What about the many countries who tried to emulate these rising stars and failed? What about the former stars who have fallen on hard times, like the Ivory Coast, which was one of the fastest developers of the 1960s and 1970s, only to become mired in a civil war? What about Mexico, which saw rapid growth until 1980 and has had slow growth ever since, despite embracing the experts' reforms?

The experts in Developmentalism's Politburo don't bother themselves with such questions. All the previous answers were right; they were just missing one more "necessary condition" that the experts have only just now added to the list. Like all ideologies, Development is at the same time too rigid to predict what will work in the messy real world and yet flexible enough to forever escape falsification by real-world events. The high church of Development, the World Bank, has guaranteed it can never be wrong by making statements such as, "different policies can yield the same result, and the same policy can yield different results, depending on country institutional contexts and underlying growth strategies." Of course, you still need experts to figure out the contexts and strategies.

Resistance is Futile

Perhaps more hypocritical yet is Development's simple theory of historical inevitability. Poor societies are not just poor, the experts tell us, they are "developing" until they reach the final stage of history, or "development," in which poverty will soon end. Under this historiography, an end to starvation, tyranny, and war are thrown in like a free toaster on an infomercial. The experts judge all societies on a straight line, per capita income,

with the superior countries showing the inferior countries the image of their own future. And the experts heap scorn on those who resist the inevitabilities on the path to development.

One of today's leading Developmentalists, *New York Times* columnist Thomas Friedman, can hardly conceal his mockery of those who resist the march of history, or "the flattening of the world." "When you are Mexico," Friedman has written, "and your claim to fame is that you are a low-wage manufacturing country, and some of your people are importing statuettes of your own patron saint from China, because China can make them and ship them all the way across the Pacific more cheaply than you can produce them . . . you have got a problem. [T]he only way for Mexico to thrive is with a strategy of reform . . . the more Mexico just sits there, the more it is going to get run over." Friedman seems blissfully unaware that poor Mexico, so far from God yet so close to American pundits, has already tried much harder than China to implement the experts' "strategy of reform."

The self-confidence of Developmentalists like Friedman is so strong that they impose themselves even on those who accept their strategies. This year, for instance, Ghana celebrated its 50th anniversary as the first black African nation to gain independence. Official international aid donors to Ghana told its allegedly independent government, in the words of the World Bank: "We Partners are here giving you our pledge to give our best to make lives easier for you in running your country." Among the things they will do to make your life easier is to run your country for you.

Unfortunately, Development ideology has a dismal record of helping any country actually develop. The regions where the ideology has been most influential, Latin America and Africa, have done the worst. Luckless Latins and Africans are left chasing yesterday's formulas for success while those who ignored the Developmentalists found homegrown paths to success. The nations that have been the most successful in the past 40 years did so in such a variety of different ways that it would be hard to argue that they discovered the "correct answer" from development ideology. In fact, they often conspicuously violated whatever it was the experts said at the time. The East Asian tigers, for instance, chose outward orientation on their own in the 1960s, when the experts' conventional wisdom was industrialization for the home market. The rapid growth of China over the past quarter century came when it was hardly a poster child for either the 1980s Washington Consensus or the 1990s institutionalism of democracy and cracking down on corruption.

What explains the appeal of development ideology despite its dismal track record? Ideologies usually arise in response to tragic situations in which people are hungry for clear and comprehensive solutions. The inequality of the Industrial Revolution bred Marxism, and the backwardness of Russia its Leninist offshoot. Germany's defeat and demoralization in World War I birthed Nazism. Economic hardship accompanied by threats to identity led to both Christian and Islamic fundamentalism. Similarly, development ideology appeals to those who want a definitive, complete answer to the tragedy of world poverty and inequality. It answers the question, "What is to be done?" to borrow the title of Lenin's 1902 tract. It stresses collective social outcomes that must be remedied by collective, top-down action by the intelligentsia, the revolutionary vanguard, the development expert. As Sachs explains, "I have . . . gradually come to understand through my scientific research and on the ground advisory work the awesome power in our generation's hands to end the massive suffering of the extreme poor . . . although introductory economics textbooks preach individualism and decentralized markets, our safety and prosperity depend at least as much on collective decisions."

Freeing the Poor

Few realize that Americans in 1776 had the same income level as the average African today. Yet, like all the present-day developed nations, the United States was lucky enough to escape poverty before there were Developmentalists. In the words of former IMF First Deputy Managing Director Anne Krueger, development in the rich nations "just happened." George Washington did not have to deal with aid partners, getting structurally adjusted by them, or preparing poverty-reduction strategy papers for them. Abraham Lincoln did not celebrate a government of the donors, by the donors, and for the donors. Today's developed nations were free to experiment with their own pragmatic paths toward more government accountability and freer markets. Individualism and decentralized markets were good enough to give rise to penicillin, air conditioning, high-yield corn, and the automobile—not to mention better living standards, lower mortality, and the iPod.

The opposite of ideology is freedom, the ability of societies to be unchained from foreign control. The only "answer" to poverty reduction is freedom from being told the answer. Free societies and individuals are not guaranteed to succeed. They will make bad choices. But at least they bear the cost of those mistakes, and learn from them. That stands in stark contrast to

accountability-free Developmentalism. This process of learning from mistakes is what produced the repositories of common sense that make up mainstream economics. The opposite of Development ideology is not anything goes, but the pragmatic use of time-tested economic ideas—the benefits of specialization, comparative advantage, gains from trade, market-clearing prices, trade-offs, budget constraints—by individuals, firms, governments, and societies as they find their own success.

History proves just how much good can come from individuals who both bear the costs and reap the benefits of their own choices when they are free to make them. That includes local politicians, activists, and businesspeople who are groping their way toward greater freedom, contrary to the Developmentalists who oxymoronically impose freedom of choice on other people. Those who best understood the lessons of the 20th century were not the ideologues asking, "What is to be done?" They were those asking, "How can people be more free to find their own solutions?"

The ideology of Development should be packed up in crates and sent off to the Museum of Dead Ideologies, just down the hall from Communism, Socialism, and Fascism. It's time to recognize that the attempt to impose a rigid development ideology on the world's poor has failed miserably. Fortunately, many poor societies are forging their own path toward greater freedom and prosperity anyway. That is how true revolutions happen.

Critical Thinking

1. What is William Easterly's critique of "developmentalism"?
2. Compare and contrast Easterly's point of view with that of Sachs.

WILLIAM EASTERLY is professor of economics at New York University.

Reprinted in entirety by McGraw-Hill with permission from *Foreign Policy,* July/August 2007. www.foreignpolicy.com. © 2007 Washingtonpost.Newsweek Interactive, LLC.

The Quiet Coup

The crash has laid bare many unpleasant truths about the United States. One of the most alarming; says a former chief economist of the International Monetary Fund, is that the finance industry has effectively captured our government—a state of affairs that more typically describes emerging markets, and is at the center of many emerging-market crises. If the IMF's staff could speak freely about the U.S., it would tell us what it tells all countries in this situation: Recovery will fail unless we break the financial oligarchy that is blocking essential reform. And if we are to prevent a true depression, we're running out of time.

SIMON JOHNSON

One thing you learn rather quickly when working at the International Monetary Fund is that no one is ever very happy to see you. Typically, your "clients" come in only after private capital has abandoned them, after regional trading-bloc partners have been unable to throw a strong enough lifeline, after last-ditch attempts to borrow from powerful friends like China or the European Union have fallen through. You're never at the top of anyone's dance card.

The reason, of course, is that the IMF specializes in telling its clients what they don't want to hear. I should know; I pressed painful changes on many foreign officials during my time there as chief economist in 2007 and 2008. And I felt the effects of IMF pressure, at least indirectly, when I worked with governments in Eastern Europe as they struggled after 1989, and with the private sector in Asia and Latin America during the crises of the late 1990s and early 2000s. Over that time, from every vantage point, I saw firsthand the steady flow of officials—from Ukraine, Russia, Thailand, Indonesia, South Korea, and elsewhere—trudging to the fund when circumstances were dire and all else had failed.

Every crisis is different, of course. Ukraine faced hyperinflation in 1994; Russia desperately needed help when its short-term-debt rollover scheme exploded in the summer of 1998; the Indonesian rupiah plunged in 1997, nearly leveling the corporate economy; that same year, South Korea's 30-year economic miracle ground to a halt when foreign banks suddenly refused to extend new credit.

But I must tell you, to IMF officials, all of these crises looked depressingly similar. Each country, of course, needed a loan, but more than that, each needed to make big changes so that the loan could really work. Almost always, countries in crisis need to learn to live within their means after a period of excess—exports must be increased, and imports cut—and

the goal is to do this without the most horrible of recessions. Naturally, the fund's economists spend time figuring out the policies—budget, money supply, and the like—that make sense in this context. Yet the economic solution is seldom very hard to work out.

No, the real concern of the fund's senior staff, and the biggest obstacle to recovery, is almost invariably the politics of countries in crisis.

Typically, these countries are in a desperate economic situation for one simple reason—the powerful elites within them overreached in good times and took too many risks. Emerging-market governments and their private-sector allies commonly form a tight-knit—and, most of the time, genteel—oligarchy, running the country rather like a profit-seeking company in which they are the controlling shareholders. When a country like Indonesia or South Korea or Russia grows, so do the ambitions of its captains of industry. As masters of their mini-universe, these people make some investments that clearly benefit the broader economy, but they also start making bigger and riskier bets. They reckon—correctly, in most cases—that their political connections will allow them to push onto the government any substantial problems that arise.

In Russia, for instance, the private sector is now in serious trouble because, over the past five years or so, it borrowed at least $490 billion from global banks and investors on the assumption that the country's energy sector could support a permanent increase in consumption throughout the economy. As Russia's oligarchs spent this capital, acquiring other companies and embarking on ambitious investment plans that generated jobs, their importance to the political elite increased. Growing political support meant better access to lucrative contracts, tax breaks, and subsidies. And foreign investors could not have been more pleased; all other things being equal, they prefer to lend money to people who have the implicit backing of their national governments, even if that backing gives off the faint whiff of corruption.

But inevitably, emerging-market oligarchs get carried away; they waste money and build massive business empires on a mountain of debt. Local banks, sometimes pressured by the government, become too willing to extend credit to the elite and to those who depend on them. Overborrowing always ends badly, whether for an individual, a company, or a country. Sooner or later, credit conditions become tighter and no one will lend you money on anything close to affordable terms.

The downward spiral that follows is remarkably steep. Enormous companies teeter on the brink of default, and the local banks that have lent to them collapse. Yesterday's "public-private partnerships" are relabeled "crony capitalism." With credit unavailable, economic paralysis ensues, and conditions just get worse and worse. The government is forced to draw down its foreign-currency reserves to pay for imports, service debt, and cover private losses. But these reserves will eventually run out. If the country cannot right itself before that happens, it will default on its sovereign debt and become an economic pariah. The government, in its race to stop the bleeding, will typically need to wipe out some of the national champions—now hemorrhaging cash—and usually restructure a banking system that's gone badly out of balance. It will, in other words, need to squeeze at least some of its oligarchs.

Squeezing the oligarchs, though, is seldom the strategy of choice among emerging-market governments. Quite the contrary: at the outset of the crisis, the oligarchs are usually among the first to get extra help from the government, such as preferential access to foreign currency, or maybe a nice tax break, or—here's a classic Kremlin bailout technique—the assumption of private debt obligations by the government. Under duress, generosity toward old friends takes many innovative forms. Meanwhile, needing to squeeze *someone,* most emerging-market governments look first to ordinary working folk—at least until the riots grow too large.

Treasury and the Fed just worked out a transaction and claimed it was the best that could be done. This was late-night, backroom dealing, pure and simple.

Eventually, as the oligarchs in Putin's Russia now realize, some within the elite have to lose out before recovery can begin. It's a game of musical chairs: there just aren't enough currency reserves to take care of everyone, and the government cannot afford to take over private-sector debt completely.

So the IMF staff looks into the eyes of the minister of finance and decides whether the government is serious yet. The fund will give even a country like Russia a loan eventually, but first it wants to make sure Prime Minister Putin is ready, willing, and able to be tough on some of his friends. If he is not ready to throw former pals to the wolves, the fund can wait. And when he is ready, the fund is happy to make helpful suggestions—particularly with regard to wresting control of the banking system from the hands of the most incompetent and avaricious "entrepreneurs."

Of course, Putin's ex-friends will fight back. They'll mobilize allies, work the system, and put pressure on other parts of the government to get additional subsidies. In extreme cases, they'll even try subversion—including calling up their contacts in the American foreign-policy establishment, as the Ukrainians did with some success in the late 1990s.

Many IMF programs "go off track" (a euphemism) precisely because the government can't stay tough on erstwhile cronies, and the consequences are massive inflation or other disasters. A program "goes back on track" once the government prevails or powerful oligarchs sort out among themselves who will govern—and thus win or lose—under the IMF-supported plan. The real fight in Thailand and Indonesia in 1997 was about which powerful families would lose their banks. In Thailand, it was handled relatively smoothly. In Indonesia, it led to the fall of President Suharto and economic chaos.

From long years of experience, the IMF staff knows its program will succeed—stabilizing the economy and enabling growth—only if at least some of the powerful oligarchs who did so much to create the underlying problems take a hit. This is the problem of all emerging markets.

Becoming a Banana Republic

In its depth and suddenness, the U.S. economic and financial crisis is shockingly reminiscent of moments we have recently seen in emerging markets (and only in emerging markets): South Korea (1997), Malaysia (1998), Russia and Argentina (time and again). In each of those cases, global investors, afraid that the country or its financial sector wouldn't be able to pay off mountainous debt, suddenly stopped lending. And in each case, that fear became self-fulfilling, as banks that couldn't roll over their debt did, in fact, become unable to pay. This is precisely what drove Lehman Brothers into bankruptcy on September 15, causing all sources of funding to the U.S. financial sector to dry up overnight. Just as in emerging-market crises, the weakness in the banking system has quickly rippled out into the rest of the economy, causing a severe economic contraction and hardship for millions of people.

But there's a deeper and more disturbing similarity: elite business interests—financiers, in the case of the U.S.—played a central role in creating the crisis, making ever-larger gambles, with the implicit backing of the government, until the inevitable collapse. More alarming, they are now using their influence to prevent precisely the sorts of reforms that are needed, and fast, to pull the economy out of its nosedive. The government seems helpless, or unwilling, to act against them.

Top investment bankers and government officials like to lay the blame for the current crisis on the lowering of U.S. interest rates after the dotcom bust or, even better—in a "buck stops somewhere else" sort of way—on the flow of savings out of China. Some on the right like to complain about Fannie Mae or Freddie Mac, or even about longer-standing efforts to promote broader homeownership. And, of course, it is axiomatic to everyone that the regulators responsible for "safety and soundness" were fast asleep at the wheel.

But these various policies—lightweight regulation, cheap money, the unwritten Chinese-American economic alliance, the promotion of homeownership—had something in common. Even though some are traditionally associated with Democrats and some with Republicans, they *all* benefited the financial sector. Policy changes that might have forestalled the crisis but would have limited the financial sector's profits—such as Brooksley Born's now-famous attempts to regulate credit-default swaps at the Commodity Futures Trading Commission, in 1998—were ignored or swept aside.

The financial industry has not always enjoyed such favored treatment. But for the past 25 years or so, finance has boomed, becoming ever more powerful. The boom began with the Reagan years, and it only gained strength with the deregulatory policies of the Clinton and George W. Bush administrations. Several other factors helped fuel the financial industry's ascent. Paul Volcker's monetary policy in the 1980s, and the increased volatility in interest rates that accompanied it, made bond trading much more lucrative. The invention of securitization, interest-rate swaps, and credit-default swaps greatly increased the volume of transactions that bankers could make money on. And an aging and increasingly wealthy population invested more and more money in securities, helped by the invention of the IRA and the 401(k) plan. Together, these developments vastly increased the profit opportunities in financial services.

Not surprisingly, Wall Street ran with these opportunities. From 1973 to 1985, the financial sector never earned more than 16 percent of domestic corporate profits. In 1986, that figure reached 19 percent. In the 1990s, it oscillated between 21 percent and 30 percent, higher than it had ever been in the postwar period. This decade, it reached 41 percent. Pay rose just as dramatically. From 1948 to 1982, average compensation in the financial sector ranged between 99 percent and 108 percent of the average for all domestic private industries. From 1983, it shot upward, reaching 181 percent in 2007.

The great wealth that the financial sector created and concentrated gave bankers enormous political weight—a weight not seen in the U.S. since the era of J.P. Morgan (the man). In that period, the banking panic of 1907 could be stopped only by coordination among private-sector bankers: no government entity was able to offer an effective

Financial-industry profits as a share of U.S. business profits.

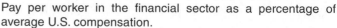

Pay per worker in the financial sector as a percentage of average U.S. compensation.

response. But that first age of banking oligarchs came to an end with the passage of significant banking regulation in response to the Great Depression; the reemergence of an American financial oligarchy is quite recent.

The Wall Street—Washington Corridor

Of course, the U.S. is unique. And just as we have the world's most advanced economy, military, and technology, we also have its most advanced oligarchy.

In a primitive political system, power is transmitted through violence, or the threat of violence: military coups, private militias, and so on. In a less primitive system more typical of emerging markets, power is transmitted via money: bribes, kickbacks, and offshore bank accounts. Although lobbying and campaign contributions certainly play major roles in the American political system, old-fashioned corruption—envelopes stuffed with $100 bills—is probably a sideshow today, Jack Abramoff notwithstanding.

Instead, the American financial industry gained political power by amassing a kind of cultural capital—a belief system. Once, perhaps, what was good for General Motors was good for the country. Over the past decade, the attitude took hold that what was good for Wall Street was good for the country. The banking-and-securities industry has become one of the top contributors to political campaigns, but at the peak of its influence, it did not have to buy favors the way, for example, the tobacco companies or military contractors might have to. Instead, it benefited from the fact that Washington insiders already believed that large financial institutions and free-flowing capital markets were crucial to America's position in the world.

One channel of influence was, of course, the flow of individuals between Wall Street and Washington. Robert Rubin, once the co-chairman of Goldman Sachs, served in Washington as Treasury secretary under Clinton, and later became chairman of Citigroup's executive committee. Henry Paulson, CEO of Goldman Sachs during the long boom, became Treasury secretary under George W. Bush. John Snow, Paulson's predecessor, left to become chairman of Cerberus Capital Management, a large private-equity firm that also counts Dan Quayle among its executives. Alan Greenspan, after leaving the Federal Reserve, became a consultant to Pimco, perhaps the biggest player in international bond markets.

These personal connections were multiplied many times over at the lower levels of the past three presidential administrations, strengthening the ties between Washington and Wall Street. It has become something of a tradition for Goldman Sachs employees to go into public service after they leave the firm. The flow of Goldman alumni—including Jon Corzine, now the governor of New Jersey, along with Rubin and Paulson—not only placed people with Wall Street's worldview in the halls of power; it also helped create an image of Goldman (inside the Beltway, at least) as an institution that was itself almost a form of public service.

Wall Street is a very seductive place, imbued with an air of power. Its executives truly believe that they control the levers that make the world go round. A civil servant from Washington invited into their conference rooms, even if just for a meeting, could be forgiven for falling under their sway. Throughout my time at the IMF, I was struck by the easy access of leading financiers to the highest U.S. government officials, and the interweaving of the two career tracks. I vividly remember a meeting in early 2008—attended by top policy makers from a handful of rich countries—at which the chair casually proclaimed, to the room's general approval, that the best preparation for becoming a central-bank governor was to work first as an investment banker.

A whole generation of policy makers has been mesmerized by Wall Street, always and utterly convinced that whatever the banks said was true. Alan Greenspan's pronouncements in favor of unregulated financial markets are well known. Yet Greenspan was hardly alone. This is what Ben Bernanke, the man who succeeded him, said in 2006: "The management of market risk and credit risk has become increasingly sophisticated . . . Banking organizations of all sizes have made substantial strides over the past two decades in their ability to measure and manage risks."

Of course, this was mostly an illusion. Regulators, legislators, and academics almost all assumed that the managers of these banks knew what they were doing. In retrospect, they didn't. AIG's Financial Products division, for instance, made $2.5 billion in pretax profits in 2005, largely by selling underpriced insurance on complex, poorly understood securities. Often described as "picking up nickels in front of a steamroller," this strategy is profitable in ordinary years, and catastrophic in bad ones. As of last fall, AIG had outstanding insurance on more than $400 billion in securities. To date, the U.S. government, in an effort to rescue the company, has committed about $180 billion in investments and loans to cover losses that AIG's sophisticated risk modeling had said were virtually impossible.

Wall Street's seductive power extended even (or especially) to finance and economics professors, historically confined to the cramped offices of universities and the pursuit of Nobel Prizes. As mathematical finance became more and more essential to practical finance, professors increasingly took positions as consultants or partners at financial institutions. Myron Scholes and Robert Merton, Nobel laureates both, were perhaps the most famous; they took board seats at the hedge fund Long-Term Capital Management in 1994, before the fund famously flamed out at the end of the decade. But many others beat similar paths. This migration gave the stamp of academic legitimacy (and the intimidating aura of intellectual rigor) to the burgeoning world of high finance.

As more and more of the rich made their money in finance, the cult of finance seeped into the culture at large. Works like *Barbarians at the Gate, Wall Street,* and *Bonfire of the Vanities*—all intended as cautionary tales—served only to increase Wall Street's mystique. Michael Lewis noted in *Portfolio* last year that when he wrote *Liar's Poker,* an insider's account of the financial industry, in 1989, he had hoped the book might provoke outrage at Wall Street's hubris and excess. Instead, he found himself "knee-deep in letters from students at Ohio State who wanted to know if I had any other secrets to share . . . They'd read my book as a how-to manual." Even Wall Street's criminals, like Michael Milken and Ivan Boesky, became larger than life. In a society that celebrates the idea of making money, it was easy to infer that the interests of the financial sector were the same as the interests of the country—and that the winners in the financial sector knew better what was good for America than did the career civil servants in Washington. Faith in free financial markets grew into conventional wisdom—trumpeted on the editorial pages of *The Wall Street Journal* and on the floor of Congress.

From this confluence of campaign finance, personal connections, and ideology there flowed, in just the past decade, a river of deregulatory policies that is, in hindsight, astonishing:

- insistence on free movement of capital across borders;
- the repeal of Depression-era regulations separating commercial and investment banking;

- a congressional ban on the regulation of credit-default swaps;
- major increases in the amount of leverage allowed to investment banks;
- a light (dare I say *invisible?*) hand at the Securities and Exchange Commission in its regulatory enforcement;
- an international agreement to allow banks to measure their own riskiness;
- and an intentional failure to update regulations so as to keep up with the tremendous pace of financial innovation.

The mood that accompanied these measures in Washington seemed to swing between nonchalance and outright celebration: finance unleashed, it was thought, would continue to propel the economy to greater heights.

America's Oligarchs and the Financial Crisis

The oligarchy and the government policies that aided it did not alone cause the financial crisis that exploded last year. Many other factors contributed, including excessive borrowing by households and lax lending standards out on the fringes of the financial world. But major commercial and investment banks—and the hedge funds that ran alongside them—were the big beneficiaries of the twin housing and equity-market bubbles of this decade, their profits fed by an ever-increasing volume of transactions founded on a relatively small base of actual physical assets. Each time a loan was sold, packaged, securitized, and resold, banks took their transaction fees, and the hedge funds buying those securities reaped ever-larger fees as their holdings grew.

Because everyone was getting richer, and the health of the national economy depended so heavily on growth in real estate and finance, no one in Washington had any incentive to question what was going on. Instead, Fed Chairman Greenspan and President Bush insisted metronomically that the economy was fundamentally sound and that the tremendous growth in complex securities and credit-default swaps was evidence of a healthy economy where risk was distributed safely.

In the summer of 2007, signs of strain started appearing. The boom had produced so much debt that even a small economic stumble could cause major problems, and rising delinquencies in subprime mortgages proved the stumbling block. Ever since, the financial sector and the federal government have been behaving exactly the way one would expect them to, in light of past emerging-market crises.

By now, the princes of the financial world have of course been stripped naked as leaders and strategists—at least in the eyes of most Americans. But as the months have rolled by, financial elites have continued to assume that their position as the economy's favored children is safe, despite the wreckage they have caused.

Stanley O'Neal, the CEO of Merrill Lynch, pushed his firm heavily into the mortgage-backed-securities market at its peak in 2005 and 2006; in October 2007, he acknowledged, "The bottom line is, we—I—got it wrong by being overexposed to subprime, and we suffered as a result of impaired liquidity in that market. No one is more disappointed than I am in that result." O'Neal took home a $14 million bonus in 2006; in 2007, he walked away from Merrill with a severance package worth $162 million, although it is presumably worth much less today.

In October, John Thain, Merrill Lynch's final CEO, reportedly lobbied his board of directors for a bonus of $30 million or more, eventually reducing his demand to $10 million in December; he withdrew the request, under a firestorm of protest, only after it was leaked to *The Wall Street Journal.* Merrill Lynch as a whole was no better: it moved its bonus payments, $4 billion in total, forward to December, presumably to avoid the possibility that they would be reduced by Bank of America, which would own Merrill beginning on January 1. Wall Street paid out $18 billion in year-end bonuses last year to its New York City employees, after the government disbursed $243 billion in emergency assistance to the financial sector.

In a financial panic, the government must respond with both speed and overwhelming force. The root problem is uncertainty—in our case, uncertainty about whether the major banks have sufficient assets to cover their liabilities. Half measures combined with wishful thinking and a wait-and-see attitude cannot overcome this uncertainty. And the longer the response takes, the longer the uncertainty will stymie the flow of credit, sap consumer confidence, and cripple the economy—ultimately making the problem much harder to solve. Yet the principal characteristics of the government's response to the financial crisis have been delay, lack of transparency, and an unwillingness to upset the financial sector.

The response so far is perhaps best described as "policy by deal": when a major financial institution gets into trouble, the Treasury Department and the Federal Reserve engineer a bailout over the weekend and announce on Monday that everything is fine. In March 2008, Bear Stearns was sold to JPMorgan Chase in what looked to many like a gift to JPMorgan. (Jamie Dimon, JPMorgan's CEO, sits on the board of directors of the Federal Reserve Bank of New York, which, along with the Treasury Department, brokered the deal.) In September, we saw the sale of Merrill Lynch to Bank of America, the first bailout of AIG, and the takeover and immediate sale of Washington Mutual to JPMorgan—all of which were brokered by the government. In October, nine large banks were recapitalized on the same day behind closed doors in Washington. This, in turn, was followed by additional bailouts for Citigroup, AIG, Bank of America, Citigroup (again), and AIG (again).

Some of these deals may have been reasonable responses to the immediate situation. But it was never clear (and still isn't) what combination of interests was being served, and how. Treasury and the Fed did not act according to any publicly articulated principles, but just worked out a transaction and claimed it was the best that could be done under the circumstances. This was late-night, backroom dealing, pure and simple.

Throughout the crisis, the government has taken extreme care not to upset the interests of the financial institutions, or to question the basic outlines of the system that got us here. In September 2008, Henry Paulson asked Congress for $700 billion to buy toxic assets from banks, with no strings attached and no judicial review of his purchase decisions. Many observers suspected that the purpose was to overpay for those assets and thereby take the problem off the banks' hands—indeed, that is the only way that buying toxic assets would have helped anything. Perhaps because there was no way to make such a blatant subsidy politically acceptable, that plan was shelved.

Instead, the money was used to recapitalize banks, buying shares in them on terms that were grossly favorable to the banks themselves. As the crisis has deepened and financial institutions have needed more help, the government has gotten more and more creative in figuring out ways to provide banks with subsidies that are too complex for the general public to understand. The first AIG bailout, which was on relatively good terms for the taxpayer, was supplemented by three further bailouts whose terms were more AIG-friendly. The second Citigroup bailout and the Bank of America bailout included complex asset guarantees that provided the banks with insurance at below-market rates. The third Citigroup bailout, in late February, converted government-owned preferred stock to common stock at a price significantly higher than the market price—a subsidy that probably even most *Wall Street Journal* readers would miss on first reading. And the convertible preferred shares that the Treasury will buy under the new Financial Stability Plan give the conversion option (and thus the upside) to the banks, not the government.

This latest plan—which is likely to provide cheap loans to hedge funds and others so that they can buy distressed bank assets at relatively high prices—has been heavily influenced by the financial sector, and Treasury has made no secret of that. As Neel Kashkari, a senior Treasury official under both Henry Paulson and Tim Geithner (and a Goldman alum) told Congress in March, "We had received inbound unsolicited proposals from people in the private sector saying, 'We have capital on the sidelines; we want to go after [distressed bank] assets.'" And the plan lets them do just that: "By marrying government capital—taxpayer capital—with private-sector capital and providing financing, you can enable those investors to then go after those assets at a price that makes sense for the investors and at a price that makes sense for the banks." Kashkari didn't mention anything about what makes sense for the third group involved: the taxpayers.

Even leaving aside fairness to taxpayers, the government's velvet-glove approach with the banks is deeply troubling, for one simple reason: it is inadequate to change the behavior of a financial sector accustomed to doing business on its own terms, at a time when that behavior *must* change. As an unnamed senior bank official said to *The New York Times* last fall, "It doesn't matter how much Hank Paulson gives us, no one is going to lend a nickel until the economy turns." But there's the rub: the economy can't recover until the banks are healthy and willing to lend.

The Way Out

Looking just at the financial crisis (and leaving aside some problems of the larger economy), we face at least two major, interrelated problems. The first is a desperately ill banking sector that threatens to choke off any incipient recovery that the fiscal stimulus might generate. The second is a political balance of power that gives the financial sector a veto over public policy, even as that sector loses popular support.

Big banks, it seems, have only gained political strength since the crisis began. And this is not surprising. With the financial system so fragile, the damage that a major bank failure could cause—Lehman was small relative to Citigroup or Bank of America—is much greater than it would be during ordinary times. The banks have been exploiting this fear as they wring favorable deals out of Washington. Bank of America obtained its second bailout package (in January) after warning the government that it might not be able to go through with the acquisition of Merrill Lynch, a prospect that Treasury did not want to consider.

The challenges the United States faces are familiar territory to the people at the IMF. If you hid the name of the country and just showed them the numbers, there is no doubt what old IMF hands would say: nationalize troubled banks and break them up as necessary.

If you hid the name of the country and just showed them the numbers, there is no doubt what old IMF hands would say: nationalize troubled banks and break them up.

In some ways, of course, the government has already taken control of the banking system. It has essentially guaranteed the liabilities of the biggest banks, and it is their only plausible source of capital today. Meanwhile, the Federal Reserve has taken on a major role in providing credit to the economy—the function that the private banking sector is supposed to be performing, but isn't. Yet there are limits to what the Fed can do on its own; consumers and businesses are still dependent on banks that lack the balance sheets and the incentives to make the loans the economy needs, and the government has no real control over who runs the banks, or over what they do.

At the root of the banks' problems are the large losses they have undoubtedly taken on their securities and loan portfolios. But they don't want to recognize the full extent of their losses, because that would likely expose them as insolvent. So they talk down the problem, and ask for handouts that aren't enough to make them healthy (again, they can't reveal the size of the handouts that would be necessary for that), but are enough to keep them upright a little longer. This behavior is corrosive: unhealthy banks either don't lend (hoarding money to shore up reserves) or they make desperate gambles on high-risk loans and investments that could pay off big, but probably won't pay off at all. In either case, the economy suffers further, and as it does, bank assets themselves continue to deteriorate—creating a highly destructive vicious cycle.

To break this cycle, the government must force the banks to acknowledge the scale of their problems. As the IMF understands (and as the U.S. government itself has insisted to multiple emerging-market countries in the past), the most direct way to do this is nationalization. Instead, Treasury is trying to negotiate bailouts bank by bank, and behaving as if the banks hold all the cards—contorting the terms of each deal to minimize government ownership while forswearing government influence over bank strategy or operations. Under these conditions, cleaning up bank balance sheets is impossible.

Nationalization would not imply permanent state ownership. The IMF's advice would be, essentially: scale up the standard Federal Deposit Insurance Corporation process. An FDIC "intervention" is basically a government-managed bankruptcy procedure for banks. It would allow the government to wipe out bank shareholders, replace failed management, clean up the balance sheets, and then sell the banks back to the private sector. The main advantage is immediate recognition of the problem so that it can be solved before it grows worse.

The government needs to inspect the balance sheets and identify the banks that cannot survive a severe recession. These banks should face a choice: write down your assets to their true value and raise private capital within 30 days, or be taken over by the government. The government would write down the toxic assets of banks taken into receivership—recognizing reality—and transfer those assets to a separate government entity, which would attempt to salvage whatever value is possible for the taxpayer (as the Resolution Trust Corporation did after the savings-and-loan debacle of the 1980s). The rump banks—cleansed and able to lend safely, and hence trusted again by other lenders and investors—could then be sold off.

Cleaning up the megabanks will be complex. And it will be expensive for the taxpayer; according to the latest IMF numbers, the cleanup of the banking system would probably cost close to $1.5 trillion (or 10 percent of our GDP) in the long term. But only decisive government action—exposing the full extent of the financial rot and restoring some set of banks to publicly verifiable health—can cure the financial sector as a whole.

This may seem like strong medicine. But in fact, while necessary, it is insufficient. The second problem the U.S. faces—the power of the oligarchy—is just as important as the immediate crisis of lending. And the advice from the IMF on this front would again be simple: break the oligarchy.

Oversize institutions disproportionately influence public policy; the major banks we have today draw much of their power from being too big to fail. Nationalization and re-privatization would not change that; while the replacement of the bank executives who got us into this crisis would be just and sensible, ultimately, the swapping-out of one set of powerful managers for another would change only the names of the oligarchs.

Ideally, big banks should be sold in medium-size pieces, divided regionally or by type of business. Where this proves impractical—since we'll want to sell the banks quickly—they could be sold whole, but with the requirement of being broken up within a short time. Banks that remain in private hands should also be subject to size limitations.

This may seem like a crude and arbitrary step, but it is the best way to limit the power of individual institutions in a sector that is essential to the economy as a whole. Of course, some people will complain about the "efficiency costs" of a more fragmented banking system, and these costs are real. But so are the costs when a bank that is too big to fail—a financial weapon of mass self-destruction—explodes. Anything that is too big to fail is too big to exist.

To ensure systematic bank breakup, and to prevent the eventual reemergence of dangerous behemoths, we also need to overhaul our antitrust legislation. Laws put in place more than 100 years ago to combat industrial monopolies were not designed to address the problem we now face. The problem in the financial sector today is not that a given firm might have enough market share to influence prices; it is that one firm or a small set of interconnected firms, by failing, can bring down the economy. The Obama administration's fiscal stimulus evokes FDR, but what we need to imitate here is Teddy Roosevelt's trust-busting.

Caps on executive compensation, while redolent of populism, might help restore the political balance of power and deter the emergence of a new oligarchy. Wall Street's main attraction—to the people who work there and to the government officials who were only too happy to bask in its reflected glory—has been the astounding amount of money that could be made. Limiting that money would reduce the allure of the financial sector and make it more like any other industry.

Still, outright pay caps are clumsy, especially in the long run. And most money is now made in largely unregulated private hedge funds and private-equity firms, so lowering pay would be complicated. Regulation and taxation should be part of the solution. Over time, though, the largest part may involve more transparency and competition, which would bring financial-industry fees down. To those who say this would drive financial activities to other countries, we can now safely say: fine.

Two Paths

To paraphrase Joseph Schumpeter, the early-20th-century economist, everyone has elites; the important thing is to change them from time to time. If the U.S. were just another country, coming to the IMF with hat in hand, I might be fairly optimistic about its future. Most of the emerging-market crises that I've mentioned ended relatively quickly, and gave way, for the most part, to relatively strong recoveries. But this, alas, brings us to the limit of the analogy between the U.S. and emerging markets.

Emerging-market countries have only a precarious hold on wealth, and are weaklings globally. When they get into trouble, they quite literally run out of money—or at least out of foreign currency, without which they cannot survive. They must make difficult decisions; ultimately, aggressive action is baked into the cake. But the U.S., of course, is the world's most powerful nation, rich beyond measure, and blessed with the exorbitant privilege of paying its foreign debts in its own currency, which it can print. As a result, it could very well stumble along for years—as Japan did during its lost decade—never summoning the courage to do what it needs to do, and never really recovering. A clean break with the past—involving the takeover and cleanup of major banks—hardly looks like a sure thing right now. Certainly no one at the IMF can force it.

In my view, the U.S. faces two plausible scenarios. The first involves complicated bank-by-bank deals and a continual drumbeat of (repeated) bailouts, like the ones we saw in February with Citigroup and AIG. The administration will try to muddle through, and confusion will reign.

Boris Fyodorov, the late finance minister of Russia, struggled for much of the past 20 years against oligarchs, corruption, and abuse of authority in all its forms. He liked to say that confusion and chaos were very much in the interests of the powerful—letting them take things, legally and illegally, with impunity. When inflation is high, who can say what a piece of property is really worth? When the credit system is supported by byzantine government arrangements and backroom deals, how do you know that you aren't being fleeced?

Our future could be one in which continued tumult feeds the looting of the financial system, and we talk more and more about exactly how our oligarchs became bandits and how the economy just can't seem to get into gear.

The second scenario begins more bleakly, and might end that way too. But it does provide at least some hope that we'll be shaken out of our torpor. It goes like this: the global economy continues to deteriorate, the banking system in east-central Europe collapses, and—because eastern Europe's banks are mostly owned by western European banks—justifiable fears of government insolvency spread throughout the Continent. Creditors take further hits and confidence falls further. The Asian economies that export manufactured goods are devastated, and the commodity producers in Latin America and Africa are not much better off. A dramatic worsening of the global environment forces the U.S. economy, already staggering, down onto both knees. The baseline growth rates used in the administration's current budget are increasingly seen as unrealistic, and the rosy "stress scenario" that the U.S. Treasury is currently using to evaluate banks' balance sheets becomes a source of great embarrassment.

Under this kind of pressure, and faced with the prospect of a national and global collapse, minds may become more concentrated.

The conventional wisdom among the elite is still that the current slump "cannot be as bad as the Great Depression." This view is wrong.

The conventional wisdom among the elite is still that the current slump "cannot be as bad as the Great Depression." This view is wrong. What we face now could, in fact, be worse than the Great Depression—because the world is now so much more interconnected and because the banking sector is now so big. We face a synchronized downturn in almost all countries, a weakening of confidence among individuals and firms, and major problems for government finances. If our leadership wakes up to the potential consequences, we may yet see dramatic action on the banking system and a breaking of the old elite. Let us hope it is not then too late.

Critical Thinking

1. What does Simon Johnson mean by oligarchs?
2. What is Johnson's point of view?
3. What reasons does he offer to support his point of view?
4. Does Johnson's argument support or contradict the central point of view of articles 1 and 4?

SIMON JOHNSON, a professor at MIT's Sloan School of Management, was the chief economist at the International Monetary Fund during 2007 and 2008. He blogs about the financial crisis at baselinescenario.com, along with James Kwak, who also contributed to this essay.

The Case against the West
America and Europe in the Asian Century

KISHORE MAHBUBANI

There is a fundamental flaw in the West's strategic thinking. In all its analyses of global challenges, the West assumes that it is the source of the solutions to the world's key problems. In fact, however, the West is also a major source of these problems. Unless key Western policymakers learn to understand and deal with this reality, the world is headed for an even more troubled phase.

The West is understandably reluctant to accept that the era of its domination is ending and that the Asian century has come. No civilization cedes power easily, and the West's resistance to giving up control of key global institutions and processes is natural. Yet the West is engaging in an extraordinary act of self-deception by believing that it is open to change. In fact, the West has become the most powerful force preventing the emergence of a new wave of history, clinging to its privileged position in key global forums, such as the UN Security Council, the International Monetary Fund, the World Bank, and the G-8 (the group of highly industrialized states), and refusing to contemplate how the West will have to adjust to the Asian century.

Partly as a result of its growing insecurity, the West has also become increasingly incompetent in its handling of key global problems. Many Western commentators can readily identify specific failures, such as the Bush administration's botched invasion and occupation of Iraq. But few can see that this reflects a deeper structural problem: the West's inability to see that the world has entered a new era.

Apart from representing a specific failure of policy execution, the war in Iraq has also highlighted the gap between the reality and what the West had expected would happen after the invasion. Arguably, the United States and the United Kingdom intended only to free the Iraqi people from a despotic ruler and to rid the world of a dangerous man, Saddam Hussein. Even if George W. Bush and Tony Blair had no malevolent intentions, however, their approaches were trapped in the Western mindset of believing that their interventions could lead only to good, not harm or disaster. This led them to believe that the invading U.S. troops would be welcomed with roses thrown at their feet by happy Iraqis. But the twentieth century showed that no country welcomes foreign invaders. The notion that any Islamic nation would approve of Western military boots on its soil was ridiculous. Even in the early twentieth century, the British invasion and occupation of Iraq was met with armed resistance. In 1920, Winston Churchill, then British secretary for war and air, quelled the rebellion of Kurds and Arabs in British-occupied Iraq by authorizing his troops to use chemical weapons. "I am strongly in favor of using poisoned gas against uncivilized tribes," Churchill said. The world has moved on from this era, but many Western officials have not abandoned the old assumption that an army of Christian soldiers can successfully invade, occupy, and transform an Islamic society.

Many Western leaders often begin their speeches by remarking on how perilous the world is becoming. Speaking after the August 2006 discovery of a plot to blow up transatlantic flights originating from London, President Bush said, "The American people need to know we live in a dangerous world." But even as Western leaders speak of such threats, they seem incapable of conceding that the West itself could be the fundamental source of these dangers. After all, the West includes the best-managed states in the world, the most economically developed, those with the strongest democratic institutions. But one cannot assume that a government that rules competently at home will be equally good at addressing challenges abroad. In fact, the converse is more likely to be true. Although the Western mind is obsessed with the Islamist terrorist threat, the West is mishandling the two immediate and pressing challenges of Afghanistan and Iraq. And despite the grave threat of nuclear terrorism, the Western custodians of the nonproliferation regime have allowed that regime to weaken significantly. The challenge posed by Iran's efforts to enrich uranium has been aggravated by the incompetence of the United States and the European Union. On the economic front, for the first time since World War II, the demise of a round of global trade negotiations, the Doha Round, seems imminent. Finally, the danger of global warming, too, is being mismanaged.

Yet Westerners seldom look inward to understand the deeper reasons these global problems are being mismanaged. Are there domestic structural reasons that explain this? Have Western democracies been hijacked by competitive populism and structural short-termism, preventing them from addressing long-term challenges from a broader global perspective?

Fortunately, some Asian states may now be capable of taking on more responsibilities, as they have been strengthened by implementing Western principles. In September 2005, Robert Zoellick, then U.S. deputy secretary of state, called on China to become a "responsible stakeholder" in the international system. China has responded positively, as have other Asian states. In recent decades, Asians have been among the greatest beneficiaries of the open multilateral order created by the United States and the other victors of World War II, and few today want to destabilize it. The number of Asians seeking a comfortable middle-class existence has never been higher. For centuries, the Chinese and the Indians could only dream of such an accomplishment; now it is within the reach of around half a billion people in China and India. Their ideal is to achieve what the United States and Europe did. They want to replicate, not dominate, the West. The universalization of the Western dream represents a moment of triumph for the West. And so the West should welcome the fact that the Asian states are becoming competent at handling regional and global challenges.

The Middle East Mess

Western Policies have been most harmful in the Middle East. The Middle East is also the most dangerous region in the world. Trouble there affects not just seven million Israelis, around four million Palestinians, and 200 million Arabs; it also affects more than a billion Muslims worldwide. Every time there is a major flare-up in the Middle East, such as the U.S. invasion of Iraq or the Israeli bombing of Lebanon, Islamic communities around the world become concerned, distressed, and angered. And few of them doubt the problems origin: the West.

The invasion and occupation of Iraq, for example, was a multi-dimensional error. The theory and practice of international law legitimizes the use of force only when it is an act of self-defense or is authorized by the UN Security Council. The U.S.-led invasion of Iraq could not be justified on either count. The United States and the United Kingdom sought the Security Council's authorization to invade Iraq, but the council denied it. It was therefore clear to the international community that the subsequent war was illegal and that it would do huge damage to international law.

This has created an enormous problem, partly because until this point both the United States and the United Kingdom had been among the primary custodians of international law. American and British minds, such as James Brierly,

Philip Jessup, Hersch Lauterpacht, and Hans Morgenthau, developed the conceptual infrastructure underlying international law, and American and British leaders provided the political will to have it accepted in practice. But neither the United States nor the United Kingdom will admit that the invasion and the occupation of Iraq were illegal or give up their historical roles as the chief caretakers of international law. Since 2003, both nations have frequently called for Iran and North Korea to implement UN Security Council resolutions. But how can the violators of UN principles also be their enforcers?

One rare benefit of the Iraq war may be that it has awakened a new fear of Iran among the Sunni Arab states. Egypt, Jordan, and Saudi Arabia, among others, do not want to deal with two adversaries and so are inclined to make peace with Israel. Saudi Arabia's King Abdullah used the opportunity of the special Arab League summit meeting in March 2007 to relaunch his long-standing proposal for a two-state solution to the Israeli-Palestinian conflict. Unfortunately, the Bush administration did not seize the opportunity—or revive the Taba accords that President Bill Clinton had worked out in January 2001, even though they could provide a basis for a lasting settlement and the Saudis were prepared to back them. In its early days, the Bush administration appeared ready to support a two-state solution. It was the first U.S. administration to vote in favor of a UN Security Council resolution calling for the creation of a Palestinian state, and it announced in March 2002 that it would try to achieve such a result by 2005. But here it is 2008, and little progress has been made.

The United States has made the already complicated Israeli-Palestinian conflict even more of a mess. Many extremist voices in Tel Aviv and Washington believe that time will always be on Israel's side. The pro-Israel lobby's stranglehold on the U.S. Congress, the political cowardice of U.S. politicians when it comes to creating a Palestinian state, and the sustained track record of U.S. aid to Israel support this view. But no great power forever sacrifices its larger national interests in favor of the interests of a small state. If Israel fails to accept the Taba accords, it will inevitably come to grief. If and when it does, Western incompetence will be seen as a major cause.

Never Say Never

Nuclear nonproliferation is another area in which the West, especially the United States, has made matters worse. The West has long been obsessed with the danger of the proliferation of weapons of mass destruction, particularly nuclear weapons. It pushed successfully for the near-universal ratification of the Biological and Toxin Weapons Convention, the Chemical Weapons Convention, and the Nuclear Nonproliferation Treaty (NPT).

But the West has squandered many of those gains. Today, the NPT is legally alive but spiritually dead. The NPT was inherently problematic since it divided the world into nuclear haves (the states that had tested a nuclear device by 1967) and nuclear have-nots (those that had not). But for two decades it was reasonably effective in preventing horizontal proliferation (the spread of nuclear weapons to other states). Unfortunately, the NPT has done nothing to prevent vertical proliferation, namely, the increase in the numbers and sophistication of nuclear weapons among the existing nuclear weapons states. During the Cold War, the United States and the Soviet Union agreed to work together to limit proliferation. The governments of several countries that could have developed nuclear weapons, such as Argentina, Brazil, Germany, Japan, and South Korea, restrained themselves because they believed the NPT reflected a fair bargain between China, France, the Soviet Union, the United Kingdom, and the United States (the five official nuclear weapons states and five permanent members of the UN Security Council) and the rest of the world. Both sides agreed that the world would be safer if the five nuclear states took steps to reduce their arsenals and worked toward the eventual goal of universal disarmament and the other states refrained from acquiring nuclear weapons at all.

So what went wrong? The first problem was that the NPT's principal progenitor, the United States, decided to walk away from the postwar rule-based order it had created, thus eroding the infrastructure on which the NPT's enforcement depends. During the time I was Singapore's ambassador to the UN, between 1984 and 1989, Jeane Kirkpatrick, the U.S. ambassador to the UN, treated the organization with contempt. She infamously said, "What takes place in the Security Council more closely resembles a mugging than either a political debate or an effort at problem-solving." She saw the postwar order as a set of constraints, not as a set of rules that the world should follow and the United States should help preserve. This undermined the NPT, because with no teeth of its own, no self-regulating or sanctioning mechanisms, and a clause allowing signatories to ignore obligations in the name of "supreme national interest," the treaty could only really be enforced by the UN Security Council. And once the United States began tearing holes in the fabric of the overall system, it created openings for violations of the NPT and its principles. Finally, by going to war with Iraq without UN authorization, the United States lost its moral authority to ask, for example, Iran to abide by Security Council resolutions.

Another problem has been the United States'—and other nuclear weapons states'—direct assault on the treaty. The NPT is fundamentally a social contract between the five nuclear weapons states and the rest of the world, based partly on the understanding that the nuclear powers will eventually give up their weapons. Instead, during the Cold War, the United States and the Soviet Union increased both the quantity and the sophistication of their nuclear weapons: the United States' nuclear stockpile peaked in 1966 at 31,700 warheads, and the Soviet Union's peaked in 1986 at 40,723. In fact, the United States and the Soviet Union developed their nuclear stockpiles so much that they actually ran out of militarily or economically significant targets. The numbers have declined dramatically since then, but even the current number of nuclear weapons held by the United States and Russia can wreak enormous damage on human civilization.

The nuclear states' decision to ignore Israel's nuclear weapons program was especially damaging to their authority. No nuclear weapons state has ever publicly acknowledged Israel's possession of nuclear weapons. Their silence has created a loophole in the NPT and delegitimized it in the eyes of Muslim nations. The consequences have been profound. When the West sermonizes that the world will become a more dangerous place when Iran acquires nuclear weapons, the Muslim world now shrugs.

India and Pakistan were already shrugging by 1998, when they tested their first nuclear weapons. When the international community responded by condemning the tests and applying sanctions on India, virtually all Indians saw through the hypocrisy and double standards of their critics. By not respecting their own obligations under the NPT, the five nuclear states had robbed their condemnations of any moral legitimacy; criticisms from Australia and Canada, which have also remained silent about Israel's bomb, similarly had no moral authority. The near-unanimous rejection of the NPT by the Indian establishment, which is otherwise very conscious of international opinion, showed how dead the treaty already was.

The world has lost its trust in the five nuclear weapons states and now sees them as the NPT's primary violators.

From time to time, common sense has entered discussions on nuclear weapons. President Ronald Reagan said more categorically than any U.S. president that the world would be better off without nuclear weapons. Last year, with the NPT in its death throes and the growing threat of loose nuclear weapons falling into the hands of terrorists forefront in everyone's mind, former Secretary of State George Shultz, former Defense Secretary William Perry, former Secretary of State Henry Kissinger, and former Senator Sam Nunn warned in *The Wall Street Journal* that the world was "now on the precipice of a new and dangerous nuclear era." They argued, "Unless urgent new actions are taken, the U.S. soon will be compelled to enter a new nuclear era that will be more precarious, psychologically disorienting, and economically even more costly than was Cold War deterrence." But these calls may have come too late. The world has lost its trust in the five nuclear weapons states and now sees them as the NPT's primary violators rather than its custodians. Those states' private cynicism about their obligations to the NPT has become public knowledge.

Contrary to what the West wants the rest of the world to believe, the nuclear weapons states, especially the United States and Russia, which continue to maintain thousands of nuclear weapons, are the biggest source of nuclear proliferation. Mohamed ElBaradei, the director general of the International Atomic Energy Agency, warned in *The Economist* in 2003, "The very existence of nuclear weapons gives rise to the pursuit of them. They are seen as a source of global influence, and are valued for their perceived deterrent effect. And as long as some countries possess them (or are protected by them in alliances) and others do not, this asymmetry breeds chronic global insecurity." Despite the Cold War, the second half of the twentieth century seemed to be moving the world toward a more civilized order. As the twenty-first century unfurls, the world seems to be sliding backward.

Irresponsible Stakeholders

After leading the world toward a period of spectacular economic growth in the second half of the twentieth century by promoting global free trade, the West has recently been faltering in its global economic leadership. Believing that low trade barriers and increasing trade interdependence would result in higher standards of living for all, European and U.S. economists and policymakers pushed for global economic liberalization. As a result, global trade grew from seven percent of the world's GDP in 1940 to 30 percent in 2005.

But a seismic shift has taken place in Western attitudes since the end of the Cold War. Suddenly, the United States and Europe no longer have a vested interest in the success of the East Asian economies, which they see less as allies and more as competitors. That change in Western interests was reflected in the fact that the West provided little real help to East Asia during the Asian financial crisis of 1997–98. The entry of China into the global marketplace, especially after its admission to the World Trade Organization, has made a huge difference in both economic and psychological terms. Many Europeans have lost confidence in their ability to compete with the Asians. And many Americans have lost confidence in the virtues of competition.

There are some knotty issues that need to be resolved in the current global trade talks, but fundamentally the negotiations are stalled because the conviction of the Western "champions" of free trade that free trade is good has begun to waver. When Americans and Europeans start to perceive themselves as losers in international trade, they also lose their drive to push for further trade liberalization. Unfortunately, on this front at least, neither China nor India (nor Brazil nor South Africa nor any other major developing country) is ready to take over the West's mantle. China, for example, is afraid that any effort to seek leadership in this area will stoke U.S. fears that it is striving for global hegemony. Hence, China is lying low. So, too, are the United States and Europe. Hence, the trade talks are stalled. The end of the West's promotion of global trade liberalization could well mean the end of the most spectacular economic growth the world has ever seen. Few in the West seem to be reflecting on the consequences of walking away from one of the West's most successful policies, which is what it will be doing if it allows the Doha Round to fail.

At the same time that the Western governments are relinquishing their stewardship of the global economy, they are also failing to take the lead on battling global warming. The awarding of the Nobel Peace Prize to former U.S. Vice President Al Gore, a longtime environmentalist, and the UN's Intergovernmental Panel on Climate Change confirms there is international consensus that global warning is a real threat. The most assertive advocates for tackling this problem come from the U.S. and European scientific communities, but the greatest resistance to any effective action is coming from the U.S. government. This has left the rest of the world confused and puzzled. Most people believe that the greenhouse effect is caused mostly by the flow of current emissions. Current emissions do aggravate the problem, but the fundamental cause is the stock of emissions that has accumulated since the Industrial Revolution. Finding a just and equitable solution to the problem of greenhouse gas emissions must begin with assigning responsibility both for the current flow and for the stock of greenhouse gases already accumulated. And on both counts the Western nations should bear a greater burden.

The West has to learn to share power and responsibility for the management of global issues with the rest of the world.

When it comes to addressing any problem pertaining to the global commons, such as the environment, it seems only fair that the wealthier members of the international community should shoulder more responsibility. This is a natural principle of justice. It is also fair in this particular case given the developed countries' primary role in releasing harmful gases into the atmosphere. R. K. Pachauri, chair of the Intergovernmental Panel on Climate Change, argued last year, "China and India are certainly increasing their share, but they are not increasing their per capita emissions anywhere close to the levels that you have in the developed world." Since 1850, China has contributed less than 8 percent of the world's total emissions of carbon dioxide, whereas the United States is responsible for 29 percent and western Europe is responsible for 27 percent. Today, India's per capita greenhouse gas emissions are equivalent to only 4 percent of those of the United States and 12 percent of those of the European Union. Still, the Western governments are not clearly acknowledging their responsibilities and are allowing many of their citizens to believe that China and India are the fundamental obstacles to any solution to global warming.

Washington might become more responsible on this front if a Democratic president replaces Bush in 2009. But people in the West will have to make some real concessions if they are to reduce significantly their per capita share of global emissions. A cap-and-trade program may do the trick. Western countries will probably have to make economic sacrifices. One option might be, as the journalist Thomas Friedman has suggested, to impose a dollar-per-gallon tax on Americans' gasoline consumption. Gore has proposed a carbon tax. So far, however, few U.S. politicians have dared to make such suggestions publicly.

Temptations of the East

The Middle East, nuclear proliferation, stalled trade liberalization, and global warming are all challenges that the West is essentially failing to address. And this failure suggests that a systemic problem is emerging in the West's stewardship of the international order—one that Western minds are reluctant to analyze or confront openly. After having enjoyed centuries of global domination, the West has to learn to share power and responsibility for the management of global issues with the rest of the world. It has to forgo outdated organizations, such as the Organization for Economic Cooperation and Development, and outdated processes, such as the G-8, and deal with organizations and processes with a broader scope and broader representation. It was always unnatural for the 12 percent of the world population that lived in the West to enjoy so much global power. Understandably, the other 88 percent of the world population increasingly wants also to drive the bus of world history.

First and foremost, the West needs to acknowledge that sharing the power it has accumulated in global forums would serve its interests. Restructuring international institutions to reflect the current world order will be complicated by the absence of natural leaders to do the job. The West has become part of the problem, and the Asian countries are not yet ready to step in. On the other hand, the world does not need to invent any new principles to improve global governance; the concepts of domestic good governance can and should be applied to the international community. The Western principles of democracy, the rule of law, and social justice are among the world's best bets. The ancient virtues of partnership and pragmatism can complement them.

Democracy, the foundation of government in the West, is based on the premise that each human being in a society is an equal stakeholder in the domestic order. Thus, governments are selected on the basis of "one person, one vote." This has produced long-term stability and order in Western societies. In order to produce long-term stability and order worldwide, democracy should be the cornerstone of global society, and the planet's 6.6 billion inhabitants should become equal stakeholders. To inject the spirit of democracy into global governance and global decision-making, one must turn to institutions with universal representation, especially the UN. UN institutions such as the World Health Organization and the World Meteorological Organization enjoy widespread legitimacy because of their universal membership, which

means their decisions are generally accepted by all the countries of the world.

The problem today is that although many Western actors are willing to work with specialized UN agencies, they are reluctant to strengthen the UN's core institution, the UN General Assembly, from which all these specialized agencies come. The UN General Assembly is the most representative body on the planet, and yet many Western countries are deeply skeptical of it. They are right to point out its imperfections. But they overlook the fact that this imperfect assembly enjoys legitimacy in the eyes of the people of this imperfect world. Moreover, the General Assembly has at times shown more common sense and prudence than some of the most sophisticated Western democracies. Of course, it takes time to persuade all of the UN's members to march in the same direction, but consensus building is precisely what gives legitimacy to the result. Most countries in the world respect and abide by most UN decisions because they believe in the authority of the UN. Used well, the body can be a powerful vehicle for making critical decisions on global governance.

The world today is run not through the General Assembly but through the Security Council, which is effectively run by the five permanent member states. If this model were adopted in the United States, the U.S. Congress would be replaced by a selective council comprised of only the representatives from the country's five most powerful states. Would the populations of the other 45 states not deem any such proposal absurd? The West must cease its efforts to prolong its undemocratic management of the global order and find ways to effectively engage the majority of the world's population in global decision-making.

Another fundamental principle that should underpin the global order is the rule of law. This hallowed Western principle insists that no person, regardless of his or her status, is above the law. Ironically, while being exemplary in implementing the rule of law at home, the United States is a leading international outlaw in its refusal to recognize the constraints of international law. Many Americans live comfortably with this contradiction while expecting other countries to abide by widely accepted treaties. Americans react with horror when Iran tries to walk away from the NPT. Yet they are surprised that the world is equally shocked when Washington abandons a universally accepted treaty such as the Comprehensive Test Ban Treaty.

The Bush administration's decision to exempt the United States from the provisions of international law on human rights is even more damaging. For over half a century, since Eleanor Roosevelt led the fight for the adoption of the Universal Declaration of Human Rights, the United States was the global champion of human rights. This was the result of a strong ideological conviction that it was the United States' God-given duty to create a more civilized world. It also made for a good ideological weapon during the Cold War: the free United States was fighting the unfree Soviet Union. But the Bush administration has stunned the world by walking away from universally accepted human rights conventions, especially those on torture. And much as the U.S. electorate could not be expected to tolerate an attorney general who broke his own laws from time to time, how can the global body politic be expected to respect a custodian of international law that violates these very rules?

Finally, on social justice, Westerns nations have slackened. Social justice is the cornerstone of order and stability in modern Western societies and the rest of the world. People accept inequality as long as some kind of social safety net exists to help the dispossessed. Most western European governments took this principle to heart after World War II and introduced welfare provisions as a way to ward off Marxist revolutions seeking to create socialist societies. Today, many Westerners believe that they are spreading social justice globally with their massive foreign aid to the developing world. Indeed, each year, the members of the Organization for Economic Cooperation and Development, according to the organization's own estimates, give approximately $104 billion to the developing world. But the story of Western aid to the developing world is essentially a myth. Western countries have put significant amounts of money into their overseas development assistance budgets, but these funds' primary purpose is to serve the immediate and short-term security and national interests of the donors rather than the long-term interests of the recipients.

Some Asian countries are now ready to join the West in becoming responsible custodians of the global order.

The experience of Asia shows that where Western aid has failed to do the job, domestic good governance can succeed. This is likely to be Asia's greatest contribution to world history. The success of Asia will inspire other societies on different continents to emulate it. In addition, Asia's march to modernity can help produce a more stable world order. Some Asian countries are now ready to join the West in becoming responsible custodians of the global order; as the biggest beneficiaries of the current system, they have powerful incentives to do so. The West is not welcoming Asia's progress, and its short-term interests in preserving its privileged position in various global institutions are trumping its long-term interests in creating a more just and stable world order. Unfortunately, the West has gone from being the world's primary problem solver to being its single biggest liability.

Critical Thinking

1. According to Kishore Mahbubani, what is the fundamental flaw in the West's strategic thinking?

2. What are the reasons, according to Mahbubani, for the West's declining influence?

3. Does Mahbubani's argument support or contradict the central arguments of articles 1 and 4?

KISHORE MAHBUBANI is Dean of the Lee Kuan Yew School of Public Policy at the National University of Singapore. This essay is adapted from his latest book, *The New Asian Hemisphere: The Irresistible Shift of Global Power to the East* (Public Affairs, 2008).

From *Foreign Affairs*, May/June 2008, pp. 111–124. Copyright © 2008 by Council on Foreign Relations, Inc. Reprinted by permission of Foreign Affairs. www.ForeignAffairs.com

Bolivia and Its Lithium

Can the "Gold of the 21st Century" help lift a nation out of poverty?

REBECCA HOLLENDER AND JIM SHULTZ

Executive Summary

The resource curse refers to the paradox that countries and regions with an abundance of natural resources, especially minerals and fuels, tend to have less economic growth and worse development outcomes than countries with fewer natural resources.

Bolivia has a long history with that curse, dating back to the theft of its sliver at the hands of the Spanish during the colonial era. Today Bolivia seeks to break that curse with what some call "the gold of the 21st century": lithium. This report examines Bolivia's prospects for doing so.

I. Lithium—The Super Hero of Metals

Every time we pick up a cell phone or iPod, look at our watch, or plug-in a laptop we are relying on batteries that contain lithium. It is also used in ceramics and glass production, bi-polar medication, air conditioners, lubricants, nuclear weaponry, and other products. The lightest metal on Earth, lithium is mined from many sources, but most cheaply from underground brines like those found in abundance under Bolivia's vast Salar de Uyuni.

Today the global focus on lithium is about its potential as a key ingredient in a new generation of electric cars batteries. Powerful global players are investing billions of dollars in lithium's future. Some predictions speculate that lithium car battery sales could jump from $100 million per year to $103 billion per year in the next 2 decades. If so, the countries that possess lithium are poised to become much bigger players in the global economy.

Despite the growing enthusiasm about lithium's future, there are also real doubts as well. The process for transforming lithium into its commercially valuable form, lithium carbonate, is complex and expensive. The electric vehicle batteries currently being developed with lithium are still too large and heavy, and too slow to charge. The batteries are so expensive that they put the cost of electric cars beyond the reach of most consumers. Lithium batteries also have a record of catching fire. So while lithium car batteries might become a massive global market, they could also turn out to be the energy equivalent of the 8-track tape.

II. The Race for Bolivia's Lithium

Based even on conservative estimates, Bolivia's lithium reserves are the largest in the world. The Salar de Uyuni, a 10,000 square kilometer (3,860 square miles) expanse of salt-embedded minerals, located in Bolivia's department of Southwest Potosí, is ground zero for Bolivia's lithium dreams.

Foreign corporations and governments alike are lining up to court a Bolivian government intent on getting the best deal possible for its people. Among the major players are two Japanese giants, Mitsubishi and Sumitomo, the latter of which already has a stake in the controversial San Cristobal Mine known for contaminating the same region. The French electric vehicle manufacturer, Bolloré, is also courting the Morales government, as are the governments of South Korea, Brazil, and Iran.

The Bolivian government has sketched out a general plan for the various phases of its lithium ambitions, but many of the details of how all this will be done have yet to be defined. To get its feet wet in the technical and economic waters of lithium, the government of Bolivia has invested $5.7 million in the development of a "pilot plant" at the edge of the Salar de Uyuni. The plant is intended to test drive the steps in getting the lithium-rich brine out from under the Salar's crust and separating it into its distinct (and marketable) parts. Based on the experience of this pilot plant, the government aims to then construct a much larger industrial-scale plant, capable of producing up to 30,000 to 40,000 metric tons of lithium carbonate per year. This will be followed by a third phase to produce marketable lithium compounds, which the government plans to undertake in partnership with foreign investors.

To get help in meeting the formidable challenges it faces, the government has assembled a Scientific Advisory Committee (Scientific Research Committee for the Industrialization of the Evaporitic Resources of Bolivia) comprised of experts from universities, private companies, and governments, to give free, and mutually beneficial, advice.

III. The Challenges Ahead on Bolivia's Lithium Highway

At heart, Bolivia's lithium ambitions are simple: to lift a people out of poverty by squeezing the maximum benefit possible from a natural resource on the cutting edge of global markets. But between where Bolivia sits today and where it aims to go on its lithium highway there are major challenges that it will need to face:

Getting the Economics Right

Bolivia's dreams of lithium wealth involve hitting a complicated moving target. The electric car battery market looks like the most lucrative for lithium development, and is the one the Morales government says it's aiming for (Morales also claims that Bolivia will produce electric vehicles), but how big that market will be, and when it will peak, is still just a guessing game. Bolivia could aim for more traditional lithium markets, such as glass and ceramics, but they aren't nearly so potentially profitable. A middle option would be established types of lithium batteries for products such as watches, cell phones, iPods, laptops and other electronic gadgets.

How much will it cost to build a lithium battery industry in Bolivia? That number is one of the most elusive pieces of information in the picture. If Bolivia kicks into full industrial mode the budget would be $200 million or higher just for the main plant. But that still doesn't include massive additional investments in supporting chemical industries and huge infrastructure development in a region where today even keeping the lights on is a technological challenge. One Bolivian official has placed the potential cost at as high as $1 billion. Because of this, Bolivia is looking for serious partnerships with investors, an approach that some local community groups do not support.

The fact that the government might suddenly have substantial new revenues from lithium is also no guarantee that the Bolivian people will end up any better off. Those revenues could easily become a magnet for corruption, waste and favoritism and there will be a constant tension between the demand to use the funds for public goods and reinvesting them into state-controlled lithium production.

Environmental Impacts

Lost in the great Bolivian lithium race is a set of very deep and real environmental concerns. In the name of providing cleaner cars to the wealthy countries of the north, Bolivia's beautiful and rare Salar could end up an environmental wasteland. The adequacy of Bolivia's environmental strategy for lithium development in Southwest Potosí is doubted by several well-regarded Bolivian environmental organizations.

One major problem that lithium development could cause is a major water crisis. The region already suffers from a serious water shortage, impacting quinoa farmers, llama herders, the region's vital tourism industry, and drinking water sources. While Bolivian officials contend that the lithium project's water requirements will be minimal, their estimates are based on very limited and incomplete information.

Contamination of the air, water and soil is also a major concern. Large quantities of toxic chemicals will be needed to process the predicted 30,000 to 40,000 tons of lithium per year that the project expects to mine. The escape of such chemicals via leaching, spills, or air emissions is a danger that threatens the communities and the ecosystem as a whole. Reports from Chile's Salar de Atacama describe a landscape scarred by mountains of discarded salt and huge canals filled with blue chemically contaminated water.

Bolivian officials have dismissed those risks, and the government system in place to protect the environment is inadequate at best. Public institutions, such as Bolivia's Ministry of the Environment and Water, which are responsible for ensuring compliance with environmental requirements, clearly lack the capacity or authority to intervene in an effective way.

The Threat to Communities

How do the people and communities who live in Southwest Potosí feel about their homeland becoming the site of what could soon become one of the biggest industrial projects their nation has ever built? To be sure, many groups in the region have long supported lithium development, seeing it as a vital opportunity for increased income and development. But there are deep concerns as well.

Quinoa producers and tourism operators have expressed concern about supposed benefits that the Bolivian government has promised from lithium, saying that the benefits are irrelevant to local needs and could easily damage the two industries that are thriving in the region—agriculture and tourism. But Bolivia's laws that guarantee community involvement in planning are as weak as its environmental protections. While some local organizations—especially ones that actively support Evo Morales' political party (MAS)—have been engaged, others say they have not.

The Capacity of the Bolivian Government to Manage the Program

Finally, there are concerns about the chronic problems faced by the Bolivian government to manage such an ambitious program—problems that pre-date President Morales. To pull off its lithium ambitions, Bolivia will need highly trained and qualified experts, in the technical and scientific aspects of lithium, in business management and economics, and in social and environmental impacts. And these experts need to be solely accountable to the Bolivian people, not to foreign governments or corporations.

IV. Conclusion—Can Bolivia Beat the Resource Curse?

Whether these challenges are surmountable for the people of Bolivia and their leaders is an open debate. To be certain, there is real potential here. The demand for lithium is clearly on the rise, and with the possibility in the future of a very big rise. Bolivia is indeed sitting on the world's largest supply of lithium and it is being courted by some serious players. And importantly, all this is happening just as Bolivia has a government that has committed itself to a different way of doing resource business.

In practical terms, the government is also doing some important things right, such as beginning with a pilot effort to test the technological and economic waters. But there are many things that can go badly wrong on the lithium road ahead. In the uphill battle to make Bolivia's lithium dreams a reality, clearly the first step is to acknowledge and understand the economic, environmental, social, and capacity challenges.

What Bolivia is trying to do is hard—very hard. It is trying to break a curse—the paradox of plenty—that few impoverished nations escape. Its effort to escape that curse is extremely important, which is why so much of the world is watching. It is an experiment that is economic, social, political, technological and practical all at the same time. The fate of its success lies in the hands of the Bolivian people and in their ability to hold their leaders accountable, both for their own benefit and the planet's.

Critical Thinking

1. Why has lithium become an important raw material?

2. What do the authors mean by a "development paradox"?

3. Is Bolivia's approach to the development of its lithium reserves similar to Sachs or Easterly's development approach?

Not Your Father's Latin America

Its troubles continue, but the region has made real progress.

DUNCAN CURRIE

Hugo Chávez likes to boast that history is on his side. During a recent broadcast of his talk show, *Aló Presidente,* the Venezuelan leader informed Barack Obama that "the process of change in Latin America is not going to stop," even if the U.S. deploys naval fleets and fighter planes. It's easy to dismiss such rhetoric as typical Chávez bluster. But is there a nugget of truth in it? Is Venezuela's illiberal "Bolivarian revolution" really sweeping Latin America?

The short answer is no. The longer answer is that, while various small countries have embraced Chávez-style populism, most of the region's large economic powers have not. In general, Latin American officials have greatly improved their fiscal and monetary policies, making their economies less sensitive to external shocks. Though Latin America has not escaped the global recession and is still plagued by many of its perennial troubles—such as widespread corruption, high levels of violent crime, ethnic fissures, and yawning inequality—its recent progress offers grounds for optimism.

We must appreciate just how far Latin America has come. From the late 1970s through the early 2000s, the region went through a seemingly endless series of economic and financial implosions. Meanwhile, frequent military coups and prolonged civil wars stifled its movement toward liberal democracy.

Even after free elections and constitutional government became the norm, inflation remained a scourge, and currency meltdowns continued to wreak havoc. The 2001–02 Argentine financial crisis sparked a full-blown economic collapse and a massive debt default, which fueled severe turmoil in neighboring countries. In mid-2002, the Bush administration endorsed a $30 billion International Monetary Fund bailout for Brazil (which was suffering from its own domestic woes) and dispatched a $1.5 billion Treasury loan to Uruguay. The U.S. took a stemer line on Argentina but eventually supported a new IMF loan package after Argentine economy minister Roberto Lavagna implemented some prudent reforms that mitigated the crisis.

As the global economy recovered, so did Latin America's. Between 2002 and 2008, the region enjoyed its most robust expansion in decades. Unlike the growth spurt during the 1990s, this one led to substantial poverty reduction. According to World Bank estimates, the poverty rate in Latin America and the Caribbean—that is, the share of the population living on less than $4 a day (in purchasing-power-parity terms)—fell from 45.4 percent in 2002 to 32.5 percent in 2008. Over that same period, the rate of extreme poverty (the portion living on less than $2 a day) dropped from 21.5 percent to 13.1 percent.

Had Latin America just gotten lucky? After all, its anti-poverty gains occurred during an era of abundant liquidity, high commodity prices, and booming global trade. But that wasn't the whole story: Latin America also strengthened its fundamentals, taming inflation and accumulating foreign-exchange reserves while slashing its external debt. An April 2008 Inter-American Development Bank study pointed to lingering vulnerabilities but affirmed that economic management in the region had "noticeably improved." More recently, a May 2009 IMF survey said that many Latin American countries "have made strides in strengthening fiscal positions and public debt structures, solidifying financial systems and their regulation, anchoring inflation expectations, and building more credible policy frameworks."

Latin America's experience during the current global slump has underscored these achievements. The downturn has been painful (in some countries, deeply painful) but not cataclysmic. Previous recessions in Latin America triggered banking and currency disasters. Not this one. The region has demonstrated that it is much more resilient now than it was in the past. Alberto Ramos, senior Latin America economist at Goldman Sachs, says the difference is "night and day."

Perhaps the most pleasant surprise of recent Latin American history has been the performance of Brazilian president Luiz. Inácio Lula da Silva, a former union boss whose 2002 election spooked the investment community. Lula's predecessor, Fernando Henrique Cardoso, was a more conservative social democrat who had helped devise and manage the anti-inflationary "Plano Real" during his tenures as Brazilian finance minister (1993–94) and president (1995–2003). As former Federal Reserve chairman Alan Greenspan writes in *The Age of Turbulence,* the Plano Real "successfully brought the nation's roaring inflation to a halt after it had surged more than 5,000 percent during the twelve months between mid-1993 and mid-1994."

Lula, a member of the left-wing Workers' Party and a long-time friend of Cuban dictator Fidel Castro, had fiercely opposed the Plano Real. He had also spent years attacking free-market economics and calling for major social changes. How would he govern as president? "To the surprise of most, myself included," writes Greenspan, "he has largely followed the sensible policies embodied in the Plano Real." Indeed, there has been a great deal of continuity between the Cardoso and Lula administrations. Despite being dogged by assorted scandals, Lula has acquired enormous popularity and international stature.

He is part of a bigger trend: Throughout Latin America, there is a growing center-left political class that broadly agrees with conservatives about the basic tenets of good economic stewardship. "This is a very positive development for the region," says economist Luis Oganes, head of Latin America research at J. P. Morgan. In a 2007 *New Republic* article, foreign-affairs scholar Walter Russell Mcad wrote that "Latin America is now beginning to acquire something it has sorely lacked: a left-of-center political leadership able to combine its mission of serving the poor with a firm commitment to currency stability, the rule of law, and the development of a favorable business climate."

This can be seen in countries such as Chile, Uruguay, and Peru. The Chilean economy remains the most dynamic in Latin America. Since 1990, it has been piloted by the center-left Concertación coalition, which inherited a slew of free-market reforms from the Pinochet dictatorship. Successive Concentación governments "kept the broad thrust of the dictatorship's economic policies, deepened some of them and reformed others," writes journalist Michael Reid in *Forgotten Continent.* "That bestowed democratic legitimacy on the 'Chilean model.'" During the recent commodity boom, Chile saved a hefty chunk of its copper windfall. As the *Wall Street Journal* reports, this enabled it to craft "one of the largest stimulus packages in the world relative to the size of its economy."

In Uruguay, the center-left administration of Pres. Tabaré Vázquez has promoted a solid economic agenda and completed a "trade and investment framework agreement" with the United States. In Peru, Pres. Alan García has effectively repudiated his earlier stint as chief executive in the late 1980s, when he espoused economic populism and unleashed hyper-inflation. Since returning to the presidency in 2006, Garcia has governed as a born-again neoliberal.

His 2006 election campaign reflected a larger ideological struggle. García defeated Ollanta Humala, a radical populist favored by Chávez, after telling voters to choose "between Hugo Chávez and Peru." That same year, conservative Felipe Calderón won a razor-thin victory over leftist Andrés Manuel López Obrador to capture the Mexican presidency. Just as García did in Peru, Calderòn linked his opponent to Chávez. It proved a smart strategy, as Calderón came from behind to triumph.

All of these countries—Brazil, Chile, Uruguay, Peru, and Mexico—have rejected *Chavismo.* All five have inflation-targeting central banks. So does Colombia, which has made greater progress over the past half-decade than any other country in the hemisphere. Pres. Álvaro Uribe took office in 2002 amid a horrendous guerrilla war that threatened to turn Colombia into a failed state. Since then, the government has reclaimed Bogotá, Medellín, and other cities from left-wing rebels; demobilized thousands of right-wing paramilitaries; dramatically reduced violence; and fostered a more attractive business environment. Prior to the recession, Colombia's GDP was growing at its fastest rate since the 1970s. National police data show that in 2008, the country had 44 percent fewer homicides and 75 percent fewer massacres than it did in 2002.

Yet the number of massacres increased slightly from 2007 to 2008, and new scandals have emerged concerning extrajudicial killings by the army. Uribe helped expose paramilitary infiltration of the political system, but the subsequent discoveries have implicated many of his supporters. As for the drug war, an October 2008 Government Accountability Office report said that Plan Colombia, the vast U.S. aid package begun under President Clinton, had "not fully achieved" its drug-reduction goals but had nonetheless contributed to "major security advances." Uribe is still immensely popular, though he has raised eyebrows by musing about a third term in office. (His current term expires in 2010.) Colombian lawmakers already amended their constitution to let him run for a second term in 2006.

It would be the height of moral confusion to associate Uribe, a staunch democrat, with Latin America's populist rabble. But revising constitutions to extend or abolish term limits is the preferred strategy of Chávez and his ilk. That's what ousted Honduran president Manuel Zelaya was trying to do, via an illegal "referendum," before the supreme court and the military intervened.

His removal trimmed the ranks of Chávez allies. In 2008, Honduras had joined the "Bolivarian Alternative for the Americas," a Chávez-led trade group whose members now include Venezuela, Cuba, Bolivia, Nicaragua, Ecuador, and a few tiny Caribbean nations. Heavily dependent on tourism, the impoverished Caribbean islands are especially susceptible to Chávez's petro-diplomacy. The governments of Bolivia, Nicaragua, and Ecuador feel an ideological attachment to Venezuela. All of them have, to varying degrees, embraced illiberal populism. So has Argentina, where Pres. Cristina Kirchner nationalized the private-pension system late last year.

Though Venezuela, Argentina, and Ecuador posted impressive growth rates when commodity prices were booming, they are now dealing with the consequences of reckless policy decisions. The Kirchner government suffered a crushing setback in Argentina's June 28 congressional elections. "There was definitely a shift to the right in Argentina," says Oganes. In Venezuela, unfortunately, Chávez won a referendum on scrapping term limits this past February, and he has intensified his attacks on independent media outlets and opposition politicians. Chávez is also lending full-throated support to Zelaya as the deposed Honduran leader seeks to reclaim his former office.

Beyond the unrest in Honduras, Central America faces a raft of economic and security challenges. Costa Rica and Panama remain its most stable and prosperous countries. The latter is now led by a conservative supermarket baron named Ricardo Martinelli. El Salvador also has a new president, Mauricio Funes, who represents the FMLN, a former leftist guerrilla outfit turned political party. Funes cites Lula as his model and "has filled the cabinet mostly with moderates," says Michael Shifter, a vice president at the Inter-American Dialogue. But it is unclear whether Funes can genuinely transform the FMLN and curb soaring crime. In neighboring Guatemala, Pres. Álvaro Colom has been hobbled by a sensational murder scandal at a time when his country is being over-whelmed by drug violence.

Meanwhile, such violence continues to generate grisly headlines in Mexico. It has exacerbated a nasty recession (the worst in Latin America), as has the swine-flu panic. President Calderón deserves credit for tackling the narco-gangs with military force. Though his anti-crime campaign is still widely popular, his party got thrashed in Mexico's July 5 congressional elections. That makes it even less likely that Calderón will be able to undertake the tax, energy, and labor-market reforms necessary to boost his country's long-term economic performance.

"To change Mexico, you really need an extraordinary leader," says economist Rafael Amiel, regional managing director for Latin America at IHS Global Insight. "I'm more hopeful about Brazil than Mexico." Like other Latin American countries, both Brazil and Mexico require deep structural changes in order to realize their full growth potential. "The Latin American experience has laid bare the fact that private ownership and fiscal prudence yield only limited benefits in a regime of overbearing taxation and regulation," writes Harvard economist Andrei Shleifer.

While the ongoing recession has aggravated social tensions and reversed some of the region's anti-poverty gains, Latin America's recent record is one of significant progress. "Many countries are on the right track," says Amiel. But a smaller cluster—the Chávez bloc—is clearly on the wrong track. As Shifter puts it, "We have different Latin Americas, and they're moving in very different directions."

Critical Thinking

1. Describe the economic progress made in Latin America.

2. How does this article complement or contradict the point of view of articles 1, 18 and 24?

More Aid Is Not the Answer

"Most analysts on the continent do not share donor nations' optimism that a big push in aid will make a big difference in the lives of poor Africans."

JONATHAN GLENNIE

Africa needs help—of this there should be no doubt. Some African countries in the past decade saw encouragingly strong growth in gross domestic product (GDP), and this can be an important part of poverty reduction. Yet hopes that the region would be somewhat immune to the recent global financial crisis have proved unfounded, and the continent remains by far the world's poorest.

In the past two years, not only has global demand for African commodity exports shrunk (except in China), but the region's financial architecture has turned out to be not as independent from the rest of the world as had been supposed. And while Africa receives relatively little foreign investment compared to other parts of the world, even that has fallen significantly.

So Africa does need aid. The question is, what kind of aid? The simple (and simplistic) calculation at the heart of the developed world's present attitude toward Africa is this: Sub-Saharan Africa is poor; if rich countries send it more money, it will be less poor, and people living in poverty will be better off.

The theory seems both logical and fair. More aid should mean less poverty, more schools and hospitals, fewer children dying of preventable diseases, and more roads and infrastructure to support developing economies. But, unfortunately, it is not that simple. Official aid to Africa (as distinct from private charity) has often meant more poverty, more hungry people, worse basic services for poor people, and increased damage to already precarious democratic institutions.

For African nations, along with other developing countries, the recent financial crisis and the ongoing global downturn present an opportunity to emerge from a vicious cycle of aid dependency and lack of accountability, and to move toward a virtuous circle of accountability and independence. The many options and decisions regarding aid currently on the international community's and African nations' table should be judged in this light. And they should be assessed with the understanding that what matters are not just economic consequences, but also shifts in power and accountability.

The New Aid Era

According to the World Bank, developing countries in 2010 face a financing shortfall of up to $700 billion, as a consequence of falling export receipts, remittances, and foreign investment. Aid has been the standard response to cash shortages in the past and, predictably, it is again one of the central issues under debate. Pressure has mounted both to reduce aid (as donor governments seek to balance their budgets and focus on national priorities) and to increase aid (to help poor countries that, according to the accepted wisdom, are not responsible for the global crisis yet are suffering its consequences).

As donor governments look for ways to cut expenditures on non-priority activities, some aid campaigners are shifting away from calling for a doubling of aid to Africa, instead trying to ensure that assistance at least does not tail off. But to continue to focus attention on the amount of aid provided would be both to ignore mistakes of the past and to miss opportunities that the present offers.

Aid to Africa has risen year on year since the turn of the millennium, though ambitious targets set by donors have not been reached. Official data show development aid to Africa, depending on which figures you use, either doubling or almost tripling since 2000, with predictions of more increases in years to come. As Angel Gurría, the secretary general of the Organization for Economic Cooperation and Development, has observed, "We are talking here about an increase in official development assistance of a magnitude and in a time frame that has never been attempted before in the history of the aid effort."

Underpinning the impressive numbers are influential studies published in the past few years (such as a 2005 report on the United Nations' Millennium Project, directed by the globe-trotting American economist Jeffrey Sachs, and a 2005 report by the Commission for Africa, chaired by then–Prime Minister Tony Blair of Britain) that provide the theoretical and evidentiary basis for this new era of aid. These reports buttress the aid optimism that is now the political consensus in donor countries, and they seek to turn back a tide of literature that, beginning in the 1990s, has questioned the impact of aid on poverty reduction.

But most analysts on the continent do not share donor nations' optimism that a big push in aid will make a big difference in the lives of poor Africans. It is hard to find a single African. non-governmental organization that is actively campaigning for aid increases, while many explicitly reject the idea that huge increases in assistance are the way to achieve growth and development.

It is hard to find a single African nongovernmental organization that is actively campaigning for aid increases.

In a 2005 literature review, Moses Isooba of Uganda's Community Development Resource Network found that "a majority of civil society actors in Africa see aid as a fundamental cause of Africa's deepening poverty." He went on to acknowledge that foreign assistance can make "a lasting difference in helping people to lift themselves out of poverty," but he called for a radical rethinking regarding the purpose and nature of aid giving. Charles Lwanga-Ntale of Development Research and Training, another Ugandan NGO, has observed "almost unanimous pessimism among African civil society and academia about the unworkable nature of aid, given the way in which it is structured and delivered."

According to Siapha Kamara of the Social Enterprise Development Foundation of West Africa: "Official Africa tends to be more enthusiastic about the anticipated increase in international aid than civil society. . . . The more African governments are dependent on international aid, the less ordinary citizens such as farmers, workers, teachers, or nurses have a meaningful say in politics and economic policies."

Good, Bad, Ugly

Why should so many experts in Africa question the good that aid is doing their countries? Because, while most people in rich countries consider aid to be a simple act of generosity, Africans understand it is far more complex.

To get a clearer picture of what is happening, it helps to distinguish among the various effects of foreign aid in Africa. One category is direct impacts. These are easiest to measure, and they are the ones about which we hear the most in the media—how many people have been vaccinated, how many schools have been built, and so on. Direct impacts also include less publicized and often harmful side effects such as, for example, the displacement of people by large projects like dams or mines.

A second type of impact is indirect macroeconomic consequences. Large inflows of foreign money affect prices and incentives, and the effects can be damaging to poor people if the inflows are not managed well. For example, increases in aid to Tanzania in the late 1990s led to inflation, which in turn led authorities to tighten credit, which meant private firms found it harder to expand. The syndrome that economists call Dutch Disease is a potentially serious problem for African aid recipients. When a country's exchange rate is allowed to fluctuate, large aid inflows strengthen the national currency, which makes exports less competitive and imports cheaper. As a result, people depending on export industries suffer, as do domestic producers that compete with imports.

Constituting a third and highly controversial category are the impacts of aid conditionality. Official development assistance provided by multilateral institutions and foreign governments often comes with conditions attached, and these in effect dictate policy making. These policy prescriptions have not always been helpful. For example, international demands during economic downturns for reduced deficits and increased interest rates have reflected the policies that many developed countries, with the sovereignty to make their own decisions, typically avoid.

But even more problematic than the policies promoted by donors is a fourth impact of aid—its effect on the relationship between governments and the governed. It is generally agreed that African governments' shortcomings in accountability and effectiveness over recent decades have been a major factor in the region's low growth and insignificant poverty reduction. What is less discussed, but is becoming increasingly clear, is that dependency on aid from foreign donors has undermined development of the basic institutions needed to govern and the vital link of accountability between state and citizen.

In Mali, a recent study by Isaline Bergamaschi found that, as donors' influence over policy has grown, the government's will and capacity to take the lead and manage the aid relationship has declined. "If the current political situation seems characterized by a certain degree of inertia, a lack of development strategy, weak capacities, and compliance with donors," wrote Bergamaschi, "it can only be understood as the result of the weakening of the state and donor entanglement in national institutions and politics, and several decades of aid dependence." Likewise, observers have described Ghana's federal budget as a façade, aimed at satisfying aid donors rather than serving as a genuine and thought-through spending plan.

The effect of such dependency has been to retard African civic development in fundamental and long-lasting ways. It is what Kamara was referring to when he talked about ordinary people not having a meaningful say in decisions about how their countries are run.

Optimists and Pessimists

In response to gradually building pressure around the globe for more aid, the Group of Eight industrial nations in July 2005 met in Scotland and released a communiqué promising substantially more assistance, though not all that was being demanded. On top of an agreement to forgive large amounts of debt, the G-8 members pledged $50 billion (some of it previously announced) in aid to developing nations by 2010, of which half would go to Africa.

A spokesman for Oxfam International, a leading British NGO, commented at the time that "The G-8's aid increase could save the lives of 5 million children by 2010—but 50 million children's lives will still be lost because the G-8 didn't go as far as they should have done. If the $50 billion increase had kicked in immediately, it could have lifted 300 million people out of poverty in the next five years."

This kind of claim is common on the aid campaigning circuit. Campaigners need to make clear statements about the impacts of policies. But even allowing for the fact that mega-calculations will always be more than slightly arbitrary, yet are still important to convey the magnitude of what is at stake, this statement was highly misleading. Why? Because it was made on the basis of a very lop-sided analysis, which looks only at the most direct and beneficial outcomes of aid.

If one considers only the positive column on the balance sheet, ignoring all the damaging consequences of aid, it is certainly possible that, if spent well, aid money could have the kinds of benefits alluded to. Aid spent well can put children through school, build infrastructure, and save lives.

But what about all the other impacts? What about the possibly harmful effects on exchange rates and prices, with the serious consequences these might have on workers and consumers? What about the long-term consequences of consistently immature and unaccountable state institutions? Where are these impacts taken into account when we calculate millions of lives saved per billions of aid dollars spent?

At the other extreme in debates about aid to Africa are the aid pessimists. The economist Dambisa Moyo is currently the most notable of these, having attracted wide attention with her 2009 book *Dead Aid: Why Aid Is Not Working and How There Is Another Way for Africa.* Moyo's critique of aid dependency is valid. She is right about the harm done to the development of effective and accountable governance in Africa by high levels of government-to-government aid. But hers is not a serious analytical study. It is an anti-aid polemic of a sort common in the conservative media of the United States, where the only facts cited are ones that bolster a case, and where exaggeration is considered par for the course.

Rather than accepting simplistic notions—that more aid equals less poverty, or that aid only and always increases poverty—we need to look at the evidence. All the evidence. In contrast to aid optimists and aid pessimists, who selectively use evidence either to support or to dismiss aid, we need to recognize that the impacts of aid are complex. Only when we assess these effects dispassionately and systematically can we have any real expectation of making a positive and sustained impact on human rights, development, and poverty reduction in Africa.

Aid Realism

This approach can be termed aid realism. Aid realism means not getting swept away by the ethical clamor to "do something" when a proper analysis shows that what is being done is ineffective or harmful. And it means not bowing to an ideological anti-aid position in the face of the rights and urgent needs of millions of people. It means carefully analyzing the overall impact of foreign aid in African nations—first, to see how aid in itself can be improved, and, second, to question its importance in relation to other policies and factors that influence development and poverty reduction in the region.

Such an analysis emphatically does not lead to the conclusion that the West should leave Africa alone. African civil society, while heavily critical of foreign assistance, is not sitting on its haunches in despair, and neither should anyone else. There are many positive measures that rich countries should take right now to help Africans reduce poverty and improve human rights.

For example, far more money flows out of the continent each year than arrives there in aid, but where are the campaign to stem illegal capital flows via tax havens? Likewise, rich countries need to overhaul rules on international property rights and foreign investment. They should act on climate change, and invest more in transferable technology. They should better regulate an arms trade that causes turmoil in Africa. They should do many things they are not doing now.

In fact, it will be almost impossible for African states to reduce their reliance on aid without the international community's adopting a range of supporting measures. If the first reason to stop campaigning for aid increases is that aid may be doing more harm than good in some countries, the second is that all the emphasis on aid is obscuring more important policies that the West should be adopting to help Africans escape poverty.

The dominance of aid in the West's thinking about Africa is one of the reasons that other, more important, actions are not taken. Rich-country leaders are not feeling enough political pressure to make the important changes. Aid is easier—never mind all the problems it brings with it—and it benefits donors.

After all, geopolitical considerations, not analyses of poverty, have governed most donor choices about aid spending. Assistance to Africa swelled during the cold war and then declined in the 1990s, when poverty on the continent was increasing sharply. Now, in the context of a global war on terrorism, donor nations—including particularly the United States—again want to use aid to influence the politics of other countries. But aid is not always good for the recipient nations' citizens and institutions.

Decades of Dependency

Dependency is the one issue that, more than any other, separates the current period from previous episodes of aid enthusiasm. Aid dependency can be measured by looking at aid as a percentage of a recipient country's GDP, and seeing how that ratio changes over time. When official development assistance started in the 1960s, it accounted for 2.3 percent of African GDP, similar to the proportion in South Asia (home to large aid recipients like India and Bangladesh).

What has happened since is instructive. While aid to South Asia has steadily declined, and now makes up around 1 per cent of GDP, aid to Africa has trended the other way, skyrocketing in the 1980s and hardly falling since. It now averages around 9 percent of GDP across Africa (excluding South Africa and Nigeria), with many countries receiving much more than that.

Since the turn of the millennium, when this new era of aid began, aid increases have been directed not to countries hoping for a boost to help them out of short-term trouble, but to countries now severely dependent on aid. When we look at aid levels in the rest of the developing world, the contrast is stark. Only a handful of countries scattered elsewhere across the globe, such as Nicaragua and Haiti and the small islands of Oceania, come close to the type of aid dependence seen in Africa. Vietnam, which has seen aid rise significantly since the 1980s, still relies on it for only 4 percent or less of its GDP. Aid to poor countries in the Americas has progressively shrunk from 0.7 percent of GDP in the 1960s to under 0.3 percent today.

It is not that no other countries have ever received large amounts of aid before. The key factor is that, in Africa, very high aid receipts have now lasted for decades and have become the norm. Never has any group of countries been so dependent on foreign aid for their basic functioning, for so long. There is a big difference between receiving aid as a welcome support and needing it as a fundamental part of the national budget.

Very high aid receipts have now lasted for decades and have become the norm.

Dependence on foreign governments for financial assistance has undermined development efforts in Africa, and it will continue to do so despite the modern (and laudable) emphasis on "good governance" and "country ownership." Although aid dependency has drawn considerable comment both in Africa and among the rich nations, the fretting has had virtually no impact on donor policy. Instead, the trend continues—and it will get worse if promised aid increases actually do kick in. While the rest of the world (with some exceptions) appears to be moving on from aid, Africa is getting more and more aid-dependent.

Government-to-government aid will always have an important supporting role, a role it has played with occasional success over the years. In some countries, depending on their economic and political contexts, aid increases may be appropriate and helpful. But most countries in Africa, rather than seeking more aid, should be reducing the amount they accept. Why? Because when the whole range of aid's impacts are taken into account, it becomes clear that aid at present levels is hindering rather than helping many countries' development prospects.

Less Aid, More Help

The biggest headline from the London Group of 20 Summit in 2009 was, as usual, a huge pledge of aid (over $1 trillion, much of it double-counted) to help poor countries. And yet, for all the efforts put into "aid effectiveness," the undermining of institutions continues to be endemic in the aid relationship. A course needs to be set to reduce, rather than entrench, aid dependency. In this regard, in response to the recent global crisis, an overhaul of the global financial system would provide a unique opportunity to undo measures that until now have prevented developing countries from maximizing their development resources.

One issue coming under increasing scrutiny, for example, is the complex global web of tax havens that serves no serious purpose for rich nations or poor, but is responsible for allowing dodgy deals, theft, and other crimes to abound. Poor African countries lose far more every year through capital flight to tax havens than they receive in aid. Plugging this leak, cracking down on corruption, and building better national financial systems could make more credit available to small and medium-sized businesses—and would also open an avenue toward reduced dependence on aid. The likelihood of such reforms has grown since the global financial crisis erupted.

Other measures that have been considered or adopted at a range of global meetings in 2009 and 2010 could have repercussions for decades to come, as the financial architecture is redrawn, and crucial issues that were previously considered off the table are suddenly on it. Reform of financial institutions such as the International Monetary Fund has been discussed for decades, but the political will to do something may finally emerge as a result of the crisis.

Aid will certainly continue to play a role in this new context, and some African countries could benefit from aid increases. Botswana is one example. It received high levels of assistance in the 1960s and 1970s (averaging 17 percent of GDP), and during that period its growth performance exceeded the growth rates of Hong Kong, Taiwan, Malaysia, and Thailand. In contrast to almost all other African countries, aid to Botswana has steadily declined over the decades. Today it receives negligible levels of assistance. Yet its economic boom has been brought to a tragic end by an AIDS pandemic that slashed life expectancy from 56 years to 35 in a decade. Botswana could use more aid again as it seeks to recover.

Other countries, however, should ideally receive less. Rwanda already funds half its government spending with aid. Rather than seeking to increase this proportion, Rwanda should set itself the goal of reducing it over time. So should other nations. Developing countries have reduced poverty when they have implemented the right policies, and when foreign governments have taken supportive measures. Aid has been at best marginal to this effort, and at worst has undermined it.

On the other hand, while government-to government aid can have adverse effects, support for civil society and provision of global public goods, such as climate change measures and health technologies, would be a constructive use of increased aid resources. Politicians promise more aid when they do not want to make changes that are more fundamental. Now is the time for substantial reform, not for counting aid dollars.

Critical Thinking

1. What is Glennie's point of view?
2. What reasons does Glennie offer to support his point of view?
3. How does this article fit into the debate between Sachs and Easterly?

JONATHAN GLENNIE, a country representative for Christian Aid, is the author of *The Trouble with Aid: Why Less Could Mean More for Africa* (Zed Books, 2008).

From *Current History,* May 2010, pp. 205–209. Copyright © 2010 by Current History, Inc. Reprinted by permission.

It's Still the One

Oil's very future is now being seriously questioned, debated, and challenged. The author of an acclaimed history explains why, just as we need more oil than ever, it is changing faster than we can keep up with.

DANIEL YERGIN

On a still afternoon under a hot Oklahoma sun, neither a cloud nor an ounce of "volatility" was in sight. Anything but. All one saw were the somnolent tanks filled with oil, hundreds of them, spread over the rolling hills, some brand-new, some more than 70 years old, and some holding, inside their silver or rust-orange skins, more than half a million barrels of oil each.

This is Cushing, Oklahoma, the gathering point for the light, sweet crude oil known as West Texas Intermediate—or just WTI. It is the oil whose price you hear announced every day, as in "WTI closed today at. . . ." Cushing proclaims itself, as the sign says when you ride into town, the "pipeline crossroads of the world." Through it passes the network of pipes that carry oil from Texas and Oklahoma and New Mexico, from Louisiana and the Gulf Coast, and from Canada too, into Cushing's tanks, where buyers take title before moving the oil onward to refineries where it is turned into gasoline, jet fuel, diesel, home heating oil, and all the other products that people actually use.

But that is not what makes Cushing so significant. After all, there are other places in the world through which much more oil flows. Cushing plays a unique role in the new global oil industry because WTI is the preeminent benchmark against which other oils are priced. Every day, billions of "paper barrels" of light, sweet crude are traded on the floor of the New York Mercantile Exchange in lower Manhattan and, in ever increasing volumes, at electron speed around the world, an astonishing virtual commerce that no matter how massive in scale, still connects back somehow to a barrel of oil in Cushing changing owners.

That frenetic daily trading has helped turn oil into something new—not only a physical commodity critical to the security and economic viability of nations but also a financial asset, part of that great instantaneous exchange of stocks, bonds, currencies, and everything else that makes up the world's financial portfolio. Today, the daily trade in those "paper barrels"—crude oil futures—is more than 10 times the world's daily consumption of physical barrels of oil. Add in the trades that take place on other exchanges or outside them entirely, and the ratio may be as much as 30 times greater. And though the oil may flow steadily in and out of Cushing at a stately 4 miles per hour, the global oil market is anything but stable.

That's why, as I sat down to work on a new edition of *The Prize* and considered what had changed since the early 1990s, when I wrote this history of the world's most valuable, and misunderstood, commodity, the word "volatility" kept springing to mind. How could it not? Indeed, when people are talking about volatility, they are often thinking oil. On July 11, 2008, WTI hit $147.27. Exactly a year later, it was $59.87. In between, in December, it fell as low as $32.40. (And don't forget a little more than a decade ago, when it was as low as $10 a barrel and consumers were supposedly going to swim forever in a sea of cheap oil.)

These wild swings don't just affect the "hedgers" (oil producers, airlines, heating oil dealers, etc.) and the "speculators," the financial players. They show up in the changing prices at the gasoline station. They stir political passions and feed consumers' suspicions. Volatility also makes it more difficult to plan future energy investments, whether in oil and gas or in renewable and alternative fuels. And it can have a cataclysmic impact on the world economy. After all, Detroit was knocked flat on its back by what happened at the gasoline pump in 2007 and 2008 even before the credit crisis. The enormous impact of these swings is why British Prime Minister Gordon Brown and French President Nicolas Sarkozy were recently moved to call for a global solution to "destructive volatility." But, they were forced to add, "There are no easy solutions."

This volatility is part of the new age of oil. For though Cushing looks pretty much the same as it did when *The Prize* came out, the world of oil looks very different. Some talk today about "the end of oil." If so, others reply, we are entering its very long goodbye. One characteristic of this new age is that oil has developed a split personality—as a physical commodity but also now as a financial asset. Three other defining characteristics of this new age are the globalization of the demand for oil, a vast shift from even a decade ago; the rise of climate change as a political factor shaping decisions on how we will use oil, and how much of it, in the future; and the drive for new technologies that could dramatically affect oil along with the rest of the energy portfolio.

The cast of characters in the oil business has also grown and changed. Some oil companies have become "supermajors," such as ExxonMobil and Chevron, while others, such as Amoco and ARCO, have just disappeared. "Big oil" no longer means the traditional international oil companies, their logos instantly recognizable from corner gas stations, but rather much larger state-owned companies, which, along with governments, today control more than 80 percent of the world's oil reserves. Fifteen of the world's 20 largest oil companies are now state-owned.

The cast of oil traders has also much expanded. Today's global oil game now includes pension funds, institutional money managers, endowments, and hedge funds, as well as individual investors and day traders. The managers at the pension funds and the university endowments see themselves as engaged in "asset allocation," hedging risks and diversifying to protect retirees' incomes and faculty salaries. But, technically, they too are part of the massive growth in the ranks of the new oil speculators.

With all these changes, the very future of this most vital commodity is now being seriously questioned, debated, and challenged, even as the world will need more of it than ever before. Both the U.S. Department of Energy and the International Energy Agency project that, even accounting for gains in efficiency, global energy use will increase almost 50 percent from 2006 to 2030—and that oil will continue to provide 30 percent or more of the world's energy in 2030.

But will it?

$147.27-Closing price per barrel of oil on July 11, 2008. Exactly one year later, it had fallen to $59.87.

From the beginning, oil has been a global industry, going back to 1861 when the first cargo of kerosene was sent from Pennsylvania—the Saudi Arabia of 19th-century oil—to Britain. (The potential crew was so fearful that the kerosene would catch fire that they had to be gotten drunk to shanghai them on board.) But that is globalization of supply, a familiar story. What is decisively new is the globalization of demand.

For decades, most of the market—and the markets that mattered the most—were in North America, Western Europe, and Japan. That's also where the growth was. At the time of the first Gulf War in 1991, China was still an oil exporter.

But now, the growth is in China, India, other emerging markets, and the Middle East. Between 2000 and 2007, the world's daily oil demand increased by 9.4 million barrels. Almost 85 percent of that growth was in emerging markets. There were many reasons that prices soared all the way to $147.27 last year, ranging from geopolitics to a weak dollar to the impact of financial markets and speculation (in all its manifold meanings). But the starting point was the fundamentals—the surge in oil demand driven by powerful economic growth in emerging markets. This shift may be even more powerful than people recognize: So far this year, more new cars have been sold in China than in the United States. When economic recovery

The Capital of Oil

Within three years of its discovery in 1912, the Cushing field in Oklahoma was producing almost 20 percent of U.S. oil. Two years later, it was supplying a substantial part of the fuel used by the U.S. Army in Europe during World War I. The Cushing area was so prolific that it became known as "the Queen of the Oil Fields," and Cushing became one of those classic wild oil boomtowns of the early 20th century. "Any man with red blood gets oil fever" was the diagnosis of one reporter who visited the area during those days. Production grew so fast around Cushing that pipelines had to be hurriedly built and storage tanks quickly thrown up to hold surplus supplies. By the time production began to decline, a great deal of infrastructure was in place, and Cushing turned into a key oil hub, its network of pipelines used to bring in supplies from elsewhere in Oklahoma and West Texas. Those supplies were stored in the tanks at Cushing before being put into other pipelines and shipped to refineries. When the New York Mercantile Exchange—the NYMEX—started to trade oil futures in 1983, it needed a physical delivery point. Cushing, its boom days long gone, but with its network of pipelines and tank farms and its central location, was the obvious answer. As much as 1.1 million barrels per day pass in and out of Cushing—equivalent to about 6 percent of U.S. oil consumption. But prices for much of the world's crude oil are set against the benchmark of the West Texas Intermediate crude oil—also known as "domestic sweet"—sitting in those 300 or so tanks in Cushing, making this sedate Oklahoma town not only an oil hub but one of the hubs of the world economy.

—Daniel Yergin

takes hold again, what happens to oil demand in such emerging countries will be crucial.

The math is clear: More consumers mean more demand, which means more supplies are needed. But what about the politics? There the forecasts are murkier, feeding a new scenario for international tension—a competition, even a clash, between China and the United States over "scarce" oil resources. This scenario even comes with a well-known historical model—the rivalry between Britain and "rising" Germany that ended in the disaster of World War I.

This scenario, though compelling reading, does not really accord with the way that the world oil market works. The Chinese are definitely new players, willing and able to pay top dollar to gain access to existing and new oil sources and, lately, also making loans to oil-producing countries to ensure future supplies. With more than $2 trillion in foreign reserves, China certainly has the wherewithal to be in the lending business.

But the global petroleum industry is not a go-it-alone business. Because of the risk and costs of large-scale development, companies tend to work in consortia with other companies.

Oil-exporting countries seek to diversify the countries and companies they work with. Inevitably, any country in China's position—whose demand had grown from 2.5 million barrels per day to 8 million in a decade and a half—would be worrying about supplies. Such an increase, however, is not a forecast of inevitable strife; it is a message about economic growth and rising standards of living. It would be much more worrying if, in the face of rising demand, Chinese companies were not investing in production both inside China (the source of half of its supply) and outside its borders.

There are potential flash points in this new world of oil. But they will not come from standard commercial competition. Rather, they arise when oil (along with natural gas) gets caught up in larger foreign-policy issues—most notably today, the potentially explosive crisis over the nuclear ambitions of oil- and gas-rich Iran.

Yet, despite all the talk of an "oil clash" scenario, there seems to be less overall concern than a few years ago and much more discussion about "energy dialogue." The Chinese themselves appear more confident about their increasingly important place in this globalized oil market. Although the risks are still there, the Chinese—and the Indians right alongside them—have the same stake as other consumers in an adequately supplied world market that is part of the larger global economy. Disruption of that economy, as the last year has so vividly demonstrated, does not serve their purposes. Why would the Chinese want to get into a confrontation over oil with the United States when the U.S. export market is so central to their economic growth and when the two countries are so financially interdependent?

Oil is not even the most important energy issue between China and the United States. It is coal. The two countries have the world's largest coal resources, and they are the world's biggest consumers of it. In a carbon-constrained world, they share a strong common interest in finding technological solutions for the emissions released when coal is burned.

And that leads directly to the second defining feature of the new age of oil: climate change. Global warming was already on the agenda when *The Prize* came out. It was back in 1992 that 154 countries signed the Rio Convention, pledging to dramatically reduce CO_2 concentrations in the atmosphere. But only in recent years has climate change really gained traction as a political issue—in Europe early in this decade, in the United States around 2005. Whatever the outcome of December's U.N. climate change conference in Copenhagen, carbon regulation is now part of the future of oil. And that means a continuing drive to reduce oil demand.

How does that get done? How does the world at once meet both the challenge of climate change and the challenge of economic growth—steady expansion in the industrial countries and more dramatic growth in China, India, and other emerging markets as tens of millions of their citizens rise from poverty and buy appliances and cars?

The answer has to be in another defining change—an emphasis on technology to a degree never before seen. The energy business has always been a technology business. After all, the men who figured out in 1859, exactly 150 years ago, how to drill that first oil well—Colonel Drake and his New Haven, Conn., investors—would, in today's lingo, be described as a group of disruptive technology entrepreneurs and venture capitalists. Again and again, in researching oil's history, I was struck by how seemingly insurmountable barriers and obstacles were overcome by technological progress, often unanticipated.

9.4 million-Number of barrels by which the world's daily oil demand rose from 2000 to 2007, with 85 percent coming from the developing world.

But the focus today on technology—all across the energy spectrum—is of unprecedented intensity. In the mid-1990s, I chaired a task force for the U.S. Department of Energy on "strategic energy R&D." Our panel worked very hard for a year and a half and produced what many considered a very worthy report. But there was not all that much follow-through. The Gulf War was over, and the energy problem looked like it had been "solved."

Today, by contrast, the interest in energy technology is enormous. And it will only be further stoked by the substantial increases that are ahead in government support for energy R&D. Much of that spending and effort is aimed at finding alternatives to oil. Yet the challenge is not merely to find alternatives; it is to find alternatives that can be competitive at the massive scale required.

What will those alternatives be? The electric car, which is the hottest energy topic today? Advanced biofuels? Solar systems? New building designs? Massive investment in wind? The evolving smart grid, which can integrate electric cars with the electricity industry? Something else that is hardly on the radar screen yet? Or perhaps a revolution in the internal combustion engine, making it two to three times as efficient as the ones in cars today?

We can make educated guesses. But, in truth, we don't know, and we won't know until we do know. For now, it is clear that the much higher levels of support for innovation—along with considerable government incentives and subsidies—will inevitably drive technological change and thus redraw the curve in the future demand for oil.

Indeed, the biggest surprises might come on the demand side, through conservation and improved energy efficiency. The United States is twice as energy efficient as it was in the 1970s. Perhaps we will see a doubling once again. Certainly, energy efficiency has never before received the intense focus and support that it does today.

Just because we have entered this new age of high-velocity change does not mean this story is about the imminent end of oil. Consider the "peak oil" thesis—shorthand for the presumption that the world has reached the high point of production and is headed for a downward slope. Historically, peak-oil thinking gains attention during times when markets are tight and prices are rising, stoking fears of a permanent shortage. In 2007 and 2008, the belief system built around peak oil helped drive prices to $147.27. (It was actually the fifth time that the world had supposedly "run out" of oil. The first such episode was in the 1880s; the last instance before this most recent time was in the 1970s.)

However, careful examination of the world's resource base—including my own firm's analysis of more than 800 of the largest oil fields—indicates that the resource endowment of the planet is sufficient to keep up with demand for decades to come. That, of course, does not mean that the oil will actually make it to consumers. Any number of "aboveground" risks and obstacles can stand in the way, from government policies that restrict access to tax systems to civil conflict to geopolitics to rising costs of exploration and production to uncertainties about demand. As has been the case for decades and decades, the shifting relations between producing and consuming countries, between traditional oil companies and state-owned oil companies, will do much to determine what resources are developed, and when, and thus to define the future of the industry.

There are two further caveats. Many of the new projects will be bigger, more complex, and more expensive. In the 1990s, a "megaproject" might have cost $500 million to $1 billion. Today, the price tag is more like $5 billion to $10 billion. And an increasing part of the new petroleum will come in the form of so-called "unconventional oil"—from ultradeep waters, Canadian oil sands, and the liquids that are produced with natural gas.

But through all these changes, one constant of the oil market is that it is not constant. The changing balance of supply and demand—shaped by economics, politics, technologies, consumer tastes, and accidents of all sorts—will continue to move prices. Economic recovery, expectations thereof, the pent-up demand for "demand," a shift into oil as a "financial asset"— some combination of these could certainly send oil prices up again, even with the current surplus in the market. Yet, the quest for stability is also a constant for oil, whether in reaction to the boom-and-bust world of northwest Pennsylvania in the late 19th century, the 10-cents-a-barrel world of Texas oil in the 1930s, or the $147.27 barrel of West Texas Intermediate in July 2008.

Certainly, the roller-coaster ride of oil prices over the last couple of years, as oil markets and financial markets have become more integrated, has made volatility a central pre-occupation for policymakers who do not want to see their economies whip-sawed by huge price swings. Yet without the flexibility and liquidity of markets, there is no effective way to balance supply and demand, no way for consumers and producers to hedge their risks. Nor is there a way to send signals to these consumers and producers about how much oil to use and how much money to invest—or signals to would-be innovators about tomorrow's opportunities.

One part of the solution is not only enhancement of the already considerable regulation of the financial markets where oil is traded, but also greater transparency and better understanding of who the players are in the rapidly expanding financial oil markets. But regulatory changes cannot eliminate market cycles or repeal the laws of supply and demand in the world's largest organized commodity market. Those cycles may not be much in evidence amid the quiet tanks and rolling hills at Cushing. But they are inescapably part of the global landscape of the new world of oil.

Critical Thinking

1. How is the "age for oil" changing?
2. Specifically, how is the demand of oil changing?
3. How do these general and specific changes affect the US-China relationship?
4. Does Yergin's analysis complement or contradict Klare's point of view in Article 3?

DANIEL YERGIN received a Pulitzer Prize for *The Prize: The Epic Quest for Oil, Money and Power,* published in an updated edition this year. He is chairman of IHS Cambridge Energy Research Associates.

Reprinted in entirety by McGraw-Hill with permission from *Foreign Policy,* September/October 2009, pp. 90, 92–95. www.foreignpolicy.com. © 2009 Washingtonpost.Newsweek Interactive, LLC.

Seven Myths about Alternative Energy

As the world looks around anxiously for an alternative to oil, energy sources such as biofuels, solar, and - nuclear seem like they could be the magic ticket. They're not."

MICHAEL GRUNWALD

What Comes Next?
Imagining the Post-Oil World

Nothing is as fraught with myths, misperceptions, and outright flights of fancy as the conversation about oil's successors. We asked two authors—award-winning environmental journalist Michael Grunwald and energy consultant David J. Rothkopf—to take aim at some of these myths, and look over the horizon to see which technologies might win the day and which ones could cause unexpected new problems. If fossil fuels are indeed saying their very long goodbye, then their would-be replacements still have a lot to prove.

1. "We Need to Do Everything Possible to Promote Alternative Energy"

Not exactly. It's certainly clear that fossil fuels are mangling the climate and that the status quo is unsustainable. There is now a broad scientific consensus that the world needs to reduce greenhouse gas emissions more than 25 percent by 2020—and more than 80 percent by 2050. Even if the planet didn't depend on it, breaking our addictions to oil and coal would also reduce global reliance on petrothugs and vulnerability to energy-price spikes.

But though the world should do everything sensible to promote alternative energy, there's no point trying to do everything possible. There are financial, political, and technical pressures as well as time constraints that will force tough choices; solutions will need to achieve the biggest emissions reductions for the least money in the shortest time. Hydrogen cars, cold fusion, and other speculative technologies might sound cool, but they could divert valuable resources from ideas that are already achievable and cost-effective. It's nice that someone managed to run his car on liposuction leftovers, but that doesn't mean he needs to be subsidized.

Reasonable people can disagree whether governments should try to pick energy winners and losers. But why not at least agree that governments shouldn't pick losers to be winners? Unfortunately,

that's exactly what is happening. The world is rushing to promote alternative fuel sources that will actually accelerate global warming, not to mention an alternative power source that could cripple efforts to stop global warming.

We can still choose a truly alternative path. But we'd better hurry.

2. "Renewable Fuels Are the Cure for Our Addiction to Oil"

Unfortunately not. "Renewable fuels" sound great in theory, and agricultural lobbyists have persuaded European countries and the United States to enact remarkably ambitious biofuels mandates to promote farm-grown alternatives to gasoline. But so far in the real world, the cures—mostly ethanol derived from corn in the United States or biodiesel derived from palm oil, soybeans, and rapeseed in Europe—have been significantly worse than the disease.

Researchers used to agree that farm-grown fuels would cut emissions because they all made a shockingly basic error. They gave fuel crops credit for soaking up carbon while growing, but it never occurred to them that fuel crops might displace vegetation that soaked up even more carbon. It was as if they assumed that biofuels would only be grown in parking lots. Needless to say, that hasn't been the case; Indonesia, for example, destroyed so many of its lush forests and peat lands to grow palm oil for the European biodiesel market that it ranks third rather than 21st among the world's top carbon emitters.

In 2007, researchers finally began accounting for deforestation and other land-use changes created by biofuels. One study found that it would take more than 400 years of biodiesel use to "pay back" the carbon emitted by directly clearing peat for palm oil. Indirect damage can be equally devastating because on a hungry planet, food crops that get diverted to fuel usually end up getting replaced somewhere. For example, ethanol profits are prompting U.S. soybean farmers to switch to corn, so Brazilian soybean farmers are expanding into cattle pastures to pick up the slack and Brazilian ranchers are invading the Amazon rain forest, which is why another study pegged corn ethanol's payback period at 167 years. It's simple economics: The mandates increase demand for grain, which boosts prices, which makes it lucrative to ravage the wilderness.

Deforestation accounts for 20 percent of global emissions, so unless the world can eliminate emissions from all other sources—cars, coal, factories, cows—it needs to back off forests. That means limiting agriculture's footprint, a daunting task as the world's population grows—and an impossible task if vast expanses of cropland are converted to grow middling amounts of fuel. Even if the United States switched its entire grain crop to ethanol, it would only replace one fifth of U.S. gasoline consumption.

This is not just a climate disaster. The grain it takes to fill an SUV tank with ethanol could feed a hungry person for a year; biofuel mandates are exerting constant upward pressure on global food prices and have contributed to food riots in dozens of poorer countries. Still, the United States has quintupled its ethanol production in a decade and plans to quintuple its biofuel production again in the next decade. This will mean more money for well-subsidized grain farmers, but also more malnutrition, more deforestation, and more emissions. European leaders have paid a bit more attention to the alarming critiques of biofuels—including one by a British agency that was originally established to promote biofuels—but they have shown no more inclination to throw cold water on this $100 billion global industry.

3. "If Today's Biofuels Aren't the Answer, Tomorrow's Biofuels Will Be"

Doubtful. The latest U.S. rules, while continuing lavish support for corn ethanol, include enormous new mandates to jump-start "second-generation" biofuels such as cellulosic ethanol derived from switchgrass. In theory, they would be less destructive than corn ethanol, which relies on tractors, petroleum-based fertilizers, and distilleries that emit way too much carbon. Even first-generation ethanol derived from sugar cane—which already provides half of Brazil's transportation fuel—is considerably greener than corn ethanol. But recent studies suggest that any biofuels requiring good agricultural land would still be worse than gasoline for global warming. Less of a disaster than corn ethanol is still a disaster.

Back in the theoretical world, biofuels derived from algae, trash, agricultural waste, or other sources could help because they require no land or at least unspecific "degraded lands," but they always seem to be "several" years away from large-scale commercial development. And some scientists remain hopeful that fast-growing perennial grasses such as miscanthus can convert sunlight into energy efficiently enough to overcome the land-use dilemmas—someday. But for today, farmland happens to be very good at producing the food we need to feed us and storing the carbon we need to save us, and not so good at generating fuel. In fact, new studies suggest that if we really want to convert biomass into energy, we're better off turning it into electricity.

Then what should we use in our cars and trucks? In the short term . . . gasoline. We just need to use less of it.

Instead of counterproductive biofuel mandates and ethanol subsidies, governments need fuel-efficiency mandates to help the world's 1 billion drivers guzzle less gas, plus subsidies for mass transit, bike paths, rail lines, telecommuting, carpooling, and other activities to get those drivers out of their cars. Policymakers also need to eliminate subsidies for roads to nowhere, mandates that require excess parking and limit dense development in urban areas, and other sprawl-inducing policies. None of this is as enticing as inventing a magical new fuel, but it's doable, and it would cut emissions.

In the medium term, the world needs plug-in electric cars, the only plausible answer to humanity's oil addiction that isn't decades away. But electricity is already the source of even more emissions than oil. So we'll need an answer to humanity's coal addiction, too.

4. "Nuclear Power Is the Cure for Our Addiction to Coal"

Nope. Atomic energy is emissions free, so a slew of politicians and even some environmentalists have embraced it as a clean alternative to coal and natural gas that can generate power when there's no sun or wind. In the United States, which already gets nearly 20 percent of its electricity from nuclear plants, utilities are thinking about new reactors for the first time since the Three Mile Island meltdown three decades ago—despite global concerns about nuclear proliferation, local concerns about accidents or terrorist attacks, and the lack of a disposal site for the radioactive waste. France gets nearly 80 percent of its electricity from nukes, and Russia, China, and India are now gearing up for nuclear renaissances of their own.

But nuclear power cannot fix the climate crisis. The first reason is timing: The West needs major cuts in emissions within a decade, and the first new U.S. reactor is only scheduled for 2017—unless it gets delayed, like every U.S. reactor before it. Elsewhere in the developed world, most of the talk about a nuclear revival has remained just talk; there is no Western country with more than one nuclear plant under construction, and scores of existing plants will be scheduled for decommissioning in the coming decades, so there's no way nuclear could make even a tiny dent in electricity emissions before 2020.

The bigger problem is cost. Nuke plants are supposed to be expensive to build but cheap to operate. Unfortunately, they're turning out to be really, really expensive to build; their cost estimates have quadrupled in less than a decade. Energy guru Amory Lovins has calculated that new nukes will cost nearly three times as much as wind—and that was before their construction costs exploded for a variety of reasons, including the global credit crunch, the atrophying of the nuclear labor force, and a supplier squeeze symbolized by a Japanese company's worldwide monopoly on steel-forging for reactors. A new reactor in Finland that was supposed to showcase the global renaissance is already way behind schedule and way, way over budget. This is why plans for new plants were recently shelved in Canada and several U.S. states, why Moody's just warned utilities they'll risk ratings downgrades if they seek new reactors, and why renewables attracted $71 billion in worldwide private capital in 2007—while nukes attracted zero.

It's also why U.S. nuclear utilities are turning to politicians to supplement their existing loan guarantees, tax breaks, direct subsidies, and other cradle-to-grave government goodies with new public largesse. Reactors don't make much sense to build unless someone else is paying; that's why the strongest push for nukes is coming from countries where power is publicly funded. For all the talk of sanctions, if the world really wants to cripple the Iranian economy, maybe the mullahs should just be allowed to pursue nuclear energy.

Unlike biofuels, nukes don't worsen warming. But a nuclear expansion—like the recent plan by U.S. Republicans who want 100 new plants by 2030—would cost trillions of dollars for relatively modest gains in the relatively distant future.

Nuclear lobbyists do have one powerful argument: If coal is too dirty and nukes are too costly, how are we going to produce our juice? Wind is terrific, and it's on the rise, adding nearly half of new U.S. power last year and expanding its global capacity by a third in 2007. But after increasing its worldwide wattage tenfold in a decade—China is now the leading producer, and Europe is embracing wind as well—it still produces less than 2 percent of the world's electricity. Solar and geothermal are similarly wonderful and inexhaustible technologies, but they're still global rounding errors. The average U.S. household now has 26 plug-in devices, and the rest of the world is racing to catch up; the U.S. Department of Energy expects global electricity consumption to rise 77 percent by 2030. How can we meet that demand without a massive nuclear revival?

Wind is terrific, but it produces less than 2 percent of the world's electricity.

We can't. So we're going to have to prove the Department of Energy wrong.

5. "There Is No Silver Bullet to the Energy Crisis"

Probably not. But some bullets are a lot better than others; we ought to give them our best shot before we commit to evidently inferior bullets. And one renewable energy resource is the cleanest, cheapest, and most abundant of them all. It doesn't induce deforestation or require elaborate security. It doesn't depend on the weather. And it won't take years to build or bring to market; it's already universally available.

It's called "efficiency." It means wasting less energy—or more precisely, using less energy to get your beer just as cold, your shower just as hot, and your factory just as productive. It's not about some austerity scold harassing you to take cooler showers, turn off lights, turn down thermostats, drive less, fly less, buy less stuff, eat less meat, ditch your McMansion, and otherwise change your behavior to save energy. Doing less with less is called conservation. Efficiency is about doing more or

the same with less; it doesn't require much effort or sacrifice. Yet more efficient appliances, lighting, factories, and buildings, as well as vehicles, could wipe out one fifth to one third of the world's energy consumption without any real deprivation.

Efficiency isn't sexy, and the idea that we could use less energy without much trouble hangs uneasily with today's more-is-better culture. But the best way to ensure new power plants don't bankrupt us, empower petrodictators, or imperil the planet is not to build them in the first place. "Negawatts" saved by efficiency initiatives generally cost 1 to 5 cents per kilowatt-hour versus projections ranging from 12 to 30 cents per kilowatt-hour from new nukes. That's because Americans in particular and human beings in general waste amazing amounts of energy. U.S. electricity plants fritter away enough to power Japan, and American water heaters, industrial motors, and buildings are as ridiculously inefficient as American cars. Only 4 percent of the energy used to power a typical incandescent bulb produces light; the rest is wasted. China is expected to build more square feet of real estate in the next 15 years than the United States has built in its entire history, and it has no green building codes or green building experience.

But we already know that efficiency mandates can work wonders because they've already reduced U.S. energy consumption levels from astronomical to merely high. For example, thanks to federal rules, modern American refrigerators use three times less energy than 1970s models, even though they're larger and more high-tech.

The biggest obstacles to efficiency are the perverse incentives that face most utilities; they make more money when they sell more power and have to build new generating plants. But in California and the Pacific Northwest, utility profits have been decoupled from electricity sales, so utilities can help customers save energy without harming shareholders. As a result, in that part of the country, per capita power use has been flat for three decades—while skyrocketing 50 percent in the rest of the United States. If utilities around the world could make money by helping their customers use less power, the U.S. Department of Energy wouldn't be releasing such scary numbers.

6. "We Need a Technological Revolution to Save the World"

Maybe. In the long term, it's hard to imagine how (without major advances) we can reduce emissions 80 percent by 2050 while the global population increases and the developing world develops. So a clean-tech Apollo program modeled oil the Manhattan Project makes sense. And we do need carbon pricing to send a message to market makers and innovators to promote low-carbon activities; Europe's cap-and-trade scheme seems to be working well after a rocky start. The private capital already pouring into renewables might someday produce a cheap solar panel or a synthetic fuel or a superpowerful battery or a truly clean coal plant. At some point, after we've milked efficiency for all the negawatts and negabarrels we can, we might need something new.

But we already have all the technology we need to start reducing emissions by reducing consumption. Even if we only hold electricity demand flat, we can subtract a coal-fired megawatt every time we add a wind-powered megawatt. And with a smarter grid, green building codes, and strict efficiency standards for everything from light bulbs to plasma TVs to server farms, we can do better than flat. Al Gore has a reasonably plausible plan for zero-emissions power by 2020; he envisions an ambitious 28 percent decrease in demand through efficiency, plus some ambitious increases in supply from wind, solar, and geothermal energy. But we don't even have to reduce our fossil fuel use to zero to reach our 2020 targets. We just have to use less.

If somebody comes up with a better idea by 2020, great! For now, we should focus on the solutions that get the best emissions bang for the buck.

7. "Ultimately, We'll Need to Change Our Behaviors to Save the World"

Probably. These days, it's politically incorrect to suggest that going green will require even the slightest adjustment to our way of life, but let's face it: Jimmy Carter was right. It wouldn't kill you to turn down the heat and put on a sweater. Efficiency is a miracle drug, but conservation is even better; a Prius saves gas, but a Prius sitting in the driveway while you ride your bike uses no gas. Even energy-efficient dryers use more power than clotheslines.

More with less will be a great start, but to get to 80 percent less emissions, the developed world might occasionally have to do less with less. We might have to unplug a few digital picture frames, substitute teleconferencing for some business travel, and take it easy on the air conditioner. If that's an inconvenient truth, well, it's less inconvenient than trillions of dollars' worth of new reactors, perpetual dependence on hostile petrostates, or a fricasseed planet.

After all, the developing world is entitled to develop. Its people are understandably eager to eat more meat, drive more cars, and live in nicer houses. It doesn't seem fair for the developed world to say: Do as we say, not as we did. But if the developing world follows the developed world's wasteful path to prosperity, the Earth we all share won't be able to accommodate us. So we're going to have to change our ways. Then we can at least say: Do as we're going, not as we did.

Critical Thinking

1. What is Grunwald's point of view?
2. How does this article complement or contradict the point of views in articles 3, 12, 13 and 25?

MICHAEL GRUNWALD, a senior correspondent at *Time* magazine, is an award-winning environmental journalist and author of *The Swamp: The Everglades, Florida, and the Politics of Paradise.*

The End of Easy Oil

Monica Heger

Canada's tar sands will soon be our top source of imported oil. But will that energy be worth the costs?

"We have the energy," declares a road sign that welcomes visitors to Fort McMurray in Alberta, Canada. It is no idle boast: This city of 70,000 lies in the heart of Canada's oil sands, geologic formations that collectively contain 13 percent of the world's proven oil reserves. During the early 2000s, a massive oil-extraction industry boomed here, rapidly transforming vast stretches of boreal forest into strip mines. But when oil prices tumbled with the global recession, Alberta's energy industry took a big hit. In mid-2008 the Norwegian company Statoil-Hydro withdrew its application to build a $4 billion upgrading plant; Royal Dutch Shell decided to shelve a mining construction project that fall. An estimated $90 billion in development contracts were canceled or put on hold, bringing the oil sands industry to a crossroads.

To many environmentalists—and, less predictably, to many energy developers as well—the slowdown in oil sands extraction may prove to be an unexpected blessing. The United States has become deeply reliant on extreme extraction from Canada's tar sands, which this year are expected to become this country's top source of imported crude, surpassing our purchases from the vast oil fields of Saudi Arabia. The recession "has given the oil sands industry a chance to step back and breathe," says David McColl, head of oil sands studies at the Canadian Energy Research Institute, a nonprofit whose membership includes government departments, the University of Calgary, and energy companies. With the slowdown, developers must improve efficiency to stay profitable, making changes that will both help the bottom line and begin to address some of the tough environmental problems associated with tar sands oil.

Worldwide, mostly in Canada and Venezuela, oil sand reserves total a stunning 2 trillion barrels of oil. That is equivalent to 280 years of America's current consumption, although only around a tenth of that total appears to be recoverable with current technology. Unfortunately, the process of extracting, upgrading, and refining the fuel is dirty and resource-intensive. In Canada, relatively shallow oil sand deposits lie beneath a 1,500-square-mile region just north of Fort McMurray. Developers access the sands by literally scraping away the earth's surface, along with anything that happens to be living there. The raw material extracted—a thick, black goo called bitumen—makes up 10 percent of the harvested material by weight. The rest is sand and small amounts of water. Two tons of sand must be processed to yield a single barrel of oil, producing twice as

much greenhouse-gas emissions as the processing of conventional crude. (Deeper reserves must be forced to the surface by an injection of pressurized steam, with even greater emissions; about 40 percent of Canadian oil from the sands is produced this way.) Each barrel of bitumen also generates more than 500 gallons of tailings, a liquid by-product laced with traces of bitumen and other pollutants. Operators hold the tailings in giant ponds, many located adjacent to the Athabasca River, which runs through eastern Alberta. Those ponds already cover an estimated 50 square miles, and an analysis of the industry's seepage records by the Canadian environmental advocacy group Environmental Defense suggests that every day around 3 million gallons of contaminated fluid leaks into the surrounding area.

Even more unnerving are the findings of a recent study by ecologist David Schindler at the University of Alberta. He and his colleagues found that over the course of four months, 11,400 tons of particulate matter—including bitumen and cancer-causing polycyclic aromatic compounds—were deposited within 30 miles of oil sands upgrading facilities belonging to two of Canada's major oil sands development companies, Suncor and Syncrude. Sampling of the Athabasca River revealed that pollutants appeared in greater concentrations downstream from the facilities and were not Hotected in comparable sites farther away, the researchers say. "The concentrations there are in the range where deformities and mortalities would be expected in fish," Schindler says, "and the compounds that we found are known carcinogens in humans."

Environmental concerns that were brushed aside when oil prices spiked a few years back have gained traction since the economy cooled. In February the Whole Foods grocery chain threw its weight behind a campaign to boycott companies that use fuel generated from the oil sands. And in June Syncrude was found guilty of violating provincial and federal law when 1,600 waterbirds died in one of its tailings ponds near Fort McMurray (the company may appeal the decision). Regulators have also started to assert themselves more forcefully. Last year Canada's Energy Resources Conservation Board issued new rules requiring at least 20 percent of the fine particles from new tailings to be captured starting in 2011, and 50 percent by 2013. Suncor has since begun developing a new technology that would mix some refining by-products with a polymer, creating a dry solid that can be more easily contained and reducing the amount of liquid that ends up in the toxic ponds.

Such changes will become increasingly important as the world economy recovers. Oil sands development has begun to pick up, with a projected $13 billion in new investment in

2010, a $2 billion increase from 2009. A recent industry report estimates that oil sands production, which currently stands at around 1.5 million barrels a day, could jump 46 percent by 2015. The United States now imports 22 percent of its oil from our northern neighbor, and China has also shown interest in Canada's sands, taking a $1.7 billion, 60 percent stake in two new projects in northern Alberta. In short, the tar sands—like deep oil—will probably remain an important part of the energy picture for the foreseeable future.

"Oil sands and offshore drilling are both symptoms of the same problem: We're running out of easy oil," says Simon Dyer, oil sands director at the Pembina Institute, a nonprofit sustainable energy research organization. But with ingenuity, smart regulation, and better enforcement, government and industry may be able to find a path that meets our needs until clean—or at least cleaner—energy sources can step up to the task.

Critical Thinking

1. What is meant by "extreme extraction"?

2. How do Canadian tar sands fit into the changing supply and demand equation for oil?

3. How does this case study illustrate the relationship between natural resources and social structures?

On Clean Energy, China Skirts Rules

Keith Bradsher

Until very recently, Hunan Province was known mainly for lip-searing spicy food, smoggy cities and destitute pig farmers. Mao was born in a village on the outskirts of Changsha, the provincial capital here in south-central China.

Now, Changsha and two adjacent cities are emerging as a center of clean energy manufacturing. They are churning out solar panels for the American and European markets, developing new equipment to manufacture the panels and branching into turbines that generate electricity from wind. By contrast, clean energy companies in the United States and Europe are struggling. Some have started cutting jobs and moving operations to China in ventures with local partners.

The booming Chinese clean energy sector, now more than a million jobs strong, is quickly coming to dominate the production of technologies essential to slowing global warming and other forms of air pollution. Such technologies are needed to assure adequate energy as the world's population grows by nearly a third, to nine billion people by the middle of the century, while oil and coal reserves dwindle.

But much of China's clean energy success lies in aggressive government policies that help this crucial export industry in ways most other governments do not. These measures risk breaking international rules to which China and almost all other nations subscribe, according to some trade experts interviewed by The New York Times.

A visit to one of Changsha's newest success stories offers an example of the government's methods. Hunan Sunzone Optoelectronics, a two-year-old company, makes solar panels and ships close to 95 percent of them to Europe. Now it is opening sales offices in New York, Chicago and Los Angeles in preparation for a push into the American market next February.

To help Sunzone, the municipal government transferred to the company 22 acres of valuable urban land close to downtown at a bargain-basement price. That reduced the company's costs and greatly increased its worth and attractiveness to investors.

Meanwhile, a state bank is preparing to lend to the company at a low interest rate, and the provincial government is sweetening the deal by reimbursing the company for most of the interest payments, to help Sunzone double its production capacity.

Heavily subsidized land and loans for an exporter like Sunzone are the rule, not the exception, for clean energy businesses in Changsha and across China, Chinese executives said in interviews over the last three months.

But this kind of help violates World Trade Organization rules banning virtually all subsidies to exporters, and could be successfully challenged at the agency's tribunals in Geneva, said Charlene Barshefsky, who was the United States trade representative during the second Clinton administration and negotiated the terms of China's entry to the organization in 2001.

If the country with the subsidies fails to remove them, other countries can retaliate by imposing steep tariffs on imports from that country. But multinational companies and trade associations in the clean energy business, as in many other industries, have been wary of filing trade cases, fearing Chinese officials' reputation for retaliating against joint ventures in their country and potentially denying market access to any company that takes sides against China.

W.T.O. rules allow countries to subsidize goods and services in their home markets, as long as those subsidies do not discriminate against imports. But the rules prohibit export subsidies, to prevent governments from trying to help their companies gain in world markets.

The W.T.O. also requires countries to declare all national, state and local subsidies every two years, so that if one country's exports surge suspiciously, other countries' trade officials can easily check to see if that product is being subsidized.

But China has virtually ignored the requirement since joining the W.T.O. Contending that it is still a developing country struggling to understand its commitments, China has filed just one list of subsidies, which were in place between 2001 and 2004. And that one list covered only central government policies while omitting local or provincial subsidies.

The Chinese mission to the W.T.O., which is part of China's commerce ministry, would not comment for this article. After reading questions The New York Times submitted by fax last week, mission officials declined to respond, saying that any comments might affect China's standing in other trade disputes.

Sunzone and other Chinese clean energy companies also benefit from the fact that the government spends $1 billion a day intervening in the currency markets so that Chinese exports become more affordable in foreign markets. Systematic intervention in currency markets to obtain an advantage in trade violates the rules of the International Monetary Fund, of which China is a member, although the I.M.F. has little power to punish violators.

Chinese wind and solar power manufacturers further benefit from the government's imposition of sharp reductions this summer in exports of raw materials, known as rare earths, that are crucial for solar panels and wind turbines. China mines almost all of the world's rare earths. W.T.O. rules ban most export restrictions.

Of course, China's success in clean energy also stems from assets enjoyed by many of the nation's industries: low labor costs, expanding universities that groom lots of engineering talent, inexpensive construction and ever-improving transportation and telecommunications networks.

For example, engineers with freshly issued bachelor's degrees can be found here in Hunan Province for a salary of only about $2,640 a year—not significantly more than blue-collar workers with vocational school degrees can make. But the fuel propelling clean energy companies in China lies in advantages provided by the government, executives say.

Other countries also try to help their clean energy industries, too, but not to the extent that China does—and not, so far at least, to the point of potentially running afoul of W.T.O. rules.

No doubt China's aggressive tactics are making clean energy more affordable. Solar panel prices have dropped by nearly half in the last two years, and wind turbine prices have fallen by a quarter—partly because of the global financial crisis but mainly because of China's rapid expansion in these sectors and the accompanying economies of scale. Large Chinese wind turbines now sell for about $685,000 per megawatt of capacity, while Western wind turbines cost $850,000 a megawatt.

The question is whether China is building this industry in ways that are unfair to overseas competitors and make other nations overly dependent on a Chinese industry whose approach to the business may not be economically or politically sustainable.

Because China's clean energy industry has relied so heavily on land deals and cheap state-supported loans, the industry could be vulnerable if China's real estate bubble bursts, or if the banks' loose lending creates financial problems of the sort that have plagued Western financial markets in recent years.

Other countries may also become less enthusiastic about subsidizing renewable energy if it means importing more goods from China instead of creating jobs at home.

The rapid rise of China's solar and wind industries illuminates how the government helps many export industries, as well as the challenges for the West now that the country has emerged as the world's second-largest economy, surpassing Japan and gradually gaining on the United States.

Winning Big

Barely a player in the solar industry five years ago, China is on track to produce more than half the world's solar panels this year. More than 95 percent of them will be exported to countries like the United States and Germany that offer generous subsidies for consumers who buy solar panels.

By contrast, the Chinese government has relatively modest solar subsidies for its citizens. Instead it has devoted more money to helping manufacturers, allowing them to cash in on other countries' consumer subsidy programs.

China is also on track to make nearly half of the world's wind turbines this year. China offers financial incentives for utilities to use wind power, which is less costly than solar power, and the country passed the United States last year as the world's largest wind turbine market. Government-subsidized turbine makers are now preparing for large-scale exports to the United States and Europe, which could also result in violations of W.T.O. rules.

Meanwhile, China itself imports virtually no wind turbines or solar panels, instead protecting those developing industries. For example, China until late last year required that 70 percent of the content of each wind turbine and 80 percent of the content of each solar panel be made within China. China quietly dropped that rule after objections from American officials, but also because its own industries had become the world's largest, lowest-cost producers.

Now China strongly opposes suggestions in Congress that the United States or Europe follow China's example and impose "local content" rules to help their own struggling renewable energy industries.

"Now if the U.S. sets up that kind of regulation, it will really be a problem" said Li Junfeng, a senior Chinese energy policy maker. "We need to buy from each other."

China's expansion has been traumatic for American and European solar power manufacturers, and Western wind turbine makers are now bracing to compete with low-cost Chinese exports. This year, BP shut down its solar panel manufacturing in Frederick, Md., and in Spain, and laid off most of the employees while expanding a joint venture in China.

Evergreen Solar of Marlboro, Mass., plans to move the final manufacturing steps for its solar panels from Devens, Mass., to China next summer, eliminating 300 American jobs, after struggling to borrow money in the United States and after finding that costs in China were lower.

The Obama administration has begun high-level discussions on how to respond to China's industrial policies, Treasury Secretary Timothy F. Geithner said in an interview in Washington in July.

"We are concerned about the depth and breadth of the measures they have taken," Mr. Geithner said, later adding, "We will be aggressive on the trade front in terms of fighting anything that is clearly discriminatory."

Helping Hand

Here in Changsha, Sunzone's general manager and chief engineer, Zhao Feng, represents a new breed of Chinese clean energy entrepreneurs. Tall and fit, he is an avid painter, fisherman and golfer.

Mr. Zhao is quick to point out that state and federal governments in the United States have also encouraged the development of the clean energy industry. "Our provincial governor has come several times to our plant, just as Gov. Arnold Schwarzenegger has made several visits to solar power companies" in California, he said.

But the Hunan government's backing of Sunzone is much more extensive than anything in the United States.

With government help, Sunzone lined up financing and received all the permits necessary to build a factory in just three months under an expedited approval system for clean energy businesses. It took only eight more months to build and equip the factory. "The construction teams worked 24 hours a day, seven days a week in three shifts," Mr. Zhao said.

Building and equipping a solar panel factory in the United States takes 14 to 16 months, and getting environmental and other permits can take years, said Tom Zarrella, the former chief executive of GT Solar in Merrimack, N.H., a big supplier of solar manufacturing equipment to factories in the United States and China.

A strong symbol of the government's commitment to the clean energy industry in China may be Sunzone's walled 22-acre compound here.

The company has only 360 employees, who work in a modest two-story building and small factory. Many of them live in a six-story dormitory. The compound also has a demonstration house powered by solar panels.

But the government has granted Sunzone enough cheap land to make room for an orchard of orange trees, a nearly finished golf driving range and winding country lanes—all of it across the street from 17-story apartment buildings near the heart of downtown Changsha. A lone trellis-covered swing that sits on Sunzone's vast plot seems to signal how little occupied the land is.

As a clean energy business, Sunzone was allowed to buy the land two years ago for $90,000 an acre, Mr. Zhao said. That was one-third of the official price then for industrial land from the government.

Industrial land in this desirable neighborhood now sells for $720,000 an acre, giving Sunzone an eightfold profit on paper. The company carries the land on its books at this market price, and can borrow against it, Mr. Zhao said. The valuable land also means the company has big assets and little debt on its balance sheet, which should help attract investors for a planned initial public offering in 2012.

Executives at three other clean energy companies in and around Changsha said they, too, had been allowed to buy government land for a third of the regulated price.

Mr. Zhao defended the size of his corporate park as necessary for his business and said it was not a real estate investment. The driving range will be made available to all employees for their relaxation, he said. And he said Sunzone hoped to build a nine-story solar research center on part of its land someday.

The local government of Zhuzhou, a city near Changsha, is even more generous. "For really good projects, we can give them the land for free," said He Jianbo, the deputy director of the city's flourishing high-tech zone, which already makes everything from electric buses to solar panels, and is preparing to build electric cars. "This land subsidy is not available to traditional industries, only high-tech industries."

Many state and local governments in the United States have also built roads, installed power lines and made other infrastructure improvements that have increased the value of private land as part of programs to attract clean energy. Tax holidays for such businesses are common in the United States, as in China.

But according to Commerce Department experts in Washington, government agencies in the United States have generally refrained from the sale of deeply discounted government land

to export industries, while infrastructure improvements have been made to benefit all road and telecommunications users, not just specific export industries. A wide range of international trade agreements, including W.T.O. rules, allow governments to provide infrastructure and some types of tax breaks, but bar subsidies in the form of cheap transfers of valuable government assets like land to exporters.

Mr. Zhao said that whatever the global trade rules might be on export subsidies, the world should appreciate the generous assistance of Chinese government agencies to the country's clean energy industries. That support has made possible a sharp drop in the price of renewable energy and has helped humanity address global warming, he said.

The subsidized land will also help Sunzone afford plans to sell solar panels below cost to poor people in western China, Mr. Zhao said, adding that he hoped the effort would build good will and lead to more sales there.

Money for Nothing

As Sunzone prepares to double its manufacturing capacity by the end of this year, state banks and the municipal government are ready to help.

The company has reached a tentative deal to borrow $11 million, to increase employment to 600 workers. The bank will lend the money at an interest rate of about 6 percent, but the provincial government will then give Sunzone a direct rebate to pay more than half the interest on the loan. "Just yesterday, the bank general manager brought his staff here to see how they could be of service to us," Mr. Zhao said. "We don't need to go to the bank; they come here."

Low-interest loans from government-run banks are crucial to China's clean energy success, some experts say, because of the high cost of factory equipment.

"If you change the interest rate half a percent or 1 percent, the difference is amazing, because the cost is all at the beginning," said Dennis Bracy, chief executive of the U.S.-China Clean Energy Forum, a discussion group of Chinese energy officials and former American cabinet officials.

In the United States, the Obama administration has approved $10 billion in grants, loan guarantees and other financing to help new entrants in the industry and aid existing companies, and has promised another $10 billion, said Matt Rogers, the senior adviser to Energy Secretary Steven Chu for economic stimulus programs. Almost all the money is for projects that will generate electricity for the United States.

But the American clean energy programs carry many time-consuming and difficult requirements. Companies must show they can repay loans and have innovative technology. The department has given conditional approval to 18 renewable energy loan guarantees, although only four have led to the actual issuance of loans so far. But the administration is moving quickly to accelerate the process, said Jonathan Silver, the executive director of the Energy Department's loan guarantee program.

China has been pumping loans into clean energy so rapidly that even $23 billion in credit offered by the China Development Bank to three solar panel exporters and a wind turbine maker since April has barely raised eyebrows. China Development Bank, owned by the government, exists to lend money for strategic priorities.

Western clean energy companies complain of much higher financing costs—when they can raise money at all. Banks have been cautious about the sector, which leans heavily on venture capitalists and private equity firms that demand implicit interest rates of up to 9 percent right now in the United States, said Thomas Maslin, a senior solar analyst at IHS Emerging Energy Research.

Evergreen Solar, the Massachusetts company, struggled for three years to raise money in the States, but had no trouble doing so in China. Chinese state banks were happy to lend most of the money for the factory on very attractive terms, like a five-year loan with no payments of interest or principal until the end of the loan, said Michael El-Hillow, the company's chief financial officer.

"You can't get a penny in the United States, it doesn't matter who you call—banks, government. It's awful," he said. "Therein lies the hidden advantage of being in China."

Many Chinese clean energy executives argue that China should offer more subsidies for its own people to buy renewable energy, in addition to helping export-oriented manufacturers. But until domestic demand takes off, government support will remain crucial.

"Who wins this clean energy race," Mr. Zhao of Sunzone said, "really depends on how much support the government gives."

Critical Thinking

1. What is the point of view of Keith Bradsher's case study?

2. What reasons does he offer to support this point of view?

3. Describe how this case study complements or contradicts the point of view of articles 4 and 24.

UNIT 5
Conflict

Unit Selections

Learning Outcomes

After reading this unit you should be able to:

- Identify the dynamics of different types of international conflicts.

- Make some predictions on future hot spots where war might break out.

- Discuss the basic issues surrounding the proliferation of nuclear weapons.

- Offer insights into additional international relations theories that are summarized in some the articles.

- Assess your on-going effort at identifying your theory of international relations and how this unit changes/complements it.

Student Website
www.mhhe.com/cls

Internet References

DefenseLINK
   www.defenselink.mil
Federation of American Scientists (FAS)
   www.fas.org
ISN International Relations and Security Network
   www.isn.ethz.ch
The NATO Integrated Data Service (NIDS)
   www.nato.int/structur/nids/nids.htm

Do you lock your doors at night? Do you secure your personal property to avoid theft? These are basic questions that have to do with your sense of personal security. Most individuals take steps to protect what they have, including their lives. The same is true for groups of people, including countries.

In the international arena, governments frequently pursue their national interest by entering into mutually agreeable "deals" with other governments. Social scientists call these types of arrangements "exchanges" (i.e., each side gives up something it values in order to gain something in return that it values even more). On an economic level, it functions like this: "I have the oil that you need and am willing to sell it. In return I want to buy from you the agricultural products that I lack." Whether on the governmental level or the personal level ("If you help me with my homework, then I will drive you home this weekend."), exchanges are the process used by most individuals and groups to obtain and protect what is of value. The exchange process, however, can break down. When threats and punishments replace mutual exchanges, conflict ensues. Neither side benefits, and there are costs to both. Further, each may use threats with the expectation that the other will capitulate. But if efforts at intimidation and coercion fail, the conflict may escalate into violent confrontation.

With the end of the cold war, issues of national security and the nature of international conflict have changed. In the late 1980s agreements between the former Soviet Union and the United States led to the elimination of superpower support for participants in low-intensity conflicts in Central America, Africa, and Southeast Asia. Fighting the cold war by proxy is now a thing of the past. In addition, cold war military alliances have either collapsed or have been significantly redefined. Despite these historic changes, there is no shortage of conflicts in the world today.

Many experts initially predicted that the collapse of the Soviet Union would decrease the arms race and diminish the threat of nuclear war. However, some analysts now believe that the threat of nuclear war has in fact increased as control of nuclear weapons has become less centralized and the command structure less reliable. In addition, the proliferation of nuclear weapons into North Korea and South Asia (India and Pakistan) is a growing security issue. Further, there are concerns about both dictatorial governments and terrorist organizations obtaining weapons of mass destruction. What these changing circumstances mean for U.S. policy is a topic of considerable debate.

The unit begins with a unique perspective on the sources of international conflict. It is followed by a series of case studies that provide insights into the roots of the drug war in Mexico,

© Royalty-Free/CORBIS

terrorism and conflict in the Middle East, and the foreign policy objectives of emerging regional and global powers. The unit concludes with an article on the increasingly complex problem of nuclear weapons proliferation.

As in the case of the other global issues described in this anthology, international conflict is a dynamic problem. It is important to understand that conflicts are not random events, but follow patterns and trends. Forty-five years of cold war established discernable patterns of international conflict as the superpowers deterred each other with vast expenditures of money and technological know-how. The consequence of this stalemate was often a shift to the developing world for conflict by superpower proxy.

The changing circumstances of the post-cold war era generate a series of important new policy questions: Will there be more nuclear proliferation? Is there an increased danger of so-called "rogue" states destabilizing the international arena? Is the threat of terror a temporary or permanent feature of world affairs? Will there be a growing emphasis on low-intensity conflicts related to the interdiction of drugs, or will some other unforeseen issue determine the world's hot spots? Will the United States and its European allies lose interest in security issues that do not directly involve their economic interests and simply look the other way, for example, as age-old ethnic conflicts become brutally violent? Can the international community develop viable institutions to mediate and resolve disputes before they become violent? The answers to these and related questions will determine the patterns of conflict in the twenty-first century.

The Revenge of Geography

People and ideas influence events, but geography largely determines them, now more than ever. To understand the coming struggles, it's time to dust off the Victorian thinkers who knew the physical world best. A journalist who has covered the ends of the Earth offers a guide to the relief map—and a primer on the next phase of conflict.

ROBERT D. KAPLAN

When rapturous Germans tore down the Berlin Wall 20 years ago it symbolized far more than the overcoming of an arbitrary boundary. It began an intellectual cycle that saw all divisions, geographic and otherwise, as surmountable; that referred to "realism" and "pragmatism" only as pejoratives; and that invoked the humanism of Isaiah Berlin or the appeasement of Hitler at Munich to launch one international intervention after the next. In this way, the armed liberalism and the democracy-promoting neoconservatism of the 1990s shared the same universalist aspirations. But alas, when a fear of Munich leads to overreach the result is Vietnam—or in the current case, Iraq.

And thus began the rehabilitation of realism, and with it another intellectual cycle. "Realist" is now a mark of respect, "neo-con" a term of derision. The Vietnam analogy has vanquished that of Munich. Thomas Hobbes, who extolled the moral benefits of fear and saw anarchy as the chief threat to society, has elbowed out Isaiah Berlin as the philosopher of the present cycle. The focus now is less on universal ideals than particular distinctions, from ethnicity to culture to religion. Those who pointed this out a decade ago were sneered at for being "fatalists" or "determinists." Now they are applauded as "pragmatists." And this is the key insight of the past two decades—that there are worse things in the world than extreme tyranny, and in Iraq we brought them about ourselves. I say this having supported the war.

So now, chastened, we have all become realists. Or so we believe. But realism is about more than merely opposing a war in Iraq that we know from hindsight turned out badly. Realism means recognizing that international relations are ruled by a sadder, more limited reality than the one governing domestic affairs. It means valuing order above freedom, for the latter becomes important only after the former has been established. It means focusing on what divides humanity rather than on what unites it, as the high priests of globalization would have it. In short, realism is about recognizing and embracing those forces beyond our control that constrain human action—culture, tradition, history, the bleaker tides of passion that lie just beneath the veneer of civilization. This poses what, for realists, is the central question in foreign affairs: Who can do what to whom? And of all the unsavory truths in which realism is rooted, the bluntest, most uncomfortable, and most deterministic of all is geography.

Indeed, what is at work in the recent return of realism is the revenge of geography in the most old-fashioned sense. In the 18th and 19th centuries, before the arrival of political science as an academic specialty, geography was an honored, if not always formalized, discipline in which politics, culture, and economics were often conceived of in reference to the relief map. Thus, in the Victorian and Edwardian eras, mountains and the men who grow out of them were the first order of reality; ideas, however uplifting, were only the second.

And yet, to embrace geography is not to accept it as an implacable force against which humankind is powerless. Rather, it serves to qualify human freedom and choice with a modest acceptance of fate. This is all the more important today, because rather than eliminating the relevance of geography, globalization is reinforcing it. Mass communications and economic integration are weakening many states, exposing a Hobbesian world of small, fractious regions. Within them, local, ethnic, and religious sources of identity are reasserting themselves, and because they are anchored to specific terrains, they are best explained by reference to geography. Like the faults that determine earthquakes, the political future will be defined by conflict and instability with a similar geographic logic. The upheaval spawned by the ongoing economic crisis is increasing the relevance of geography even further, by weakening social orders and other creations of humankind, leaving the natural frontiers of the globe as the only restraint.

So we, too, need to return to the map, and particularly to what I call the "shatter zones" of Eurasia. We need to reclaim those thinkers who knew the landscape best. And we need to update their theories for the revenge of geography in our time.

If you want to understand the insights of geography, you need to seek out those thinkers who make liberal humanists profoundly uneasy—those authors who thought the map determined nearly everything, leaving little room for human agency.

One such person is the French historian Fernand Braudel, who in 1949 published *The Mediterranean and the Mediterranean World in the Age of Philip II.* By bringing demography and nature itself into history, Braudel helped restore geography to its proper place. In his narrative, permanent environmental forces lead to enduring historical trends that preordain political events and regional wars. To Braudel, for example, the poor, precarious soils along the Mediterranean, combined with an uncertain, drought-afflicted climate, spurred ancient Greek and Roman conquest. In other words, we delude ourselves by thinking that we control our own destinies. To understand the present challenges of climate change, warming Arctic seas, and the scarcity of resources such as oil and water, we must reclaim Braudel's environmental interpretation of events.

So, too, must we reexamine the blue-water strategizing of Alfred Thayer Mahan, a U.S. naval captain and author of *The Influence of Sea Power Upon History, 1660–1783.* Viewing the sea as the great "commons" of civilization, Mahan thought that naval power had always been the decisive factor in global political struggles. It was Mahan who, in 1902, coined the term "Middle East" to denote the area between Arabia and India that held particular importance for naval strategy. Indeed, Mahan saw the Indian and Pacific oceans as the hinges of geopolitical destiny, for they would allow a maritime nation to project power all around the Eurasian rim and thereby affect political developments deep into Central Asia. Mahan's thinking helps to explain why the Indian Ocean will be the heart of geopolitical competition in the 21st century—and why his books are now all the rage among Chinese and Indian strategists.

Similarly, the Dutch-American strategist Nicholas Spykman saw the seaboards of the Indian and Pacific oceans as the keys to dominance in Eurasia and the natural means to check the land power of Russia. Before he died in 1943, while the United States was fighting Japan, Spykman predicted the rise of China and the consequent need for the United States to defend Japan. And even as the United States was fighting to liberate Europe, Spykman warned that the postwar emergence of an integrated European power would eventually become inconvenient for the United States. Such is the foresight of geographical determinism.

But perhaps the most significant guide to the revenge of geography is the father of modern geopolitics himself—Sir Halford J. Mackinder—who is famous not for a book but a single article, "The Geographical Pivot of History," which began as a 1904 lecture to the Royal Geographical Society in London. Mackinder's work is the archetype of the geographical discipline, and he summarizes its theme nicely: "Man and not nature initiates, but nature in large measure controls."

His thesis is that Russia, Eastern Europe, and Central Asia are the "pivot" around which the fate of world empire revolves. He would refer to this area of Eurasia as the "heartland" in a later book. Surrounding it are four "marginal" regions of the Eurasian landmass that correspond, not coincidentally, to the four great religions, because faith, too, is merely a function of geography for Mackinder. There are two "monsoon lands": one in the east generally facing the Pacific Ocean, the home of Buddhism; the other in the south facing the Indian Ocean, the home of Hinduism. The third marginal region is Europe, watered by the Atlantic to the west and the home of Christianity. But the most fragile of the four marginal regions is the Middle East, home of Islam, "deprived of moisture by the proximity of Africa" and for the most part "thinly peopled" (in 1904, that is).

Realism is about recognizing and embracing those forces beyond our control that constrain human action. And of all the unsavory truths in which realism is rooted, the bluntest, most uncomfortable, and most deterministic of all is geography.

This Eurasian relief map, and the events playing out on it at the dawn of the 20th century, are Mackinder's subject, and the opening sentence presages its grand sweep:

> When historians in the remote future come to look back on the group of centuries through which we are now passing, and see them fore-shortened, as we to-day see the Egyptian dynasties, it may well be that they will describe the last 400 years as the Columbian epoch, and will say that it ended soon after the year 1900.

Mackinder explains that, while medieval Christendom was "pent into a narrow region and threatened by external barbarism," the Columbian age—the Age of Discovery—saw Europe expand across the oceans to new lands. Thus at the turn of the 20th century, "we shall again have to deal with a closed political system," and this time one of "world-wide scope."

> Every explosion of social forces, instead of being dissipated in a surrounding circuit of unknown space and barbaric chaos, will [henceforth] be sharply re-echoed from the far side of the globe, and weak elements in the political and economic organism of the world will be shattered in consequence.

By perceiving that European empires had no more room to expand, thereby making their conflicts global, Mackinder foresaw, however vaguely, the scope of both world wars.

Mackinder looked at European history as "subordinate" to that of Asia, for he saw European civilization as merely the outcome of the struggle against Asiatic invasion. Europe, he writes, became the cultural phenomenon it is only because of its geography: an intricate array of mountains, valleys, and peninsulas; bounded by northern ice and a western ocean; blocked by seas and the Sahara to the south; and set against the immense, threatening flatland of Russia to the east. Into this confined landscape poured a succession of nomadic, Asian invaders from the naked steppe. The union of Franks, Goths, and Roman provincials against these invaders produced the basis for modern France. Likewise, other European powers originated, or at least matured, through their encounters with Asian nomads. Indeed, it was the Seljuk Turks' supposed ill treatment of Christian pilgrims in Jerusalem that ostensibly led to the Crusades, which Mackinder considers the beginning of Europe's collective modern history.

Russia, meanwhile, though protected by forest glades against many a rampaging host, nevertheless fell prey in the 13th century to the Golden Horde of the Mongols. These invaders decimated and subsequently changed Russia. But because most of Europe knew no such level of destruction, it was able to emerge as the world's political cockpit, while Russia was largely denied access to the European Renaissance. The ultimate land-based empire, with few natural barriers against invasion, Russia would know forevermore what it was like to be brutally conquered. As a result, it would become perennially obsessed with expanding and holding territory.

Key discoveries of the Columbian epoch, Mackinder writes, only reinforced the cruel facts of geography. In the Middle Ages, the peoples of Europe were largely confined to the land. But when the sea route to India was found around the Cape of Good Hope, Europeans suddenly had access to the entire rimland of southern Asia, to say nothing of strategic discoveries in the New World. While Western Europeans "covered the ocean with their fleets," Mackinder tells us, Russia was expanding equally impressively on land, "emerging from her northern forests" to police the steppe with her Cossacks, sweeping into Siberia, and sending peasants to sow the southwestern steppe with wheat. It was an old story: Europe versus Russia, a liberal sea power (like Athens and Venice) against a reactionary land power (like Sparta and Prussia). For the sea, beyond the cosmopolitan influences it bestows by virtue of access to distant harbors, provides the inviolate border security that democracy needs to take root.

In the 19th century, Mackinder notes, the advent of steam engines and the creation of the Suez Canal increased the mobility of European sea power around the southern rim of Eurasia, just as railways were beginning to do the same for land power in the Eurasian heartland. So the struggle was set for the mastery of Eurasia, bringing Mackinder to his thesis:

> As we consider this rapid review of the broader currents of history, does not a certain persistence of geographical relationship become evident? Is not the pivot region of the world's politics that vast area of Euro-Asia which is inaccessible to ships, but in antiquity lay open to the horse-riding nomads, and is today about to be covered with a network of railways?

Just as the Mongols banged at, and often broke down, the gates to the marginal regions surrounding Eurasia, Russia would now play the same conquering role, for as Mackinder writes, "the geographical quantities in the calculation are more measurable and more nearly constant than the human." Forget the czars and the commissars-yet-to-be in 1904; they are but trivia compared with the deeper tectonic forces of geography.

Mackinder's determinism prepared us for the rise of the Soviet Union and its vast zone of influence in the second half of the 20th century, as well as for the two world wars preceding it. After all, as historian Paul Kennedy notes, these conflicts were struggles over Mackinder's "marginal" regions, running from Eastern Europe to the Himalayas and beyond. Cold War containment strategy, moreover, depended heavily on rimland bases across the greater Middle East and the Indian Ocean. Indeed, the U.S. projection of power into Afghanistan and Iraq, and today's tensions with Russia over the political fate of Central Asia and the Caucasus have only bolstered Mackinder's thesis. In his article's last paragraph, Mackinder even raises the specter of Chinese conquests of the "pivot" area, which would make China the dominant geopolitical power. Look at how Chinese migrants are now demographically claiming parts of Siberia as Russia's political control of its eastern reaches is being strained. One can envision Mackinder's being right yet again.

The wisdom of geographical determinism endures across the chasm of a century because it recognizes that the most profound struggles of humanity are not about ideas but about control over territory, specifically the heartland and rimlands of Eurasia. Of course, ideas matter, and they span geography. And yet there is a certain geographic logic to where certain ideas take hold. Communist Eastern Europe, Mongolia, China, and North Korea were all contiguous to the great land power of the Soviet Union. Classic fascism was a predominantly European affair. And liberalism nurtured its deepest roots in the United States and Great Britain, essentially island nations and sea powers both. Such determinism is easy to hate but hard to dismiss.

To discern where the battle of ideas will lead, we must revise Mackinder for our time. After all, Mackinder could not foresee how a century's worth of change would redefine—and enhance—the importance of geography in today's world. One author who did is Yale University professor Paul Bracken, who in 1999 published *Fire in the East*. Bracken draws a conceptual map of Eurasia defined by the collapse of time and distance and the filling of empty spaces. This idea leads him to declare a "crisis of room." In the past, sparsely populated geography acted as a safety mechanism. Yet this is no longer the case, Bracken argues, for as empty space increasingly disappears, the very "finite size of the earth" becomes a force for instability. And as I learned at the U.S. Army's Command and General Staff College, "attrition of the same adds up to big change."

One force that is shrinking the map of Eurasia is technology, particularly the military applications of it and the rising power it confers on states. In the early Cold War, Asian militaries were mostly lumbering, heavy forces whose primary purpose was national consolidation. They focused inward. But as national wealth accumulated and the computer revolution took hold, Asian militaries from the oil-rich Middle East to the tiger economies of the Pacific developed full-fledged, military-civilian postindustrial complexes, with missiles and fiber optics and satellite phones. These states also became bureaucratically more cohesive, allowing their militaries to focus outward, toward other states. Geography in Eurasia, rather than a cushion, was becoming a prison from which there was no escape.

Now there is an "unbroken belt of countries," in Bracken's words, from Israel to North Korea, which are developing ballistic missiles and destructive arsenals. A map of these countries' missile ranges shows a series of overlapping circles: Not only is no one safe, but a 1914-style chain reaction leading to wider war is easily conceivable. "The spread of missiles and weapons of mass destruction in Asia is like the spread of the six-shooter in the American Old West," Bracken writes—a cheap, deadly equalizer of states.

The other force driving the revenge of geography is population growth, which makes the map of Eurasia more claustrophobic still. In the 1990s, many intellectuals viewed the 18th-century English philosopher Thomas Malthus as an overly deterministic thinker because he treated humankind as a species reacting to its physical environment, not a body of autonomous individuals. But as the years pass, and world food and energy prices fluctuate, Malthus is getting more respect. If you wander through the slums of Karachi or Gaza, which wall off multitudes of angry lumpen faithful—young men mostly—one can easily see the conflicts over scarce resources that Malthus predicted coming to pass. In three decades covering the Middle East, I have watched it evolve from a largely rural society to a realm of teeming megacities. In the next 20 years, the Arab world's population will nearly double while supplies of groundwater will diminish.

A Eurasia of vast urban areas, overlapping missile ranges, and sensational media will be one of constantly enraged crowds, fed by rumors transported at the speed of light from one Third World megalopolis to another. So in addition to Malthus, we will also hear much about Elias Canetti, the 20th-century philosopher of crowd psychology: the phenomenon of a mass of people abandoning their individuality for an intoxicating collective symbol. It is in the cities of Eurasia principally where crowd psychology will have its greatest geopolitical impact. Alas, ideas do matter. And it is the very compression of geography that will provide optimum breeding grounds for dangerous ideologies and channels for them to spread.

All of this requires major revisions to Mackinder's theories of geopolitics. For as the map of Eurasia shrinks and fills up with people, it not only obliterates the artificial regions of area studies; it also erases Mackinder's division of Eurasia into a specific "pivot" and adjacent "marginal" zones. Military assistance from China and North Korea to Iran can cause Israel to take military actions. The U.S. Air Force can attack landlocked Afghanistan from Diego Garcia, an island in the middle of the Indian Ocean. The Chinese and Indian navies can project power from the Gulf of Aden to the South China Sea—out of their own regions and along the whole rimland. In short, contra Mackinder, Eurasia has been reconfigured into an organic whole.

The map's new seamlessness can be seen in the Pakistani outpost of Gwadar. There, on the Indian Ocean, near the Iranian border, the Chinese have constructed a spanking new deep-water port. Land prices are booming, and people talk of this still sleepy fishing village as the next Dubai, which may one day link towns in Central Asia to the burgeoning middle-class fleshpots of India and China through pipelines, supertankers, and the Strait of Malacca. The Chinese also have plans for developing other Indian Ocean ports in order to transport oil by pipelines directly into western and central China, even as a canal and land bridge are possibly built across Thailand's Isthmus of Kra. Afraid of being outflanked by the Chinese, the Indians are expanding their own naval ports and strengthening ties with both Iran and Burma, where the Indian-Chinese rivalry will be fiercest.

Much of Eurasia will eventually be as claustrophobic as the Levant, with geography controlling everything and no room to maneuver. The battle over land between Israelis and Palestinians is a case of utter geographical determinism. This is Eurasia's future as well.

These deepening connections are transforming the Middle East, Central Asia, and the Indian and Pacific oceans into a vast continuum, in which the narrow and vulnerable Strait of Malacca will be the Fulda Gap of the 21st century. The fates of the Islamic Middle East and Islamic Indonesia are therefore becoming inextricable. But it is the geographic connections, not religious ones, that matter most.

This new map of Eurasia—tighter, more integrated, and more crowded—will be even less stable than Mackinder thought. Rather than heartlands and marginal zones that imply separateness, we will have a series of inner and outer cores that are fused together through mass politics and shared paranoia. In fact, much of Eurasia will eventually be as claustrophobic as Israel and the Palestinian territories, with geography controlling everything and no room to maneuver. Although Zionism shows the power of ideas, the battle over land between Israelis and Palestinians is a case of utter geographical determinism. This is Eurasia's future as well.

The ability of states to control events will be diluted, in some cases destroyed. Artificial borders will crumble and become more fissiparous, leaving only rivers, deserts, mountains, and other enduring facts of geography. Indeed, the physical features of the landscape may be the only reliable guides left to understanding the shape of future conflict. Like rifts in the Earth's crust that produce physical instability, there are areas in Eurasia that are more prone to conflict than others. These "shatter zones" threaten to implode, explode, or maintain a fragile equilibrium. And not surprisingly, they fall within that unstable inner core of Eurasia: the greater Middle East, the vast way station between the Mediterranean world and the Indian subcontinent that registers all the primary shifts in global power politics.

This inner core, for Mackinder, was the ultimate unstable region. And yet, writing in an age before oil pipelines and ballistic missiles, he saw this region as inherently volatile, geographically speaking, but also somewhat of a secondary concern. A century's worth of technological advancement and population explosion has rendered the greater Middle East no less volatile but dramatically more relevant, and where Eurasia is most prone to fall apart now is in the greater Middle East's several shatter zones.

I'll never forget what a U.S. military expert told me in Sanaa: "Terrorism is an entrepreneurial activity, and in Yemen you've got over 20 million aggressive, commercial-minded, and well-armed people, all extremely hard-working compared with the Saudis next door. It's the future, and it terrifies the hell out of the government in Riyadh."

The Indian subcontinent is one such shatter zone. It is defined on its landward sides by the hard geographic borders of the Himalayas to the north, the Burmese jungle to the east, and the somewhat softer border of the Indus River to the west. Indeed, the border going westward comes in three stages: the Indus; the unruly crags and canyons that push upward to the shaved wastes of Central Asia, home to the Pashtun tribes; and, finally, the granite, snow-mantled massifs of the Hindu Kush, transecting Afghanistan itself. Because these geographic impediments are not contiguous with legal borders, and because barely any of India's neighbors are functional states, the current political organization of the subcontinent should not be taken for granted. You see this acutely as you walk up to and around any of these land borders, the weakest of which, in my experience, are the official ones—a mere collection of tables where cranky bureaucrats inspect your luggage. Especially in the west, the only border that lives up to the name is the Hindu Kush, making me think that in our own lifetimes the whole semblance of order in Pakistan and southeastern Afghanistan could unravel, and return, in effect, to vague elements of greater India.

In Nepal, the government barely controls the countryside where 85 percent of its people live. Despite the aura bequeathed by the Himalayas, nearly half of Nepal's population lives in the dank and humid lowlands along the barely policed border with India. Driving throughout this region, it appears in many ways indistinguishable from the Ganges plain. If the Maoists now ruling Nepal cannot increase state capacity, the state itself could dissolve.

The same holds true for Bangladesh. Even more so than Nepal, it has no geographic defense to marshal as a state. The view from my window during a recent bus journey was of the same ruler-flat, aquatic landscape of paddy fields and scrub on both sides of the line with India. The border posts are disorganized, ramshackle affairs. This artificial blotch of territory on the Indian subcontinent could metamorphose yet again, amid the gale forces of regional politics, Muslim extremism, and nature itself.

Like Pakistan, no Bangladeshi government, military or civilian, has ever functioned even remotely well. Millions of Bangladeshi refugees have already crossed the border into India illegally. With 150 million people—a population larger than Russia—crammed together at sea level, Bangladesh is vulnerable to the slightest climatic variation, never mind the changes caused by global warming. Simply because of its geography, tens of millions of people in Bangladesh could be inundated with salt water, necessitating the mother of all humanitarian relief efforts. In the process, the state itself could collapse.

Of course, the worst nightmare on the subcontinent is Pakistan, whose dysfunction is directly the result of its utter lack of geographic logic. The Indus should be a border of sorts, but Pakistan sits astride both its banks, just as the fertile and teeming Punjab plain is bisected by the India-Pakistan border. Only the Thar Desert and the swamps to its south act as natural frontiers between Pakistan and India. And though these are formidable barriers, they are insufficient to frame a state composed of disparate, geographically based, ethnic groups—Punjabis, Sindhis, Baluchis, and Pashtuns—for whom Islam has provided insufficient glue to hold them together. All the other groups in Pakistan hate the Punjabis and the army they control, just as the groups in the former Yugoslavia hated the Serbs and the army they controlled. Pakistan's raison d'être is that it supposedly provides a homeland for subcontinental Muslims, but 154 million of them, almost the same number as the entire population of Pakistan, live over the border in India.

To the west, the crags and canyons of Pakistan's North-West Frontier Province, bordering Afghanistan, are utterly porous. Of all the times I crossed the Pakistan-Afghanistan border, I never did so legally. In reality, the two countries are inseparable. On both sides live the Pashtuns. The wide belt of territory between the Hindu Kush mountains and the Indus River is really Pashtunistan, an entity that threatens to emerge were Pakistan to fall apart. That would, in turn, lead to the dissolution of Afghanistan.

The Taliban constitute merely the latest incarnation of Pashtun nationalism. Indeed, much of the fighting in Afghanistan today occurs in Pashtunistan: southern and eastern Afghanistan and the tribal areas of Pakistan. The north of Afghanistan, beyond the Hindu Kush, has seen less fighting and is in the midst of reconstruction and the forging of closer links to the former Soviet republics in Central Asia, inhabited by the same ethnic groups that populate northern Afghanistan. Here is the ultimate world of Mackinder, of mountains and men, where the facts of geography are asserted daily, to the chagrin of U.S.-led forces—and of India, whose own destiny and borders are hostage to what plays out in the vicinity of the 20,000-foot wall of the Hindu Kush.

Another shatter zone is the Arabian Peninsula. The vast tract of land controlled by the Saudi royal family is synonymous with Arabia in the way that India is synonymous with the subcontinent. But while India is heavily populated throughout, Saudi Arabia constitutes a geographically nebulous network of oases separated by massive waterless tracts. Highways and domestic air links are crucial to Saudi Arabia's cohesion. Though India is built on an idea of democracy and religious pluralism, Saudi Arabia is built on loyalty to an extended family. But while India is virtually surrounded by troubling geography and dysfunctional states, Saudi Arabia's borders disappear into harmless desert to the north and are shielded by sturdy, well-governed, self-contained sheikhdoms to the east and southeast.

Where Saudi Arabia is truly vulnerable, and where the shatter zone of Arabia is most acute, is in highly populous Yemen to the south. Although it has only a quarter of Saudi Arabia's land area, Yemen's population is almost as large, so the all-important demographic core of the Arabian Peninsula is crammed into its mountainous southwest corner, where sweeping besalt plateaus, rearing up into sandcastle formations and volcanic plugs, embrace a network of oases densely inhabited since antiquity. Because the Turks and the British never really controlled Yemen, they did not leave behind the strong bureaucratic institutions that other former colonies inherited.

When I traveled the Saudi-Yemen border some years back, it was crowded with pickup trucks filled with armed young men, loyal to this sheikh or that, while the presence of the Yemeni government was negligible. Mudbrick battlements hid the encampments of these rebellious sheikhs, some with their own artillery. Estimates of the number of firearms in Yemen vary, but any Yemeni who wants a weapon can get one easily. Meanwhile, groundwater supplies will last no more than a generation or two.

I'll never forget what a U.S. military expert told me in the capital, Sanaa: "Terrorism is an entrepreneurial activity, and in Yemen you've got over 20 million aggressive, commercial-minded, and well-armed people, all extremely hard-working compared with the Saudis next door. It's the future, and it terrifies the hell out of the government in Riyadh." The future of teeming, tribal Yemen will go a long way to determining the future of Saudi Arabia. And geography, not ideas, has everything to do with it.

The Fertile Crescent, wedged between the Mediterranean Sea and the Iranian plateau, constitutes another shatter zone. The countries of this region—Jordan, Lebanon, Syria, and Iraq—are vague geographic expressions that had little meaning before the 20th century. When the official lines on the map are removed, we find a crude finger-painting of Sunni and Shiite clusters that contradict national borders. Inside these borders, the governing authorities of Lebanon and Iraq barely exist. The one in Syria is tyrannical and fundamentally unstable; the one in Jordan is rational but under quiet siege. (Jordan's main reason for being at all is to act as a buffer for other Arab regimes that fear having a land border with Israel.) Indeed, the Levant is characterized by tired authoritarian regimes and ineffective democracies.

Of all the geographically illogical states in the Fertile Crescent, none is more so than Iraq. Saddam Hussein's tyranny, by far the worst in the Arab world, was itself geographically determined: Every Iraqi dictator going back to the first military coup in 1958 had to be more repressive than the previous one just to hold together a country with no natural borders that seethes with ethnic and sectarian consciousness. The mountains that separate Kurdistan from the rest of Iraq, and the division of the Mesopotamian plain between Sunnis in the center and Shiites in the south, may prove more pivotal to Iraq's stability than the yearning after the ideal of democracy. If democracy doesn't in fairly short order establish sturdy institutional roots, Iraq's geography will likely lead it back to tyranny or anarchy again.

But for all the recent focus on Iraq, geography and history tell us that Syria might be at the real heart of future turbulence in the Arab world. Aleppo in northern Syria is a bazaar city with greater historical links to Mosul, Baghdad, and Anatolia than to Damascus. Whenever Damascus's fortunes declined with the rise of Baghdad to the east, Aleppo recovered its greatness. Wandering through the souks of Aleppo, it is striking how distant and irrelevant Damascus seems: The bazzars are dominated by Kurds, Turks, Circassians, Arab Christians, Armenians, and others, unlike the Damascus souk, which is more a world of Sunni Arabs. As in Pakistan and the former Yugoslavia, each sect and religion in Syria has a specific location. Between Aleppo and Damascus in the increasingly Islamist Sunni heartland. Between Damascus and the Jordanian border are the Druse, and in the mountain stronghold contiguous with Lebanon are the Alawites—both remnants of a wave of Shiism from Persia and Mesopotamia that swept over Syria a thousand years ago.

Elections in Syria in 1947, 1949, and 1954 exacerbated these divisions by polarizing the vote along sectarian lines. The late Hafez al-assad came to power in 1970 after 21 changes of government in 24 years. For three decades, he was the Leonid Brezhnev of the Arab world, staving off the future by failing to build a civil society at home. His sone Bashar will have to open the political system eventually, if only to keep pace with a dynamically changing society armed with satellite dishes and the Internet. But no one knows how stable a post-authoritarian Syria would be. Policymakers must fear the worst. Yet a post-Assad Syria may well do better than post-Saddam Iraq, precisely because its tyranny has been much less severe. Indeed, traveling from Saddam's Iraq to Assad's Syria was like coming up for air.

In addition to its inability to solve the problem of political legitimacy, the Arab world is unable to secure its own environment. The plateau peoples of Turkey will dominate the Arabs in the 21st century because the Turks have water and the Arabs don't. Indeed, to develop its own desperately poor southeast and thereby suppress Kurdish separatism, Turkey will need to divert increasingly large amounts of the Euphrates River from Syria and Iraq. As the Middle East becomes a realm of parched urban areas, water will grow in value relative to oil. The countries with it will retain the ability—and thus the power—to blackmail those without it. Water will be like nuclear energy, thereby making desalinization and dual-use power facilities primary targets of missile strikes in future wars. Not just in the West Bank, but everywhere there is less room to maneuver.

A final shatter zone is the Persian core, stretching from the Caspian Sea to Iran's north to the Persian Gulf to its south. Virtually all of the greater Middle East's oil and natural gas lies in this region. Just as shipping lanes radiate from the Persian Gulf, pipelines are increasingly radiating from the Caspian region to the Mediterranean, the Black Sea, China, and the Indian Ocean. The only country that straddles both energy-producing areas is Iran, as Geoffrey Kemp and

Robert E. Harkavy note in *Strategic Geography and the Changing Middle East*. The Persian Gulf possesses 55 percent of the world's crude-oil reserves, and Iran dominates the whole gulf, from the Shatt al-Arab on the Iraqi border to the Strait of Hormuz in the southeast—a coastline of 1,317 nautical miles, thanks to its many bays, inlets, coves, and islands that offer plenty of excellent places for hiding tanker-ramming speedboats.

It is not an accident that Iran was the ancient world's first superpower. There was a certain geographic logic to it. Iran is the greater Middle East's universal joint, tightly fused to all of the outer cores. Its border roughly traces and conforms to the natural contours of the landscape—plateaus to the west, mountains and seas to the north and south, and desert expanse in the east toward Afghanistan. For this reason, Iran has a far more venerable record as a nation-state and urbane civilization than most places in the Arab world and all the places in the Fertile Crescent. Unlike the geographically illogical countries of that adjacent region, there is nothing artificial about Iran. Not surprisingly, Iran is now being wooed by both India and China, whose navies will come to dominate the Eurasian sea lanes in the 21st century.

Of all the shatter zones in the greater Middle East, the Iranian core is unique: The instability Iran will cause will not come from its implosion, but from a strong, internally coherent Iranian nation that explodes outward from a natural geographic platform to shatter the region around it. The security provided to Iran by its own natural boundaries has historically been a potent force for power projection. The present is no different. Through its uncompromising ideology and nimble intelligence services, Iran runs an unconventional, postmodern empire of substate entities in the greater Middle East: Hamas in Palestine, Hezbollah in Lebanon, and the Sadrist movement in southern Iraq. If the geographic logic of Iranian expansion sounds eerily similar to that of Russian expansion in Mackinder's original telling, it is.

The geography of Iran today, like that of Russia before, determines the most realistic strategy to securing this shatter zone: containment. As with Russia, the goal of containing Iran must be to impose pressure on the contradictions of the unpopular, theocratic regime in Tehran, such that it eventually changes from within. The battle for Eurasia has many, increasingly interlocking fronts. But the primary one is for Iranian hearts and minds, just as it was for those of Eastern Europeans during the Cold War. Iran is home to one of the Muslim world's most sophisticated populations, and traveling there, one encounters less anti-Americanism and anti-Semitism than in Egypt. This is where the battle of ideas meets the dictates of geography.

In this century's fight for Eurasia, like that of the last century, Mackinder's axiom holds true: Man will initiate, but nature will control. Liberal universalism and the individualism of Isaiah Berlin aren't going away, but it is becoming clear that the success of these ideas is in large measure bound and determined by geography. This was always the case, and it is harder to deny now, as the ongoing recession will likely cause the global economy to contract for the first time in six decades. Not only wealth, but political and social order, will erode in many places, leaving only nature's frontiers and men's passions as the main arbiters of that age-old question: Who can coerce whom? We thought globalization had gotten rid of this antiquarian world of musty maps, but now it is returning with a vengeance.

We all must learn to think like Victorians. That is what must guide and inform our newly rediscovered realism. Geographical determinists must be seated at the same honored table as liberal humanists, thereby merging the analogies of Vietnam and Munich. Embracing the dictates and limitations of geography will be especially hard for Americans, who like to think that no constraint, natural or otherwise, applies to them. But denying the facts of geography only invites disasters that, in turn, make us victims of geography.

Better, instead, to look hard at the map for ingenious ways to stretch the limits it imposes, which will make any support for liberal principles in the world far more effective. Amid the revenge of geography, that is the essence of realism and the crux of wise policymaking—working near the edge of what is possible, without slipping into the precipice.

Critical Thinking

1. What does Robert Kaplan mean by "realism?"

2. According to Kaplan, what role does geography have in understanding global issues?

3. Identify Mackinder's "heartland" and what its modern implications are.

4. What are the main reasons that the "map of Eurasia is more claustrophobic"?

5. What are some of the most important "shatter zones?"

6. How does this article complement/contradict articles 1, 4, 24 and 28?

ROBERT D. KAPLAN is national correspondent for *The Atlantic* and senior fellow at the Center for a New American Security.

A Himalayan Rivalry

Asia's two giants are still unsure what to make of each other. But as they grow, they are coming closer—for good and bad.

Memories of a war between India and China are still vivid in the Tawang valley, a lovely, cloud-blown place high on the south-eastern flank of the Himalayas. They are nurtured first by the Indian army, humiliated in 1962 when the People's Liberation Army swept into Tawang from next-door Tibet. India now has three army corps—about 100,000 troops—in its far north-eastern state of Arunachal Pradesh, which includes Tawang.

With another corps in reserve, and a few Sukhoi fighter planes deployed last year to neighbouring Assam, they are a meaty border force, unlike their hapless predecessors. In 1962 many Indian troops were sent shivering to the front in light cotton uniforms issued for Punjab's fiery plains. In a weeklong assault the Chinese seized much of Arunachal, as well as a slab of Kashmir in the western Himalayas, and killed 3,000 Indian officers and men. Outside Tawang's district headquarters a roadside memorial, built in the local Buddhist style, commemorates these dead. At a famous battle site, below the 14,000-foot pass that leads into Tawang, army convoys go slow, and salute their ghosts.

In wayside villages of solid white houses fluttering with coloured prayer-flags, China's two-week occupation of Tawang is also remembered. Local peasants, aged 60 and more but with youthful Tibetan features, light-brown and creased by the wind, recall playing Sho (Tibetan Mahjong) with the invaders. Many say they remember them fondly: the Chinese, they note, helped get in the wheat harvest that year. "They were little men, but they were always ready to help. We had no problem with them," says Mem Nansey, an aged potato farmer. The Chinese withdrew to Tibet, their superiority established but their supply lines overstretched, barely a fortnight after they had come. "We weren't sorry to see the back of them, either," says Mr Nansey, concerned, it seems, that no one should doubt his loyalty to Delhi, 1,500km (930 miles) to the west.

His ambivalence is widely shared. China and India, repositories of 40% of the world's people, are often unsure what to make of each other. Since re-establishing diplomatic ties in 1976, after a post-war pause, they and their relationship have in many ways been transformed. The 1962 war was an act of Chinese aggression most obviously springing from China's desire for western Aksai Chin, a lofty plain linking Xinjiang to Tibet. But its deeper causes included a famine in China and economic malaise in both countries. China and India are now the world's

fastest-growing big economies, however, and in a year or two, when India overtakes Japan on a purchasing-power-parity basis, they will be the world's second- and third-biggest. And as they grow, Asia's giants have come closer.

Their two-way trade is roaring: only $270m in 1990, it is expected to exceed $60 billion this year. They are also tentatively co-operating, for their mutual enrichment, in other ways: for example, by co-ordinating their bids for the African oil supplies that both rely on. Given their contrasting economic strengths—China's in manufacturing, India's in services—some see an opportunity for much deeper co-operation. There is even a word for this vision, "Chindia". On important international issues, notably climate-change policy and world trade, their alignment is already imposing.

Their leaders naturally talk up these pluses: at the summit of the BRICs (Brazil, Russia, India, China) in Brasília in April, for example, and during celebrations in Beijing earlier this year to commemorate the 60th anniversary of India's recognition of the People's Republic. "India and China are not in competition," India's sage-like prime minister, Manmohan Singh, often says. "There is enough economic space for us both."

China's president, Hu Jintao, says the same. And no doubt both want to believe it. The booms in their countries have already moved millions out of poverty, especially in China, which is far ahead on almost every such measure of progress (and also dismissive of the notion that India could ever rival it). A return to confrontation, besides hugely damaging the improved image of both countries, would plainly jeopardise this movement forward. That is why the secular trend in China-India relations is positive.

Yet China and India are in many ways rivals, not Asian brothers, and their relationship is by any standard vexed—as recent quarrelling has made abundantly plain. If you then consider that they are, despite their mutual good wishes, old enemies, bad neighbours and nuclear powers, and have two of the world's biggest armies—with almost 4m troops between them—this may seem troubling.

Forget Chindia

There are many caveats to the recent improvement in their relationship. As the world's oil wells run dry, many—including sober analysts in both countries—foresee China-India rivalry redrawn as a cut-throat contest for an increasingly scarce resource. The two oil-gluggers' recent co-operation on energy was, after all, as unusual as it was tentative. More often, Chinese state-backed energy firms compete with all-comers, for Sudanese oil and Burmese gas, and win.

Rivalry over gas supplies is a bigger concern for Indian policymakers. They fear China would be more able to "capture" gas by building massive pipelines overnight. Water is already an object of contention, given that several of the big rivers of north India, including the Brahmaputra, on which millions depend, rise in Tibet. China recently announced that it is building a dam on the Brahmaputra, which it calls the Yarlung Tsangpo, exacerbating an old Indian fear that the Beijing regime means to divert the river's waters to Chinese farmers.

As for Chindia, it can seem almost too naive to bother about. Over 70% of India's exports to China by value are raw materials, chiefly iron ore, bespeaking a colonial-style trade relationship that is hugely favourable to China. A proliferating range of Chinese non-tariff barriers to Indian companies, which India grumbles about, is a small part of this. The fault lies chiefly with India's uncompetitive manufacturing. It is currently cheaper, an Indian businessman says ruefully, to export plastic granules to China and then import them again in bucket-form, than it is to make buckets in India.

This is a source of tension. India's great priority is to create millions of jobs for its young, bulging and little-skilled population, which will be possible only if it makes huge strides in manufacturing. Similarly, if China trails India in IT services at present, its recent investments in the industry suggest it does not plan to lag for long.

Yet there is another, more obvious bone of contention, which exacerbates all these others and lies at the root of them: the 4,000km border that runs between the two countries. Nearly half a century after China's invasion, it remains largely undefined and bitterly contested.

The basic problem is twofold. In the undefined northern part of the frontier India claims an area the size of Switzerland, occupied by China, for its region of Ladakh. In the eastern part, China claims an Indian-occupied area three times bigger, including most of Arunachal. This 890km stretch of frontier was settled in 1914 by the governments of Britain and Tibet, which was then in effect independent, and named the McMahon Line after its creator, Sir Henry McMahon, foreign secretary of British-ruled India. For China—which was afforded mere observer status at the negotiations preceding the agreement—the McMahon Line represents a dire humiliation.

China also particularly resents being deprived of Tawang, which—though south of the McMahon Line—was occupied by Indian troops only in 1951, shortly after China's new Communist rulers dispatched troops to Tibet. This district of almost 40,000 people, scattered over 2,000 square kilometres of valley and high mountains, was the birthplace in the 17th century of the sixth Dalai Lama (the incumbent incarnation is the 14th). Tawang is a centre of Tibet's Buddhist culture, with one of the biggest Tibetan monasteries outside Lhasa. Traditionally, its ethnic Monpa inhabitants offered fealty to Tibet's rulers—which those aged peasants around Tawang also remember. "the Tibetans came for money and did nothing for us," said Mr Nansey, referring to the fur-cloaked Tibetan officials who until the late 1940s went from village to village extracting a share of the harvest.

Making matters worse, the McMahon Line was drawn with a fat nib, establishing a ten-kilometre margin for error, and it has never been demarcated. With more confusion in the central sector, bordering India's northern state of Uttarakhand, there are in all a dozen stretches of frontier where neither side knows where even the disputed border should be. In these "pockets", as they are called, Indian and Chinese border guards circle each other endlessly while littering the Himalayan hillsides—as dogs mark lampposts—to make their presence known. When China-India relations are strained, this gives rise to tit-for-tat and mostly bogus accusations of illegal border incursions—for which each side can offer the other's empty cigarette and noodle packets as evidence. In official Indian parlance such proof is grimly referred to as "telltale signs". It is plainly garbage. Yet this is a carefully rehearsed and mutually comprehensible ritual for which both sides deserve credit, of a sort. Despite several threatened dust-ups—including one in 1986 that saw 200,000 Indian troops rushed to northern Tawang district—there has been no confirmed exchange of fire between Indian and Chinese troops since 1967.

Hands Extended— and Withdrawn

It would be even better if the two countries would actually settle their dispute, and, until recently, that seemed imaginable. The obvious solution, whereby both sides more or less accept the status quo, exchanging just a few bits of turf to save face, was long ago advocated by China, including in the 1980s by the then prime minister, Deng Xiaoping. India's leaders long considered this politically impossible. But in 2003 a coalition government led by the Hindu-nationalist Bharatiya Janata Party—which in 1998 had cited the Chinese threat to justify its decision to test a nuclear bomb—launched an impressive bid for peace. For the first time India declared itself ready to compromise on territory, and China appeared ready to meet it halfway. Both countries appointed special envoys, who have since met 13 times, to lead the negotiations that followed. This led to an outline deal in 2005, containing the "guiding principles and political parameters" for a final settlement. Those included an agreement that it would involve no exchange of "settled populations"—which implied that China had dropped its historical demand for Tawang.

Yet the hopes this inspired have faded. In ad hoc comments from Chinese diplomats and through its state-controlled media—which often refer to Arunachal as Chinese South Tibet—China appears to have reasserted its demand for most of India's far north-eastern state. Annoying the Indians further, it started issuing special visas to Indians from Arunachal and Kashmir—after having denied a visa to an Indian official from Arunachal on the basis that he was, in fact, Chinese. It also objected to a $60m loan to India from the Asian Development Bank, on the basis that some of the money was earmarked for irrigation schemes in Arunachal. Its spokesman described a visit to Tawang by Mr Singh, ahead of a general election last year, as "provocative and dangerous". Chinese analysts warn against understanding from these hints that China has formally revised its position on the border. But that is India's suspicion. And no one, in either country, is predicting a border settlement soon.

In fact, the relationship has generally soured. Having belatedly woken up to the huge improvements China has made in its border infrastructure, enabling a far swifter mobilisation of Chinese troops there, India announced last year that it would deploy another 60,000 troops to Arunachal. It also began upgrading its airfields in Assam and deploying the Sukhois to them. India's media meanwhile reported a spate of "incursions" by Chinese troops. China's state-controlled media was more restrained, with striking exceptions. Last year an editorial in the *Global Times,* an English-language tabloid in Beijing, warned that "India needs to consider whether or not it can afford the consequences of a potential confrontation with China." Early this year India's outgoing national security adviser and special envoy to China, M.K. Narayanan, accused Chinese hackers of attacking his website, as well as those of other Indian government departments.

Recent diplomacy has brought more calm. Officials on both sides were especially pleased by their show of unity at the United Nations climate meeting in Copenhagen last December, where China and India, the world's biggest and fourth-biggest emitters of carbon gas, faced down American-led demands for them to undertake tougher anti-warming measures. A slight cooling in the America-India relationship, which President George Bush had pushed with gusto, has also helped. So, India hopes, has its appointment of a shrewd Mandarin-speaker, Shivshankar Menon, as its latest national security adviser and special envoy to China. He made his first visit to Beijing in this role last month; a 14th round of border talks is expected. And yet the China-India relationship has been bruised.

Negative Views

In China, whose Communist leaders are neither voluble nor particularly focused on India, this bruising is mostly clear from last year's quarrel itself. The Chinese, many of whom consider India a dirty, third-rate sort of place, were perhaps most obviously to blame for it. This is despite China's conspicuous recent success in settling its other land disputes, including with Russia and Vietnam—a fact Chinese commentators often cite to indicate Indian intransigence. Chinese public opinion also seems to be turning against India, a country the Chinese have been wont to remark on fondly, if at all, as the birthplace of Buddhism. According to a recent survey of global opinion released by the BBC, the Chinese show a "distinct cooling" towards India, which 47% viewed negatively.

In garrulous, democratic India, the fallout is easier to gauge. According to the BBC poll, 38% of Indians have a negative view of China. In fact, this has been more or less the case since the defeat of 1962. Lamenting the failure of Indian public opinion to move on, Patricia Uberoi, a sociologist at Delhi's Centre for the Study of Developing Societies, notes that while there have been many Indian films on the subcontinent's violent partition, including star-crossed Indo-Pakistani romances, there has been only one notable Indian movie on the 1962 war: a

propaganda film called "Haqeeqat", or "Truth", supported by the Indian defence ministry.

Hawkish Indian commentators are meanwhile up in arms. "China, in my view, does not want a rival in Asia," says Brajesh Mishra, a former national security adviser and special envoy to China, who drafted the 2005 agreement and is revered by the hawks. "Its main agenda is to keep India preoccupied with events in South Asia so it is constrained from playing a more important role in Asian and global affairs." Senior officials present a more nuanced analysis, noting, for example, that India has hardly been alone in getting heat from China: many countries, Asian and Western, have similarly been singed. Yet they admit to heightened concern over China's intentions in South Asia, and foresee no hope for a settlement of the border. Nicholas Burns, a former American diplomat who led the negotiations for an America-India nuclear co-operation deal that was concluded in 2008, and who now teaches at Harvard University, suspects that over the past year China has supplanted Pakistan as the main worry of Indian policymakers. He considers the China-India relationship "exceedingly troubled and perturbed" and thinks that it will remain "uneasy for many years to come".

Fear of Encirclement

For foreign-policy realists, who see China and India locked in a battle for Asian supremacy, this is inevitable. Even fixing the border could hardly mitigate the tension. More optimistic analysts, and there are many, even if currently hushed, consider this old-school nonsense. Though both India and China have their rabid fringe, they say, they are rational enough to know that a strategic struggle would be sapping and, given each other's vast size, unwinnable. Both are therefore committed, as they claim, to fixing the border and fostering better relations. Yet there are a few impediments to this—of which two are most often cited by analysts in Beijing and Delhi.

One is represented by the America-India nuclear deal, agreed in principle between Mr Singh and Mr Bush in 2005. Not unreasonably, China took this as a sign that America wanted to use India as a counterweight to China's rise. It also considered the pact hypocritical: America, while venting against China's ally, North Korea, going nuclear (which it did a year later), was offering India a free pass to nuclear-power status, despite its refusal to sign the Nuclear Non-Proliferation Treaty. Indian analysts believe that China, in a cautious way, tried to scupper the deal by encouraging some of its opponents, including Ireland and Sweden, to vote against it in the Nuclear Suppliers Group, a 46-member club from which it required unanimous approval.

This glitch reflects a bigger Chinese fear of encirclement by America and its allies, a fear heightened by a recent burst of American activity in Asia. The United States has sought to strengthen security ties with South-East Asian countries, including Vietnam and Indonesia. It has also called on China, in an unusually public fashion, to be more accommodating over contested areas of the South China Sea—where America and India share concerns about a Chinese naval build-up, including the construction of a nuclear-submarine base on the Chinese island of Hainan. In north-east Asia, America has launched military exercises with South Korea in response to North Korea's alleged sinking of a South Korean warship in March. Some Chinese analysts, with ties to the government, consider these a direct challenge to China.

China is deeply suspicious of America's military campaign in nearby Afghanistan (and covertly in Pakistan), which is supported from bases in Central Asian countries. It is also unimpressed by a growing closeness between India and Japan, its main Asian rival. Japanese firms are, for example, expected to invest $10 billion, and perhaps much more, in a 1,500km "industrial corridor" between Delhi and Mumbai. In 2007 Japanese warships took part in a naval exercise in the Bay of Bengal, also involving Indian, Australian and Singaporean ships and the American nuclear-powered vessels *USS Nimitz* and *USS Chicago,* which was hosted by India and was the biggest ever held in the region.

This seemed to back a proposal, put about by American think-tankers, for an "axis of democracies" to balance China. Officially, India would want no part of this. "We don't want to balance China," says a senior Indian official. But, he adds, "all the democracies do feel it is safer to be together. Is China going to be peaceful or not? We don't know. In the event that China leaves the path of peaceful rise, we would work very closely together."

India also fears encirclement, and with reason. America's Pentagon, in an annual report on China's military power released on August 16th, said China's armed forces were developing "new capabilities" that might extend their reach into the Indian Ocean. China has also made big investments in all India's neighbours. It is building deepwater ports in Pakistan and Bangladesh, roads in Nepal and oil and gas pipelines in Myanmar. Worse, it agreed in 2008 to build two nuclear-power plants for its main regional ally, Pakistan—a deal that also worried America, who saw it as a tit-for-tat response to its nuclear deal with India. (China has become Pakistan's biggest supplier of military hardware, including fighter jets and guided-missile frigates, and in the past has given it weapons-grade fissile material and a tested bomb design as part of its nuclear support.)

Muffling Tibet

Hawkish Indians consider these Chinese investments as a "string of pearls" to throttle India. Wiser ones point out that India is too big to throttle—and that China's rising influence in South Asia is an indictment of India's past inability to get on with almost any of its neighbours. Under Mr Singh, India has sought to redress this. It is boosting trade with Sri Lanka and Bangladesh, and sticking, with commendable doggedness in the face of little encouragement, to the task of making peace with Pakistan. That would be glorious for both countries; it would also remove a significant China-India bugbear.

The other great impediment to better relations is Tibet. Its fugitive Dalai Lama and his "government-in-exile" have found refuge in India since 1959—and China blames him, and by extension his hosts, for the continued rebelliousness in his homeland. A Tibetan uprising in March 2008, the biggest in decades, was therefore a major factor in last year's China-India spat. It led to China putting huge pressure on India to stifle the anti-China Tibetan protests that erupted in India—especially one intended to disrupt the passage of the Olympic torch through Delhi en route to Beijing. It also objected to a visit to Tawang by the Dalai Lama last November, which it predictably called a "separatist action". This visit, from which leftover banners of welcome still festoon the town's main bazaar, perhaps reminded China why it is so fixated on Tawang—as a centre of the Tibetan Buddhist culture that it is struggling, all too visibly, to control.

Mindful of the huge support the Dalai Lama enjoys in India, its government says it can do little to restrict him. Yet it policed the protest tightly, and also barred foreign journalists from accompanying him to Tawang. India would perhaps rather be spared discreet balancing acts of this sort. "But we're stuck with him, he's our guest," says V.R. Raghavan, a retired Indian general and veteran of the 1962 war. Indeed, many Indian pundits consider that China will never settle the border, and so relinquish a potential source of leverage over India, while the 75-year-old lama is alive.

After his death, China will attempt to control his holy office as it has those of other senior lamas. It will "discover" the reincarnated Dalai Lama in Tibet, or at least endorse the choice of its agents, and attempt to groom him into a more biddable monk. In theory that would end a major cause of China-India discord, but only if the Chinese can convince Tibetans that their choice is the right one, which seems unlikely. The Dalai Lama has already indicated that he may choose to be "reborn" outside China. There is talk of the important role Tawang has often played in identifying incarnations of the Dalai Lama, or even that the 14th may choose to reincarnate in Tawang itself.

For the abbot of Tawang's main monastery, Guru Tulku Rinpoche, that would be a great blessing. "If his holiness chooses to be born in Tawang, we would be so happy," he says in his red-carpeted monastic office, as half a dozen skinny lads file in to be inducted into monkhood. Silently, they prostrate themselves before the abbot, while he scribbles down their new monastic names. Outside his window, the early morning sun sparkles through the white clouds that hang low over Tawang. It is hard to think that this remote and tranquil spot could have caused such a continent-sized ruckus. Yet, if the abbot has his wish, it will cause a lot more trouble yet.

Critical Thinking

1. What is the point of view of this article?

2. What reasons are offered to support this point of view?

3. How does this article complement/contradict Kaplan's geopolitical analysis in Article 32?

4. How does this article complement/contradict the points of view presented in articles 1 and 4?

Living with a Nuclear Iran

Iran can be contained. The path to follow? A course laid out half a century ago by a young Henry Kissinger, who argued that American chances of checking revolutionary powers such as the Soviet Union depended on our credible willingness to engage them in limited war.

ROBERT D. KAPLAN

IN 1957, A 34-year-old Harvard faculty member, Henry Kissinger, published a book, *Nuclear Weapons and Foreign Policy,* putting forth a counterintuitive proposition: that at the height of the Cold War, with the United States and the Soviet Union amassing enough hydrogen bombs for Armageddon, a messy, limited war featuring conventional forces and a tactical nuclear exchange or two was still possible, and the United States had to be prepared for such a conflict. Fresh in Kissinger's mind was the Korean War, which had concluded with a truce only four years earlier—"a war to which," as he wrote, "an all-out strategy seemed particularly unsuited." But President Dwight D. Eisenhower believed that any armed conflict with Moscow would accelerate into a thermonuclear holocaust, and he rejected outright this notion of "limited" nuclear war.

The absence of a nuclear exchange during the Cold War makes Eisenhower and what became the doctrine of mutual assured destruction look wise in hindsight. But more than half a century after *Nuclear Weapons and Foreign Policy* was published, it still offers swift, searing insights into human nature and a deeply troubling contemporary relevance. Eurasia—from the Mediterranean Sea to the Sea of Japan—is today an almost unbroken belt of overlapping ballistic-missile ranges: those of Israel, Syria, Iran, Pakistan, India, China, and North Korea. Many of these nations have or seek to acquire nuclear arsenals; some are stirred by religious zealotry; and only a few have robust bureaucratic control mechanisms to inhibit the use of these weapons. This conjunction of circumstances increases the prospect of limited nuclear war in this century. Kissinger long ago considered this problem in full, and the current nuclear impasse with Iran gives fresh reason to bring his book back into the debate.

Kissinger begins his study by challenging the idea that peace constitutes the "'normal' pattern of relations among states." Indeed, he describes a world that seems anything but peaceful:

On the ideological plane, the contemporary ferment is fed by the rapidity with which ideas can be communicated and by the inherent impossibility of fulfilling the expectations aroused by revolutionary slogans. On the economic and social plane, millions are rebelling against standards of living as well as against social and racial barriers which had remained unchanged for centuries.

Continuing his description of a world that matches our own, he writes, "International relationships have become truly global . . . There are no longer any isolated areas." In 2010, that sounds utterly mundane; but then again, in Eisenhower's day, The idea that North Korea would help Syria to build a nuclear plant and thereby precipitate an Israeli military raid (as happened in 2007) would have seemed wildly improbable. Kissinger foresaw an interconnected world incessantly roiled by unsettling ideologies and unmet expectations.

Out of this turbulence inevitably come revolutionary powers, whose emergence is a critical theme in Kissinger's book:

Time and again states appear which boldly proclaim that their purpose is to destroy the existing structure and to recast it completely. And time and again, the powers that are the declared victims stand by indifferent or inactive, while the balance of power is overturned.

Obviously, Kissinger was concerned here with the Soviet Union. As he told me in an interview last spring in his Manhattan office, he considered Moscow a revolutionary power because of its instigation of the 1948—49 Berlin blockade, and its encouragement of the Korean War in 1950, which were very much recent history when he wrote—Stalin had been dead for only four years. Over nearly five decades, thanks at least in part to a Western strategy of containment that resulted in no limited nuclear exchanges, the behavior of the Soviet regime evolved. The revolutionary power had been tamed, if not by us, then by its own longevity.

To insert a nuclearizing Iran in place of the mid-20th-century Soviet Union is to raise several tantalizing possibilities. In his book, Kissinger writes that, by acquiring nuclear weapons, a nation becomes able, for the first time, to change the regional or global balance of power without an invasion or a declaration of war. Let us assume that Iran develops a nuclear capability—an outcome that seems likely despite the imposition of sanctions and the threat by Israel of some kind of preemptive military strike. Would a nuclear Iran be as dangerous a revolutionary power as the old Soviet Union? More broadly, how should the United States contend with the threat posed by Iran, North Korea, and other would-be revolutionary powers that seek to use their possession of nuclear weapons to overturn the status quo?

Kissinger's 1957 analysis of how the status quo powers respond to revolutionary powers seems sadly applicable to the situation with Iran today: "All their instincts will cause them to seek to integrate the revolutionary power into the legitimate framework with which they are familiar and which to them seems 'natural.'" They see negotiations as the preferred way to manage emerging differences. The problem is that for a revolutionary power, a negotiation is not "in itself a symptom of reduced tension," as the status quo powers would have us believe, but merely a tactic to gain time. Whereas for normal nations, a treaty has legal and moral weight, for the revolutionary power, treaty talks are merely a concessionary phase in the continuing struggle. Think of how North Korea has skillfully—and repeatedly—used the promise of giving up its nuclear capability as a negotiating tool to secure other benefits, from fuel oil to relief from sanctions.

"Iran," Kissinger told me, "merely by pursuing nuclear weapons, has given itself a role in the region out of proportion to its actual power, and it gains further by the psychological impact of its being able to successfully defy the United Nations Security Council." Nevertheless, he went on, he does not consider Iran a threat of the "same order of magnitude" as the 1950s' Soviet Union, even as it "ideologically and militarily challenges the Middle East order."

When I asked Kissinger whether a nuclear Iran would be containable, he suggested that he would want to take tough measures to prevent a nuclear Iran in the first place. He did tell me that the United States had "different deterrence equations" to consider: Iran versus Israel, Iran versus the Sunni Arabs, Iran versus its own dissidents, and Islam versus the West. All of these dynamics, he explained, would interact in the event of an Iran that goes nuclear, and lead to "even more-frequent crises" than we currently have in the Middle East.

But in spite of Iran's refusal thus far to avail itself of "the genuine opportunity to transform itself from a cause to a nation," Kissinger told me, the country's true strategic interests should "run parallel with our own." For example, Iran should want to limit Russia's influence in the Caucasus and Central Asia, it should want to limit the Taliban's influence in neighboring Afghanistan, it should accept stability in Iraq, and it should want to serve as a peaceful balancing power in the Sunni Arab world.

Indeed, I would argue that because Sunni Arabs from Saudi Arabia, the United Arab Emirates, Lebanon, and Egypt perpetrated the attacks of September 11, 2001, and because Sunni hostility to American and Israeli interests remains a conspicuous problem, the United States should theoretically welcome a strengthened Shiite role in the Middle East, were Iran to go through an even partial political transformation. And demographic, cultural, and other indicators all point to a positive ideological and philosophical shift in Iran in the medium to long term. Given this prognosis, and the high cost and poor

chances for success of any military effort to eliminate Iran's nuclear program, I believe that containment of a nuclear Iran is the most sensible policy for the United States.

The success of containment will depend on a host of regional factors. But its sine qua non will be the ability of the United States to underline any policy toward a nuclear-armed Iran with the credible threat of military action. As Kissinger told me, "I want America to sustain whatever measures it takes about Iran." As he writes in *Nuclear Weapons and Foreign Policy,* "Deterrence . . . is achieved when one side's readiness to run risks in relation to the other is high; it is least effective when the willingness to run risks is low, however powerful The military capability."

Kissinger well knows from personal experience that domestic politics temper U.S. willingness to run such risks. Limited wars—those conflicts when a nation chooses for political reasons not to bring to bear all the weapons at its disposal—have always been difficult for Americans. "My book" he told me, "was written after one limited war, in Korea, where the U.S. achieved some of its objectives. Since the book was published, we had a limited war in Vietnam, in which a sector of the U.S. population wanted to lose the war in order to purify America's soul. To a lesser extent, that was also the case in Iraq. That is a new experience. You can't fight a war for an exit strategy." His conclusion: "America can no longer engage in a conflict unless it knows it can win it."

The crux of Kissinger's book and, in many ways, his professional life is this ongoing tension between his belief that limited war is something that the United States must be prepared to wage and his recognition of the domestic upheavals that such wars inevitably trigger. To refuse as a matter of principle to fight limited wars is to leave America powerless, with only an inflexible and reactive policy against the subtle maneuvers of adversaries: "Our empiricism," Kissinger writes, "dooms us" to requiring all the facts of a case beforehand, by which point it is too late to act. The search for certainty, he goes on, reduces us to dealing with emergencies, not preventing them. But for a democracy that needs to mobilize an entire population through patient argument in order to deploy troops for war—and, therefore, requires a good-versus-evil cause to ensure public support—limited wars, with their nuanced objectives, are far more challenging than all-out ones.

We must be more willing, not only to accept the prospect of limited war but, as Kissinger does in his book of a half century ago, to accept the prospect of a limited nuclear war between states. For most of the 1950s, observes Lawrence Freedman, a strategic theorist and historian at King's College London, in *The Evolution of Nuclear Strategy,* "the imminence of a strategic stalemate was taken as a basic premise." Although Kissinger was not the first or only thinker to advocate that the West develop strategies for the limited use of nuclear weapons, his "challenging, confident, and assertive style" made him easily the most forceful and articulate.

Kissinger recognizes the inherent dangers of this new strategic approach. Indeed, writing in 1957 about a possible superpower confrontation, he is also describing a possible 21st-century India-Pakistan one:

A limited nuclear war which had to be improvised in the midst of military operations would be undertaken under the worst possible conditions. . . . Because of the need for rapid reaction which is imposed by the speed and power of modern weapons, a misinterpretation of the opponent's intentions . . . may well produce a cataclysm . . . And [the two adversaries'] difficulties would be compounded by the fact that they would have had no previous experience to serve as a guide.

As Kissinger argues in his book, the psychological advantage in limited war will constantly shift in favor of the side that convincingly conveys the intention of escalating, particularly if the escalation entails nuclear weapons. Armed with nuclear weapons, in other words, a cornered Pakistan in a limited war with India would be a fearsome thing to behold.

At the time of his writing *Nuclear Weapons and Foreign Policy,* some analysts took Kissinger to task for what one reviewer called "wishful thinking"—in particular, his insufficient consideration of civilian casualties in a limited nuclear exchange. Moreover, Kissinger himself later moved away from his advocacy of a NATO strategy that relied on short-range, tactical nuclear weapons to counterbalance the might of the Soviet Union's conventional forces. (The doctrinal willingness to suffer millions of West German civilian casualties to repel a Soviet attack seemed a poor way to demonstrate the American commitment to the security and freedom of its allies.) But that does not diminish the utility of Kissinger's thinking the unthinkable. Indeed, now that the nuclear club has grown, and nuclear weaponry has become more versatile and sophisticated, the questions that his book raises are even more relevant. The dreadful prospect of limited nuclear exchanges is inherent in a world no longer protected by the carapace of mutual assured destruction. Yet much as limited war has brought us to grief, our willingness to wage it may one day save us from revolutionary powers that have cleverly obscured their intentions—Iran not least among them.

Critical Thinking

1. What is the central premise of Kissinger's containment policy toward revolutionary powers?

2. How does Robert Kaplan interpret this 1950s-era doctrine in the context of contemporary Iran?

3. Robert Kaplan is the author of articles 32 and 34. How does this article complement/contradict Article 32?

ROBERT D. KAPLAN is an *Atlantic* national correspondent, a senior fellow at the Center for a New American Security, and a member of the Defense Policy Board. His newest book is *Monsoon: The Indian Ocean and the Future of American Power.*

The Border of Madness

In the almost three years since President Felipe Calderón launched a war on drug cartels, border towns in Mexico have turned into halls of mirrors where no one knows who is on which side or what chance remark could get you murdered. Some 14,000 people have been killed in that time—the worst carnage since the Mexican Revolution—and part of the country is effectively under martial law. Is this evidence of a creeping coup by the military? A war between drug cartels? Between the president and his opposition? Or just collateral damage from the (U.S.-supported) war on drugs? Nobody knows: Mexico is where facts, like people, simply disappear. The stakes for the U.S. are high, especially as the prospect of a failed state on our southern border begins to seem all too real.

PHILIP CAPUTO

Those famous words came to mind when another man named Díaz offered me an equally concise observation about the realities of life in the country today: "In Mexico it is dangerous to speak the truth. It is even dangerous to know the truth."

His full name is Fernando Díaz Santana. He hosts two AM-radio news-and-commentary shows in the small Chihuahuan city of Nuevo Casas Grandes. A stocky, broad-faced man in late middle age. he projects an air of warmth, openness, and intelligence. As he tells me that it's dangerous to speak or know the truth, the half-rueful, half-apologetic expression in his eyes makes it plain that he'd rather not keep his mouth shut and his mind closed.

He's received text messages from listeners cautioning him to be careful of what he says on the air. He takes these friendly warnings seriously; failure to heed them could bring a death sentence like the one meted out to Armando Rodríguez, a crime reporter murdered by an unidentified gunman in November 2008 in Juárez, the violent border city across the Rio Grande from El Paso, Texas. The fear of suffering a similar fate is a powerful incentive for self-censorship, for training a naturally inquisitive mind to acquire ignorance.

Poor Mexico. So far from God and so close to the United States.

—Porfirio Díaz, dictator of Mexico from 1876 to 1880 and 1884 to 1911

"So now we give just the objective facts," Díaz says as he sits facing me in a stuffy, windowless rear room of the radio station, in Nuevo Casas Grandes's central business district. He and the co-host of his afternoon show, David Andrew (pronounced Da-*veed* An-*dray*-oo), explain that the "objective facts" are those reported by the police or city hall or some other official source. Though the accuracy of such facts is often questionable, no questions dare be asked. "We say nothing more," Díaz adds. "As long as we don't get too deeply into a story, we are safe."

I am reminded of Winnie Verloc, the character in Joseph Conrad's *The Secret Agent* who "felt profoundly that things do not stand much looking into."

More than 14,000 people have been killed in the almost three years since President Felipe Calderón mobilized the army to fight Mexico's half-dozen major drug cartels. Virtually none of those homicides has been solved, partly because witnesses suffer short-term memory loss when questioned, and partly because the police, for various reasons, also feel profoundly that things do not stand much looking into.

Rodríguez's death is illustrative. His colleagues believe he was killed for an article he wrote linking relatives of Patricia González, the Chihuahuan state attorney general, to narcotics trafficking.

That is not idle theorizing. Jorge Luis Aguirre, a writer for LaPotaka.com, an online Juárez news service, had written extensively about corruption in the Chihuahuan state government, and did not spare González either. On the night of November 13, 2008, as he was driving to Rodríguez's wake, he got a call on his cell phone. The male caller said, "You're next, son of a bitch!" and hung up.

Aguirre immediately packed up his wife and sons and fled to El Paso, where he sought asylum. In March, testifying at a hearing of the U.S. Senate Judiciary Subcommittee on Crime and Drugs, he stated that he'd identified the source of the threats:

"Victor Valencia, a representative of the governor of the state of Chihuahua, had sent people to warn me to 'tone down' my

150

criticisms of the prosecutor, Patricia González, because if I didn't, he was going to kill me, using the Juárez cartel's preferred method of kidnapping followed by execution."

The aftermath reveals a lot about today's Mexico. Patricia González remains in her post. Victor Valencia has been promoted to chief of public security in Juárez. The federal deputy attorney general handling the Rodríguez murder case, Jesús Martín Huerta Yedra, was shot to death in his car, along with his secretary. The investigation has since gone nowhere, to no one's surprise. As the newspaper *El Diario* editorialized.

Friends of the journalist, who preferred not to give their names for security reasons, mentioned that they do not feel frustrated by the lack of advances in the case since from the beginning, they felt that the authorities had no intention of doing anything to clarify the crime.

To *clarify* the crime. Of the many things Mexico lacks these days, clarity is near the top of the list, It is dangerous to know the truth. Finding it is frustrating. Statements by U.S. and Mexican government officials, repeated by a news media that prefers simple story lines, have fostered the impression in the United States that the conflict in Mexico is between Calderón's white hats and the crime syndicates' black hats. The reality is far more complicated, as suggested by this statistic: out of those 14,000 dead, fewer than 100 have been soldiers. Presumably, army casualties would be far higher if the war were as straightforward as it's often made out to be.

What, then, accounts for the carnage, the worst Mexico has suffered since the revolution, a century ago? To be sure, many of the dead have been cartel criminals. Some were killed in firefights with the army, others in battles between the cartels for control of smuggling routes, and still others in power struggles within the cartels. The toll includes more than 1,000 police officers, some of whom, according to Mexican press reports, were executed by soldiers for suspected links to drug traffickers. Conversely, a number of the fallen soldiers may have been killed by policemen moonlighting as cartel hit men, though that cannot be proved. Meanwhile, human-rights groups have accused the military of unleashing a reign of terror—carrying out forced disappearances, illegal detentions, acts of torture, and assassinations—not only to fight organized crime but also to suppress dissidents and other political troublemakers. What began as a war on drug trafficking has evolved into a low-intensity civil war with more than two sides and no white hats, only shades of black. The ordinary Mexican citizen—never sure who is on what side, or who is fighting whom and for what reason—retreats into a private world where he becomes willfully blind, deaf, and above all, dumb.

The ordinary Mexican citizen-never sure who is on what side, or who is fighting whom and for what reason-retreats into a private world where he becomes willfully blind, deaf, and above all, dumb.

Which brings us back to Fernando Díaz and his avoidance of truth.

I have come to see him at the suggestion of Emilio Gutiérrez, who fled to the U.S. because army officers threatened him with death. During an interview at his hiding place north of the border, Gutiérrez told me about a mysterious event that occurred on February 12, 2008. Teams of gunmen, riding in SUVs and pickup trucks and described by witnesses as "dressed like soldiers," swept through Nuevo Casas Grandes and six neighboring communities between midnight and dawn, kidnapping and executing people.

The convoys covered 170 miles altogether, rolling through military checkpoints unimpeded. In Nuevo Casas Grandes, the "armed commandos," as they were called by the Mexican media, set fire to the house of a police subcommander and shot him to death as he ran outside. Two other people, one of them the uncle of a midlevel narcotics trafficker, were also executed. The press reported that 14 more were abducted, but the actual number was believed to be much higher. All the victims, except two who were apparently snatched by mistake and later released, vanished without a trace.

Gutiérrez, a reporter in *El Diario*'s Ascensión bureau, covered the operation. From what he'd seen with his own eyes and from interviews with eyewitnesses, he concluded that the perpetrators were dressed like soldiers for the simple reason that they *were* soldiers. An operation on that scale, he reasoned, could not have been conducted by gangs of pistoleros hastily thrown together: it required thorough planning, accurate intelligence, discipline, and coordination. Nor could pistoleros have driven through army roadblocks without being stopped. If the raid wasn't military, it must have been conducted with the army's cooperation.

That wasn't what Gutiérrez reported, however. He told me that his boss, José Martínez Valdéz, the editor of *El Diario*'s editions in northwest Chihuahua, instructed him to "not cause problems by writing that this was military." Gutiérrez's silence did not win him any points with the army. Five months later, he was warned that the military was going to kill him, and he was forced to leave the country.

But why, I asked, would soldiers maraud the countryside on a murder-and-kidnapping spree? He replied that the raid was not part of the Mexican government's war *on* the drug cartels but a struggle *between* two powerful cartels: the Juárez organization, headed by Vicente Carillo, and the Sinaloa federation, whose boss, Joaquin "El Chapo" Guzmán, is the most-wanted man in Mexico. Gutiérrez said that in this instance the gunmen, whoever they were, had been after people they thought were working for the Juárez cartel.

"It's an open secret in Mexico," he said, "that the army is fighting the [Juárez] cartel to weaken them and pave the way for Guzmán."

Open secret or no, an allegation that soldiers may have acted on behalf of a drug lord needs to be substantiated. After all, Calderón's counter-narcotics strategy relies, with U.S. support, almost exclusively on the military.

With a short list of contacts provided by Gutiérrez, my interpreter, Molly Molloy, and I enter Mexico through the Palomas border crossing and head south into the Chihuahuan Desert. I have just been in Juárez and am relieved to not be going back to that industrialized border city—utterly charmless in the best of times, and these are far from the best of times. Juárez's main product now is the corpse. Last year, drug-related violence there claimed more than 1,600 lives, and the toll for the first nine months of this year soared beyond 1,800, and mounts daily. That makes Juárez, population 1.5 million, the most violent city in the world. Two lines of graffiti summed up a place where not only law and order but civilization itself has broken down: MI CIUDAD PIDE CLEMENCIA EN SU DEMENTIA ("My city asks for mercy in its madness"), and MI CIUDAD ES UN NEGRO LAMENTO UN AULLIDO INFINITO ("My city is a black lament, an eternal howl").

Nuevo Casas Grandes lies on a plateau near a fertile valley—cowboy-and-farmer country where cattle graze on the high desert ranges and apple and pecan orchards form tidy ranks on the city's outskirts. The city itself, with some 51,000 people, is known to archaeologicaliy minded tourists for its proximity to Paquimé, the site of ancient pueblo ruins. It looks prosperous by the standards of interior Mexico, with wide streets, a few decent hotels and restaurants, an airport, and several auto dealerships selling Fords and Jeeps and other familiar makes. If it weren't for all the Mexican license plates, I could believe we were in a town in the southwestern United States.

Our first call is at the offices of *El Diario,* housed in a whitewashed villa on the main drag. Molloy and I are hoping to meet with José Martínez Valdéz, who is Gutiérrez's former editor, and the news director, Victor Valdovinos. They can answer some of our questions and provide introductions to city officials. But repeated attempts to see Martinez are unsuccessful—he manages to dodge us all afternoon. We do get a very brief audience with Valdovinos. When we tell him what we are there for, he flinches and says, "You don't want to talk to me," then vanishes.

That leaves Fernando Díaz, whom we find at the radio station as he and David Andrew wrap up their afternoon show. They are willing to talk to us, and we go into the back room. Andrew, a heavyset, 30-ish man with dense carbon-black hair, shuts the door, either to muffle the noise from outside or to make sure no one overhears our conversation.

In the Mexico Mexicans have to live in, Díaz begins, life is "very hard, very bad," a statement he underscores with a statistic: last year, 115 homicides were committed in Nuevo Casas Grandes and its surrounding communities. That works out to a murder rate more than 20 times as high as New York City's.

It's at this juncture that he makes his comment about the dangers of speaking or knowing the truth. I begin inquiring about the February 2008 incident, but Díaz and his younger colleague aren't eager to discuss it.

I don't get anywhere, though Díaz casts doubt on Gutierrez's assertion that the raid was a military operation. All of this talk about human-rights abuses by the army is "a myth," Díaz insists. He is in fact cheered that an army battalion has been making rounds to bolster security in Nuevo Casas Grandes: "We are abandoned and unprotected here in northwest Chihuahua. It is a very big wish that the soldiers will bring peace. The

army is the only group we can trust," He adds by way of illustration that several sicarios, as professional assassins are called in Mexico, were arrested and confessed to killing 19 people in town.

Two of the *sicarios,* Andrew interjects, were his neighbors: "One guy worked in a car wash, the other guy was an army deserter." Two others turned out to be auto salesmen—"nice guys in the day, killers by night." Díaz says, as if he's voicing over a trailer for *Dr. Jekyll and Mr. Hyde.* "You are talking to me, a radio announcer, but you can't be sure that I'm not a sicario," Díaz adds. "You say you're an American reporter, but I don't know that you're not a *sicario.* You cannot trust anybody." He doesn't seem to notice that he's contradicted his earlier remark that only the army can be trusted.

> ## "You say you're an American reporter," Díaz tells me, "but i don't know that you're not a *sicario*"—a professional assassin. "You cannot trust anybody."

The question is, can the army be trusted, and if so, can it win this latest—and biggest—battle in the seemingly eadless "war on drugs"? Calderón has deployed more than 45,000 troops (out of a total force of 230,000) throughout the country. Of that number, about 7,000, reinforced by 2,300 federal policemen, occupy Juárez as part of Operación Conjunta Chihuahua—the Joint Chihuahuan Operation. The army has taken over all the policing functions. The city is under undeclared martial law.

Although many ordinary Mexicans welcome the army's intervention, certain that things would be far worse without it, approval has been far from universal. Claims of grievous abuses by the armed forces—unlawful detentions, disappearances, thefts, rapes, and murders—have increased sixfold in the past three years, according to Human Rights Watch. One hundred and seventy complaints have been filed in Chihuahua alone, says Gustavo de la Rosa, the former Chihuahua state ombudsman for Mexico's National Human Rights Commission.

Leaving aside the question of whether militarizing the antinarcotics campaign is the best way to go about things (a similar strategy in Colombia has been only partially successful), the fact is that, by destroying public trust in the armed forces, military misconduct undermines the entire effort, as I learned from a 50-year-old cleaning woman who now lives in Arizona and who asked to remain anonymous. She was visiting her aunt in Juárez last December when soldiers broke into a neighbor's house, claiming that they were looking for a suspect.

"They didn't say who," the woman told me. "They tore her house apart, took her jewelry and her money, and said that if she complained about what they did they were going to come back and kill her. People are more afraid of the police and soldiers than they are of the narcos, because they're very mean guys—not all, but many."

The fear goes beyond undisciplined soldiers running amok. In an interview, de la Rosa told me that the president, elected in 2006 by a margin as thin as an ATM card, called out the army not merely to fight the cartels and eliminate a threat to national sovereignty but to consolidate his power and confer legitimacy on his presidency. "Calderón wants to show the Congress that the military is with him," de la Rosa said. "And the military promised to support Calderón in exchange for being allowed out of the barracks, because the army wants to govern. Chihuahua is an experiment. What is happening here is in essence a military coup, a regional coup." To support this contention, he cited a change he has had to make in his own work. Under normal circumstances, he would file complaints of abuse with the state governor, but now. he said, "the governor is ineffective, so I have to go to General Felipe de Jesús Espitia, the *comandante* of the 5th Military District."

I was somewhat incredulous that the military was staging a creeping coup. To what end? I asked.

De la Rosa shrugged. "Actually, nobody really knows or understands what the military is up to," he answered, hedging a bit. Then he asserted that the army intends not to stamp out drug trafficking but to "control" it. "So now if a drug cartel wants to move drugs into the U.S., who would they go to? To the governor? No, to the general." (*El Universal,* Mexico's largest newspaper, reported in September that de la Rosa had received death threats from the army, apparently because of his sharp criticisms; sources have told me he has taken temporary refuge in the U.S.)

As de la Rosa suggested, there is a dismal history of collusion between the armed forces and organized crime. In the late 1980s, the Mexican defense secretary was caught peddling protection to three drug organizations, which paid him a total of $10 million. In 1997, Mexico's chief anti-narcotics officer was indicted for providing the Juárez cartel with classified drug-enforcement information in exchange for millions of dollars in bribes. In a 2001 essay in the *Journal of Contemporary Criminal Justice,* a University of Texas criminologist, Patrick O'Day, cited several instances of Mexican soldiers' guarding narcotics shipments and transporting them into the United States in military vehicles or by other means. These operations were so extensive and went on for so long that O'Day concluded that the army was a cartel unto itself.

But let us make the risky assumption that today's army is no longer involved in drug trafficking. The belief that it is exploiting a weak government to advance agendas beyond its declared mission is widespread, and not without reason. While many of the crimes alleged to have been committed by the armed forces appear to be the random acts of rogue troops, others may be part of a directed campaign with three possible objectives.

One objective is laudable—to get information about drug trafficking. The problem is that, in de la Rosa's words, "the army's investigative techniques are kidnapping and torture." But according to Cipriana Jurado, a veteran labor organizer and women's-rights activist, the military has another

purpose: trying to stifle dissent, she said, citing numerous arrests of political troublemakers. And, as Gutiérrez's case indicates, the generals also may be seeking to clamp down on Mexico's freewheeling press.

In seeking, much less speaking, the truth about what the army is up to, one often runs into the paradox of the Mexican reality: something dreadful happens and is then treated as if it hadn't happened. Facts, like people, simply disappear.

I experience this myself as I tour the ruins of a Juárez drug-rehabilitation center with my friend Julián Cardona, a photographer and Reuters correspondent. The rehab clinic is in a shabby two-story building on an unpaved street lined with cinder-block hovels, old cars, and derelict buses. A wind-whipped urban grit that feels dirtier than desert dust pelts our faces as we enter the rectangular patio strewn with rubble, its walls gouged by bullet holes. Small rooms lead off the patio, each with a hand-painted phrase above its door—COCINA for kitchen, SALA DE JUNTAS for meeting room D-TOX, which needs no translation.

We enter the meeting room. Votive candles gutter in glass jars arranged around an image of Jesus Christ propped up in one corner. The walls are peppered with bullet holes and spattered with dried blood. Cardona tells me what happened here on a Wednesday evening. August 13, 2008, as an Assembly of God pastor named Socorro García and her deacon, Joel Valle, conducted a service for the patients. After they and about 20 addicts gathered in the meeting room to sing hymns and hold a prayer service, García took the podium for altar call. "Is there anyone here who was a Christian in the past," she asked, "but who fell away into drugs and who would like to reconcile with God?" Several patients raised their hands. García summoned them.

Outside, a Ford pickup carrying a detachment of Mexican paratroopers was parked at an intersection no more than 50 yards away. Two other trucks pulled up in front of the rehab center. Eight men armed with assault rifles and 9-millimeter pistols and wearing bulletproof vests and ski masks piled out of the vehicles and rushed inside.

The shooting started in the patio, just as the patients were walking up to the podium in answer to García's call. Some flung themselves to the floor, others ran for their lives or huddled against a wall. García stood at the podium, crying out. "Muchachos! Ask God for another chance to live!" At that moment, four gunmen burst inside and, in her words, started "shooting in all directions."

García raised her hands and hollered above the gunshots, "Lord, send your angels to protect us!" A gunman looked at her through the eyeholes of his ski mask and she looked back. He stopped shooting. "I was right there in front of him," Garcia told Cardona. "He had already shot a lot of people, and one more life would have meant nothing to him, but he didn't shoot. Why? Maybe God did not allow it."

Neighbors called the Emergency Response Center, the equivalent of 911, but got no response. Accounts of the actions taken by the soldiers parked at the street corner differ. According to one, the soldiers stood by passively as the assassins jumped in their trucks and fled. According to another. they drove past the rehab center at high speed while the massacre was going on. People shouted to them to put a stop to it, but the soldiers kept going. This led one of the neighbors to conclude that they "were guarding the killers or came with them so that the police would not intervene."

In all, nine people were killed and five wounded. Among the dead was Joel Valle, the deacon. It was the worst mass murder in Juárez in years, Cardona says as I gaze at the flickering votives, the bloodstains and bullet holes framing the picture of Christ.

Of course, I have questions: Were any of the killers identified or captured? No. Was their motive determined? No, although there were rumors that they were after members of a street gang, the Aztecas, said to be hiding in the facility. Were the soldiers involved in the massacre? That's what eyewitnesses claimed, Cardona replies. I keep grasping for facts, hut realize it's futile. Cardona says, "This is the black hole of Mexico. You cannot see inside of it, and nothing gets out,"

Despite the heavy military and police presence, six rehabilitation clinics have been attacked in Juárez over the past two years. The deadliest incident occurred on September 2, when 18 people were executed. Government authorities claimed the massacres were part of a war of extermination between the Sinaloa and Juárez cartels.

The conduct of the Mexican military goes to the heart of U.S. counter-narcotics policy. In the past year, experts like General Barry McCaffrey (the drug czar in the Clinton administration) and political figures have warned that if the cartels are not contained, Mexico could become a failed state and the U.S. could find itself with an Afghanistan or a Pakistan on its southern border. Such forecasts are hyperbole, but the fact is that drug trafficking and its attendant corruption are a malignancy that has spread into Mexico's lymph system. To extend the metaphor, Calderón is attempting to perform radical surgery with the only instrument at his disposal—the army. It may be a tainted instrument, so the reasoning goes, but it is less tainted than the law-enforcement agencies.

Washington supports, indeed encourages, this approach through the Mérida Initiative, a security-cooperation agreement between the two countries that Congress passed and George W. Bush signed into law. Its aim is to provide $1.4 billion in funding, spread over several years, for military and law-enforcement training, equipment such as helicopters and surveillance aircraft, and judicial reforms. The aid package also includes conditions for improvements to Mexico's less-than-enviable record on human-rights issues. Fifteen percent of the funds can be withheld if Mexico fails to show progress on matters such as prosecuting human-rights violators and prohibiting the use of torture to obtain evidence and testimony.

And that is where U.S. policy becomes contradictory. It calls for a military solution to the trafficking problem. But there are very few, if any, civil safeguards on the actions of the Mexican military. Its soldiers are subject only to military law, even when deployed in their current crime-fighting capacity, and the country's military-justice system is, to understate things, opaque.

A good example is the case of Javier Rosales, a medical technician who died after he and a friend were captured and tortured by soldiers. Members of his family went to the state justice office and the federal attorney general's office to file a complaint against the soldiers and demand an investigation. They were turned away because, the officials said, charges of army misconduct fall under military jurisdiction. However, Enrique Torres, a spokesman for the Joint Chihuahuan Operation, told me that the army looks into such allegations only through internal investigations or when formal charges have been filed by state or federal prosecutors. It's pure catch-22: state or federal authorities will not receive complaints against soldiers, and the army will not investigate unless charges have been filed by state or federal authorities.

That is among the reasons why, out of the more than 2,000 complaints brought before Mexico's National Human Rights Commission, not one has resulted in the prosecution of a single soldier.

The provisions of the Mérida Initiative would appear to give the U.S. considerable leverage in compelling the Mexican army to act with more restraint and greater respect for the civil rights of the country's citizens. Financial leverage, that is. The moral authority of the U.S. has been eroded by accusations that it has employed torture and illegal detentions in the "war on terror," as well as by its status as the drug cartels' biggest market and its singularly unsuccessful efforts to dry up demand.

Every year, under the Foreign Assistance Act, the State Department is required to certify that its southern neighbor is fully cooperating in efforts to stem the export of illegal narcotics into the United States, Without certification, Mexico would be ineligible to receive the vast majority of American aid. But the U.S. government often soft-pedals criticisms of Mexico on matters such as corruption and human-rights offenses, for two reasons. One is U.S. sensitivity to the Mexican elite, which can be thin-skinned about what it regards as infringements from the north on its national sovereignty. The second is money. In the highly unlikely event that Mexico were decertified, the cutoff in U.S. aid would strain bilateral relations, trade agreements would be imperiled, and American businessmen would find it harder to operate south of the border. Also, of all the countries that export oil to the United States, Mexico, at 985,000 barrels a day, ranks third, behind Canada and Saudi Arabia.

That makes speaking the truth about Mexico politically and economically dangerous in official U.S. circles.

But a larger question arises. Even if tomorrow the Mexican military began waging its anti-narcotics campaign with the probity of, say, the Swiss Guard, could it overcome the power of cartels? The drug bosses and their organizations have become integrated into Mexican society, corrupting every aspect of the nation's life.

The U.S. government estimates that the cultivation and trafficking of illegal drugs directly employs 450,000 people in Mexico. Unknown numbers of people, possibly in the millions, are indirectly linked to the drug industry, which has revenues estimated to be as high as $25 billion a year, exceeded only by Mexico's annual income from manufacturing and oil exports. Dr. Edgardo Buscaglia, a law professor at the Autonomous Technological Institute in Mexico City and a senior legal and economic adviser to the UN and the World Bank, concluded in a recent report that 17 of Mexico's 31 states have become virtual narco-republics, where organized crime has infiltrated government, the courts, and the police so extensively that there is almost no way they can be cleaned up. The drug gangs have acquired a "military capacity" that enables them to confront the army on an almost equal footing.

"This in itself does not prove that we are in a situation of a failed state today," Buscaglia wrote. He seemed to be suggesting that the situation could change tomorrow—and not for the better.

Critical Thinking

1. What does the term "failed state" mean? Is it used in the same way as Lester Brown uses the term in Article #2?

2. What does Philip Caputo mean by "halls of mirrors"?

3. What role does the U.S. play in Mexico's drug wars?

PHILIP CAPUTO is the author of 14 books, including *A Rumor of War, Acts of Faith,* and most recently, *Crossers,* a novel about life on the Mexican border.

From *The Atlantic,* December 2009, pp. 62–69. Copyright © 2009 by Atlantic Monthly Group. Reprinted by permission of Tribune Media Services.

The Jihad against the Jihadis: How Moderate Muslim Leaders Waged War on Extremists—and Won

FAREED ZAKARIA

September 11, 2001, was gruesome enough on its own terms, but for many of us, the real fear was of what might follow. Not only had al-Qaeda shown it was capable of sophisticated and ruthless attacks, but a far greater concern was that the group had or could establish a powerful hold on the hearts and minds of Muslims. And if Muslims sympathized with al-Qaeda's cause, we were in for a herculean struggle. There are more than 1.5 billion Muslims living in more than 150 countries across the world. If jihadist ideology became attractive to a significant part of this population, the West faced a clash of civilizations without end, one marked by blood and tears.

These fears were well founded. The 9/11 attacks opened the curtain on a world of radical and violent Islam that had been festering in the Arab lands and had been exported across the globe, from London to Jakarta. Polls all over the Muslim world revealed deep anger against America and the West and a surprising degree of support for Osama bin Laden. Governments in most of these countries were ambivalent about this phenomenon, assuming that the Islamists' wrath would focus on the United States and not themselves. Large, important countries like Saudi Arabia and Indonesia seemed vulnerable.

More than eight eventful years have passed, but in some ways it still feels like 2001. Republicans have clearly decided that fanning the public's fears of rampant jihadism continues to be a winning strategy. Commentators furnish examples of backwardness and brutality from various parts of the Muslim world—and there are many—to highlight the grave threat we face.

But, in fact, the entire terrain of the war on terror has evolved dramatically. Put simply, the moderates are fighting back and the tide is turning. We no longer fear the possibility of a major country succumbing to jihadist ideology. In most Muslim nations, mainstream rulers have stabilized their regimes and their societies, and extremists have been isolated. This has not led to the flowering of Jeffersonian democracy or liberalism. But modern, somewhat secular forces are clearly in control and widely supported across the Muslim world. Polls, elections, and in-depth studies all confirm this trend.

The focus of our concern now is not a broad political movement but a handful of fanatics scattered across the globe. Yet Washington's vast nation-building machinery continues to spend tens of billions of dollars in Iraq and Afghanistan, and there are calls to do more in Yemen and Somalia. What we have to ask ourselves is whether any of that really will deter these small bands of extremists. Some of them come out of the established democracies of the West, hardly places where nation building will help. We have to understand the changes in the landscape of Islam if we are going to effectively fight the enemy on the ground, rather than the enemy in our minds.

Once, no country was more worrying than bin Laden's homeland. The Kingdom of Saudi Arabia, steward of the holy cities of Mecca and Medina, had surpassed Egypt as the de facto leader of the Arab world because of the vast sums of money it doled out to Islamic causes—usually those consonant with its puritanical Wahhabi doctrines. Since 1979 the Saudi regime had openly appeased its home-grown Islamists, handing over key ministries and funds to reactionary mullahs. Visitors to Saudi Arabia after 9/11 were shocked by what they heard there. Educated Saudis—including senior members of the government—publicly endorsed wild conspiracy theories and denied that any Saudis had been involved in the 9/11 attacks. Even those who accepted reality argued that the fury of some Arabs was inevitable, given America's one-sided foreign policy on the Arab–Israeli issue.

America's initial reaction to 9/11 was to focus on al-Qaeda. The group was driven out of its base in Afghanistan and was pursued wherever it went. Its money was tracked and blocked, its fighters arrested and killed. Many other nations joined in, from France to Malaysia. After all, no government wanted to let terrorists run loose in its land.

But a broader conversation also began, one that asked, "Why is this happening, and what can we do about it?" The most influential statement on Islam to come out of the post-9/11 era was not a presidential speech or an intellectual's essay. It was, believe it or not, a United Nations report. In 2002 the U.N. Development Program published a detailed study of the Arab world. The paper made plain that in an era of globalization, openness, diversity, and tolerance, the Arabs were the world's great laggards. Using hard data, the report painted a picture of political, social, and intellectual stagnation in countries from the Maghreb to the Gulf. And it was written by a team of Arab scholars. This was not paternalism or imperialism. It was truth.

The report, and many essays and speeches by political figures and intellectuals in the West, launched a process of reflection in the Arab world. The debate did not take the form that many in the West wanted—no one said, "You're right, we are backward." But still, leaders in Arab countries were forced to advocate modernity and moderation openly rather than hoping that they could quietly reap its fruits by day while palling around with the mullahs at night. The Bush administration launched a series of programs across the Muslim world to strengthen moderates, shore up civil society, and build forces of tolerance and pluralism. All this has had an effect. From Dubai to Amman to Cairo, in some form or another, authorities have begun opening up economic and political systems that had been tightly closed. The changes have sometimes been small, but the arrows are finally moving in the right direction.

Ultimately, the catalyst for change was something more lethal than a report. After 9/11, al-Qaeda was full of bluster: recall the videotapes of bin Laden and his deputy, Ayman al-Zawahiri, boasting of their plans. Yet they confronted a far less permissive environment. Moving money, people, and materials had all become much more difficult. So they, and local groups inspired by them, began attacking where they could—striking local targets rather than global ones, including a nightclub and hotel in Indonesia, a wedding party in Jordan, cafés in Casablanca and Istanbul, and resorts in Egypt. They threatened the regimes that, either by accident or design, had allowed them to live and breathe.

Over the course of 2003 and 2004, Saudi Arabia was rocked by a series of such terrorist attacks, some directed against foreigners, but others at the heart of the Saudi regime—the Ministry of the Interior and compounds within the oil industry. The monarchy recognized that it had spawned dark forces that were now endangering its very existence. In 2005 a man of wisdom and moderation, King Abdullah, formally ascended to the throne and inaugurated a large-scale political and intellectual effort aimed at discrediting the ideology of jihadism. Mullahs were ordered to denounce suicide bombings and violence more generally. Education was pried out of the hands of the clerics. Terrorists and terror suspects were "rehabilitated" through extensive programs of education, job training, and counseling. Central Command chief Gen. David Petraeus said to me, "The Saudi role in taking on al-Qaeda, both by force but also using political, social, religious, and educational tools, is one of the most important, least reported positive developments in the war on terror."

Perhaps the most successful country to combat jihadism has been the world's most populous Muslim nation, Indonesia. In 2002 that country seemed destined for a long and painful struggle with the forces of radical Islam. The nation was rocked by terror attacks, and a local Qaeda affiliate, Jemaah Islamiah, appeared to be gaining strength. But eight years later, JI has

been marginalized and mainstream political parties have gained ground, all while a young democracy has flowered after the collapse of the Suharto dictatorship.

Magnus Ranstorp of Stockholm's Center for Asymmetric Threat Studies recently published a careful study examining Indonesia's success in beating back extremism. The main lesson, he writes, is to involve not just government but civil society as a whole, including media and cultural figures who can act as counterforces to terrorism. (That approach obviously has greater potential in regions and countries with open and vibrant political systems—Southeast Asia, Turkey, and India—than in the Arab world.)

Iraq occupies an odd place in this narrative. While the invasion of Iraq inflamed the Muslim world and the series of blunders during the initial occupation period created dangerous chaos at the heart of the Middle East, Iraq also became a stage on which al-Qaeda played a deadly hand, and lost. As al-Qaeda in Iraq gained militarily, it began losing politically. It turned from its broader global ideology to focus on a narrow sectarian agenda, killing Shias and fueling a Sunni–Shia civil war. In doing so, the group also employed a level of brutality and violence that shocked most Iraqis. Where the group gained control, even pious people were repulsed by its reactionary behavior. In Anbar province, the heart of the Sunni insurgency, al-Qaeda in Iraq would routinely cut off the fingers of smokers. Even those Sunnis who feared the new Iraq began to prefer Shia rule to such medievalism.

Since 9/11, Western commentators have been calling on moderate Muslim leaders to condemn jihadist ideology, issue *fatwas* against suicide bombing, and denounce al-Qaeda. Since about 2006, they've begun to do so in significant numbers. In 2007 one of bin Laden's most prominent Saudi mentors, the preacher and scholar Salman al-Odah, wrote an open letter criticizing him for "fostering a culture of suicide bombings that has caused bloodshed and suffering, and brought ruin to entire Muslim communities and families." That same year Abdulaziz al ash-Sheikh, the grand mufti of Saudi Arabia, issued a *fatwa* prohibiting Saudis from engaging in jihad abroad and accused both bin Laden and Arab regimes of "transforming our youth into walking bombs to accomplish their own political and military aims." One of al-Qaeda's own top theorists, Abdul-Aziz el-Sherif, renounced its extremism, including the killing of civilians and the choosing of targets based on religion and nationality. Sherif—a longtime associate of Zawahiri who crafted what became known as al-Qaeda's guide to jihad—has called on militants to desist from terrorism, and authored a rebuttal of his former cohorts.

Al-Azhar University in Cairo, the oldest and most prestigious school of Islamic learning, now routinely condemns jihadism. The Darul Uloom Deoband movement in India, home to the original radicalism that influenced al-Qaeda, has inveighed against suicide bombing since 2008. None of these groups or people have become pro-American or liberal, but they have become anti-jihadist.

This might seem like an esoteric debate. But consider: the most important moderates to denounce militants have been the families of radicals. In the case of both the five young

American Muslims from Virginia arrested in Pakistan last year and Christmas bomber Umar Farouk Abdulmutallab, parents were the ones to report their worries about their own children to the U.S. government—an act so stunning that it requires far more examination, and praise, than it has gotten. This is where soft power becomes critical. Were the fathers of these boys convinced that the United States would torture, maim, and execute their children without any sense of justice, they would not have come forward. I doubt that any Chechen father has turned his child over to Vladimir Putin's regime.

The data on public opinion in the Muslim world are now overwhelming. London School of Economics professor Fawaz Gerges has analyzed polls from dozens of Muslim countries over the past few years. He notes that in a range of places— Jordan, Pakistan, Indonesia, Lebanon, and Bangladesh—there have been substantial declines in the number of people who say suicide bombing and other forms of violence against civilian targets can be justified to defend Islam. Wide majorities say such attacks are, at most, rarely acceptable.

The shift has been especially dramatic in Jordan, where only 12 percent of Jordanians view suicide attacks as "often or sometimes justified" (down from 57 percent in 2005). In Indonesia, 85 percent of respondents agree that terrorist attacks are "rarely/never justified" (in 2002, by contrast, only 70 percent opposed such attacks). In Pakistan, that figure is 90 percent, up from 43 percent in 2002.

Gerges points out that, by comparison, only 46 percent of Americans say that "bombing and other attacks intentionally aimed at civilians" are "never justified," while 24 percent believe these attacks are "often or sometimes justified."

This shift does not reflect a turn away from religiosity or even from a backward conception of Islam. That ideological struggle persists and will take decades, not years, to resolve itself. But the battle against jihadism has fared much better, much sooner, than anyone could have imagined.

The exceptions to this picture readily spring to mind— Afghanistan, Pakistan, Yemen. But consider the conditions in those countries. In Afghanistan, jihadist ideology has wrapped itself around a genuine ethnic struggle in which Pashtuns feel that they are being dispossessed by rival groups. In Pakistan, the regime is still where Saudi Arabia was in 2003 and 2004: slowly coming to realize that the extremism it had fostered has now become a threat to its own survival. In Yemen, the state simply lacks the basic capacity to fight back. So the rule might simply be that in those places where a government lacks the desire, will, or capacity to fight jihadism, al-Qaeda can continue to thrive.

But the nature of the enemy is now quite different. It is not a movement capable of winning over the Arab street. Its political appeal does not make rulers tremble. The video messages of bin Laden and Zawahiri once unsettled moderate regimes. Now they are mostly dismissed as almost comical attempts to find popular causes to latch onto. (After the financial crash, bin Laden tried his hand at bashing greedy bankers.)

This is not an argument to relax our efforts to hunt down militants. AlQaeda remains a group of relentless, ruthless killers who are trying to recruit other fanatics to carry out hideous attacks that would do terrible damage to civilized society. But the group's aura is gone, its political influence limited. Its few remaining fighters are spread thinly throughout the world and face hostile environments almost everywhere.

America is no longer engaged in a civilizational struggle throughout the Muslim world, but a military and intelligence campaign in a set of discrete places. Now, that latter struggle might well require politics, diplomacy, and development assistance—in the manner that good foreign policy always does (Petraeus calls this a "whole-of-government strategy"). We have allies; we need to support them. But the target is only a handful of extremist organizations that have found a small group of fanatics to carry out their plans. To put it another way, even if the United States pursues a broad and successful effort at nation building in Afghanistan and Yemen, does anyone really think that will deter the next Nigerian misfit—or fanatic from Detroit—from getting on a plane with chemicals in his underwear? Such people cannot be won over. They cannot be reasoned with; they can only be captured or killed.

The enemy is not vast; the swamp is being drained. Al-Qaeda has already lost in the realm of ideology. What remains is the battle to defeat it in the nooks, crannies, and crevices of the real world.

Critical Thinking

1. What is Fareed Zakaria's point of view?
2. What sources does he identify that provide data to support his point of view?
3. What are some of the long-term implications of his analysis?

War in the Fifth Domain

Are the mouse and keyboard the new weapons of conflict?

At the height of the cold war, in June 1982, an American early-warning satellite detected a large blast in Siberia. A missile being fired? A nuclear test? It was, it seems, an explosion on a Soviet gas pipeline. The cause was a malfunction in the computer-control system that Soviet spies had stolen from a firm in Canada. They did not know that the CIA had tampered with the software so that it would "go haywire, after a decent interval, to reset pump speeds and valve settings to produce pressures far beyond those acceptable to pipeline joints and welds," according to the memoirs of Thomas Reed, a former air force secretary. The result, he said, "was the most monumental non-nuclear explosion and fire ever seen from space."

This was one of the earliest demonstrations of the power of a "logic bomb". Three decades later, with more and more vital computer systems linked up to the internet, could enemies use logic bombs to, say, turn off the electricity from the other side of the world? Could terrorists or hackers cause financial chaos by tampering with Wall Street's computerised trading systems? And given that computer chips and software are produced globally, could a foreign power infect high-tech military equipment with computer bugs? "It scares me to death," says one senior military source. "The destructive potential is so great."

After land, sea, air and space, warfare has entered the fifth domain: cyberspace. President Barack Obama has declared America's digital infrastructure to be a "strategic national asset" and appointed Howard Schmidt, the former head of security at Microsoft, as his cyber-security tsar. In May the Pentagon set up its new Cyber Command (Cybercom) headed by General Keith Alexander, director of the National Security Agency (NSA). His mandate is to conduct "full-spectrum" operations—to defend American military networks and attack other countries' systems. Precisely how, and by what rules, is secret.

Britain, too, has set up a cyber-security policy outfit, and an "operations centre" based in GCHQ, the British equivalent of the NSA. China talks of "winning informationised wars by the mid-21st century". Many other countries are organising for cyberwar, among them Russia, Israel and North Korea. Iran boasts of having the world's second-largest cyber-army.

What will cyberwar look like? In a new book Richard Clarke, a former White House staffer in charge of counter-terrorism and cyber-security, envisages a catastrophic breakdown within 15 minutes. Computer bugs bring down military e-mail systems; oil refineries and pipelines explode; air-traffic-control systems collapse; freight and metro trains derail; financial data are scrambled; the electrical grid goes down in the eastern United States; orbiting satellites spin out of control. Society soon breaks down as food becomes scarce and money runs out. Worst of all, the identity of the attacker may remain a mystery.

In the view of Mike McConnell, a former spy chief, the effects of full-blown cyberwar are much like nuclear attack. Cyberwar has already started, he says, "and we are losing it." Not so, retorts Mr Schmidt. There is no cyberwar. Bruce Schneier, an IT industry security guru, accuses securocrats like Mr Clarke of scaremongering. Cyberspace will certainly be part of any future war, he says, but an apocalyptic attack on America is both difficult to achieve technically ("movie-script stuff") and implausible except in the context of a real war, in which case the perpetrator is likely to be obvious.

For the top brass, computer technology is both a blessing and a curse. Bombs are guided by GPS satellites; drones are piloted remotely from across the world; fighter planes and warships are now huge data-processing centres; even the ordinary foot-soldier is being wired up. Yet growing connectivity over an insecure internet multiplies the avenues for e-attack; and growing dependence on computers increases the harm they can cause.

By breaking up data and sending it over multiple routes, the internet can survive the loss of large parts of the network. Yet some of the global digital infrastructure is more fragile. More than nine-tenths of internet traffic travels through undersea fibre-optic cables, and these are dangerously bunched up in a few choke-points, for instance around New York, the Red Sea or the Luzon Strait in the Philippines. Internet traffic is directed by just 13 clusters of potentially vulnerable domain-name servers. Other dangers are coming: weakly governed swathes of Africa are being connected up to fibre-optic cables, potentially creating new havens for cyber-criminals. And the spread of mobile internet will bring new means of attack.

The internet was designed for convenience and reliability, not security. Yet in wiring together the globe, it has merged the garden and the wilderness. No passport is required in cyberspace. And although police are constrained by national borders, criminals roam freely. Enemy states are no longer on the other side of the ocean, but just behind the firewall. The ill-intentioned can mask their identity and location, impersonate others and con their way into the buildings that hold the digitised wealth of the electronic age: money, personal data and intellectual property.

Mr Obama has quoted a figure of $1 trillion lost last year to cybercrime—a bigger underworld than the drugs trade, though such figures are disputed. Banks and other companies do not like to admit how much data they lose. In 2008 alone Verizon, a telecoms company, recorded the loss of 285m personal-data records, including credit-card and bank-account details, in investigations conducted for clients.

About nine-tenths of the 140 billion e-mails sent daily are spam; of these about 16% contain moneymaking scams, including "phishing" attacks that seek to dupe recipients into giving out passwords or bank details, according to Symantec, a security-software vendor. The amount of information now available online about individuals makes it ever easier to attack a computer by crafting a personalised e-mail that is more likely to be trusted and opened. This is known as "spear-phishing".

The ostentatious hackers and virus-writers who once wrecked computers for fun are all but gone, replaced by criminal gangs seeking to harvest data. "Hacking used to be about making noise. Now it's about staying silent," says Greg Day of McAfee, a vendor of IT security products. Hackers have become wholesale providers of malware—viruses, worms and Trojans that infect computers—for others to use. Websites are now the favoured means of spreading malware, partly because the unwary are directed to them through spam or links posted on social-networking sites. And poorly designed websites often provide a window into valuable databases.

Malware is typically used to steal passwords and other data, or to open a "back door" to a computer so that it can be taken over by outsiders. Such "zombie" machines can be linked up to thousands, if not millions, of others around the world to create a "botnet". Estimates for the number of infected machines range up to 100m. Botnets are used to send spam, spread malware or launch distributed denial-of-service (DDoS) attacks, which seek to bring down a targeted computer by overloading it with countless bogus requests.

The Spy Who Spammed Me

Criminals usually look for easy prey. But states can combine the criminal hacker's tricks, such as spear-phishing, with the intelligence apparatus to reconnoitre a target, the computing power to break codes and passwords, and the patience to probe a system until it finds a weakness—usually a fallible human being. Steven Chabinsky, a senior FBI official responsible for cyberse-curity, recently said that "given enough time, motivation and funding, a determined adversary will always—always—be able to penetrate a targeted system."

Traditional human spies risk arrest or execution by trying to smuggle out copies of documents. But those in the cyberworld face no such risks. "A spy might once have been able to take out a few books' worth of material," says one senior American military source. "Now they take the whole library. And if you restock the shelves, they will steal it again."

China, in particular, is accused of wholesale espionage, attacking the computers of major Western defence contractors and reputedly taking classified details of the F-35 fighter, the mainstay of future American air power. At the end of 2009 it appears to have targeted Google and more than a score of other IT companies. Experts at a cyber-test-range built in Maryland

by Lockheed Martin, a defence contractor (which denies losing the F-35 data), say "advanced persistent threats" are hard to fend off amid the countless minor probing of its networks. Sometimes attackers try to slip information out slowly, hidden in ordinary internet traffic. At other times they have tried to break in by leaving infected memory-sticks in the car park, hoping somebody would plug them into the network. Even unclassified e-mails can contain a wealth of useful information about projects under development.

"Cyber-espionage is the biggest intelligence disaster since the loss of the nuclear secrets [in the late 1940s]," says Jim Lewis of the Centre for Strategic and International Studies, a think-tank in Washington, DC. Spying probably presents the most immediate danger to the West: the loss of high-tech know-how that could erode its economic lead or, if it ever came to a shooting war, blunt its military edge.

Western spooks think China deploys the most assiduous, and most shameless, cyberspies, but Russian ones are probably more skilled and subtle. Top of the league, say the spooks, are still America's NSA and Britain's GCHQ, which may explain why Western countries have until recently been reluctant to complain too loudly about computer snooping.

The next step after penetrating networks to steal data is to disrupt or manipulate them. If military targeting information could be attacked, for example, ballistic missiles would be useless. Those who play war games speak of being able to "change the red and blue dots": make friendly (blue) forces appear to be the enemy (red), and vice versa.

General Alexander says the Pentagon and NSA started co-operating on cyberwarfare in late 2008 after "a serious intrusion into our classified networks". Mr Lewis says this refers to the penetration of Central Command, which oversees the wars in Iraq and Afghanistan, through an infected thumb-drive. It took a week to winkle out the intruder. Nobody knows what, if any, damage was caused. But the thought of an enemy lurking in battle-fighting systems alarms the top brass.

That said, an attacker might prefer to go after unclassified military logistics supply systems, or even the civilian infrastructure. A loss of confidence in financial data and electronic transfers could cause economic upheaval. An even bigger worry is an attack on the power grid. Power companies tend not to keep many spares of expensive generator parts, which can take months to replace. Emergency diesel generators cannot make up for the loss of the grid, and cannot operate indefinitely. Without electricity and other critical services, communications systems and cash-dispensers cease to work. A loss of power lasting just a few days, reckon some, starts to cause a cascade of economic damage.

Experts disagree about the vulnerability of systems that run industrial plants, known as supervisory control and data acquisition (SCADA). But more and more of these are being connected to the internet, raising the risk of remote attack. "Smart" "grids", which relay information about energy use to the utilities, are promoted as ways of reducing energy waste. But they also increase security worries about both crime (eg, allowing bills to be falsified) and exposing SCADA networks to attack.

General Alexander has spoken of "hints that some penetrations are targeting systems for remote sabotage". But precisely what is happening is unclear: are outsiders probing SCADA systems only for reconnaissance, or to open "back doors" for future use? One senior American military source said that if any country were found to be planting logic bombs on the grid, it would provoke the equivalent of the Cuban missile crisis.

Estonia, Georgia and WWI

Important thinking about the tactical and legal concepts of cyber-warfare is taking place in a former Soviet barracks in Estonia, now home to NATO's "centre of excellence" for cyber-defence. It was established in response to what has become known as "Web War I", a concerted denial-of-service attack on Estonian government, media and bank web servers that was precipitated by the decision to move a Soviet-era war memorial in central Tallinn in 2007. This was more a cyber-riot than a war, but it forced Estonia more or less to cut itself off from the internet.

Similar attacks during Russia's war with Georgia the next year looked more ominous, because they seemed to be coordinated with the advance of Russian military columns. Government and media websites went down and telephone lines were jammed, crippling Georgia's ability to present its case abroad. President Mikheil Saakashvili's website had to be moved to an American server better able to fight off the attack. Estonian experts were dispatched to Georgia to help out.

Many assume that both these attacks were instigated by the Kremlin. But investigations traced them only to Russian "hacktivists" and criminal botnets; many of the attacking computers were in Western countries. There are wider issues: did the cyber-attack on Estonia, a member of NATO, count as an armed attack, and should the alliance have defended it? And did Estonia's assistance to Georgia, which is not in NATO, risk drawing Estonia into the war, and NATO along with it?

Such questions permeate discussions of NATO's new "strategic concept", to be adopted later this year. A panel of experts headed by Madeleine Albright, a former American secretary of state, reported in May that cyber-attacks are among the three most likely threats to the alliance. The next significant attack, it said, "may well come down a fibre-optic cable" and may be serious enough to merit a response under the mutual-defence provisions of Article 5.

During his confirmation hearing, senators sent General Alexander several questions. Would he have "significant" offensive cyber-weapons? Might these encourage others to follow suit? How sure would he need to be about the identity of an attacker to "fire back"? Answers to these were restricted to a classified supplement. In public the general said that the president would be the judge of what constituted cyberwar; if America responded with force in cyberspace it would be in keeping with the rules of war and the "principles of military necessity, discrimination, and proportionality".

General Alexander's seven-month confirmation process is a sign of the qualms senators felt at the merging of military and espionage functions, the militarisation of cyberspace and the fear that it may undermine Americans' right to privacy. Cyber-command will protect only the military ".mil" domain. The government domain, ".gov", and the corporate infrastructure, ".com" will be the responsibility respectively of the Department of Homeland Security and private companies, with support from Cybercom.

One senior military official says General Alexander's priority will be to improve the defences of military networks. Another bigwig casts some doubt on cyber-offence. "It's hard to do it at a specific time," he says. "If a cyber-attack is used as a military weapon, you want a predictable time and effect. If you are using it for espionage it does not matter; you can wait." He implies that cyber-weapons would be used mainly as an adjunct to conventional operations in a narrow theatre.

The Chinese may be thinking the same way. A report on China's cyber-warfare doctrine, written for the congressionally mandated US-China Economic and Security Review Commission, envisages China using cyber-weapons not to defeat America, but to disrupt and slow down its forces long enough for China to seize Taiwan without having to fight a shooting war.

Apocalypse or Asymmetry?

Deterrence in cyber-warfare is more uncertain than, say, in nuclear strategy: there is no mutually assured destruction, the dividing line between criminality and war is blurred and identifying attacking computers, let alone the fingers on the keyboards, is difficult. Retaliation need not be confined to cyberspace; the one system that is certainly not linked to the public internet is America's nuclear firing chain. Still, the more likely use of cyber-weapons is probably not to bring about electronic apocalypse, but as tools of limited warfare.

Cyber-weapons are most effective in the hands of big states. But because they are cheap, they may be most useful to the comparatively weak. They may well suit terrorists. Fortunately, perhaps, the likes of al-Qaeda have mostly used the internet for propaganda and communication. It may be that jihadists lack the ability to, say, induce a refinery to blow itself up. Or it may be that they prefer the gory theatre of suicide-bombings to the anonymity of computer sabotage—for now.

Critical Thinking

1. What is meant by the term "cyberwar?"
2. In addition to hostile governments, what other types of international actors employ this tactic?
3. How serious a problem is cyberwar and what efforts are being made to address it?

Banning the Bomb

A New Approach

WARD WILSON

In July of 1945, U.S. president Harry Truman wrote in his diary, "It is certainly a good thing for the world that Hitler's crowd or Stalin's did not discover this atomic bomb. It seems to be the most terrible thing ever discovered, but it can be made the most useful." Terrible and useful. For sixty years, people have focused on the terrible aspects of nuclear weapons. They have made films about nuclear war, detailed the horrors of Hiroshima and Nagasaki, and imagined the end of life on earth. In those sixty years, on the other hand, people have rarely talked seriously about the usefulness of nuclear weapons. Do they really win wars? Are they effective threats? Fear—engendered by real and imagined cold war dangers—constrained real inquiry. Absorbed by images of destruction, most people didn't ask practical questions. But it turns out that the area that we've explored the most—the terribleness of nuclear weapons—is not the key to understanding them. The key is investigating whether or not they are really useful.

I am not urging the familiar argument that nuclear weapons are too dangerous to be useful; I am suggesting that even if one could use them with impunity, nuclear weapons would still have little practical value. Sixty years of experience, recent reevaluations of the track record of nuclear weapons, and reinterpretations of Hiroshima and Nagasaki based on new research make it possible to argue that there are very few situations in which nuclear weapons are useful. It might, in fact, be possible to demonstrate that nuclear weapons are functionally the equivalent of biological and chemical weapons: powerful and dangerous weapons, but with very few real applications. And therefore it might also be possible to make the case that—as with chemical and biological weapons—there are practical, prudential reasons for banning nuclear weapons.

Current Strategies

To date, two related strategies have been used to oppose the use of nuclear weapons: the horror strategy and the risk strategy. The former relies on moral feelings and tries to persuade people that using nuclear weapons is too immoral to contemplate. The latter relies on calculations of the possibility that a small war could become an all-out nuclear war and tries to persuade people that the danger is too great.

Those who use the horror strategy often make Hiroshima and Nagasaki the centerpiece of their case. They try to drive home the immorality of using nuclear weapons by forcing their listeners to experience vicariously the horror of these cities. Doctors increased the emotional impact of this approach in the 1980s by talking unflinchingly and in detail about the medical consequences of nuclear attacks.

The risk strategy has been more widely embraced than the horror strategy. Vividly given a story line by Nevil Shute in *On the Beach* (a novel later made into a movie in which a nuclear war extinguishes all human life), it has remained a staple of antinuclear argument, used by radicals and sober policymakers alike.

Jonathan Schell updated and expanded the risk strategy in *The Fate of the Earth*. Schell eschewed the normal tack of emphasizing the risks of escalation, arguing instead that an all-out nuclear war might lead to the destruction of all life on earth. So it didn't matter how big or small the risk of escalation was, the consequences were so terrible that no amount of risk was worth running. In 1983, Carl Sagan and four others further buttressed Schell's case with evidence suggesting that severe climatic disruption, dubbed "nuclear winter," could be triggered by a nuclear war.

Sound as their reasoning might be, both these strategies have weaknesses. The horror argument's weakness is that in a crisis necessity almost always trumps morality. People will say, "Yes, it's wrong. But we have to do it. We have no other choice." If the Bomb seems likely to be militarily effective most people will decide to use it, even if they know it is wrong to do so.

The risk strategy has been eroded by the end of the cold war, which led to lowered tensions and significantly reduced the likelihood of nuclear escalation. Another key—but often overlooked—change is the end of "extended deterrence"—the threat by the United States and the Soviet Union to respond to attacks on their client states with nuclear counterattacks. At one time, all of Europe, all of Latin America, some of Asia, and even parts of Africa were covered by extended deterrence. With the collapse of the cold war client-state system, many nations are now out from under the nuclear umbrella. It is now possible for the United States to attack, say, Syria, with nuclear weapons without the threat of a nuclear response from Russia. As the risk of escalation has decreased, the strength of the risk argument has also decreased.

Bigger Is Not Better

It is often said that every weapon that man has invented has been used in war. This statement misses the point. The important issue is not whether this or that weapon has ever been used, it is whether such a weapon—once tried—has become a fixture in the arsenals of warlike nations. Horrible weapons have been imagined and tried. But are they still used?

Consider the Paris Gun. Built by the Germans in World War I, it was more than 90 feet long, weighed 256 tons, and moved on rails. It fired a 210-pound projectile more than 80 miles. Often confused with its smaller cousin, the large mortar called "Big Bertha," in its day it was the largest cannon ever built. It was a terrifying weapon. From March until August of 1918, the Germans used it to rain shells down on Paris without warning. The Parisians were bewildered and terrified. In all, the Paris Gun fired about 360 shells, killing 250 people and wounding 620.

Only a handful of other superguns have since been built (Schwerer Gustav and V3 among them). Their impact on the wars in which they participated was minimal. Today, nations do not race to build their own superguns. African nations, torn by strife, do not try to trade their oil or diamond resources for superguns bought from arms dealers. There are no angry diatribes in liberal papers about the horror of these weapons and the necessity of banning them.

"But of course this is so," someone might say, "because these weapons were not very effective." And that is the point. Decisions about acquiring or banning weapons are not based on their horribleness but on their ability or inability to help win wars.

There are four general ways that nuclear weapons might be used: in a war intended to exterminate an opponent, in a war of coercion, as a threat, and to create terror. For two of these categories—coercion and threats—it is relatively easy to show that nuclear weapons are not ideal weapons and, in some circumstances, are so seriously mismatched to the task at hand as to be useless.

On the other hand, nuclear weapons are admirably suited for wars of extermination. If you have decided on a war in which your goal is to annihilate your opponent, nuclear weapons are your best choice. In this case it is necessary to argue not that the weapons wouldn't be useful, but that such wars are morally wrong. This is not a demanding task. No case can be made that the capability to wage a war of annihilation is valuable or necessary. And this moral judgment is borne out by the practical experience of history: the actual number of wars of extermination is small. (Wars of extermination are distinct from genocide or other murderous actions within a country's own boundaries.) A careful review of human history unearthed only one clear case, the Third Punic War.

The vast majority of wars are wars of coercion. The conventional wisdom has been that nuclear weapons are decisive in this kind of war. After all, they won the war in the Pacific. But when examined closely, the presumption of decisiveness evaporates. Recent reinterpretations of the Japanese surrender call into question the notion that the bombings of Hiroshima and Nagasaki were in any way connected with that decision. The Soviet intervention radically altered the strategic situation and was the decisive event.

The power to destroy cities is not the power to win wars. Freeman Dyson makes this point vividly in an example drawn from the Falklands War. Someone had said loosely about the war that if the British had wanted to they could have "blown Buenos Aires off the map." This was true, but Dyson points out that the British would still have had to send soldiers to re-conquer the Falklands. And destroying Buenos Aires would probably have made the Argentine soldiers defending the islands fight more fiercely. Or the British could have nuked the Falklands themselves, but that would have destroyed the islands. The British abstained from using nuclear weapons not because they have admirable restraint, but because there was no practical application for the weapons.

Sixty years of experience with nuclear weapons does not support the notion that they are singularly useful to their possessors. Despite its nuclear arsenal, the United States was fought to a draw in Korea, lost a war in Vietnam, did not stop genocides in Cambodia or Rwanda, and is currently mired in conflict in Iraq. Despite its sizable nuclear arsenal, the Soviet Union suffered humiliation in its own guerrilla war in Afghanistan. Nuclear nations have fought many wars, but these supposedly powerful weapons have not played a decisive role in any of them.

Nuclear weapons do not appear to be suited to the battlefield. This inutility has already been ratified by two of the most authoritative bodies in a position to make a judgment: the military establishments of the United States and the Soviet Union. If tactical nuclear weapons were really militarily useful, would these two military establishments have allowed almost all tactical weapons to be retired in the 1980s?

Nuclear weapons are also of questionable effectiveness in attacks on economic targets. Most economic targets are roughly building-sized, and with today's precision-guided munitions, conventional weapons are more than adequate. Nuclear weapons, on the other hand, require destruction of an area many times larger than the target. What is the point of destroying a quarter of a city in order to knock out an oil refinery? It is true that a large-scale nuclear attack could effectively shatter a nation's economic infrastructure, but at what point does this become a war of extermination?

Diplomatic Influence

When the United States first got nuclear weapons, there were high hopes that they would provide not just military might, but international influence as well. Truman, when he talked about nuclear weapons being "useful" in the diary entry quoted above, was probably thinking of the upcoming negotiations he faced with the Soviet Union over the shape of the post–World War II world. His secretary of state, James F. Byrnes, told him with a touch of euphoria that nuclear weapons would probably allow the United States to "dictate our own terms after the war." Byrnes returned from the bargaining table a chastened man. The Soviets, he reported ruefully afterward, "are stubborn, obstinate, and they don't scare." Perhaps this is not surprising. Joseph Stalin said in a 1946 interview in *Pravda,* "Atomic bombs are meant to frighten those with weak nerves."

The U.S. nuclear monopoly did not prevent communist domination of Eastern Europe in the years after the Second World War. It did not prevent the Berlin Crisis of 1948. It did not prevent the communist takeover of China in 1949. Of course, any threat will work some percentage of the time—some people scare easily. The question is, are nuclear weapons reliable tools of coercion? Clearly not.

Some people argue that nuclear weapons have kept the United States and other nations safe by deterring nuclear war. This is difficult to prove. Imagine a man who says that the lucky penny he keeps on his dresser has prevented nuclear war. When you ask for proof, he says, "Well, I've kept that penny on the dresser for sixty-two years and there's been no war, so it must be working!" Nuclear weapons may provide crucial safety and security, although it is hard to imagine how dangerous weapons that cannot be defended against are the best means of providing safety. Another—perhaps more certain—way to prevent nuclear war is to ban nuclear weapons.

Of What Use Today?

Another way to assess the usefulness of nuclear weapons is to think about the role they might play in a crisis today. Imagine, for example, that the North Koreans used a nuclear weapon to attack Seoul or Tokyo. The United States, Russia, Great Britain, France, or China would all be in a position to retaliate against Pyongyang. Some might argue that this would be the right way to deter future nuclear attacks against cities. But wouldn't a far more practical deterrent be for the United States, Russia, and China to form an alliance, invade North Korea, and set up a new government? Nuking Pyongyang only punishes the innocent. North Korea's leaders would surely have left the city shortly before the North Korean nuclear strike was launched. Nuking Pyongyang kills North Korean civilians, who, because they live under a dictatorship, have no responsibility for the decision to attack. Rogue states that use nuclear weapons are unlikely to be democratic states, and because what nuclear weapons do best is kill people, nuclear weapons will never be well suited to punishing such a regime.

Many people believe that the most likely use of nuclear weapons in the next few years (barring a war in the Middle East or the Asian subcontinent) is a terrorist attack against a city. Terrorists, whose aim is to coerce political change by irregular attacks on innocents, are the people most likely to imagine that nuclear weapons are useful. On the other hand, it is difficult to imagine nuclear deterrence against terrorists. Imagine that a nuclear bomb hidden in a cargo container is detonated in Baltimore Harbor. What effective nuclear retaliation options are there? It would be very difficult to identify the attackers. But even assuming that a terrorist group takes responsibility—say, al-Qaeda—how can nuclear weapons be used to redress this evil? Would you use a nuclear weapon against a city in Pakistan in which you think Osama bin Laden is hiding? Again, the vast majority of those who die will be innocent, and if faulty intelligence leads you to attack the wrong city you risk punishing *only* the innocent.

A good deal of energy has been devoted to imagining circumstances in which nuclear weapons would be exactly the right weapons to use. But why is it necessary to imagine unlikely or outlandish scenarios in order to justify these weapons?

The current U.S. administration supports research into developing "bunker buster" nuclear weapons that could destroy targets deeply buried or secreted in caves. There are two telling objections to such a weapon. First, as with most applications of nuclear weapons, conventional weapons already provide a fairly extensive bunker buster capability. Nuclear bunker busters would only extend existing capabilities a few hundred meters (to three hundred meters below the surface at most). It is within the capabilities of almost any enemy simply to dig deeper. The second is that the intelligence necessary for such a strike is unimaginable. Even with the sophisticated technology currently available to the U.S. government, for example, we were unable to identify chemical and biological facilities in Iraq, a country with barren, cloud-free, best-case topography. This is an indication of how hard it is to locate secret facilities. And we were looking for facilities on the surface.

The current administration also imagines that mini-nukes would be useful. These are weapons with roughly a third the destructive power of the bomb that destroyed Hiroshima—about the same destructive power that was deployed in the conventional raids against Japanese cities in the summer of 1945. Why build a nuclear weapon with an end result you can already achieve using conventional weapons?

In this connection, the size of nuclear weapons raises a question. Early on in the nuclear age, physicists warned that there was no theoretical limit to the size of hydrogen bombs. The Soviets tested a bomb with a yield of roughly fifty-two megatons in 1962. Larger bombs could have been built. Yet they have not been. In fact, the size of nuclear warheads in the U.S. and Russian arsenals has been shrinking. At one time one megaton (or larger) warheads were common, but today the yield of an average warhead in the U.S. strategic arsenal is only about a third of a megaton. How can nuclear bombs be shrinking if the greater the destructive power the greater the military usefulness? If nuclear weapons are useful, why is it that the trend is toward making them more like conventional weapons?

Benefits of Banning the Bomb

The benefits of a total ban are clear. The chief benefit is that it protects us against the danger that people are currently most concerned with in connection with these weapons: use by a terrorist group against a city. By banning nuclear weapons you substantially decrease the chances that they will fall into the hands of rogue states or terrorist organizations. The only reason that the director of the Pakistani nuclear project was able to sell nuclear technology to the North Koreans is that proliferation had gained such widespread acceptance. The more nations that have nuclear weapons, the more likely someone is to put them into the hands of irresponsible people. (As I write this in

October 2006, North Korea has just tested a nuclear weapon. The international reaction serves as a strong reminder that it is important to keep nuclear weapons out of the hands of unstable leaders.)

Any international ban would have to include careful monitoring of all formerly nuclear nations and inspection of nuclear power reactors. (If nuclear nations are unwilling to give up their weapons entirely, perhaps each could warehouse a small stockpile under UN administration in their own countries. The weapons could be retrieved by their owner, but only by publicly breaking the treaty.) With no military weapons floating around, and access to nuclear power monitored and controlled by international organizations, building a rogue bomb or stealing one becomes almost impossible.

None of the arguments sketched here is the final word on the usefulness of nuclear weapons. There is considerable work still to be done. The Hiroshima argument needs to be more thoroughly researched. The case against city attacks needs to be strengthened with historical examples. And along with work on each of its parts, a systematic treatment of the entire subject is needed. But it should be clear from the limited treatment here that there is enough substance in the approach to merit further work.

In 1775, Edmund Burke rose in Parliament to oppose the use of force against the American colonies. Burke believed strongly that the application of force was not the best way to bind the colonies to the British Empire. Burke said that he opposed force not because it was an "odious" instrument of policy but because it was a "feeble" one. His assertion must have been especially surprising because the British army and navy at that time were the most powerful in the world. Using force, he argued, could intimidate and coerce, but raw power alone would not create obedience in the colonies. In some situations brute force is less effective (or more "feeble") than other means.

It may seem paradoxical to think of them as "feeble," but I want to make something of the same argument about nuclear weapons. The strongest arguments against the use of nuclear weapons are not those that demonstrate that they are horrible or dangerous (although they are certainly both), but those that show that they aren't very useful. Weapons, like tools, are situational: their "power" is measured not by their raw force but by the extent to which their capabilities match the circumstances. A jackhammer is a very powerful tool; it's not much help in repairing a watch. A howitzer is of no use underwater; a shotgun blast doesn't help where stealth is required; a knife has little effect at a thousand yards. It's not the size of the bang, it's the match between the situation at hand and the weapon's capabilities. In most military situations, conventional weapons are better suited to the task at hand than nuclear ones. Only in blowing up cities are nuclear weapons singularly well suited to a task. This is an objective, however, that only terrorists pursue enthusiastically.

If there are hardly any circumstances in which nuclear weapons are militarily useful, and if it seems likely that the more nations that have nuclear arsenals the more likely the weapons are to fall into the hands of terrorists or madmen, then it makes practical sense to ban them.

Critical Thinking

1. What is Ward Wilson's point of view?

2. What reasons does he offer to support this point of view?

3. According to Wilson, what would be some of the benefits of banning nuclear weapons?

4. How does this discussion complement/contradict articles 1, 4, and 32?

WARD WILSON is an independent scholar living in Trenton, N.J. He is currently at work on a book about the military usefulness of destroying cities throughout history. He writes regularly at www.rethinking nuclearweapons.org.

UNIT 6
Cooperation

Unit Selections

Learning Outcomes

After reading this unit you should be able to:

• Describe the role of non-governmental organizations in developing international cooperative processes.

• Assess the prospects for major, multilateral international agreements to address problems such as climate change and human trafficking.

• Describe challenges to existing international agreements such as the Geneva Conventions.

• Summarize case studies where NGOs and celebrities have contributed to solving serious social and environmental problems.

• Assess your on-going effort at identifying your theory of international relations and how this unit changes/complements it.

Student Website
www.mhhe.com/cls

Internet References

Carnegie Endowment for International Peace
www.ceip.org
OECD/FDI Statistics
www.oecd.org/statistics
U.S. Institute of Peace
www.usip.org

An individual can write a letter and, assuming it is properly addressed, be relatively certain that it will be delivered to just about any location in the world. This is true even though the sender pays for postage only in the country of origin and not in the country where it is delivered. A similar pattern of international cooperation is true when a traveler boards an airplane and never gives a thought to the issue of potential language and technical barriers, even though the flight's destination is halfway around the world.

Many of the most basic activities of our lives are the direct result of governments cooperating across borders. International organizational structures, for example, have been created to eliminate barriers to trade; monitor, and respond to public health threats; set standards for international telecommunications; arrest and judge war criminals; and monitor changing atmospheric conditions. Individual governments, in other words, have recognized that their self-interest directly benefits from cooperation (in most cases by giving up some of their sovereignty through the creation of international governmental organizations, or IGOs).

Transnational activities are not limited to the governmental level. There are now tens of thousands of international nongovernmental organizations (INGOs). The activities of INGOs range from staging the Olympic Games to organizing scientific meetings to actively discouraging the hunting of seals. The number of INGOs, along with their influence, has grown tremendously in the past 60 years.

During the same period in which the growth in importance of IGOs and INGOs has taken place, there also has been a parallel expansion of corporate activity across international borders. Most U.S. consumers are as familiar with Japanese or German brand-name products as they are with items made in their own country. The multinational corporation (MNC) is an important non-state actor. The value of goods and services produced by the biggest MNCs is far greater than the gross domestic product (GDP) of many countries. The international structures that make it possible to buy a German automobile in Sacramento or a South Korean television in Buenos Aires have been developed

© Royalty-Free/CORBIS

over many years. They are the result of governments negotiating treaties that create IGOs to implement the agreements (e.g., the World Trade Organization). As a result, corporations engaged in international trade and manufacturing have created complex transnational networks of sales, distribution, and service that employ millions of people.

To some observers these trends indicate that the era of the nation-state as the dominant player in international politics is passing. Other experts have observed these same trends and have concluded that the state system has a monopoly of power and that the diverse variety of transnational organizations depends on the state system and, in significant ways, perpetuates it.

In many of the articles that appear elsewhere in this book, the authors have concluded their analysis by calling for greater international cooperation to solve the world's most pressing problems. The articles in this section provide examples of successful cooperation. In the midst of a lot of bad news, it is easy to overlook the fact that we are surrounded by international cooperation and that basic day-to-day activities in our lives often directly benefit from it.

Climate Change after Copenhagen: Beyond Doom and Gloom

BERNICE LEE

Critics of multilateral climate action have stepped up their attacks. They argue that change is not possible; that failure in last year's Copenhagen climate summit was inevitable as the public would never accept the cost of change towards a low-carbon future; nations will never concede their immediate economic interests; and that there is no prospect of collective climate change action. In their version of reality, the lowest common denominator rules. This narrative can be persuasive in times of austerity, but overlooks two critical points. Despite the political setback, investments in clean energy and efficiency continue to rise in response to policy change in developed economics like the European Union and the United States, or in emerging countries like China and India. International cooperation—together with solid national action—best serves even narrowly defined national interests on climate change. National welfare cannot be safeguarded if the world fails to deal with climate change and its resource challenges.

The Copenhagen summit on climate change last December is often described as a game-changer in global geopolitics. The world not only saw disagreements between developed and developing countries but also in the developing world, with plenty of cloak and dagger politics as well as megaphone diplomacy.

Fights over the level of ambition ended in procedural delays in Copenhagen, culminating in a last-minute dash by frustrated world leaders to come up with an acceptable political outcome. The BASIC countries—China, Brazil, South Africa and India—became critical brokers in the final political compromise, sidelining the European Union, Japan and others.

Eight months on, the international community remains divided over how to manage climate change collectively. The capacity of the international system to deliver global action in a multipolar context has been called into question; as has the effectiveness of the United Nations negotiating process. Developments so far this year have not produced renewed optimism.

These events have strengthened those who have long been vociferous against multilateral action—or any action at all—to reduce global greenhouse gas emissions. Some hailed the end of top-down climate solutions imposed by elites. Others questioned the ability of politicians to make meaningful compromises in global negotiations in a world of Twitter and instant news. The political appetite for such action is also dampened by the protracted economic downturn and controversy over climate science.

At this critical moment, it is important to get to the heart of the political disputes that surround the Copenhagen disappointment. Beyond the doom and gloom, the practical reality is more encouraging than purely political narratives. The key to unlocking the climate deadlock will lie in the ability of politicians to align global ambition with emerging realities.

A New Global Order?

For many commentators, the wrangling over the substance of the Copenhagen Accord reflected the dawning of a new world political order in which decision-making shifts to a smaller group of emerging powerful nations and away from traditional powers. Discussions on the final Copenhagen outcome were dominated largely by the United States, China, India, Brazil and South Africa. Connie Hedegaard, who part-presided over the Copenhagen conference, said that in 'the last hours in Copenhagen—China, India, the US, Russia and Japan—each spoke with one voice while Europe spoke with many different voices. We are almost unable to negotiate'. The EU has also been portrayed by the media as a minor player in brokering and drafting the accord.

China was widely characterised by many as a villain in the negotiations. Representatives, especially those from Sweden and Britain, openly lambasted Beijing for attempting to block the inclusion of the emissions target of two degrees Celsius above pre-industrial levels in the final text, as well as its rejection of the eighty percent emissions reduction target by developed countries by 2050.

Perhaps more curious is the lack of a public and international defence of Beijing's position by China or its allies. This is surprising because its view is in line with a long-standing G77 developing countries' stance that these two targets would imply a far higher per capita emissions level for developed countries, which is regarded as unfair by poorer economies. That said, there is no doubt the Chinese miscalculated the expectations not only of developed countries but also the vulnerable economies whose survival is at stake. There will be more teething pains as China juggles its two increasingly divergent profiles: as an emerging great power and as the largest developing country.

Competing Realities

Geopolitical manoeuvring aside, at the heart of the Copenhagen discord is the failure of many nations to view a strong global climate deal as central to their national interest. Many simply did not see the benefits of acting beyond the lowest common denominator. The often technical, jargonistic nature of climate talks also alienates the general public.

Other intractable issues abound: from the historical responsibility over carbon already in the atmosphere, to a process that can ill-accommodate the increasingly blurred dividing lines between developed and emerging economies, as well as multiple alliances. Many governments ended up treating climate negotiations like zero sum games that resemble trade bargaining, rather than focusing on collective problem-solving to deliver global public benefits.

Private sector groups, including the Confederation of British Industry, describe Copenhagen as a missed opportunity. Energy companies like E.ON and Britain's Centrica suggest they are likely to wait until ageing reactors and coal plants close over the next decade before investing in clean power generation.

But the overall picture is less clear-cut. The Nex index of clean energy stocks did stumble in the immediate aftermath of Copenhagen, but shares across a range of sectors surged from December 1 to early January. The Nex rose a further 4.1 percent in the first week of this year.

Following Copenhagen, many in the cleantech community believe new investments will be driven by local and national policies, mandates and incentive programmes, rather than carbon markets. Deutsche Bank identified 270 climate policies around the world, including Renewable Portfolio Standards in various US States, feed-in tariffs in Europe and energy intensity targets in China.

Low-Carbon Leaders

In any case, the change towards a low-carbon world economy continues. According to Bloomberg New Energy Finance, investment in clean energy sources globally reached $112 billion last year, up from just $18 billion in 2004. Tougher emission standards are anticipated across major sectors. This is already visible in transport, with binding legislation or voluntary standards in the world's major vehicle markets.

As competition heats up, the race for leadership in low carbon technology will be as important as the contest for energy supply. Research and development activity in low carbon options will be an important benchmark to judge company performance. The carbon portfolio and exposure of companies and governments will continue to come under increasing public scrutiny.

At the political level, it is too early to declare that all is lost. After all the Copenhagen process did attract the largest numbers of world leaders to discuss multilateral action on climate action. It is the first time developed and developing countries both agreed to take-on carbon-related commitments to limit greenhouse gas emissions.

Also, despite the unconvincing outcome, without the political momentum in the run-up to Copenhagen, the world would not have seen such a wide variety of nations taking on new national commitments to reduce carbon. Climate diplomacy did make a difference, even if it is inadequate so far.

Grim Prospects

The short-term prospects for a comprehensive global treaty on emissions reduction are grim. The Copenhagen process itself has dampened trust between many countries—and in the negotiation process—which will take time to get back on track.

Politically, activist governments will call for 'coalitions of the willing' which are likely to result in alliances that cut across developed and developing economies; certainly something to watch. More attention will also be paid to the question of variable geometry, and the extent to which different international groups like the Major Economies Forum or the G20 developed and emerging economies have helped or complicated international decision-making.

To rebuild trust, developed countries must focus on delivering the $30 billion of 'fast-start' finance pledged at Copenhagen for the next two years. It should be used to demonstrate low-carbon development models on a larger scale, in addition to incremental efficiency improvements.

On a positive note, it is now widely accepted that strong national action is a foundation for—not a result of—any future global agreement. The global focus is likely to shift onto national policy and increasing the scale of low carbon investment.

For example, the EU is considering raising its 2020 target for reducing greenhouse gas emissions from twenty to thirty percent on 1990 levels. China has proposed reducing the carbon intensity of its economy by forty to forty-five percent by 2020, from a 2005 base line. The more bottom up approach maybe less efficient, but it is delivering change, which is important to build confidence. It also demonstrates the economic and technical viability of moving towards a low carbon economy.

Technical Fixes

At the global level, technology will be a key part of any policy package on the transformation towards a low-carbon world. Many of the necessary technologies like concentrated solar power, heat pumps and offshore wind are already commercially available; others are near-to-market. The next great energy investment wave will be missed if these are not deployed globally in twenty to thirty years.

But there will be some setbacks. To hedge against this risk, greater investment in innovation and demonstrations of technology like carbon capture and storage and smart grids are needed today to create a wide portfolio of commercially available lower carbon options by 2020. This will require new public-private cooperation as well as stronger policy to provide market incentives for rapid diffusion and innovation.

Meanwhile, there must be rapid progress in finalising the process to generate and distribute climate funds, and in the design of innovative financial arrangement to enhance low carbon and efficiency investments. This will underpin the technology cooperation mechanism proposed in the Copenhagen Accord. Measurement, reporting and verification systems will also need to proceed apace. There is the challenging task too of building consensus on reforms to the UN climate process, as well as strengthening the institutional capacity for scaling-up finance beyond 2012.

Short-term political calculations must not set the terms of our future. Even though there are dangers in navigating the low carbon transition, the perception of risks of change must be balanced by a greater understanding of economic and security opportunities.

Critical Thinking

1. What are some the reasons the Copenhagen Summit failed to reach an international agreement addressing climate change?

2. What are some of the reasons Bernice Lee identifies for the prospect of continued progress towards a low-carbon economy without a broad international agreement?

3. What are some specific examples of progress towards this low-carbon goal?

From *The World Today,* August 2010. Copyright © 2010 by The World Today. Reprinted by permission.

Geneva Conventions

They help protect civilians and soldiers from the atrocities of war. But these hard-won rules of battle are falling by the wayside: Terrorists ignore them, and governments increasingly find them quaint and outdated. With every violation, war only gets deadlier for everyone.

STEVEN R. RATNER

"The Geneva Conventions Are Obsolete"

Only in the minor details. The laws of armed conflict are old; they date back millennia to warrior codes used in ancient Greece. But the modern Geneva Conventions, which govern the treatment of soldiers and civilians in war, can trace their direct origin to 1859, when Swiss businessman Henri Dunant happened upon the bloody aftermath of the Battle of Solferino. His outrage at the suffering of the wounded led him to establish what would become the International Committee of the Red Cross, which later lobbied for rules improving the treatment of injured combatants. Decades later, when the devastation of World War II demonstrated that broader protections were necessary, the modern Geneva Conventions were created, producing a kind of international "bill of rights" that governs the handling of casualties, prisoners of war (POWS), and civilians in war zones. Today, the conventions have been ratified by every nation on the planet.

Of course, the drafters probably never imagined a conflict like the war on terror or combatants like al Qaeda. The conventions were always primarily concerned with wars between states. That can leave some of the protections enshrined in the laws feeling a little old-fashioned today. It seems slightly absurd to worry too much about captured terrorists' tobacco rations or the fate of a prisoner's horse, as the conventions do. So, when then White House Counsel Alberto Gonzales wrote President George W. Bush in 2002 arguing that the "new paradigm" of armed conflict rendered parts of the conventions "obsolete" and "quaint," he had a point. In very specific—and minor—details, the conventions have been superseded by time and technology.

But the core provisions and, more crucially, the spirit of the conventions remain enormously relevant for modern warfare. For one, the world is still home to dozens of wars, for which the conventions have important, unambiguous rules, such as forbidding pillaging and prohibiting the use of child soldiers.

These rules apply to both aggressor and defending nations, and, in civil wars, to governments and insurgent groups.

The conventions won't prevent wars—they were never intended to—but they can and do protect innocent bystanders, shield soldiers from unnecessary harm, limit the physical damage caused by war, and even enhance the chances for cease-fires and peace. The fundamental bedrock of the conventions is to prevent suffering in war, and that gives them a legitimacy for anyone touched by conflict, anywhere and at any time. That is hardly quaint or old-fashioned.

"The Conventions Don't Apply to Al Qaeda"

Wrong. The Bush administration's position since Sept. 11, 2001, has been that the global war on terror is a different kind of war, one in which the Geneva Conventions do not apply. It is true that the laws do not specifically mention wars against nonstate actors such as al Qaeda. But there have always been "irregular" forces that participate in warfare, and the conflicts of the 20th century were no exception. The French Resistance during World War II operated without uniforms. Vietcong guerrillas fighting in South Vietnam were not part of any formal army, but the United States nonetheless treated those they captured as POWS.

So what treatment should al Qaeda get? The conventions contain one section—Article 3—that protects all persons regardless of their status, whether spy, mercenary, or terrorist, and regardless of the type of war in which they are fighting. That same article prohibits torture, cruel treatment, and murder of all detainees, requires the wounded to be cared for, and says that any trials must be conducted by regular courts respecting due process. In a landmark 2006 opinion, the U.S. Supreme Court declared that *at a minimum* Article 3 applies to detained al Qaeda suspects. In other words, the rules apply, even if al Qaeda ignores them.

And it may be that even tougher rules should be used in such a fight. Many other governments, particularly in Europe, believe that a "war" against terror—a war without temporal or geographic limits—is complete folly, insisting instead that the fight against terrorist groups should be a law enforcement, not a military, matter. For decades, Europe has prevented and punished terrorists by treating them as criminals. Courts in Britain and Spain have tried suspects for major bombings in London and Madrid. The prosecutors and investigators there did so while largely complying with obligations enshrined in human rights treaties, which constrain them far more than do the Geneva Conventions.

"The Geneva Conventions Turn Soldiers into War Criminals"

Only if they commit war crimes. For centuries, states have punished their own soldiers for violations of the laws of war, such as the mistreatment of prisoners or murder of civilians. The Geneva Conventions identify certain violations that states must prosecute, including murder outside of battle, causing civilians great suffering, and denying POWs fair trials, and most countries have laws on the books that punish such crimes. The U.S. military, for example, has investigated hundreds of servicemembers for abuses in Iraq and Afghanistan, leading to dozens of prosecutions. Canada prosecuted a group of its peacekeepers for the murder of a young Somali in 1993.

Yet the idea that ordinary soldiers could be prosecuted in a foreign country for being, in effect, soldiers fighting a war is ridiculous. Yes, many countries, including the United States, have laws allowing foreigners to be tried for various abuses of war committed anywhere. Yet the risk of prosecution abroad, particularly of U.S. forces, is minuscule. Those foreign laws only address bona fide war crimes, and it is rarely in the interest of foreign governments to aggravate relations with the United States over spurious prosecutions.

The idea that the International Criminal Court could one day put U.S. commanders on trial is unlikely in the extreme. That court could theoretically prosecute U.S. personnel for crimes committed in, say, Afghanistan, but only if the United States failed to do so first. What's more, the court is by its charter dedicated to trying large-scale, horrendous atrocities like those in Sudan. It is virtually inconceivable that this new institution will want to pick a fight with the United States over a relatively small number of abuses.

"The Conventions Prevent Interrogations of Terrorists"

False. If you've seen a classic war movie such as *The Great Escape,* you know that prisoners of war are only obligated to provide name, rank, date of birth, and military serial number to their captors. But the Geneva Conventions do not ban interrogators from asking for more. In fact, the laws were written with the expectation that states will grill prisoners, and clear rules were created to manage the process. In interstate war, any form of coercion is forbidden, specifically threats, insults, or punishments if prisoners fail to answer; for all other wars, cruel or degrading treatment and torture are prohibited. But questioning detainees is perfectly legal; it simply must be done in a manner that respects human dignity. The conventions thus hardly require rolling out the red carpet for suspected terrorists. Many interrogation tactics are clearly allowed, including good cop-bad cop scenarios, repetitive or rapid questioning, silent periods, and playing to a detainee's ego.

The Bush administration has engaged in legal gymnastics to avoid the conventions' restrictions, arguing that preventing the next attack is sufficient rationale for harsh tactics such as waterboarding, sleep deprivation, painful stress positions, deafening music, and traumatic humiliation. These severe methods have been used despite the protests of a growing chorus of intelligence officials who say that such approaches are actually counterproductive to extracting quality information. Seasoned interrogators consistently say that straightforward questioning is far more successful for getting at the truth. So, by mangling the conventions, the United States has joined the company of a host of unsavory regimes that make regular use of torture. It has abandoned a system that protects U.S. military personnel from terrible treatment for one in which the rules are made on the fly.

"The Geneva Conventions Ban Assassinations"

Actually, no. War is all about killing your enemy, and though the Geneva Conventions place limits on the "unnecessary suffering" of soldiers, they certainly don't seek to outlaw war. Assassinating one's enemy when hostilities have been declared is not only permissible; it is expected. But at the core of the conventions is the "principle of distinction," which bans all deliberate targeting of civilians. The boundless scope of the war on terror makes it difficult to decide who is and is not a civilian. The United States claims that it can target and kill terrorists at any time, just like regular soldiers; but the conventions treat these individuals like quasi-civilians who can be targeted and killed only during "such time as they take a *direct* part in hostilities" [emphasis mine]. The Israeli Supreme Court recently interpreted this phrase to give Israel limited latitude to continue targeted killings, but it insisted on a high standard of proof that the target had lost protected status and that capture was impossible. What standards the United States might be using—such as when the CIA targeted and killed several al Qaeda operatives in Yemen in 2002—are highly classified, so there's no way to know how much proof is insisted upon before the trigger is pulled or the button pushed.

For European countries and others who reject the idea of a "war" against terrorists to begin with, targeted killings are especially abhorrent, as international law prohibits states in peacetime from extrajudicial killings. There are very specific exceptions to this rule, such as when a police officer must defend himself or others against imminent harm. To that end, a suicide bomber heading for a crowd could legally be assassinated as a last resort. By contrast, suspected terrorists—whether planning a new attack or on the lam—are to be captured and tried.

"The Conventions Require Closing Guantánamo"

No, but changes must be made. The Geneva Conventions allow countries to detain POWs in camps, and, if someone in enemy hands does not fit the POW category, he or she is automatically accorded civilian status, which has its own protections. But none of the residents of Guantánamo's military prison qualifies as either, according to the Bush administration, thus depriving the roughly 275 detainees who remain there of the rights accorded by the conventions, such as adequate shelter and eventual release.

The possibility that detainees could remain in legal limbo indefinitely at Guantánamo has turned the issue into a foreign-relations disaster for the United States. But let's be clear—the Geneva Conventions don't require the United States to close up shop in Cuba. The rules simply insist that a working legal framework be put in place, instead of the legal vacuum that exists now.

There are several options worth consideration. The prison at Guantánamo could be turned into a pre-trial holding area where detainees are held before they are brought before U.S. courts on formal charges. (The hiccup here is that most of the detainees haven't clearly violated any U.S. law.) Alternatively, the U.S. Congress could pass legislation installing a system of preventive detention for dangerous individuals. The courts could occasionally review detainees' particular circumstances and judge whether continued detention is necessary and lawful. (The problem here is that such a system would run against 200 years of American jurisprudence.) In the end, closing Guantánamo is probably the only option that would realistically restore America's reputation, though it isn't required by any clause in the conventions. It's just the wisest course of action.

"No Nation Flouts the Geneva Conventions More than the United States"

That's absurd. When bullets start flying, rules get broken. The degree to which any army adheres to the Geneva Conventions is typically a product of its professionalism, training, and sense of ethics. On this score, U.S. compliance with the conventions has been admirable, far surpassing many countries and guerrilla armies that routinely ignore even the most basic provisions. The U.S. military takes great pride in teaching its soldiers civilized rules of war: to preserve military honor and discipline, lessen tensions with civilians, and strive to make a final peace more durable. Contrast that training with Eritrea or Ethiopia, states whose ill-trained forces committed numerous war crimes during their recent border war, or Guatemala, whose army and paramilitaries made a policy of killing civilians on an enormous scale during its long civil conflict.

More importantly, the U.S. military cares passionately that other states and nonstate actors follow the same rules to which it adheres, because U.S. forces, who are deployed abroad in far greater numbers than troops from any other nation, are most likely to be harmed if the conventions are discarded. Career U.S. military commanders and lawyers have consistently opposed the various reinterpretations of the conventions by politically appointed lawyers in the Bush White House and Justice Department for precisely this reason.

It is enormously important that the United States reaffirms its commitment to the conventions, for the sake of the country's reputation and that of the conventions. Those who rely on the flawed logic that because al Qaeda does not treat the conventions seriously, neither should the United States fail to see not only the chaos the world will suffer in exchange for these rules; they also miss the fact that the United States will have traded basic rights and protections harshly learned through thousands of years of war for the nitpicking decisions of a small group of partisan lawyers huddled in secret. Rather than advancing U.S. interests by following an established standard of behavior in this new type of war, the United States—and any country that chooses to abandon these hard-won rules—risks basing its policies on narrow legalisms. In losing sight of the crucial protections of the conventions, the United States invites a world of wars in which laws disappear. And the horrors of such wars would far surpass anything the war on terror could ever deliver.

Critical Thinking

1. What reasons are given to support Steven Ratner's contention that the hard-won rules of battle are falling by the wayside?

2. Do the Geneva Conventions prevent the interrogation of terrorists?

3. Do the Geneva Conventions ban assassinations?

STEVEN R. RATNER is professor of law at the University of Michigan.

Is Bigger Better?

Using market incentives, Fazle Hasan Abed built the largest antipoverty group in the world and helped pull Bangladesh out of the ashes. Now he wants to take on Africa.

DAVID ARMSTRONG

From the large glass window of his modern, well-lit and spacious offices 19 floors above Dhaka, Bangladesh, Fazle Hasan Abed, a former executive for Shell Oil, can keep tabs on nearby Korail, a dense slum of 60,000 people living in single-story mud, aluminum and bamboo shacks, some built on thin stilts over the brackish water of an urban lake. Abed, 72, has more than a little interest in the slum. The organization he founded in 1972, BRAC, the largest antipoverty group in the world, with 110,000 paid employees and a $482 million annual budget, has its hands everywhere in Korail.

Down one muddy lane a teacher trained by BRAC instructs 36 students using a BRAC-designed curriculum of Bengali, math and English. Nearby a group of women in the final month of pregnancy sit shrouded in colorful saris on the floor of a BRAC-built "birthing hut," staffed with BRAC-trained health workers, getting a lesson in prenatal nutrition. Not far away, Mosammat Anwaraan, an energetic woman in her late 50s, runs a mini real estate empire, the fruits of a 3,000 taka ($44) microloan in 1997 from BRAC. She owns 25 rooms in the slum, renting out 18 for 700 to 800 taka a month, making $2,500 a year. "I think rent will go up to 1,000 taka by next year," she says proudly.

Abed has replicated all-in-one programs like these in 1,000 urban slums and 70,000 rural villages across Bangladesh (the group was originally called the Bangladesh Rural Advancement Committee). Its microfinance program has made $4.6 billion in loans versus $6.9 billion from the better-known microlender Grameen. It runs 52,000 preschools and primary schools, with 1.5 million students. Its 68,000 health care volunteers, egged on by financial incentives, cover a population of 80 million. It operates commercial dairies, silkworm-raising centers and department stores to provide markets for the goods its poor beneficiaries produce. Says Abed, "If you want to do significant work, you have to be large. Otherwise we'd be tinkering around on the periphery."

The World Bank credits BRAC in part with what it calls the "Bangladesh paradox": Despite an impotent government (leaders of the two primary political parties are currently in jail on corruption charges), this country of 145 million people has improved significantly. According to the World Bank, the fraction of the population living in poverty (defined as below $2 a day in purchasing power) dropped from 58% in 1992 to 40% in 2005; secondary school enrollment has climbed from 19% in 1990 to 43% today and childhood immunization from 1% in 1980 to 80% today.

In the 1980s a woman had, on average, seven kids. Today it's two.

Thirty years ago a woman had, on average, seven children. Today the fertility rate is two, thanks in large part to widespread delivery of contraceptives to the countryside, a practice pioneered by BRAC. The country's 5% annual average growth in GDP since 1990 (to $2,300 per capita) leads the World Bank to suggest that Bangladesh could join the list of "middle income" countries in ten years. To be sure, trade liberalization, garment exports and remittances from laborers abroad are vital, but the effectiveness of these macroeconomic advances are largely dependent on the kind of ground-level social progress BRAC has made.

"I don't know of any developing-world NGO [nongovernmental organization] that has been more successful," says Dr. Allan Rosenfield, dean of Columbia University's School of Public Health, who serves on the board of BRAC's U.S. arm. "Certainly in terms of the issues they work on, they're more like a minigovernment. If I were giving out Nobel Prizes, there is no doubt I would give it to Abed."

Born to a wealthy landowning family in the Bengal region of British India in 1936, Abed grew up in a household full of servants. His father was a government official. His mother, a religious woman, often brought poor villagers to the Abed home for food. He attended Glasgow University before going to London to study accounting and business. He stayed for 12 years, working as a corporate financial officer and enjoying the life of a professional expatriate: yearly drives through continental Europe, vacations in Italy, reading Western literature. In 1968 he returned to Dhaka with a prestigious job, managing Shell's accounting department.

On Nov. 21, 1970 a cyclone hit the Chittagong area in the southern part of the country, killing perhaps 500,000 people, still the deadliest cyclone on record. Abed and friends volunteered to help. "It really changed the way I look at things," Abed says.

At the time, Bangladesh was the eastern portion of the country of Pakistan, ruled over by an unsympathetic government in Islamabad. A crackdown on the pro-East Pakistan independence movement sent Abed back to London, where he raised funds for the millions of Bangladeshi refugees in India.

After a bloody war Bangladesh won its independence in 1971. Abed sold his London flat for $17,000 and returned to a country that lay in ruins. Hundreds of thousands had been killed and the economy was in tatters—soon after, Henry Kissinger famously called Bangladesh "an international basket case."

Abed and a small group of friends worked on aid projects, but he felt much of the work wasn't benefiting those who needed it most. "Poor people are poor because they are powerless," Abed says. He turned his attention to poverty relief, mapping villages into quartiles based on wealth and focusing his efforts on only those households at the bottom.

Using the proceeds of his London apartment sale, he formed BRAC in 1972. His biggest early success was reducing child mortality. In 1975, 25% of Bangladeshi children wouldn't live to see their fifth birthday; almost half of those deaths were caused by diarrhea. Abed trained groups of women to fan out into the countryside and teach others how to mix a solution of water, salt and sugar that would combat the potentially fatal loss of fluid and electrolytes. Monitors would grade the households based on how well family members did, and that grade would determine the pay of the instructors. This was an incentive-based "social entrepreneurship" program long before that phrase became common. The average worker made $40 a month, with most households scoring in the A or B range.

BRAC researchers estimate that the program, along with a government immunization initiative, has cut the mortality rate of Bangladeshi children ages 1 to 4 from 25% to 7%.

Abed vertically integrates many BRAC programs. A BRAC village organizer will first gather 20 to 30 women and extend microcredit. Many use the loans to set up small shops and grocery stores. If the women buy a cow, for example, BRAC will help them double the price they can get for milk

by collecting it via refrigerated truck and bringing it to one of BRAC's 67 "chilling stations," then to BRAC's commercial dairy production center, which processes 10,000 liters of milk, yogurt and ice cream an hour, and selling it in the cities. It earns BRAC $1.7 million on sales of $13.4 million, all of which goes back into the programs.

Likewise, silkworm raising is the bottom step of another commercial market. Majeda Begum, who lives in a small village a day's drive from Dhaka, used her loan to buy silkworm eggs from BRAC, paying $3 for 50 grams. She hatches them in a tin-roofed shack behind her home. Begum feeds them by spreading mulberry leaves over the top, easy enough to collect, since BRAC has planted 20 million mulberry trees around the area to support the enterprise. She'll sell the cocoons back to BRAC for $5.75 a kilo. She earns, she figures, $370 a year, and no longer needs BRAC's loans. All three of her children, including two daughters, go to school. Without the income? "I'd probably only send my son," she says.

Vertically integrated, BRAC's businesses produce $90 million in revenue.

The silk is eventually woven into clothes and sold to Aarong, a chain of upmarket department stores BRAC owns in Bangladesh's big cities. Aarong netted $4.6 million on $28 million in sales in 2006. In all, BRAC's commercial enterprises account for some $90 million in revenue; it pulls in $116 million from its interest on microloans. BRAC still relies on donor funding for 20% of its budget.

Abed uses incentives for health programs, as well. Community health workers are asked to make home visits to 15 houses a day and can resell at a small markup common medicines, balm and birth control pills that they have bought from BRAC.

Recently health volunteers have been trained to recognize the symptoms of tuberculosis, which kills 70,000 Bangladeshis a year. Volunteers collect a sample of phlegm from suspect people and send it to a BRAC health office for testing. If it's positive, the volunteer gets 200 taka (about $2.50). Patients are given medicine free of charge but must post a $3.50 bond to ensure that they continue the six-month course of medication. "There are market incentives in everything we do," Abed says. Bangladesh has upped its cure rate of known TB cases to 90%.

BRAC has recently started targeting the 14% of women too poor to take advantage of microloans. A day's drive from Dhaka, in an un-air-conditioned BRAC field office swarming with flies, Akhtar Hossain unfurls a large sheet of brown paper on which is drawn a map of a nearby village. His house-by-house survey is meant to find "beggars and those with no land." The government is supposed to give these people a card that entitles the holder to 35 kilos of rice every three months. "But they never get it," he says. "The district official in charge of disbursing the cards gives it to people he knows."

To this group BRAC distributes cows, goats or a small plot of arable land. Haliman Khatun, who once worked as a laborer in others' homes and was paid only with small amounts of rice, shares her small shack in Pakundia with her cow, proudly showing off the space where the cow sleeps next to her own bed. She sells milk from the cow at the market but has bigger ambitions: She might sell it for the end of Eid, a Muslim holiday when livestock is slaughtered; cows can fetch a premium in the marketplace, and with that she could buy a plot of land or more goats, she says.

Abed is now bringing BRAC into Africa. The Gates Foundation has given $15 million in grants and loans to replicate BRAC's microfinance, agriculture and health programs in Tanzania, and the Nike Foundation is giving $1 million to establish designated centers for teenage girls in Tanzania. BRAC has set up organizations in the U.S. and the U.K. to bring in more charitable dollars.

It remains to be seen if BRAC can repeat the success it's had in Bangladesh. But Abed is encouraged by its track record in Afghanistan, where it set up shop in 2002. Some 180,000 women have borrowed $96 million from BRAC, and 4,000 have been trained as community health workers. When Abed sets out to do something, he does it big.

Critical Thinking

1. What is a non-governmental organization (NGO)?
2. What is the mission and strategic plan of BRAC?
3. How is BRAC organized?
4. What other important NGOs can you identify?

From *Forbes Magazine*, June 2, 2008, pp. 66–70. Reprinted by permission of Forbes Magazine, © 2008 Forbes Media Inc.

A World *Enslaved*

There are now more slaves on the planet than at any time in human history. True abolition will elude us until we admit the massive scope of the problem, attack it in all its forms, and empower slaves to help free themselves.

E. Benjamin Skinner

Standing in New York City, you are five hours away from being able to negotiate the sale, in broad daylight, of a healthy boy or girl. He or she can be used for anything, though sex and domestic labor are most common. Before you go, let's be clear on what you are buying. A slave is a human being forced to work through fraud or threat of violence for no pay beyond subsistence. Agreed? Good.

Most people imagine that slavery died in the 19th century. Since 1817, more than a dozen international conventions have been signed banning the slave trade. Yet, today there are more slaves than at any time in human history.

And if you're going to buy one in five hours, you'd better get a move on. First, hail a taxi to JFK International Airport, and hop on a direct flight to Port-au-Prince, Haiti. The flight takes three hours. After landing at Toussaint L'Ouverture International Airport, you will need 50 cents for the most common form of transport in Port-au-Prince, the tap-tap, a flatbed pickup retrofitted with benches and a canopy. Three quarters of the way up Route de Delmas, the capital's main street, tap the roof and hop out. There, on a side street, you will find a group of men standing in front of Le Réseau (The Network) barbershop. As you approach, a man steps forward: "Are you looking to get a person?"

Meet Benavil Lebhom. He smiles easily. He has a trim mustache and wears a multicolored, striped golf shirt, a gold chain, and Doc Martens knockoffs. Benavil is a courtier, or broker. He holds an official real estate license and calls himself an employment agent. Two thirds of the employees he places are child slaves. The total number of Haitian children in bondage in their own country stands at 300,000. They are the *restavèks,* the "staywiths," as they are euphemistically known in Creole. Forced, unpaid, they work in captivity from before dawn until night. Benavil and thousands of other formal and informal traffickers lure these children from desperately impoverished rural parents, with promises of free schooling and a better life.

The negotiation to buy a child slave might sound a bit like this:

"How quickly do you think it would be possible to bring a child in? Somebody who could clean and cook?" you ask. "I don't have a very big place; I have a small apartment. But I'm wondering how much that would cost? And how quickly?"

"Three days," Benavil responds.

"And you could bring the child here?" you inquire. "Or are there children here already?"

"I don't have any here in Port-au-Prince right now," says Benavil, his eyes widening at the thought of a foreign client. "I would go out to the countryside."

You ask about additional expenses. "Would I have to pay for transportation?"

"*Bon,*" says Benavil. "A hundred U.S."

Smelling a rip-off, you press him, "And that's just for transportation?"

"Transportation would be about 100 Haitian," says Benavil, or around $13, "because you'd have to get out there. Plus [hotel and] food on the trip. Five hundred gourdes."

"Okay, 500 Haitian," you say.

Now you ask the big question: "And what would your fee be?" This is the moment of truth, and Benavil's eyes narrow as he determines how much he can take you for.

"A hundred. American."

"That seems like a lot," you say, with a smile so as not to kill the deal. "How much would you charge a Haitian?"

Benavil's voice rises with feigned indignation. "A hundred dollars. This is a major effort."

You hold firm. "Could you bring down your fee to 50 U.S.?"

Benavil pauses. But only for effect. He knows he's still got you for much more than a Haitian would pay. "*Oui,*" he says with a smile.

But the deal isn't done. Benavil leans in close. "This is a rather delicate question. Is this someone you want as just a worker? Or also someone who will be a 'partner'? You understand what I mean?"

You don't blink at being asked if you want the child for sex. "I mean, is it possible to have someone that could be both?"

"*Oui!*" Benavil responds enthusiastically.

If you're interested in taking your purchase back to the United States, Benavil tells you that he can "arrange" the proper papers to make it look as though you've adopted the child.

He offers you a 13-year-old girl.

"That's a little bit old," you say.

"I know of another girl who's 12. Then ones that are 10, 11," he responds.

The negotiation is finished, and you tell Benavil not to make any moves without further word from you. Here, 600 miles from the United States, and five hours from Manhattan, you have successfully arranged to buy a human being for 50 bucks.

The Cruel Truth

It would be nice if that conversation, like the description of the journey, were fictional. It is not. I recorded it on Oct. 6, 2005, as part of four years of research into slavery on five continents. In the popular consciousness, "slavery" has come to be little more than just a metaphor for undue hardship. Investment bankers routinely refer to themselves as "high-paid wage slaves." Human rights activists may call $1-an-hour sweatshop laborers slaves, regardless of the fact that they are paid and can often walk away from the job. But the reality of slavery is far different. Slavery exists today on an unprecedented scale. In Africa, tens of thousands are chattel slaves, seized in war or tucked away for generations. Across Europe, Asia, and the Americas, traffickers have forced as many as 2 million into prostitution or labor. In South Asia, which has the highest concentration of slaves on the planet, nearly 10 million languish in bondage, unable to leave their captors until they pay off "debts," legal fictions that in many cases are generations old.

Few in the developed world have a grasp of the enormity of modern-day slavery. Fewer still are doing anything to combat it. Beginning in 2001, U.S. President George W. Bush was urged by several of his key advisors to vigorously enforce the Victims of Trafficking and Violence Protection Act, a U.S. law enacted a month earlier that sought to prosecute domestic human traffickers and cajole foreign governments into doing the same. The Bush administration trumpeted the effort—at home via the Christian evangelical media and more broadly via speeches and pronouncements, including in addresses to the U.N. General Assembly in 2003 and 2004. But even the quiet and diligent work of some within the U.S. State Department, which credibly claims to have secured more than 100 antitrafficking laws and more than 10,000 trafficking convictions worldwide, has resulted in no measurable decline in the number of slaves worldwide. Between 2000 and 2006, the U.S. Justice Department increased human trafficking prosecutions from 3 to 32, and convictions from 10 to 98. By 2006, 27 states had passed antitrafficking laws. Yet, during the same period, the United States liberated less than 2 percent of its own modern-day slaves. As many as 17,500 new slaves continue to enter bondage in the United States every year.

The West's efforts have been, from the outset, hamstrung by a warped understanding of slavery. In the United States, a hard-driving coalition of feminist and evangelical activists has forced the Bush administration to focus almost exclusively on the sex trade. The official State Department line is that voluntary prostitution does not exist, and that commercial sex is the main driver of slavery today. In Europe, though Germany and the Netherlands have decriminalized most prostitution, other nations such as Bulgaria have moved in the opposite direction, bowing to U.S. pressure and cracking down on the flesh trade. But, across the Americas, Europe, and Asia, unregulated escort services are exploding with the help of the Internet. Even when enlightened governments have offered clearheaded solutions to deal with this problem, such as granting victims temporary residence, they have had little impact.

Many feel that sex slavery is particularly revolting—and it is. I saw it firsthand. In a Bucharest brothel, for instance, I was offered a mentally handicapped, suicidal girl in exchange for a used car. But for every one woman or child enslaved in commercial sex, there are at least 15 men, women, and children enslaved in other fields, such as domestic work or agricultural labor. Recent studies have shown that locking up pimps and traffickers has had a negligible effect on the aggregate rates of bondage. And though eradicating prostitution may be a just cause, Western policies based on the idea that all prostitutes are slaves and all slaves are prostitutes belittles the suffering of all victims. It's an approach that threatens to put most governments on the wrong side of history.

Indebted for Life

Save for the fact that he is male, Gonoo Lal Kol typifies the average slave of our modern age. (At his request, I have changed his first name.) Like a vast majority of the world's slaves, Gonoo is in debt bondage in South Asia. In his case, in an Indian quarry. Like most slaves, Gonoo is illiterate and unaware of the Indian laws that ban his bondage and provide for sanctions against his master. His story, told to me in more than a dozen conversations inside his 4-foot-high stone and grass hutch, represents the other side of the "Indian Miracle."

Gonoo lives in Lohagara Dhal, a forgotten corner of Uttar Pradesh, a north Indian state that contains 8 percent of the world's poor. I met him one evening in December 2005 as he walked with two dozen other laborers in tattered and filthy clothes. Behind them was the quarry. In that pit, Gonoo, a member of the historically outcast Kol tribe, worked with his family 14 hours a day. His tools were simple, a rough-hewn hammer and an iron pike. His hands were covered in calluses, his fingertips worn away.

Gonoo's master is a tall, stout, surly contractor named Ramesh Garg. Garg is one of the wealthiest men in Shankargarh, the nearest sizable town, founded under the British Raj but now run by nearly 600 quarry contractors. He makes his money by enslaving entire families forced to work for no pay beyond alcohol, grain, and bare subsistence expenses. Their only use for Garg is to turn rock into silica sand, for colored glass, or gravel, for roads or ballast. Slavery scholar Kevin Bales estimates that a slave in the 19th-century American South had to work 20 years to recoup his or her purchase price. Gonoo and the other slaves earn a profit for Garg in two years.

Every single man, woman, and child in Lohagara Dhal is a slave. But, in theory at least, Garg neither bought nor owns them. They are working off debts, which, for many, started at less than $10. But interest accrues at over 100 percent annually here. Most of the debts span at least two generations, though they have no legal standing under modern Indian law. They are a fiction that Garg constructs through fraud and maintains through violence. The seed of Gonoo's slavery, for instance, was a loan of 62 cents. In 1958, his grandfather borrowed that amount from the owner of a farm where he worked. Three generations and three slavemasters later, Gonoo's family remains in bondage.

Bringing Freedom to Millions

Recently, many bold, underfunded groups have taken up the challenge of tearing out the roots of slavery. Some gained fame through dramatic slave rescues. Most learned that freeing slaves is impossible unless the slaves themselves choose to be free. Among the Kol of Uttar Pradesh, for instance, an organization called Pragati Gramodyog Sansthan (Progressive Institute for Village Enterprises, or PGS) has helped hundreds of families break the grip of the quarry contractors. Working methodically since 1985, PGS organizers slowly built up confidence among slaves. With PGS's help, the Kol formed microcredit unions and won leases to quarries so that they could keep the proceeds of their labor. Some bought property for the first time in their lives, a cow or a goat, and their incomes, which had been nil, multiplied quickly. PGS set up primary schools and dug wells. Villages that for generations had known nothing but slavery began to become free. PGS's success demonstrates that emancipation is merely the first step in abolition. Within the developed world, some national law enforcement agencies such as those in the Czech Republic and Sweden have finally begun to pursue the most culpable of human trafficking—slave-trading pimps and unscrupulous labor contractors. But more must be done to educate local police, even in the richest of nations. Too often, these street-level law enforcement personnel do not understand that it's just as likely for a prostitute to be a trafficking victim as it is for a nanny working without proper papers to be a slave. And, after they have been discovered by law enforcement, few rich nations provide slaves with the kind of rehabilitation, retraining, and protection needed to prevent their re-trafficking. The asylum now granted to former slaves in the United States and the Netherlands is a start. But more must be done.

The United Nations, whose founding principles call for it to fight bondage in all its forms, has done almost nothing to combat modern slavery. In January, Antonio Maria Costa, executive director of the U.N. Office on Drugs and Crime, called for the international body to provide better quantification of human trafficking. Such number crunching would be valuable in combating that one particular manifestation of slavery. But there is little to suggest the United Nations, which consistently fails to hold its own member states accountable for widespread slavery, will be an effective tool in defeating the broader phenomenon.

Any lasting solutions to human trafficking must involve prevention programs in at-risk source countries. Absent an effective international body like the United Nations, such an effort will require pressure from the United States. So far, the United States has been willing to criticize some nations' records, but it

has resisted doing so where it matters most, particularly in India. India abolished debt bondage in 1976, but with poor enforcement of the law locally, millions remain in bondage. In 2006 and 2007, the U.S. State Department's Office to Monitor and Combat Trafficking in Persons pressed U.S. Secretary of State Condoleezza Rice to repudiate India's intransigence personally. And, in each instance, she did not.

The psychological, social, and economic bonds of slavery run deep, and for governments to be truly effective in eradicating slavery, they must partner with groups that can offer slaves a way to pull themselves up from bondage. One way to do that is to replicate the work of grassroots organizations such as Varanasi, India-based MSEMVS (Society for Human Development and Women's Empowerment). In 1996, the Indian group launched free transitional schools, where children who had been enslaved learned skills and acquired enough literacy to move on to formal schooling. The group also targeted mothers, providing them with training and start-up materials for microenterprises. In Thailand, a nation infamous for sex slavery, a similar group, the Labour Rights Promotion Network, works to keep desperately poor Burmese immigrants from the clutches of traffickers by, among other things, setting up schools and health programs. Even in the remote highlands of southern Haiti, activists with Limyè Lavi ("Light of Life") reach otherwise wholly isolated rural communities to warn them of the dangers of traffickers such as Benavil Lebhom and to help them organize informal schools to keep children near home. In recent years, the United States has shown an increasing willingness to help fund these kinds of organizations, one encouraging sign that the message may be getting through.

For four years, I saw dozens of people enslaved, several of whom traffickers like Benavil actually offered to sell to me. I did not pay for a human life anywhere. And, with one exception, I always withheld action to save any one person, in the hope that my research would later help to save many more. At times, that still feels like an excuse for cowardice. But the hard work of real emancipation can't be the burden of a select few. For thousands of slaves, grassroots groups like PGS and MSEMVS can help bring freedom. But, until governments define slavery in appropriately concise terms, prosecute the crime aggressively in all its forms, and encourage groups that empower slaves to free themselves, millions more will remain in bondage. And our collective promise of abolition will continue to mean nothing at all.

Critical Thinking

1. What is the scope of the modern slavery problem?
2. Is this problem confined to poor countries, or are there slaves in the US and other so-called developed countries?
3. What role do NGOs play in fighting slavery?
4. What solutions to the problem does the author propose?

E. Benjamin Skinner is the author of *A Crime So Monstrous: Face-to-Face with Modern-Day Slavery* (New York: Free Press, 2008).

Reprinted in entirety by McGraw-Hill with permission from *Foreign Policy*, March/April 2008. www.foreignpolicy.com. © 2008 Washingtonpost.Newsweek Interactive, LLC.

Chile Starts Early

Jimmy Langman

Maria Estela Ortiz, a chilean education specialist, first worked with Michelle Bachelet in the late 1980s, when Bachelet was a doctor treating children whose parents had been tortured or "disappeared" by the Pinochet regime. Today, Bachelet is Chile's president, and since she took office in March 2006, Ortiz has been helping lead one of her administration's defining projects: providing free access to health and education programs for all Chileans under the age of 4. For more than three years now, as part of the effort, Chile has been building new preschools at the astounding rate of 2.5 a day, increasing the country's total from 781 to 4,300. It has also significantly boosted health coverage and nutrition programs for kids. Ortiz, who heads Chile's National Early Education Board, calls it all a vital investment in the country's future that's especially important during the current economic crisis, when more parents are forced to work and fewer have money for school.

President Bachelet leads the way in pushing the advantages of preschool.

Chile, which happens to be led by a pediatrician who's also a single mother and a committed socialist, is a particularly dramatic example of a growing trend throughout Latin America and beyond: as countries grapple with the economic downturn and reconsider spending, more and more are heeding the advice of a coalition of economists, scientists, and experts who argue that the best way to strengthen a society and increase development is to improve health, education, and other services for its youngest citizens.

The trend's most prominent spokesperson is probably Shakira, the Colombian pop singer who is also a founder of a group known as ALAS. This coalition (its name comes from an acronym for "Latin America in Solidarity Action," but also means "wings" in Spanish) has brought together Latino businesspeople, artists, and celebrities such as Jennifer Lopez and Gabriel Garcia Marquez to help end poverty in the Western hemisphere by ensuring that all kids under 6 have access to health care, education, and proper nutrition. Last year, ALAS convinced the Mexican billionaire Carlos Slim and Howard Buffett (the philanthropist son of Warren Buffett) to pledge $185 million for early

related programs in Latin America, and the group has organized huge concerts throughout the region to raise awareness.

ALAS has also sought to affect policy by working with the development economist Jeffrey Sachs and his Earth Institute at Columbia University to persuade Latin American governments to scale up their funding for programs in a region where about 60 percent of all kids still live in poverty. "This is not the time for governments to be cutting back," says Joanna Rubinstein, director of strategic development for the Earth Institute. "No country can afford to put at a risk an entire generation because of the economic crisis."

The advocates have plenty of academic research to back them up. In October 2007, the Inter-American Development Bank brought together a panel of top economists and asked them, if they had $10 billion to solve Latin America's most pressing problems, how would they do it? The group, using cost-benefit analysis, decided that the most effective use of the cash would be to invest it in programs like day care, preschool, parenting and hygiene courses, as well as early childhood health services. Meanwhile, James Heckman, a Nobel Prize-winning economist at the University of Chicago, has found that introducing preschool education for disadvantaged kids results in at least a 10 percent annual return for society by improving students' intelligence scores and social skills, leading to better school performance and employment prospects in later years as well as reduced crime and teenage-pregnancy rates.

New research also shows how dangerous it is to neglect such programs. Work by Harvard's Jack Shonkoff, for example, has found that depriving poor children of access to good health care, nutrition, and education during their first three years increases the likelihood they'll suffer from disease, learning difficulties, and poverty. Such findings are based in part on studies that show that humans develop 80 percent of their brain in the first three years of life, making nutrition and proper mental stimulation critical during this period. Says Miguel Hoffmann, a Buenos Aires psychiatrist who specializes in early-childhood development, "all the data are showing that proper care and quality education in the first years [ensure that] we learn faster and are emotionally better able to cope with life's challenges."

To provide these goods, in April Colombia announced a new national policy guaranteeing the right to a quality education for all children under 5; as part of the plan, Bogota aims to build 60 new early education centers next year and enroll 400,000 kids in government programs. But the most enthusiastic country has been Chile. In October 2006, Bachelet's government inaugurated a groundbreaking campaign called "Chile Grows With You," which brings together state-supported day care, preschool, family counseling, and health services for all Chileans who participate in the country's public-health system (about 70 percent of the population). The program aims at kids from conception through age 4 and is entirely free for the poorest 40 percent of the population. It also offers subsidies to assist poor families with raising their kids after that.

"Chile has been amazing in its ability to create a national consensus and act on it," says Andrea Rolla, director of A Good Start, a joint early-education program of Harvard University's Graduate School of Education and Chile's Education Opportunity Foundation. Now that the infrastructure is in place, Chilean officials say the next challenge is to boost enrollment and quality. But local preschools are already reporting a dramatic rise in interest. Ortiz even credits the program with a boom in births in the first half of this year, leading to the highest birthrate in the last decade. "Chilean women see the social protections and they are emboldened to have children," she says. If she's right, it's a powerful sign of Chileans' faith in the new campaign—and a show of optimism conspicuously absent in many other parts of the world at the moment.

Critical Thinking

1. According to Jimmy Langman, what is the best way to strengthen a society?

2. What are the lessons of the Chilean case study?

UNIT 7
Values and Visions

Unit Selections

Learning Outcomes

After reading this unit you should be able to:

- Identify specific examples of the "meta" component of the Allegory of the Balloon, i.e., changing values and new ideas.

- Consider how the "meta" factor impacts social structures and natural resources.

- Assess your on-going effort at identifying your theory of international relations and how this unit changes/complements it.

- Compare your theory to the Allegory of the Balloon. How are they similar/different?

Student Website
www.mhhe.com/cls

Internet References

Human Rights Web
    www.hrweb.org
InterAction
    www.interaction.org

The final unit of this book considers how humanity's view of itself is changing. Values, like all other elements discussed in this anthology, are dynamic. Visionary people with new ideas can have a profound impact on how a society deals with problems and adapts to changing circumstances. Therefore, to understand the forces at work in the world today, values, visions, and new ideas in many ways are every bit as important as new technology or changing demographics.

Novelist Herman Wouk, in his book *War and Remembrance,* observed that many institutions have been so embedded in the social fabric of their time that people assumed that they were part of human nature; for example, human sacrifice and blood sport. However, forward-thinking people opposed these institutions. Many knew that they would never see the abolition of these social systems within their own lifetimes, but they pressed on in the hope that someday these institutions would be eliminated.

Wouk believes the same is true for warfare. He states, "Either we are finished with war or war will finish us." Aspects of society such as warfare, slavery, racism, and the secondary status of women are creations of the human mind; history suggests that they can be changed by the human spirit.

The articles of this unit have been selected with the previous six units in mind. Each explores some aspect of world affairs from the perspective of values and alternative visions of the future.

New ideas are critical to meeting these challenges. The examination of well-known issues from new perspectives can yield new insights into old problems. It was feminist Susan B. Anthony who once remarked that "social change is never made by the masses, only by educated minorities." The redefinition of human values (which, by necessity, will accompany the successful confrontation of important global issues) is a task that few people take on willingly. Nevertheless, in order to deal with the dangers of nuclear war, overpopulation, and environmental degradation, educated people must take a broad view of history. This is going to require considerable effort and much personal sacrifice.

When people first begin to consider the magnitude of contemporary global problems, many often become disheartened

© Brand X Pictures/PunchStock

and depressed. Some ask: What can I do? What does it matter? Who cares? There are no easy answers to these questions, but people need only look around to see good news as well as bad. How individuals react to the world is not solely a function of so-called objective reality but a reflection of themselves.

As stated at the beginning of the first unit, the study of global issues is the study of people. The study of people, furthermore, is the study of both values and the level of commitment supporting these values and beliefs.

It is one of the goals of this book to stimulate you, the reader, to react intellectually and emotionally to the discussion and description of various global challenges. In the process of studying these issues, hopefully you have had some new insights into your own values and commitments. In the presentation of the Allegory of the Balloon, the fourth color added represented the "meta" component, all of those qualities that make human beings unique. It is these qualities that have brought us to this unique moment in time, and it will be these same qualities that will determine the outcome of our historically unique challenges.

Humanity's Common Values
Seeking a Positive Future

Overcoming the discontents of globalization and the clashes of civilizations requires us to reexamine and reemphasize those positive values that all humans share.

WENDELL BELL

Some commentators have insisted that the terrorist attacks of September 11, 2001, and their aftermath demonstrate Samuel P. Huntington's thesis of "the clash of civilizations," articulated in a famous article published in 1993. Huntington, a professor at Harvard University and director of security planning for the National Security Council during the Carter administration, argued that "conflict between groups from differing civilizations" has become "the central and most dangerous dimension of the emerging global politics."

Huntington foresaw a future in which nation-states no longer play a decisive role in world affairs. Instead, he envisioned large alliances of states, drawn together by common culture, cooperating with each other. He warned that such collectivities are likely to be in conflict with other alliances formed of countries united around a different culture.

Cultural differences do indeed separate people between various civilizations, but they also separate groups within a single culture or state. Many countries contain militant peoples of different races, religions, languages, and cultures, and such differences do sometimes provoke incidents that lead to violent conflict—as in Bosnia, Cyprus, Northern Ireland, Rwanda, and elsewhere. Moreover, within many societies today (both Western and non-Western) and within many religions (including Islam, Judaism, and Christianity) the culture war is primarily internal, between fundamentalist orthodox believers on the one hand and universalizing moderates on the other. However, for most people most of the time, peaceful accommodation and cooperation are the norms.

Conflicts between groups often arise and continue not because of the differences between them, but because of their similarities. People everywhere, for example, share the capacities to demonize others, to be loyal to their own group (sometimes even willing to die for it), to believe that they themselves and those they identify with are virtuous while all others are wicked, and to remember past wrongs committed against their group and seek revenge. Sadly, human beings everywhere share the capacity to hate and kill each other, including their own family members and neighbors.

Discontents of Globalization

Huntington is skeptical about the implications of the McDonaldization of the world. He insists that the "essence of Western civilization is the Magna Carta not the Magna Mac." And he says further, "The fact that non-Westerners may bite into the latter has no implications for accepting the former."

His conclusion may be wrong, for if biting into a Big Mac and drinking Coca-Cola, French wine, or Jamaican coffee while watching a Hollywood film on a Japanese TV and stretched out on a Turkish rug means economic development, then demands for public liberties and some form of democratic rule may soon follow where Big Mac leads. We know from dozens of studies that economic development contributes to the conditions necessary for political democracy to flourish.

Globalization, of course, is not producing an all-Western universal culture. Although it contains many Western aspects, what is emerging is a *global* culture, with elements from many cultures of the world, Western and non-Western.

Local cultural groups sometimes do view the emerging global culture as a threat, because they fear their traditional ways will disappear or be corrupted. And they may be right. The social world, after all, is constantly in flux. But, like the clean toilets that McDonald's brought to Hong Kong restaurants, people may benefit from certain changes, even when their fears prevent them from seeing this at once.

And local traditions can still be—and are—preserved by groups participating in a global culture. Tolerance and even the celebration of many local variations, as long as they do not harm others, are hallmarks of a sustainable world community. Chinese food, Spanish art, Asian philosophies, African drumming, Egyptian history, or any major religion's version of the Golden Rule can enrich the lives of everyone. What originated locally can become universally adopted (like Arabic numbers). Most important, perhaps, the emerging global culture is a fabric woven from tens of thousands—possibly hundreds of thousands—of individual networks of communication, influence, and exchange that link people and organizations across civilizational boundaries. Aided by electronic communications systems, these networks are growing stronger and more numerous each day.

Positive shared value: Unity.

Searching for Common, *Positive* Values

Global religious resurgence is a reaction to the loss of personal identity and group stability produced by "the processes of social, economic, and cultural modernization that swept across the world in the second half of the twentieth century," according to Huntington. With traditional systems of authority disrupted, people become separated from their roots in a bewildering maze of new rules and expectations. In his view, such people need "new sources of identity, new forms of stable community, and new sets of moral precepts to provide them with a sense of meaning and purpose." Organized religious groups, both mainstream and fundamentalist, are growing today precisely to meet these needs, he believes.

Positive shared value: Love.

Although uprooted people may need new frameworks of identity and purpose, they will certainly not find them in fundamentalist religious groups, for such groups are *not* "new sources of identity." Instead, they recycle the past. Religious revival movements are reactionary, not progressive. Instead of facing the future, developing new approaches to deal with perceived threats of economic, technological, and social change, the movements attempt to retreat into the past.

Religions will likely remain among the major human belief systems for generations to come, despite—or even because of—the fact that they defy conventional logic and reason with their ultimate reliance upon otherworldly beliefs. However, it is possible that some ecumenical accommodations will be made that will allow humanity to build a generally accepted ethical system based on the many similar and overlapping moralities contained in the major religions. A person does not have to believe in supernatural beings to embrace and practice the principles of a global ethic, as exemplified in the interfaith declaration, "Towards a Global Ethic," issued by the Parliament of the World's Religions in 1993.

Positive shared value: Compassion.

Interfaith global cooperation is one way that people of different civilizations can find common cause. Another is global environmental cooperation seeking to maintain and enhance the life-sustaining capacities of the earth. Also, people everywhere have a stake in working for the freedom and welfare of future generations, not least because the future of their own children and grandchildren is at stake.

Positive shared value: Welfare of future generations.

Many more examples of cooperation among civilizations in the pursuit of common goals can be found in every area from medicine and science to moral philosophy, music, and art. A truly global commitment to the exploration, colonization, and industrialization of space offers still another way to harness the existing skills and talents of many nations, with the aim of realizing and extending worthy human capacities to their fullest. So, too, does the search for extraterrestrial intelligence. One day, many believe, contact will be made. What, then, becomes of Huntington's "clash of civilizations"? Visitors to Earth will likely find the variations among human cultures and languages insignificant compared with the many common traits all humans share.

Universal human values do exist, and many researchers, using different methodologies and data sets, have independently identified similar values. Typical of many studies into universal values is the global code of ethics compiled by Rushworth M. Kidder in *Shared Values for a Troubled World* (Wiley, 1994). Kidder's list includes love, truthfulness, fairness, freedom, unity (including cooperation, group allegiance, and oneness with others), tolerance, respect for life, and responsibility (which includes taking care of yourself, of other individuals, and showing concern for community interests). Additional values mentioned are courage, knowing right from wrong, wisdom, hospitality, obedience, and stability.

The Origins of Universal Human Values

Human values are not arbitrary or capricious. Their origins and continued existence are based in the facts of biology and in how human minds and bodies interact with their physical and social environments. These realities shape and constrain human behavior. They also shape human beliefs about the world and their evaluations of various aspects of it.

Human beings cannot exist without air, water, food, sleep, and personal security. There are also other needs that, although not absolutely necessary for the bodily survival of individuals, contribute to comfort and happiness. These include clothing, shelter, companionship, affection, and sex. The last, of course, is also necessary for reproduction and, hence, for the continued survival of the human species.

Thus, there are many constraints placed on human behavior, if individuals and groups are to continue to survive and to thrive. These are *not* matters of choice. *How* these needs are met involves some—often considerable—leeway of choice, but, obviously, these needs set limits to the possible.

Much of morality, then, derives from human biological and psychological characteristics and from our higher order capacities of choice and reasoning. If humans were invulnerable and immortal, then injunctions against murder would be unnecessary. If humans did not rely on learning from others, lying would not be a moral issue.

Some needs of human individuals, such as love, approval, and emotional support, are inherently social, because they can only be satisfied adequately by other humans. As infants, individuals are totally dependent on other people. As adults, interaction with others satisfies both emotional and survival needs. The results achieved through cooperation and division of labor within a group are nearly always superior to what can be achieved by individuals each working alone. This holds true for hunting, providing protection from beasts and hostile groups, building shelters, or carrying out large-scale community projects.

Thus, social life itself helps shape human values. As societies have evolved, they have selectively retained only some of the logically possible variations in human values as norms, rights, and obligations. These selected values function to make social life possible, to permit and encourage people to live and work together.

Socially disruptive attitudes and actions, such as greed, dishonesty, cowardice, anger, envy, promiscuity, stubbornness, and disobedience, among others, constantly threaten the survival of society. Sadly, these human traits are as universal as are societal efforts to control them. Perhaps some or all of them once had survival value for individuals. But with the growth of society, they have become obstacles to the cooperation needed to sustain large-scale, complex communities. Other actions and attitudes that individuals and societies ought to avoid are equally well-recognized: abuses of power, intolerance, theft, arrogance, brutality, terrorism, torture, fanaticism, and degradation.

Positive shared value: Honesty.

I believe the path toward a harmonious global society is well marked by widely shared human values, including patience, truthfulness, responsibility, respect for life, granting dignity to all people, empathy for others, kindliness and generosity, compassion, and forgiveness. To be comprehensive, this list must be extended to include equality between men and women, respect for human rights, nonviolence, fair treatment of all groups, encouragement of healthy and nature-friendly lifestyles, and acceptance of freedom as an ideal limited by the need to avoid harming others. These value judgments are not distinctively Islamic, Judeo-Christian, or Hindu, or Asian, Western, or African. They are *human* values that have emerged, often independently, in many different places based on the cumulative life experience of generations.

Human societies and civilizations today differ chiefly in how well they achieve these positive values and suppress negative values. No society, obviously, has fully achieved the positive values, nor fully eliminated the negative ones.

But today's shared human values do not necessarily represent the ultimate expression of human morality. Rather, they provide a current progress report, a basis for critical discourse on a global level. By building understanding and agreement across cultures, such discourse can, eventually, lead to a further evolution of global morality.

In every society, many people, groups, and institutions respect and attempt to live by these positive values, and groups such as the Institute for Global Ethics are exploring how a global ethic can be improved and implemented everywhere.

Principle for global peace: Inclusion.

The Search for Global Peace and Order

Individuals and societies are so complex that it may seem foolhardy even to attempt the ambitious task of increasing human freedom and wellbeing. Yet what alternatives do we have? In the face of violent aggressions, injustice, threats to the environment, corporate corruption, poverty, and other ills of our present world, we can find no satisfactory answers in despair, resignation, and inaction.

Rather, by viewing human society as an experiment, and monitoring the results of our efforts, we humans can gradually refine our plans and actions to bring closer an ethical future world in which every individual can realistically expect a long, peaceful, and satisfactory life.

Given the similarity in human values, I suggest three principles that might contribute to such a future: *inclusion, skepticism,* and *social control.*

1. The Principle of Inclusion

Although many moral values are common to all cultures, people too often limit their ethical treatment of others to members of their own groups. Some, for example, only show respect or concern for other people who are of their own race, religion, nationality, or social class.

Such exclusion can have disastrous effects. It can justify cheating or lying to people who are not members of one's own ingroup. At worst, it can lead to demonizing them and making them targets of aggression and violence, treating them as less than human. Those victimized by this shortsighted and counterproductive mistreatment tend to pay it back or pass it on to others, creating a nasty world in which we all must live.

Today, our individual lives and those of our descendants are so closely tied to the rest of humanity that our identities ought to include a sense of kinship with the whole human race and our circle of caring ought to embrace the welfare of people everywhere. In practical terms, this means that we should devote more effort and resources to raising the quality of life for the worst-off members of the human community; reducing disease, poverty, and illiteracy; and creating equal opportunity for all men and women. Furthermore, our circle of caring ought to include protecting natural resources, because all human life depends on preserving the planet as a livable environment.

2. The Principle of Skepticism

One of the reasons why deadly conflicts continue to occur is what has been called "the delusion of certainty." Too many people refuse to consider any view but their own. And, being sure that they are right, such people can justify doing horrendous things to others.

As I claimed in "Who Is Really Evil?" (*The Futurist,* March–April 2004), we all need a healthy dose of skepticism, especially about our own beliefs. Admitting that we might be wrong can lead to asking questions, searching for better answers, and considering alternative possibilities.

Critical realism is a theory of knowledge I recommend for everyone, because it teaches us to be skeptical. It rests on the assumption that knowledge is never fixed and final, but changes as we learn and grow. Using evidence and reason, we can evaluate our current beliefs and develop new ones in response to new information and changing conditions. Such an approach is essential to futures studies, and indeed to any planning. If your cognitive maps of reality are wrong, then using them to navigate through life will not take you where you want to go.

Critical realism also invites civility among those who disagree, encouraging peaceful resolution of controversies by investigating and discussing facts. It teaches temperance and tolerance, because it recognizes that the discovery of hitherto unsuspected facts may overturn any of our "certainties," even long-cherished and strongly held beliefs.

3. The Principle of Social Control

Obviously, there is a worldwide need for both informal and formal social controls if we hope to achieve global peace and order. For most people most of the time, informal social controls may be sufficient. By the end of childhood, for example, the norms of behavior taught and reinforced by family, peers, school, and religious and other institutions are generally internalized by individuals.

Principle for global peace: Skepticism.

Yet every society must also recognize that informal norms and even formal codes of law are not enough to guarantee ethical behavior and to protect public safety in every instance. Although the threats we most often think of are from criminals, fanatics, and the mentally ill, even "normal" individuals may occasionally lose control and behave irrationally, or choose to ignore or break the law with potentially tragic results. Thus, ideally, police and other public law enforcement, caretaking, and rehabilitation services protect us not only from "others," but also from ourselves.

Likewise, a global society needs global laws, institutions to administer them, and police/peacekeepers to enforce them. Existing international systems of social control should be strengthened and expanded to prevent killing and destruction, while peaceful negotiation and compromise to resolve disputes are encouraged. A global peacekeeping force with a monopoly on the legitimate use of force, sanctioned by democratic institutions and due process of law, and operated competently and fairly, could help prevent the illegal use of force, maintain global order, and promote a climate of civil discourse. The actions of these global peacekeepers should, of course, be bound not only by law, but also by a code of ethics. Peacekeepers should use force as a last resort and only to the degree needed, while making every effort to restrain aggressors without harming innocent people or damaging the infrastructures of society.

Expanding international law, increasing the number and variety of multinational institutions dedicated to controlling armed conflict, and strengthening efforts by the United Nations and other organizations to encourage the spread of democracy, global cooperation, and peace, will help create a win-win world.

Conclusion: Values for a Positive Global Future

The "clash of civilizations" thesis exaggerates both the degree of cultural diversity in the world and how seriously cultural differences contribute to producing violent conflicts.

In fact, many purposes, patterns, and practices are shared by all—or nearly all—peoples of the world. There is an emerging global ethic, a set of shared values that includes:

- Individual responsibility.
- Treating others as we wish them to treat us.
- Respect for life.
- Economic and social justice.
- Nature-friendly ways of life.
- Honesty.
- Moderation.
- Freedom (expressed in ways that do not harm others).
- Tolerance for diversity.

The fact that deadly human conflicts continue in many places throughout the world is due less to the differences that separate societies than to some of these common human traits and values. All humans, for example, tend to feel loyalty to their group, and

Toward Planetary Citizenship

A global economy that values competition over cooperation is an economy that will inevitably hurt people and destroy the environment. If the world's peoples are to get along better in the future, they need a better economic system, write peace activists Hazel Henderson and Daisaku Ikeda in *Planetary Citizenship*.

Henderson, an independent futurist, is one of the leading voices for a sustainable economic system; she is the author of many books and articles on her economic theories, including most recently *Beyond Globalization*. Ikeda is president of Soka Gakkai International, a peace and humanitarian organization based on Buddhist principles.

"Peace and nonviolence are now widely identified as fundamental to human survival," Henderson writes. "Competition must be balanced by cooperation and sharing. Even economists agree that peace, nonviolence, and human security are global public goods along with clean air and water, health and education—bedrock conditions for human well-being and development."

Along with materialistic values and competitive economics, the growing power of technology threatens a peaceful future, she warns. Humanity needs to find ways to harness these growing, "godlike" powers to lead us to genuine human development and away from destruction.

Henderson eloquently praises Ikeda's work at the United Nations to foster global cooperation on arms control, health, environmental protection, and other crucial issues. At the heart of these initiatives is the work of globally minded grass-root movements, or "planetary citizens," which have the potential to become the next global superpower, Henderson suggests.

One example of how nonmaterial values are starting to change how societies perceive their progress is the new Gross National Happiness indicators developed in Bhutan, which "[reflect] the goals of this Buddhist nation, [and] exemplify the importance of clarifying the goals and values of a society and creating indicators to measure what we treasure: health, happiness, education, human rights, family, country, harmony, peace, and environmental quality and restoration," Henderson writes.

The authors are optimistic that the grassroots movement will grow as more people look beyond their differences and seek common values and responsibilities for the future.

Source: *Planetary Citizenship: Your Values, Beliefs and Actions Can Shape a Sustainable World* by Hazel Henderson and Daisaku Ikeda. Middleway Press, 606 Wilshire Boulevard, Santa Monica, California 90401. 2004. 200 pages. $23.95. Order from the Futurist Bookshelf, www.wfs.org/bkshelf.htm.

may easily overreact in the group's defense, leaving excluded "outsiders" feeling marginalized and victimized. Sadly, too, all humans are capable of rage and violent acts against others.

In past eras, the killing and destruction of enemies may have helped individuals and groups to survive. But in today's interconnected world that is no longer clearly the case. Today, violence and aggression too often are blunt and imprecise instruments that fail to achieve their intended purposes, and frequently blow back on the doers of violence.

The long-term trends of history are toward an ever-widening definition of individual identity (with some people already adopting self-identities on the widest scale as "human beings"), and toward the enlargement of individual circles of caring to embrace once distant or despised "outsiders." These trends are likely to continue, because they embody values—learned from millennia of human experience—that have come to be nearly universal: from the love of life itself to the joys of belonging to a community, from the satisfaction of self-fulfillment to the excitement of pursuing knowledge, and from individual happiness to social harmony.

How long will it take for the world to become a community where every human everywhere has a good chance to live a long and satisfying life? I do not know. But people of [goodwill] can do much today to help the process along. For example, we can begin by accepting responsibility for our own life choices: the goals and actions that do much to shape our future. And we can be more generous and understanding of what we perceive as mistakes and failures in the choices and behavior of oth-

ers. We can include all people in our circle of concern, behave ethically toward everyone we deal with, recognize that every human being deserves to be treated with respect, and work to raise minimum standards of living for the least well-off people in the world.

We can also dare to question our personal views and those of the groups to which we belong, to test them and consider alternatives. Remember that knowledge is not constant, but subject to change in the light of new information and conditions. Be prepared to admit that anyone—even we ourselves—can be misinformed or reach a wrong conclusion from the limited evidence available. Because we can never have all the facts before us, let us admit to ourselves, whenever we take action, that mistakes and failure are possible. And let us be aware that certainty can become the enemy of decency.

In addition, we can control ourselves by exercising self-restraint to minimize mean or violent acts against others. Let us respond to offered friendship with honest gratitude and cooperation; but, when treated badly by another person, let us try, while defending ourselves from harm, to respond not with anger or violence but with verbal disapproval and the withdrawal of our cooperation with that person. So as not to begin a cycle of retaliation, let us not overreact. And let us always be willing to listen and to talk, to negotiate and to compromise.

Finally, we can support international law enforcement, global institutions of civil and criminal justice, international courts and global peacekeeping agencies, to build and strengthen nonviolent means for resolving disputes. Above all, we can work to ensure that global institutions are honest and fair and that they hold all countries—rich and poor, strong and weak—to the same high standards.

If the human community can learn to apply to all people the universal values that I have identified, then future terrorist acts like the events of September 11 may be minimized, because all people are more likely to be treated fairly and with dignity and because all voices will have peaceful ways to be heard, so some of the roots of discontent will be eliminated. When future terrorist acts do occur—and surely some will—they can be treated as the unethical and criminal acts that they are.

There is no clash of civilizations. Most people of the world, whatever society, culture, civilization, or religion they revere or feel a part of, simply want to live—and let others live—in peace and harmony. To achieve this, all of us must realize that the human community is inescapably bound together. More and more, as Martin Luther King Jr. reminded us, whatever affects one, sooner or later affects all.

Critical Thinking

1. How does Wendell Bell contrast his argument with Samuel Huntington's "clash of civilizations" thesis?

2. What are some of the shared values that Bell identifies?

3. What is "critical realism"? How does this concept relate to the study of global issues?

4. Describe what Bell calls an "emerging global ethic."

5. How does this article complement/contradict Article 6?

WENDELL BELL is professor emeritus of sociology and senior research scientist at Yale University's Center for Comparative Research. He is the author of more than 200 articles and nine books, including the two-volume *Foundations of Futures Studies* (Transaction Publishers, now available in paperback 2003, 2004). His address is Department of Sociology, Yale University, P.O. Box 208265, New Haven, Connecticut 06520. E-mail wendell.bell@yale.edu.

This article draws from an essay originally published in the *Journal of Futures Studies 6*.

Life, Religion and Everything

Biologist and author Rupert Sheldrake believes that the world's religions have a crucial role in restoring the earth's ecological balance. Laura Sevier meets the man trying to broker a better relationship between God, man, science and the natural world.

LAURA SEVIER

A long, low drone fills the air. We are all chanting the same sound: OOOOOOOHHHHHHHH. Whistling overtones start to ring out above the group sound and then a lone female voice sings out:

Where I sit is holy

Holy is the ground

Forest mountain river listen to my sound

Great spirit circling all around.

The voice then invites everyone to join in and we sing this verse seven or eight times. Then there is silence.

It's not often you attend a talk given by an eminent scientist that begins with a session of Mongolian overtone chanting followed by a Native American Indian song about the holiness of the earth. It's especially surreal given that we're sitting on neat little rows of chairs in a Unitarian Church in Hampstead, in London.

I was there to listen to renowned English biologist Rupert Sheldrake talk about how the world's religions can learn to live with ecological integrity. The chanting, it appears, is the warm-up act, led by Sheldrake's wife, Jill Purce, a music healer.

So far so extraordinary, but then Sheldrake is no ordinary man. A respected scientist from a largely conventional educational background, he's devoted much of the past 17 years of his life to studying the sort of phenomena that most 'serious' scientists dismiss out of hand, such as telepathy, our 'seventh sense'. But religion? Given the current trend for militant atheism within science, I'm amazed. Besides, isn't religion incompatible with science? Not according to Sheldrake, an Anglican Christian. 'One of my main concerns is the opening up of science. Another is exploring the connections between science and spirituality,' he says.

His take on religion—and science—is refreshingly unorthodox precisely because it factors in a crucial new element:

nature. 'The thrust of my work is trying to break out of the mechanistic view of nature as inanimate, dead and machine-like.' In fact his 1991 book *The Rebirth of Nature: the Greening of Science and God* (Inner Traditions Bear & Company, £11.99) was devoted to showing 'how we can once again think of nature as alive'—and sacred.

The Sacred Earth

Our culture seems to have lost touch with any idea of the land as being alive and sacred and anyone who considers it to be so is often branded a tree-hugging hippie and treated with ridicule or suspicion. Land is mostly valued purely in economic terms. Yet no value is attributed to the irreplaceable benefits derived from the normal functioning of the natural world, which assures the stability of our climate, the fertility of our soil, the replenishment of our water.

Our culture seems to have lost any idea of the land being alive and sacred, and values it only in economic terms.

Religion has, until recently, remained pretty quiet on the issue.

As Edward Goldsmith wrote in the *Ecologist* in 2000, mainstream religions have become increasingly 'otherworldly'. They have 'scarcely any interest' in the natural world at all. Traditionally, religion used to play an integral role in linking people to the natural world, imbuing people with the knowledge and values that make caring for it a priority. 'Mainstream religion' Goldsmith wrote 'has failed the earth. It has lost its way, and needs to return to its roots.'

So if the world's religions are to play a part in saving what remains of the natural world, they not only need to return to their roots but also to confront the threat and scale of the global ecological crisis we now face. This means being open to a dialogue with science. 'No religions, when they were growing up, had to deal with our present situation and ecological crisis,' says Sheldrake. 'People thought they could take the earth more or less for granted. Certainly the idea that human beings could transform the climate through their actions was unheard of. This is a new situation for everybody, for religious people and scientists, for traditional cultures and modern scientific ones. We're all in this together.'

Environmental Sin

'Religion and Ecology' is now a subject of serious academic study. The Forum on Religion and Ecology at Yale University, for example, recently explored the ecological dimension of all the major world religions. The ongoing environmental crisis has sparked a 'bringing together' of the world's religions in a series of interreligious meetings and conferences around the world on the theme of 'Religion, Science and the Environment', exploring the response that religious communities can make. These brought together scientists, bishops, rabbis, marine biologists and philosophers in a way that, according to Sheldrake, 'really worked'.

Within many religions, including all branches of Christianity, there's an attempt to recover that sense of connection with nature. 'There's a lot going on,' says Sheldrake, 'even within the group seen as lagging the furthest behind—the American Evangelicals, who are somewhat retrogressive in relation to the environment.'

Some evangelicals who believe in the Rapture and think the world is soon to end have expressed the view that there's no point in attempting to save the environment because it's all going to be discarded like a used tissue.

But a more environmentally friendly view is held by the Evangelical Environmental Network (EEN), a group of individuals and organisations including World Vision, World Relief and the International Bible Society. An Evangelical Declaration on the Care of Creation, its landmark credo published in 1991, begins: 'We believe that biblical faith is essential to the solution of our ecological problems. . . . - Because we worship and honour the Creator we seek to cherish and care for the creation. Because we have sinned, we have failed our stewardship of creation. Therefore we repent of the way we have polluted, distorted or destroyed so much of the Creator's work.'

It then commits to work for reconciliation of people and the healing of suffering creation.

The belief that environmental destruction is a sin isn't a new concept. The spirituality of native American Indians, for instance, is a land-based one. In this culture, the world is animate, natural things are alive and everything is imbued with spirit.

> **Nature informs us and it is our obligation to read nature as you would a book, to feel it as you would a poem.**

In the words of John Mohawk, native American chief: 'The natural world is our Bible. We don't have chapters and verses; we have trees and fish and animals . . . The Indian sense of natural law is that nature informs us and it is our obligation to read nature as you would a book, to feel nature as you would a poem, to touch nature as you would yourself, to be part of that and step into its cycles as much as you can.'

Most importantly, environmental destruction is seen as a sin.

Loss of the Sacred

The question is, how did we lose the sacred connection with the natural world? Where did religion and culture go wrong? According to Sheldrake, the break began in the 16th century. Until then there were pagan festivals, such as May Day, that celebrated the seasons and the fertility of the land; there were nature shrines, holy wells and sacred places.

But with the Protestant Reformation in the 16th century there was an attempt by the reformers, who couldn't find anything about these 'pagan' practices in the Bible, to stamp them out. In the 17th century the Puritans brought a further wave of suppression of these things—banning, for example, Maypole dancing (Maypoles being a symbol of male fertility). 'There was a deliberate attempt to get rid of all the things that connected people to the sacredness of the land and it largely succeeded,' says Sheldrake.

Another factor he believes severed our connection is the view of nature as a machine. 'From the time of our remotest ancestors until the 17th century, it was taken for granted that the world of nature was alive, that the universe was alive and that all animals were not only alive but had souls—the word "animal" comes from the word "anima", meaning soul. This was the standard view, even within the Church. Medieval Christianity was based on an animate form of nature—a kind of Christian animism.'

But this model of a living world was replaced by the idea of the universe as a machine, an idea that stems from the philosophy of Rene Descartes. Nature was no more than dead matter and everything was viewed as mechanical, governed by mathematical principles instead of animating souls.

'This mechanistic view of nature,' Sheldrake says, 'is an extremely limiting and alienating one. It forces the whole of our understanding of nature into a machine metaphor—the universe as a machine, animals and plants as machines, you as a machine, the brain as a machine. It's a very man-centred metaphor, as only people make machines. So looking at nature in this way projects one aspect of human activity onto the whole of nature.'

Hinduism

- The Vedas (ancient Hindu scriptures) describe how the creator god Vishnu made the universe so that every element is interlinked. A disturbance in one part will upset the balance and impact all the other elements.
- Three important principles of Hindu environmentalism are *yajna* (sacrifice), *dhana* (giving) and *tapas* (penance).
- *Yajna* entails that you should sacrifice your needs for the sake of others, for nature, the poor or future generations.
- *Dhana* entails that whatever you consume you must give back.
- *Tapas* commends self-restraint in your lifestyle.
- Mother Earth is personified in the Vedas as the goddess Bhumi, or Prithvi.
- Hindu businessman Balbir Mathur, inspired by his faith, founded Trees for Life (www.treesforlife.org), a non-profit movement that plants fruit trees in developing countries, to provide sustainable and environmentally-friendly livelihoods.

Islam

- Allah has appointed humankind *khalifah* (steward) over the created world.
- This responsibility is called *al-amanah* (the trust) and Man will be held accountable to it at the Day of Judgment.
- The Qur'an warns against disturbing God's natural balance: 'Do no mischief on the earth after it hath been set in order' (7:56).
- Shari'ah (Islamic law) designates *haram* zones, used to contain urban development in protection of natural resources, and *hima,* specific conservation areas.
- The Islamic foundation for ecology and environmental sciences www.ifes.org.uk publishes a newsletter called *Eco Islam* and organised an organic *iftar* (the evening meal during Ramadan) in 2006.
- In 2000, IFEES led an Islamic educational programme on the Muslim-majority island of Misali, in response to the destruction to the aquatic ecosystem by over-fishing and the use of dynamite in coral reefs. The environmental message based on the Qur'an initiated sustainable fishing practices.

Judaism

- The Torah prohibits harming God's earth: 'Do not cut down trees even to prevent ambush, do not foul waters, or burn crops even to cause an enemy's submission' (Devarim 20:19)
- It teaches humility in the face of nature: 'Ask the beasts, and they will teach you; the birds of the sky, and they will tell you; or speak to the earth and it will teach you; the fish of the sea, they will inform you' (Job 12:7-9)
- The Talmudic law *bal tashchit* (do not destroy) was developed by Jewish scholars into a series of specific prohibitions against wasteful actions.
- The Noah Project (www.noahproject.org.uk) is a UK-based Jewish environmental organisation, engaged in hands-on conservation work, and promoting environmental responsibility by emphasising the environmental dimensions of Jewish holidays such as Tu B'Shevat (New Year of the Trees).

Christianity

- Genesis gives a picture of God creating the heavens and earth—and when it was all finished, 'God saw all that he had made, and it was very good.' (1:31) Having made man, he 'put him in the Garden of Eden to work it and take care of it' (2:15).
- Romans 8:19-22 has been interpreted as a message of redemption for the environment, calling on Christians to work towards the time when 'the creation itself will be liberated from its bondage to decay'.
- At the UN Rio Earth Summit in 1992, the World Council of Churches formed a working group on climate change. Their manifesto expresses a concern for justice towards developing countries, who are disproportionately affected by climate change, to future generations and to the world.
- www.christian-ecology.org.uk represents Churches Together in Britain and Ireland. It includes links and a daily prayer guide with references both to the Bible and to scientific and news data. Operation Noah is the climate change campaign.

Buddhism

- Buddhist religious ecology is based on three principles: nature as teacher, as a spiritual force, and as a way of life.
- Buddhists believe that nature can teach us about the interdependence and impermanence of life, and that living near to and in tune with nature gives us spiritual strength.
- Buddha commended frugality, avoiding waste, and non-violence.
- Buddhists believe that man should be in harmonious interaction with nature, not a position of authority.
- Philosopher Dr Simon James, based at Durham University, has studied the Buddhist basis of environmentalism and virtue ethics. A spiritually enlightened individual shows compassion, equanimity and humility—qualities that are intrinsic to an environmentally friendly lifestyle.
- The Zen Environmental Studies Institute (www.mro.org/zesi) in New York runs programmes in nature study and environmental advocacy, informed by Zen Buddhist meditation.

Baha'ism

- Bahá'u'lláh, founder of the Baha'i faith and regarded as a messenger from God, stated 'nature is God's Will and is its expression in and through the contingent world' (the Tablets of Baha'u'llah).
- Baha'is believe that the world reflects God's qualities and attributes and therefore must be cherished.
- The Baha'i Office of the Environment states: 'Baha'u'llah's promise that civilisation will exist on this planet for a minimum of 5,000 centuries makes it unconscionable to ignore the long-term impact of decisions made today. The world community must, therefore, learn to make use of the earth's natural resources . . . in a manner that ensures sustainability into the distant reaches of time.'
- The Barli Rural Development Institute in India was inspired by Baha'i social activism. It has trained hundreds of rural women in conservation strategies such as rainwater harvesting and solar cooking.
- www.onecountry.org is the newsletter of the Bahai international community.

It is this view, he says, that led to our current crisis. 'If you assume that nature is inanimate, then nothing natural has a life, purpose, or value. Natural resources are there to be developed, and the only value placed on them is by market forces and official planners. And if you assume that only humans are conscious, only humans have reason, and therefore only humans have true value, then it's fine to have animals in factory farms and to exploit the world in whatever way you like, and if you do conserve any bit of the earth then you have to conserve it with human ends in mind. Everything is justified in human terms.'

The mechanistic theory has become a kind of religion that is built into the official orthodoxy of economic progress and, through technology's successes, is now triumphant on a global scale. 'So,' says Sheldrake, 'this combination of science, technology, secular humanism and rationalism—all these philosophies that dominate the modern age—open the way for untrammelled exploitation of the earth that is going on everywhere today.'

The Living Universe

It seems like a pretty bleak vision. But there is an alternative: to allow our own experience and intuition to help us see nature and the universe as alive. 'Many people have emotional connections with particular places associated with their childhood, or feel an empathy with animals or plants, or are inspired by the beauty of nature, or experience a mystical sense of unity with the natural world,' Sheldrake says. 'Our private relationship with nature presupposes that nature is alive.'

In other words, we don't need to be told by science, religion or anyone that it is alive, valuable and worthy of respect and reverence. Deep down, we can feel it for ourselves. Many people have urges to get 'back to nature' in some way, to escape the confines of concrete and head for the hills, the sea, a park or even a small patch of grass. These impulses are moving us in the right direction.

Another way forward is through new revolutionary insights within science. 'Science itself is leading us away from this view of nature as a machine towards a much more organic view of living in the world,' says Sheldrake. 'The changes are happening in independent parts of science for different reasons, but all of them are pointing in the same direction: the view of a very organic, creative world.'

The big bang theory gives a new model of the universe is more like a developing organism, growing spontaneo and forming totally new structures within it. The conce quantum physics has broken open many of our ideas mechanistic universe. The old idea of determinism has way to indeterminism and chaos theory. The old idea earth as dead has given way to Gaia, the living earth. T idea of the universe as uncreative has given way to th idea of creative evolution, first in the realm of living through Darwin, and now we see that the whole cos in creative evolution. So, if the whole universe is alive universe is like a great organism, then everything with best understood as alive.

Encouraging Dialogue

This has opened up new possibilities for a dialogue between science and religion. 'These changing frontiers of science are making it much easier to see that we're all part of, and dependent on, a living earth; and for those of us who follow a religion, to see the living God as the living world,' says Sheldrake. Such insights breathe new meaning into traditional religions, their practices and seasonal festivals.

For example, all religions provide opportunities for giving thanks, both through simple everyday rituals, like saying grace, and also in collective acts of thanksgiving. These expressions of gratitude can help to remind us that we have much to be thankful for. But as Sheldrake points out, 'It's hard to feel a sense of gratitude for an inanimate, mechanical world.'

Helping people see the land as sacred again, Sheldrake maintains, is one of the major roles of religion. 'They all point towards a larger whole: the wholeness of creation and a larger story than our own individual story. All religions tell stories about our place in the world, our relation to other people and to the world in which we live. In that sense all religions relate us to the earth and the heavens.'

Sheldrake thinks we need stories: 'It's part of our nature. Science gives us stories, too—the universe story. So does TV, fiction, books.' And these stories, in his view, unify us in a way that, for instance, some New Age practices (such as personal shrines) don't. While those things have personal value, they don't have the unifying function that a traditional religion does. 'When you go to a Hindu festival or pilgrimage, you see thousands of people coming together, the whole community united by a common story or a celebration of a sacred place.'

The fascinating thing about Rupert Sheldrake is his ability to assimilate ideas from an array of different subjects that are normally kept separate, draw new connections and conclusions and open up new dialogues. He's certainly not afraid to explore new territory or use new metaphors. Thus the big bang is like 'the
'the breaking open of the cosmic egg'.
discovery that 95 per cent of the
nown, he says, 'it is as if sci-
cious'. He embraces
es the old intu-
responses
is. 'We
ting

expands to the cosmos. If the earth is alive, if the universe is alive, if solar systems are alive, if galaxies are alive, if planets are alive, then causing harm to any of these systems really is a sin; one that we have committed all too willingly for far too long.

For Further Information

Rupert Sheldrake: www.sheldrake.org

Forum on Religion and Ecology: http://environment.harvard.edu/religion—the ecological dimension of various religions

The Alliance of Religions and Conservation (ARC): www.arcworld.org

Critical Thinking

1. What is Laura Sevier's point of view?

2. What is meant by "sacred connection"?

3. What new possibilities are discussed for a dialogue between religion and science?

4. How does this article illustrate the complex web of relationships portrayed in the Allegory of the Balloon?

LAURA SEVIER is a freelance journalist and regular contributor to the *Ecologist*.

The End of Men

HANNA ROSIN

Earlier this year, women became the majority of the workforce for the first time in U.S. history. Most managers are now women too. And for every two men who get a college degree this year, three women will do the same. For years, women's progress has been cast as a struggle for equality. But what if equality isn't the end point? What if modern, postindustrial society is simply better suited to women? A report on the unprecedented role reversal now under way—and its vast cultural consequences.

In the 1970s the biologist Ronald Ericsson came up with a way to separate sperm carrying the male-producing Y chromosome from those carrying the X. He sent the two kinds of sperm swimming down a glass tube through ever-thicker albumin barriers. The sperm with the X chromosome had a larger head and a longer tail, and so, he figured, they would get bogged down in the viscous liquid. The sperm with the Y chromosome were leaner and faster and could swim down to the bottom of the tube more efficiently. Ericsson had grown up on a ranch in South Dakota, where he'd developed an Old West, cowboy swagger. The process, he said, was like "cutting out cattle at the gate." The cattle left flailing behind the gate were of course the X's, which seemed to please him. He would sometimes demonstrate the process using cartilage from a bull's penis as a pointer.

In the late 1970s, Ericsson leased the method to clinics around the U.S., calling it the first scientifically proven method for choosing the sex of a child. Instead of a lab coat, he wore cowboy boots and a cowboy hat, and doled out his version of cowboy poetry. (*People* magazine once suggested a TV mini-series based on his life called Cowboy in the Lab.) The right prescription for life, he would say, was "breakfast at five-thirty, on the saddle by six, no room for Mr. Limp Wrist." In 1979, he loaned out his ranch as the backdrop for the iconic "Marlboro Country" ads because he believed in the campaign's central image—"a guy riding on his horse along the river, no bureaucrats, no lawyers," he recalled when I spoke to him this spring. "He's the boss." (The photographers took some 6,500 pictures, a pictorial record of the frontier that Ericsson still takes great pride in.)

Feminists of the era did not take kindly to Ericsson and his Marlboro Man veneer. To them, the lab cowboy and his sperminator portended a dystopia of mass-produced boys. "You have to be concerned about the future of all women," Roberta Steinbacher, a nun-turned-social-psychologist, said in a 1984 *People* profile of Ericsson. "There's no question that there exists a universal preference for sons." Steinbacher went on to complain about women becoming locked in as "second-class citizens" while men continued to dominate positions of control and influence. "I think women have to ask themselves, 'Where does this stop?'" she said. "A lot of us wouldn't be here right now if these practices had been in effect years ago."

Ericsson, now 74, laughed when I read him these quotes from his old antagonist. Seldom has it been so easy to prove a dire prediction wrong. In the '90s, when Ericsson looked into the numbers for the two dozen or so clinics that use his process, he discovered, to his surprise, that couples were requesting more girls than boys, a gap that has persisted, even though Ericsson advertises the method as more effective for producing boys. In some clinics, Ericsson has said, the ratio is now as high as 2 to 1. Polling data on American sex preference is sparse, and does not show a clear preference for girls. But the picture from the doctor's office unambiguously does. A newer method for sperm selection, called MicroSort, is currently completing Food and Drug Administration clinical trials. The girl requests for that method run at about 75 percent.

Even more unsettling for Ericsson, it has become clear that in choosing the sex of the next generation, he is no longer the boss. "It's the women who are driving all the decisions," he says—a change the MicroSort spokespeople I met with also mentioned. At first, Ericsson says, women who called his clinics would apologize and shyly explain that they already had two boys. "Now they just call and [say] outright, 'I want a girl.'" These mothers look at their lives and think their daughters will have a bright future their mother and grandmother didn't have, brighter than their sons, even, so why wouldn't you choose a girl?"

Why wouldn't you choose a girl? That such a statement should be so casually uttered by an old cowboy like Ericsson—or by anyone, for that matter—is monumental. For nearly as long as civilization has existed, patriarchy—enforced through the rights of the firstborn son—has been the organizing principle, with few exceptions. Men in ancient Greece tied off their left testicle in an effort to produce male heirs; women have killed themselves (or been killed) for failing to bear sons. In her iconic 1949 book, *The Second Sex*, the French feminist Simone de Beauvoir suggested that women so detested their own "feminine condition" that they regarded their newborn daughters with irritation and disgust. Now the centuries-old preference for sons is eroding—or even reversing. "Women of our generation want daughters precisely because we like who we are," breezes one woman in *Cookie* magazine. Even Ericsson, the stubborn old goat, can sigh and mark the passing of an era. "Did male dominance exist? Of course it existed. But it seems to be gone now. And the era of the firstborn son is totally gone."

Ericsson's extended family is as good an illustration of the rapidly shifting landscape as any other. His 26-year-old granddaughter—"tall, slender, brighter than hell, with a take-no-prisoners personality"—is a biochemist and works on genetic sequencing. His niece studied civil engineering at the University of Southern California. His grandsons, he says, are bright and handsome, but in school "their eyes glaze over. I have to tell 'em: 'Just don't screw up and crash your pickup truck and get some girl pregnant and ruin your life.'" Recently Ericsson joked with the old boys at his elementary-school reunion that he was going to have a sex-change operation. "Women live longer than men. They do better in this economy. More of 'em graduate from college. They go into space and do everything men do, and sometimes they do it a whole lot better. I mean, hell, get out of the way—these females are going to leave us males in the dust."

Man has been the dominant sex since, well, the dawn of mankind. But for the first time in human history, that is changing—and with shocking speed. Cultural and economic changes always reinforce each other. And the global economy is evolving in a way that is eroding the historical preference for male children, worldwide. Over several centuries, South Korea, for instance, constructed one of the most rigid patriarchal societies in the world. Many wives who failed to produce male heirs were abused and treated as domestic servants; some families prayed to spirits to kill off girl children. Then, in the 1970s and '80s, the government embraced an industrial revolution and encouraged women to enter the labor force. Women moved to the city and went to college. They advanced rapidly, from industrial jobs to clerical jobs to professional work. The traditional order began to crumble soon after. In 1990, the country's laws were revised so that women could keep custody of their children after a divorce and inherit property. In 2005, the court ruled that women could register children under their own names. As recently as 1985, about half of all women in a national survey said they "must have a son." That percentage fell slowly until 1991 and then plummeted to just over 15 percent by 2003. Male preference in South Korea "is over," says Monica Das Gupta, a demographer and Asia expert at the World Bank. "It happened so fast. It's hard to believe it, but it is." The same shift is now beginning in other rapidly industrializing countries such as India and China.

Up to a point, the reasons behind this shift are obvious. As thinking and communicating have come to eclipse physical strength and stamina as the keys to economic success, those societies that take advantage of the talents of all their adults, not just half of them, have pulled away from the rest. And because geopolitics and global culture are, ultimately, Darwinian, other societies either follow suit or end up marginalized. In 2006, the Organization for Economic Cooperation and Development devised the Gender, Institutions and Development Database, which measures the economic and political power of women in 162 countries. With few exceptions, the greater the power of women, the greater the country's economic success. Aid agencies have started to recognize this relationship and have pushed to institute political quotas in about 100 countries, essentially forcing women into power in an effort to improve those countries' fortunes. In some war-torn states, women are stepping in as a sort of maternal rescue team. Liberia's president, Ellen Johnson Sirleaf, portrayed her country as a sick child in need of her care during her campaign five years ago. Postgenocide Rwanda elected to heal itself by becoming the first country with a majority of women in parliament.

In feminist circles, these social, political, and economic changes are always cast as a slow, arduous form of catch-up in a continuing struggle for female equality. But in the U.S., the world's most advanced economy, something much more remarkable seems to be happening. American parents are beginning to choose to have girls over boys. As they imagine the pride of watching a child grow and develop and succeed as an adult, it is more often a girl that they see in their mind's eye.

What if the modern, postindustrial economy is simply more congenial to women than to men? For a long time, evolutionary psychologists have claimed that we are all imprinted with adaptive imperatives from a distant past: men are faster and stronger and hardwired to fight for scarce resources, and that shows up now as a drive to win on Wall Street; women are programmed to find good providers and to care for their offspring, and that is manifested in more-nurturing and more-flexible behavior, ordaining them to domesticity. This kind of thinking frames our sense of the natural order. But what if men and women were fulfilling not biological imperatives but social roles, based on what was more efficient throughout a long era of human history? What if that era has now come to an end? More to the point, what if the economics of the new era are better suited to women?

Once you open your eyes to this possibility, the evidence is all around you. It can be found, most immediately, in the wreckage of the Great Recession, in which three-quarters of the 8 million jobs lost were lost by men. The worst-hit industries were overwhelmingly male and deeply identified with macho: construction, manufacturing, high finance. Some of these jobs will come back, but the overall pattern of dislocation is neither temporary nor random. The recession merely revealed—and accelerated—a profound economic shift that has been going on for at least 30 years, and in some respects even longer.

Earlier this year, for the first time in American history, the balance of the workforce tipped toward women, who now hold a majority of the nation's jobs. The working class, which has long defined our notions of masculinity, is slowly turning into a matriarchy, with men increasingly absent from the home and women making all the decisions. Women dominate today's colleges and professional schools—for every two men who will receive a B.A. this year, three women will do the same. Of the 15 job categories projected to grow the most in the next decade in the U.S., all but two are occupied primarily by women. Indeed, the U.S. economy is in some ways becoming a kind of traveling sisterhood: upper-class women leave home and enter the workforce, creating domestic jobs for other women to fill.

The postindustrial economy is indifferent to men's size and strength. The attributes that are most valuable today—social intelligence, open communication, the ability to sit still and focus—are, at a minimum, not predominantly male. In fact, the opposite may be true. Women in poor parts of India are learning English faster than men to meet the demands of new global call centers. Women own more than 40 percent of private businesses in China, where a red Ferrari is the new status symbol for female entrepreneurs. Last year, Iceland elected Prime Minister Johanna Sigurdardottir, the world's first openly lesbian head of state, who campaigned explicitly against the male elite she claimed had destroyed the nation's banking system, and who vowed to end the "age of testosterone."

Yes, the U.S. still has a wage gap, one that can be convincingly explained—at least in part—by discrimination. Yes, women still do most of the child care. And yes, the upper reaches of society are still dominated by men. But given the power of the forces pushing at the economy, this setup feels like the last gasp of a dying age rather than the permanent establishment. Dozens of college women I interviewed for this story assumed that they very well might be the ones working while their husbands stayed at home, either looking for work or minding the children. Guys, one senior remarked to me, "are the new ball and chain." It may be happening slowly and unevenly, but it's unmistakably happening: in the long view, the modern economy is becoming a place where women hold the cards.

Dozens of college women I interviewed assumed that they very well might be the ones working while their husbands stayed at home. Guys, one senior remarked to me, "Are the new ball and chain."

In his final book, *The Bachelors' Ball,* published in 2007, the sociologist Pierre Bourdieu describes the changing gender dynamics of Beam, the region in southwestern France where he grew up. The eldest sons once held the privileges of patrimonial loyalty and filial inheritance in Beam. But over the decades, changing economic forces turned those privileges into curses. Although the land no longer produced the impressive income it once had, the men felt obligated to tend it. Meanwhile, modern women shunned farm life, lured away by jobs and adventure in the city. They occasionally returned for the traditional balls, but the men who awaited them had lost their prestige and become unmarriageable. This is the image that keeps recurring to me, one that Bourdieu describes in his book: at the bachelors' ball, the men, self-conscious about their diminished status, stand stiffly, their hands by their sides, as the women twirl away.

Men dominate just two of the 15 job categories projected to grow the most over the next decade: janitor and computer engineer. Women have everything else—nursing, home health

assistance, child care, food preparation. Many of the new jobs, says Heather Boushey of the Center for American Progress, "replace the things that women used to do in the home for free." None is especially high-paying. But the steady accumulation of these jobs adds up to an economy that, for the working class, has become more amenable to women than to men.

The list of growing jobs is heavy on nurturing professions, in which women, ironically, seem to benefit from old stereotypes and habits. Theoretically, there is no reason men should not be qualified. But they have proved remarkably unable to adapt. Over the course of the past century, feminism has pushed women to do things once considered against their nature—first enter the workforce as singles, then continue to work while married, then work even with small children at home. Many professions that started out as the province of men are now filled mostly with women—secretary and teacher come to mind. Yet I'm not aware of any that have gone the opposite way. Nursing schools have tried hard to recruit men in the past few years, with minimal success. Teaching schools, eager to recruit male role models, are having a similarly hard time. The range of acceptable masculine roles has changed comparatively little, and has perhaps even narrowed as men have shied away from some careers women have entered. As Jessica Grose wrote in *Slate,* men seem "fixed in cultural aspic." And with each passing day, they lag further behind.

As we recover from the Great Recession, some traditionally male jobs will return—men are almost always harder-hit than women in economic downturns because construction and manufacturing are more cyclical than service industries—but that won't change the long-term trend. When we look back on this period, argues Jamie Ladge, a business professor at Northeastern University, we will see it as a "turning point for women in the workforce."

When we look back at this period we will see it as a "Turning point for women in the workforce."

The economic and cultural power shift from men to women would be hugely significant even if it never extended beyond working-class America. But women are also starting to dominate middle management, and a surprising number of professional careers as well. According to the Bureau of Labor Statistics, women now hold 51.4 percent of managerial and professional jobs—up from 26.1 percent in 1980. They make up 54 percent of all accountants and hold about half of all banking and insurance jobs. About a third of America's physicians are now women, as are 45 percent of associates in law firms—and both those percentages are rising fast. A white-collar economy values raw intellectual horsepower, which men and women have in equal amounts. It also requires communication skills and social intelligence, areas in which women, according to many studies, have a slight edge. Perhaps most important—for better or worse—it increasingly requires formal education credentials, which women are more prone to acquire, particularly early in adulthood. Just about the only professions in which women still make up a relatively small minority of newly minted workers are engineering and those calling on a hard-science background, and even in those areas, women have made strong gains since the 1970s.

Near the top of the jobs pyramid, of course, the upward march of women stalls. Prominent female CEOs, past and present, are so rare that they count as minor celebrities, and most of us can tick off their names just from occasionally reading the business pages: Meg Whitman at eBay, Carly Fiorina at Hewlett-Packard, Anne Mulcahy and Ursula Burns at Xerox, Indra Nooyi at PepsiCo; the accomplishment is considered so extraordinary that Whitman and Fiorina are using it as the basis for political campaigns. Only 3 percent of Fortune 500 CEOs are women, and the number has never risen much above that.

But even the way this issue is now framed reveals that men's hold on power in elite circles may be loosening. In business circles, the lack of women at the top is described as a "brain drain" and a crisis of "talent retention." And while female CEOs may be rare in America's largest companies, they are highly prized: last year, they outearned their male counterparts by 43 percent, on average, and received bigger raises.

If you really want to see where the world is headed, of course, looking at the current workforce can get you only so far. To see the future—of the workforce, the economy, and the culture—you need to spend some time at America's colleges and professional schools, where a quiet revolution is under way. More than ever, college is the gateway to economic success, a necessary precondition for moving into the upper-middle class—and increasingly even the middle class. It's this broad, striving middle class that defines our society. And demographically, we can see with absolute clarity that in the coming decades the middle class will be dominated by women.

We've all heard about the collegiate gender gap. But the implications of that gap have not yet been fully digested. Women now earn 60 percent of master's degrees, about half of all law and medical degrees, and 42 percent of all M.B.A.s. Most important, women earn almost 60 percent of all bachelor's degrees—the minimum requirement, in most cases, for an affluent life. In a stark reversal since the 1970s, men are now more likely than women to hold only a high-school diploma. "One would think that if men were acting in a rational way, they would be getting the education they need to get along out there," says Tom Mortenson, a senior scholar at the Pell Institute for the Study of Opportunity in Higher Education. "But they are just failing to adapt."

Since the 1980s, as women have flooded colleges, male enrollment has grown far more slowly. And the disparities start before college. Throughout the '90s, various authors and researchers agonized over why boys seemed to be failing at every level of education, from elementary school on up, and identified various culprits: a misguided feminism that treated normal boys as incipient harassers (Christina Hoff Sommers); different brain chemistry (Michael Gurian); a demanding,

verbally focused curriculum that ignored boys' interests (Richard Whitmire). But again, it's not all that clear that boys have become more dysfunctional—or have changed in any way. What's clear is that schools, like the economy, now value the self-control, focus, and verbal aptitude that seem to come more easily to young girls.

Researchers have suggested any number of solutions. A movement is growing for more all-boys schools and classes, and for respecting the individual learning styles of boys. Some people think that boys should be able to walk around in class, or take more time on tests, or have tests and books that cater to their interests. In their desperation to reach out to boys, some colleges have formed football teams and started engineering programs. Most of these special accommodations sound very much like the kind of affirmative action proposed for women over the years—which in itself is an alarming flip.

Whether boys have changed or not, we are well past the time to start trying some experiments. It is fabulous to see girls and young women poised for success in the coming years. But allowing generations of boys to grow up feeling rootless and obsolete is not a recipe for a peaceful future. Men have few natural support groups and little access to social welfare; the men's-rights groups that do exist in the U.S. are taking on an angry, antiwoman edge. Marriages fall apart or never happen at all, and children are raised with no fathers. Far from being celebrated, women's rising power is perceived as a threat.

In fact, the more women dominate, the more they behave, fittingly, like the dominant sex. Rates of violence committed by middle-aged women have skyrocketed since the 1980s, and no one knows why. High-profile female killers have been showing up regularly in the news: Amy Bishop, the homicidal Alabama professor; Jihad Jane and her sidekick, Jihad Jamie; the latest generation of Black Widows, responsible for suicide bombings in Russia. In Roman Polanski's *The Ghost Writer,* the traditional political wife is rewritten as a cold-blooded killer at the heart of an evil conspiracy. In her recent video *Telephone,* Lady Gaga, with her infallible radar for the cultural edge, rewrites Thelma and Louise as a story not about elusive female empowerment but about sheer, ruthless power. Instead of killing themselves, she and her girlfriend (played by Beyoncé) kill a bad boyfriend and random others in a homicidal spree and then escape in their yellow pickup truck, Gaga bragging, "We did it, Honey B."

The Marlboro Man, meanwhile, master of wild beast and wild country, seems too farfetched and preposterous even for advertising. His modern equivalents are the stunted men in the Dodge Charger ad that ran during this year's Super Bowl in February. Of all the days in the year, one might think, Super Bowl Sunday should be the one most dedicated to the cinematic celebration of macho. The men in Super Bowl ads should be throwing balls and racing motorcycles and doing whatever it is men imagine they could do all day if only women were not around to restrain them.

Instead, four men stare into the camera, unsmiling, not moving except for tiny blinks and sways. They look like they've been tranquilized, like they can barely hold themselves up against the breeze. Their lips do not move, but a voice-over explains their predicament—how they've been beaten silent by the demands of tedious employers and enviro-fascists and women. Especially women. "I will put the seat down, I will separate the recycling, I will carry your lip balm." This last one—lip balm—is expressed with the mildest spit of emotion, the only hint of the suppressed rage against the dominatrix. Then the commercial abruptly cuts to the fantasy, a Dodge Charger vrooming toward the camera punctuated by bold all caps: MAN'S LAST STAND. But the motto is unconvincing. After that display of muteness and passivity, you can only imagine a woman—one with shiny lips—steering the beast.

Critical Thinking

1. What is Hanna Rosin's point of view?
2. What is a patriarchal society?
3. Why does Rosin argue that a modern economy advantages women over men?
4. How does this article complement/contradict Article 5?
5. Do the authors of Article 1 give sufficient attention to changing gender roles in their alternative future scenarios?

HANNA ROSIN is an Atlantic contributing editor and the co-editor of DoubleX.

Test-Your-Knowledge Form

We encourage you to photocopy and use this page as a tool to assess how the articles in *Annual Editions* expand on the information in your textbook. By reflecting on the articles you will gain enhanced text information. You can also access this useful form on a product's book support website at www.mhhe.com/cls.

NAME: DATE:

_____

TITLE AND NUMBER OF ARTICLE:

_____

BRIEFLY STATE THE MAIN IDEA OF THIS ARTICLE:

_____

LIST THREE IMPORTANT FACTS THAT THE AUTHOR USES TO SUPPORT THE MAIN IDEA:

_____

WHAT INFORMATION OR IDEAS DISCUSSED IN THIS ARTICLE ARE ALSO DISCUSSED IN YOUR TEXTBOOK OR OTHER READINGS THAT YOU HAVE DONE? LIST THE TEXTBOOK CHAPTERS AND PAGE NUMBERS:

_____

LIST ANY EXAMPLES OF BIAS OR FAULTY REASONING THAT YOU FOUND IN THE ARTICLE:

_____

LIST ANY NEW TERMS/CONCEPTS THAT WERE DISCUSSED IN THE ARTICLE, AND WRITE A SHORT DEFINITION:

We Want Your Advice

ANNUAL EDITIONS revisions depend on two major opinion sources: one is our Advisory Board, listed in the front of this volume, which works with us in scanning the thousands of articles published in the public press each year; the other is you—the person actually using the book. Please help us and the users of the next edition by completing the prepaid article rating form on this page and returning it to us. Thank you for your help!

ANNUAL EDITIONS: Global Issues 11/12

ARTICLE RATING FORM

Here is an opportunity for you to have direct input into the next revision of this volume.
We would like you to rate each of the articles listed below, using the following scale:

1. **Excellent: should definitely be retained**
2. **Above average: should probably be retained**
3. **Below average: should probably be deleted**
4. **Poor: should definitely be deleted**

Your ratings will play a vital part in the next revision.
Please mail this prepaid form to us as soon as possible.
Thanks for your help!

RATING	ARTICLE	RATING	ARTICLE
	1. Global Trends 2025: A Transformed World: Executive Summary		24. The Case against the West: America and Europe in the Asian Century
	2. Could Food Shortages Bring Down Civilization?		25. Bolivia and Its Lithium
	3. Navigating the Energy Transition		26. Not Your Father's Latin America
	4. Asia's Rise: Rise and Fall		27. More Aid Is Not the Answer
	5. Feminists and Fundamentalists		28. It's Still the One
	6. Get Smart		29. Seven Myths about Alternative Energy
	7. The New Population Bomb: The Four Megatrends That Will Change the World		30. The End of Easy Oil
	8. Population and Sustainability		31. On Clean Energy, China Skirts Rules
	9. Why Migration Matters		32. The Revenge of Geography
	10. Pandemic Pandemonium		33. A Himalayan Rivalry
	11. The Next Breadbasket?: How Africa Could Save the World—and Itself		34. Living with a Nuclear Iran
	12. Climate Change		35. The Border of Madness
	13. The Other Climate Changers		36. The Jihad Against the Jihadis: How Moderate Muslim Leaders Waged War on Extremists—and Won
	14. The Big Melt		37. War in the Fifth Domain
	15. Troubled Waters		38. Banning the Bomb: A New Approach
	16. Acacia Avenue: How to Save Indonesia's Dwindling Rainforests		39. Climate Change After Copenhagen: Beyond Doom and Gloom
	17. Asian Carp, Other Invasive Species Make a Splash		40. Geneva Conventions
	18. Globalization and Its Contents		41. Is Bigger Better?
	19. It's a Flat World, After All		42. A World *Enslaved*
	20. Why the World Isn't Flat		43. Chile Starts Early
	21. Can Extreme Poverty Be Eliminated?		44. Humanity's Common Values: Seeking a Positive Future
	22. The Ideology of Development		45. Life, Religion and Everything
	23. The Quiet Coup		46. The End of Men

BUSINESS REPLY MAIL
FIRST CLASS MAIL PERMIT NO. 551 DUBUQUE IA

POSTAGE WILL BE PAID BY ADDRESSEE

McGraw-Hill Contemporary Learning Series
501 BELL STREET
DUBUQUE, IA 52001

NO POSTAGE
NECESSARY
IF MAILED
IN THE
UNITED STATES

ABOUT YOU

Name   Date

Are you a teacher? ❏ A student? ❏
Your school's name

Department

Address   City   State   Zip

School telephone #

YOUR COMMENTS ARE IMPORTANT TO US!

Please fill in the following information:
For which course did you use this book?

Did you use a text with this ANNUAL EDITION? ❏ yes ❏ no
What was the title of the text?

What are your general reactions to the Annual Editions concept?

Have you read any pertinent articles recently that you think should be included in the next edition? Explain.

Are there any articles that you feel should be replaced in the next edition? Why?

Are there any World Wide Websites that you feel should be included in the next edition? Please annotate.

May we contact you for editorial input? ❏ yes ❏ no
May we quote your comments? ❏ yes ❏ no

NOTES

NOTES